A REPRESENT...

of the work of England's finest poets—
from William Blake to Dylan Thomas—is presented
in this compact anthology.

Editor Oscar Williams has chosen more than 400 selections
from 22 major British poets, selections large enough and
diverse enough to reflect each poet's individual genius as well
as his life and times. Included is a comprehensive
introduction by Julian Symons, the brilliant British critic,
describing the movement begun by the
Romantics—a revolution in poetic language, form, freedom.

The Mentor Book of Major British Poets
features, in full, such long poems as:

WILLIAM WORDSWORTH'S *Intimations of Immortality*
SAMUEL TAYLOR COLERIDGE'S *Christabel* and
The Rhyme of the Ancient Mariner
JOHN KEATS' *The Eve of Saint Agnes* and all the *Odes*
PERCY BYSSHE SHELLEY'S *Adonais*
MATTHEW ARNOLD'S *The Scholar Gypsy*
WILLIAM BUTLER YEATS' *The Tower*
LORD BYRON'S *Don Juan, Canto XIII*
ROBERT BROWNING'S *Andrea del Sarto* and *Rabbi Ben Ezra*
D. H. LAWRENCE'S *The Ship of Death*
GEORGE BARKER'S *True Confession*
and up to 35 poems each by such poets as
WILLIAM BLAKE, ALFRED LORD TENNYSON,
GERARD MANLEY HOPKINS.

Renowned Poets in SIGNET CLASSIC Editions

(0451)

☐ **THE SELECTED POETRY OF BYRON edited by W. H. Auden.** A comprehensive collection which includes *Beppo, Epistle to Augusta,* selections from *Don Juan, Childe Harold, English Bards* and *Scotch Reviewers,* and extracts from the journals and letters. Introduction, Chronology, Bibliography. (515595—$2.95)

☐ **THE SELECTED POETRY OF BROWNING edited by George Ridenour.** Includes *Pauline,* selections from *The Ring and the Book, St. Martin's Summer, Fra Lippo Lippi, Childe Roland to the Dark Tower Came,* and longer works often omitted in standard anthologies. Introduction, Chronology, Bibliography. (515994—$3.50)

☐ **THE SELECTED POETRY OF KEATS edited by Paul de Man.** Contains the major works in full: *Endymion, Hyperion, The Fall of Hyperion,* all the odes, including "On a Grecian Urn" and "To A Nightingale" as well as a representative selection of Keats's sonnets and letters. Chronology and Bibliography included. (515684—$2.95)

☐ **PARADISE LOST AND PARADISE REGAINED by John Milton.** Edited and with Introduction and Notes by Christopher Ricks, Chronology, Bibliography and Footnotes included. (517350—$3.95)

☐ **IDYLLS OF THE KING and A Selection of Poems by Alfred Lord Tennyson.** Foreword by George Barker. Includes selections from *The Princess, In Memoriam A.H.H.* and *Maud.* (516443—$2.25)

Buy them at your local bookstore or use this convenient coupon for ordering.

THE NEW AMERICAN LIBRARY, INC.,
P.O. Box 999, Bergenfield, New Jersey 07621

Please send me the books I have checked above. I am enclosing $_____ (please add $1.00 to this order to cover postage and handling). Send check or money order—no cash or C.O.D.'s. Prices and numbers are subject to change without notice.

Name_____

Address_____

City _____ State _____ Zip Code _____
Allow 4-6 weeks for delivery.
This offer is subject to withdrawal without notice.

THE MENTOR BOOK OF
MAJOR BRITISH POETS

FROM WILLIAM BLAKE TO DYLAN THOMAS

Edited by
OSCAR WILLIAMS

With an Introduction by Julian Symons

A MENTOR BOOK from
NEW AMERICAN LIBRARY
TIMES MIRROR
New York and Scarborough, Ontario

Copyright © 1963 by Oscar Williams

Introduction Copyright © 1963 by Julian Symons

All rights reserved

Library of Congress Catalog Card Number: 63-20282

ACKNOWLEDGMENTS AND COPYRIGHT NOTICES

(The following page constitutes an extension of this copyright page.)
The editor wishes to thank the various authors, publishers, and agents for
permission to reprint various poems. For the convenience of readers, these
acknowledgments are listed according to poet.

GEORGE BARKER: to George Barker, for THE TRUE CONFESSION OF GEORGE
BARKER; to Criterion Books, Inc., and Faber & Faber Ltd., for ELEGY NO. 1,
MEMORIAL FOR TWO SEAMEN, RESOLUTION OF DEPENDENCE, EPISTLE I ALLEGORY
OF THE ADOLESCENT AND THE ADULT, SONNET TO MOTHER, ELEGY V, THE DEATH
OF YEATS, SECULAR ELEGY V, AND NOW THERE IS NOTHING LEFT TO CELEBRATE, TO
ANY MEMBER OF MY GENERATION, NEWS OF THE WORLD I, 'O WHO WILL SPEAK
FROM A WOMB OR A CLOUD?', AT THE WAKE OF DYLAN THOMAS, TO FATHER
GERARD MANLEY HOPKINS, S.J., SESTINA AT 34; to Oscar Williams, for DOG, DOG
IN MY MANGER.

ROBERT GRAVES: to Willis Kingsley Wing for all the poems by Robert
Graves. THE NAKED AND THE NUDE Copyright © 1957, International Authors
N. V., from *The New Yorker.* Other poems Copyright © 1955, International
Authors N. V., from *Collected Poems.*

THOMAS HARDY: to Macmillan & Co., Ltd., London, The Macmillan Co.
of Canada Ltd., and the Trustees of the Hardy Estate, for THE DARKLING
THRUSH, THE SUBALTERNS, HAP, THE TO-BE-FORGOTTEN, NEUTRAL TONES, TO
LIZBIE BROWN, THE LAST CHRYSANTHEMUM, THE SOULS OF THE SLAIN, TO AN
UNBORN PAUPER CHILD, IN TENEBRIS, THE RUINED MAID, from *Collected Poems;*
to Macmillan & Co., Ltd., London, The Macmillan Co. of Canada Ltd., The
Macmillan Company, New York, and the Trustees of the Hardy Estate, for
WESSEX HEIGHTS, CHANNEL FIRING, AFTER A JOURNEY, IN TIME OF THE 'BREAKING
OF NATIONS,' THE GOING, THE MAN HE KILLED, THE PHANTOM HORSEWOMAN,
AFTERWARDS, from *Collected Poems,* Copyright 1925 by The Macmillan Com-
pany, and A REFUSAL, NO BUYERS, THE OXEN, WHO'S IN THE NEXT ROOM?', THE
CONVERGENCE OF THE TWAIN, from *Collectd Poems,* Copyright 1925 by The
Macmillan Company, Copyright 1953 by Lloyd's Bank Ltd.

GERARD MANLEY HOPKINS: to Oxford University Press, London, for
all of the poems by Hopkins, from *Poems of Gerard Manley Hopkins.*

A. E. HOUSMAN: to Jonathan Cape Ltd., the Society of Authors, and Holt,
Rinehart and Winston, Inc., for REVOLUTION, THE NIGHT IS FREEZING FAST,
CHESTNUT CASTS HIS FLAMBEAUX, EPITAPH ON AN ARMY OF MERCENARIES, THE
LAWS OF GOD, THE LAWS OF MAN, I DID NOT LOSE MY HEART IN SUMMER'S EVEN,
WHEN ISRAEL OUT OF EGYPT CAME, from *Complete Poems.* Copyright 1922 by
Holt, Rinehart and Winston, Inc. Copyright 1936 by Barclays Bank Ltd.
Copyright renewed 1950 by Barclays Bank Ltd.; to Jonathan Cape Ltd., and
the Society of Authors for WHEN I WAS ONE-AND-TWENTY, OH, WHEN I WAS
IN LOVE WITH YOU, LOVELIEST OF TREES, REVEILLE, OH SEE HOW THICK THE GOLD-
CUP FLOWERS, TO AN ATHLETE DYING YOUNG, BREDON HILL, THE LADS IN THEIR
HUNDREDS, IS MY TEAM PLOUGHING, OTHERS, I AM NOT THE FIRST, ON WENLOCK
EDGE THE WOOD'S IN TROUBLE, WHITE IN THE MOON THE LONE ROAD LIES, INTO

HEART AN AIR THAT KILLS, THE IMMORTAL PART, WITH RUE MY HEART IS
EN, YOU SMILE UNION YOUR FRIEND TO-DAY, TERENCE, THIS IS STUPID STUFF,
OED AND TRENCHED AND WEEDED, from *Collected Poems;* to Charles Scribner's
ns, for INFANT INNOCENCE, from *My Brother, A. E. Housman,* by Laurence
usman. Copyright 1937, 1938 Laurence Housman.

H. LAWRENCE: to The Viking Press, Inc., William Heinemann Ltd.,
urence Pollinger Ltd., and the Estate of Mrs. Frieda Lawrence, for SONG OF
AN WHO HAS COME THROUGH, HUMMING-BIRD, BABY TORTOISE, TORTOISE-SHELL,
AKE, KANGAROO, from *Collected Poems,* Copyright 1929 by Jonathan Cape
d Harrison Smith, Inc. © 1957 by Frieda Lawrence Ravagli; and for
VARIAN GENTIANS, RETORT TO WHITMAN, WHALES WEEP NOT, THE SHIP OF
ATH, THE END, THE BEGINNING, from *Last Poems,* Copyright 1933 by Frieda
wrence; to Laurence Pollinger Ltd., William Heinemann Ltd., and the
tate of Mrs. Frieda Lawrence for HOW BEASTLY THE BOURGEOIS IS, DON'TS,
N'T IT BE STRANGE—?, WHEN I WENT TO THE CIRCUS, THE MOSQUITO KNOWS,
E ELEPHANT IS SLOW TO MATE.

WIN MUIR: to Grove Press, Inc., and Faber & Faber Ltd., for all the
ems by Muir, from *Collected Poems 1921-1951,* Copyright © 1957 by Edwin
uir.

LFRED OWEN: to Chatto & Windus Ltd., for all the poems by Owen,
m *Poems.*

YLAN THOMAS: to New Directions and J. M. Dent & Sons Ld., for all
e poems by Thomas, from *Collected Poems.* Copyright 1939, 1942, 1946, by
w Directions. Copyright 1952, 1953 by Dylan Thomas. Copyright © by New
rections.

ILLIAM BUTLER YEATS: to Macmillan & Co., Ltd., The Macmillan
mpany of Canada Ltd., The Macmillan Company, New York, and Mrs. W.
Yeats, for PROLOGUE TO RESPONSIBILITIES, TWO SONGS FROM A PLAY, SAILING
BYZANTIUM, THE TOWER, AMONG SCHOOL CHILDREN, A PRAYER FOR MY
UGHTER, THE SECOND COMING, A DIALOGUE OF SELF AND SOUL, CRAZY JANE
KS WITH THE BISHOP, FOR ANNE GREGORY, BYZANTIUM, JOHN KINSELLA'S
MENT FOR MRS. MARY MOORE, A BRONZE HEAD, NEWS FOR THE DELPHIC ORACLE,
E CIRCUS ANIMALS' DESERTION, LAPIS LAZULI, THE MUNICIPAL GALLERY RE-
ITED, A STICK OF INCENSE, from *Collected Poems.* Copyright 1916, 1924,
28, 1933 by The Macmillan Company. Copyright 1940, 1952, 1956, 1961 by
rtha Georgie Yeats; to Macmillan & Co. Ltd., The Macmillan Company
Canada Ltd., and Mrs. W. B. Yeats, for WHEN YOU ARE OLD, THE LAKE ISLE
INNISFREE, DOWN BY THE SALLEY GARDENS, THE SONG OF WANDERING AENGUS,
E SORROW OF LOVE, HE THINKS OF HIS PAST GREATNESS, O'SULLIVAN RUA TO
RY LAVELL, THE EVERLASTING VOICES, THE SECRET ROSE, from *Collected Poems.*

MENTOR TRADEMARK REG. U.S. PAT. OFF. AND FOREIGN COUNTRIES

REGISTERED TRADEMARK—MARCA REGISTRADA

HECHO EN CHICAGO, U.S.A.

GNET, SIGNET CLASSICS, MENTOR, PLUME, MERIDIAN AND NAL
OKS are published *in the United States* by
e New American Library, Inc.,
33 Broadway, New York, New York 10019,
Canada by The New American Library of Canada Limited,
Mack Avenue, Scarborough, Ontario M1L 1M8

12   13   14   15   16   17   18   19   20

INTED IN THE UNITED STATES OF AMERICA

SPECIAL NOTE FROM THE EDITOR

The reader of this volume will undoubtedly wonder why certain poets, such as T. S. Eliot and W. H. Auden, who are mentioned so favorably in Julian Symons' introduction, are not, after all, represented in this anthology. Harcourt, Brace and World, Inc., Mr. Eliot's American publishers, will not allow the use of his poems in paperback anthologies. On October 30, 1962, the permissions department wrote: ". . . we must refuse permission for Mr. Eliot's work to appear in paperback books intended for the mass market." A check with the permissions department in 1963, just before this book went to press, revealed that this policy was still in force. Since the printing plates used in the American edition were used in the press run intended for sale in the United Kingdom, Mr. Eliot is, alas, missing from the British edition as well. The reader ought to know, however, that Faber and Faber, Ltd., Mr. Eliot's English publishers, did not refuse permission. W. H. Auden is not to be found in the present collection for the simple reason that he is well represented in the companion volume to this anthology, *The Mentor Book of Major American Poets* which covers an identical, but not altogether arbitrary, period of time, 1776 until now. The responsibility for the book's other shortcomings—omissions and commissions—rests, of course, exclusively with the editor.

CONTENTS

INTRODUCTION xiii

WILLIAM BLAKE *(1757-1827)*

WILLIAM WORDSWORTH *(1770-1850)*

SAMUEL TAYLOR COLERIDGE *(1772-1834)*

vii

WILLIAM BUTLER YEATS *(1865-1939)*

D. H. LAWRENCE *(1885-1930)*

EDWIN MUIR *(1887-1958)*

INTRODUCTION

THE TWO REVOLUTIONS

Poetry is made up of two elements, language and vision. The vision is what the poet sees and feels, the language is the way in which he puts these feelings down on paper. But this generalization applies to good and negligible poetry alike. It is a precondition of a good poem that its writer shall put down what he has experienced personally, not a response he has made through reading other literature or by following accepted masters: also, the language in which he writes shall be the language of his own time, that is, the language of common speech modified or heightened. To put the point very simply by example: what we see and feel when we look at a daffodil cannot possibly be the same as what Wordsworth saw and felt, and the language in which we put down what we see cannot be that of Pope or Dryden.

Part of the importance of Mr. Williams's anthology springs from the fact that it begins at a point of revolution in British poetry, a point at which our way of seeing, and of putting down what we see, was radically changed. His selection shows something new entering literature, a feeling and form of expression absolutely fresh and pure. It shows this new poetry changing, being modified, weakening, throughout the nineteenth century, until poetic form and feeling were rejuvenated by another revolution, another change in our way of hearing and seeing.

> The principal object, then, proposed in these Poems was to choose incidents and situations from common life, and to relate or describe them throughout, as far as was possible in a selection of language really used by men, and, at the same time, to throw over them a certain colouring of imagination, whereby ordinary things should be presented to the mind in an unusual aspect.

So Wordsworth succinctly described his purpose in the expanded form of the preface to *Lyrical Ballads*. To understand the nature of the revolution Wordsworth was proposing one must compare this concept of language and subjects with that which was fashionable at the end of the eighteenth century.

Wordsworth himself uses for odious comparison a sonnet by Gray, which begins:

> In vain to me the smiling mornings shine
> And reddening Phoebus lifts his golden fire:
> The birds in vain their amorous descant join,
> Or cheerful fields resume their green attire.

To compare merely the *language* of this sonnet with the opening of 'The Solitary Reaper' is to see how Gray's clichés of poetic diction ('reddening Phoebus,' 'amorous descant,' 'resume their green attire') have been changed utterly into something seen and understood:

> Behold her, single in the field,
> Yon solitary Highland Lass!
> Reaping and singing by herself;
> Stop here, or gently pass!
> Alone she cuts and binds the grain,
> And sings a melancholy strain;
> O listen! for the Vale profound
> Is overflowing with the sound.

It is not just a matter of comparing a good poem by Wordsworth with a bad one by Gray. The poetic diction that seems absurd in Gray's poem once truly represented a certain weight and balance in Augustan society, but by the end of the eighteenth century such diction no longer bore any relationship to the life of the age, and thus had no relation to poetry. Wordsworth boldly announced that little 'poetic diction' would be found in his poems, and that 'as much pains has been taken to avoid it as is ordinarily taken to produce it'. He rejected totally the abstract ideas that were taken by the Augustans as the proper material of poetry, and replied to the great body of conventional opinion which insisted that poetry had its special language that must never be debased by saying there was no essential difference between the language of prose and poetry.

> Poetry sheds no tears 'such as Angels weep',
> but natural and human tears; she can boast of no
> celestial ichor that distinguishes her vital juices
> from that of prose; the same human blood circulates
> through the veins of them both.

Every revolution in language has its roots in social change, and if we ask where this poetic revolution came from, and how it happened that a man so conspicuously conservative in his feelings as Wordsworth should have been its prime agent, the answer is to be found in the emotional effect that the French

Revolution had upon the feelings of subsequent generations, and technically in the new possibilities and dangers that opened up for mankind through the Industrial Revolution. Such great events as the French Revolution (or in our time the Russian Revolution) affect permanently and vitally the lives of those who take part in them, and affect almost as much a fellow-traveller like Wordsworth, who visited, saw, and marvelled:

> Cheered with this hope, to Paris I returned,
> And ranged, with ardour heretofore unfelt,
> The spacious city, and in progress passed
> The prison where the unhappy Monarch lay,
> Associate with his children and his wife
> In bondage; and the palace, lately stormed
> With roar of cannon by a furious host.
> I crossed the square (an empty area then!)
> Of the Carrousel, where so late had lain
> The dead, upon the dying heaped, and gazed
> On this and other spots, as doth a man
> Upon a volume whose contents he knows
> Are memorable, but from him locked up,
> Being written in a tongue he cannot read,
> So that he questions the mute leaves with pain,
> And half upbraids their silence. But that night
> I felt most deeply in what world I was,
> What ground I trod on, and what air I breathed.

Wordsworth recognized the effect of the Revolution upon him when he wrote that to make his case about poetry rationally he would have to show the interactions of language and the human mind and also 'the revolutions, not of literature alone, but likewise of society itself'.

His attitude towards the French Revolution was one of sympathy during the great productive period of his life. His feelings about the technical revolution that changed Britain within half a century from an agricultural to an industrial nation were very different. He saw 'the increasing accumulation of men in cities, where the uniformity of their occupations produces a craving for extraordinary incident', and where their 'degrading thirst after outrageous stimulation' was slaked, a little oddly as it seems to us, by 'frantic novels, sickly and stupid German Tragedies, and deluges of idle and extravagant stories in verse'. To this image of degraded metropolitan humanity Wordsworth and Coleridge opposed an ideal image of Man and Nature. The Augustans had viewed man as a unit in society; the new Romantics celebrated his uniqueness as an individual. To question in verse the ordering of society and the ways of God to man would have been unthinkable for Pope or Johnson, but for the young Wordsworth and for Shelley, this was the point at which their verse began. Wordsworth and Coleridge in their early poems, Shelley and Keats throughout their short lives, rediscovered the life of the senses through the philosophical idea that man himself was a unique and almost a divine being. And if man was divine, then, in this pantheistic philosophy, it seemed that the whole of creation might be divine, too. Wordsworth's communion with Nature was continuous from his childhood, but it was not until he became adult that he expressed clearly in such a poem as 'Ode: Intimations of Immortality' the belief that, although human perceptions falter and all physical and natural beauty fades, Nature itself is always good, always beautiful, and is imperishable. It was no more than one step on from this for Shelley to assert the divinity not merely of 'Nature' but of all human creation. When he wrote that a skylark was not a bird but a blithe spirit, Shelley expressed a point of view that is commonplace to us, but seemed deeply blasphemous to many of his contemporaries.

But of course the Romantic revolution is to be regarded as something much more than a paean to Man and Nature. To have the whole of 'The Eve of St. Agnes' and five of Keats's Odes together, as we have in this collection, is to see that these poems are a sustained, unflawed exaltation of the whole of sensual life. One could not live forever on poems like these, delicate as velvet, rich as cream, cushioned in the life of the senses, yet Keats's poems are supreme assertions of the importance of the individual, an assertion linked always with the worship of poetry as an expression of the divine element in man. For Keats, poetry is a demon; for Coleridge, under the name of the primary imagination, it is 'a repetition in the finite mind of the eternal act of creation in the infinite I AM'; for Shelley, poets are the world's unacknowledged legislators. All of these claims reflect the feeling of liberation that was the essence of the Romantic Movement at its height.

Revolutions, we have often been told, devour their children. They destroy them more subtly, too, turning the idealistic Wordsworth into the sour hermit of the Lakes, driving Coleridge to incoherence, sending Shelley and Byron—who expressed the spirit of Romanticism in their lives as well as in their work—to early death. The poets who succeeded them were romantic still, but they had no longer any certain conviction of the poet's power. Their beliefs about Man and Nature were susceptible of criticism through science and utilitarian philosophy. They were not romantic egoists, but men of feeling.

Tennyson commands the second half of the nineteenth century as Wordsworth does the first, but Tennyson's attitude towards the natural world became more and more one of scepticism. I wish Mr. Williams had included 'Locksley Hall', not because it is a great poem, but because it shows so well the difference between a conservative like Wordsworth, who was convinced through revolution of new possibilities for mankind but was at the same time disgusted by factories and urban life, and a liberal humanist like Tennyson, who felt it his duty to approve of the world of mechanical marvels made by science:

> Far along the world-wide whisper of the south-wind rush-
>   ing warm,
> With the standards of the peoples plunging thro' the
>   thunder-storm;
> Till the war-drum throbbed no longer, and the battle
>   flags were furled
> In the Parliament of man, the Federation of the world . . .
> Eye, to which all order festers, all things here are out of
>   joint:
> Science moves, but slowly slowly, creeping on from point
>   to point:
> Yet I doubt not thro' the ages one increasing purpose runs,
> And the thoughts of men are widened with the process of
>   the suns.

It has often been said of Tennyson that he had really no personality to express, and this is a view with which the poet himself seems to have been more or less in sympathy. 'There's nothing I can't do in verse', he said once. 'The worst is that there's nothing in me'. He seems indeed not so much an individual as a kind of mirror through which we can see the reactions of a typical liberal humanist in the Victorian age: feelings about science, about the relations of men and women, about the proper positions of classes within society, and disturbed feelings too about the relationship between man and God. In Tennyson the furious egoism of the early Romantics is changed to something melancholy and passive. With all the equipment of a great poet, he strangely lacks vitality. The failure can be seen most clearly, as in poetry it always can, in the language. Compare the language of 'Resolution and Independence' or 'The Lime-Tree Bower My Prison' with any poem of Tennyson's, compare one of Keats's Odes with 'The Lotos-Eaters'. What was precise in Wordsworth and Coleridge has become vague in Tennyson, the language that is magnificently luxuriant and sensual in Keats has become feebly so in the Victorian poet.

Such words as these should not be taken simply in disesteem of Tennyson. The course of his career, from the boy haunted by the mystery of personal identity to the Poet Laureate who became an institution and presented to the world a face impeccably official and respectable, shows more than anything else the immense pressures towards conformity exerted by Victorian society upon the individual. Tennyson may be called the last "universal" poet in Britain: the last, that is, who wrote quite unaffectedly for a mass audience and identified himself with it. He was the last important poet whose work was popular—so popular that editions of his poems were published at a penny a volume. With Wordsworth the Romantic revolution began, with Tennyson it effectively ended. Poets since then have been representatives of a minority culture.

The separation of English literature into compartments labelled 'Highbrow' and 'Lowbrow' is nicely marked by the publication in 1850 of the two numbers of *The Germ*. This first, and characteristically short-lived, 'little magazine' was the organ of the Pre-Raphaelites, who were themselves the first conscious artistic minority movement in Britain. The Pre-Raphaelite movement began as a gesture towards artistic simplicity, but the Pre-Raphaelites and their successors quickly developed into cults concerned with the preservation of 'literature', which was no longer identified with life but was interpreted as a kind of essence that might be extracted from the dross of daily living. Tennyson, a melancholy eagle, spread benevolent wings over the whole Victorian literary scene: but beneath those outspread wings the aesthetic revolt against the vulgarity of Victorian materialism beat strongly. In his idealistic early manhood Carlyle had said that the victory of Waterloo might be less momentous than the opening of the first Mechanics' Institute, and that education for all must be wonderfully beneficial to mankind: yet what did the Mechanics' Institute do but encourage men to rebel against their masters, and what did children do with their free education but read the lowest and most vulgar books that they could find? The revolt against materialism took many forms, from Ruskin's attempt to find salvation in physical work to Swinburne's praise of the roses and raptures of vice, from William Morris's efforts to combine the creation of beautiful wallpapers and fabrics with Guild Socialism to the shy, scholastic Pater's exhortations about burning with a hard, gemlike flame. All literary movements take on a character for those involved in them that is not apparent to historians looking in cold blood at the death of their hopes a century later. What we can see in all these movements, culminating in the 'Art for Art's Sake' of the aesthetic nineties, which Wyndham Lewis called 'the last organized expression of the English mind in art', is a desperate series of evasions, of attempts to deny the increasing dissociation of art and life. Faced, as it seemed to them, with a choice between the beauty of Art and the vulgarity of Life, the writers of the nineties preferred Art.

Probably, as Dr. Leavis says, the amount of literary talent in what may be called the amoebic stage is much the same in any generation—what varies is the use that is made of it. This depends not only upon original genius but upon the tradition in which the poet is working. In the Elizabethan period there were a dozen dramatists producing permanently memorable work, at the beginning of the Romantic Revolution a dozen poets. There is only a shade of exaggeration in saying that there are certain periods in which it is almost impossible for a poet with any talent at all to write badly, and other times when it is difficult for any but the most determined and original of poets to write well. The poets of the second half of the nineteenth century all seem to me minor when put beside Wordsworth, Byron, Coleridge, and Tennyson, but some of them may well have been as talented. Browning, Hardy, Hopkins, Meredith, and Clough all found themselves confronted with the need to fight against the inert, wholly literary language in which the characteristic poetry of the time was being written. The solutions they found to the problem of discovering a language in which ideas and feelings could be freshly expressed were often marvellously effective, and the poems they wrote were works of great power and beauty, but much of their work is inevitably that of men working within a minority culture, compelled to wrench and distort language to make it serve their purpose. We live in an age of minor poetry and so, I think, have a natural feeling for those poets who struggled against the great Victorian imperatives of morality and power. I should have been delighted if Mr. Williams had been able to find room for Meredith's great sequence, 'Modern Love', or for Clough's 'Amours des Voyages', or for some of Patmore's Odes, all of them poems in which a rebellion against Victorian standards of conduct was crystallized into poetry: but there are many compensations, particularly in the wholly felicitous, surprising choice of John Davidson. It seems worth repeating what Mr. T. S. Eliot has said about Davidson's finest poem, 'Thirty Bob a Week':

> *Thirty Bob a Week* seems to me the only poem in which Davidson freed himself completely from the poetic diction of English verse of his time . . . Davidson had a great theme, and also found an idiom which elicited the greatness of the theme, which endowed this thirty-bob-a-week clerk with a dignity that would not have

appeared if a more conventional poetic diction had
been employed. The personage that Davidson created
in this poem has haunted me all my life, and the poem
is to me a great poem for ever.

To write a poem like 'Thirty Bob a Week' at the turn of the
century, Davidson had positively to wrench himself free from
the mess of literature in which such poetry as that of James
Thomson and Francis Thompson was immersed. The poets
of the nineties were more interesting artists than is often
acknowledged. Ernest Dowson and Lionel Johnson, Arthur
Symons and Lord Alfred Douglas (and of course Davidson and
A. E. Housman and W. B. Yeats, whose work is included here)
were expressing an attitude to art that is permanent and valu-
able. Of them all, however, only Yeats was able to free himself
completely of the poetic diction that hopelessly mars for us
the work of such talented writers as Dowson and Johnson, and
emerge as a major poet.

No doubt it is right to think of the poetic revolution of the
twentieth century as something generated in America and
nursed from a spark to a flame by T. S. Eliot and Ezra Pound,*
but it should be remembered that Eliot and Pound themselves
were greatly influenced in youth by the poets of the nineties.
The purely American side of this revolution can be seen in the
line that extends from Whitman through such poets in Edwin
Arlington Robinson and Robert Frost, but a Europeanized
American influence was also at work in the effect on Eliot and
Pound of the French Symbolists and the nineties poets. The
prime effect of this revolution was to produce as great a change
in poetic diction as that achieved by the Romantics.

I doubt if any young reader to-day can really understand the
shock caused to those who read the poem forty years ago by
the outrageous image contained in the first lines of 'The Love
Song of J. Alfred Prufrock', or the shock, different in kind but
equal in degree, caused by passages like the pub conversation
in *The Waste Land*:

> When Lil's husband got demobbed, I said—
> I didn't mince my words, I said to her myself,
> HURRY UP PLEASE ITS TIME
> Now Albert's coming back, make yourself a bit smart.
> He'll want to know what you done with that money he
>   gave you
> To get yourself some teeth. He did, I was there.
> You have them all out, Lil, and get a nice set,

* Ezra Pound is represented in *The Mentor Book of Major American
Poets*.

He said, I swear, I can't bear to look at you.
And no more can't I, I said, and think of poor Albert,
He's been in the army four years, he wants a good time,
And if you don't give it to him, there's others will,
    I said.

Such English pundits of the time as J. C. Squire and Edward
Marsh, both of them subsequently knighted, were shocked,
bewildered, and disgusted. They protested that this was not
poetry, rather in the tone of voice in which an Englishman may
protest that something is not cricket. Poetry was something
written in a special 'poetic' language and written about 'poetic'
subjects. Ideally it dealt with animals or with the past or with
country scenes and ways. There were occasions, rare ones, on
which poets might be permitted to break throuh this polite and
civilized style to something rougher, as Wilfred Owen and
Siegfried Sassoon did in their war poems, but in general
Squire and Marsh had no doubt that the proper tone for poetry
was elevated and pure. It was from such an attitude that
Squire was able to say of 'The Waste Land' that a grunt would
have done as well, and that the poem might as well have been
written in double dutch—for all he knew, he added, it was.

The influence of Eliot and Pound upon modern British
poetry has been enormous, that of the homespun American
poets very slight. Eliot, in particular, showed the poets who
came to maturity in the nineteen twenties or later that there
was no such thing as poetic language, that all the words were
in the dictionary for anybody to use. The specifically English
form taken by this 'revolution of the word' was an insistence
by the poets of the thirties on using images taken from medi-
cine, politics, engineering. Intoxicated by the freedom from
Georgianism bestowed upon them by Eliot, they came roaring
into the world of the internal combustion engine.

Auden, the most notable poet of the period, has been re-
served by Mr. Williams for his companion American volume,
so there is nothing here that quite conveys the feeling of libera-
tion experienced by young English poets in this period. The
poems of George Barker and Dylan Thomas take their char-
acter from a different source, through investigation of the in-
dividual personality rather than the external world.

The great difference between the Romantic Revolution and
the revolution of the twentieth century was that the first en-
larged and the second narrowed the audience for poetry. Eliot
and Pound did not enlarge the language of poetry so that all
who run might read. Their revolution of the word went to-
gether with a desire to confine the full understanding of poetry
to an intellectual élite. The British poets of the thirties, who

looked theoretically for a wider audience, in practice used th
personal language and the private jokes of one friend speakin
to another. The twentieth-century revolution in British poetry
and I think to a lesser extent in American poetry, too, ha
simply confirmed the existence of two literary audiences, a
ever-increasing 'lowbrow' one that obtains its literary food al
most automatically, through Book-of-the-Month clubs an
popular magazines, and the comparatively tiny 'highbrow
audience that reads and seriously considers poetry. There ar
exceptions to this rule, like the very considerable sales o
Dylan Thomas's poetry during the past decade: but how man
of these copies have been sold because Thomas lived wildly
died tragically, and has been written about scandalously? Ho
many of those who have Eliot's collected poems upon thei
shelves have truly read and considered the implications of hi
work? The characteristic poet of the twentieth century is the ac
knowledged legislator of a class of bored university students
The great virtue of an anthology like this one, which can offe
a really representative selection of the work of the poets chosen
is that it really may take readers on to the collected volumes o
the poets' works, where the usual anthology snippets are unlike
ly to do anything of the kind; but no anthology can heal th
deep schism in our society that makes it inevitable that to-da
the poet should speak, not to all men, but to a chosen few

There remains the necessary word that must be said abou
who's in and who's out. *Romantic* is the word that, more tha
any other, I should choose to describe Mr. Williams's attitud
to poetry, and it seems to me very right that an anthologis
should have a personal attitude, as long as he doesn't play hi
favourites outrageously. This Mr. Williams never does. I can
not imagine, for instance, that he has any strong affinity fo
Matthew Arnold, but he recognizes Arnold's importance, an
so here he is. My own few complaints of omissions are alto
gether overweighed by the pleasures of finding a complet
canto of *Don Juan*, 'The Tower', by W. B. Yeats, 'The Wrec
of the Deutschland', and that splendidly bawdy poem, 'Th
True Confession of George Barker'. The 'surprise' selections—
John Davidson and Edwin Muir, for instance—seem to me ad
mirable. What we can fairly ask of an anthologist, in any case
is not anything so ridiculous as that every one of his choice
should be our own choice, but that his selection should hav
been made from a consistent and conscientious point of view
Such a consistency, informed by taste and intelligence, is wha
makes this an uncommonly good anthology.

Julian Symons

THE MENTOR BOOK OF
MAJOR BRITISH
POETS

WILLIAM BLAKE

(1757-1827)

AND DID THOSE FEET IN ANCIENT TIME

And did those feet in ancient time
  Walk upon England's mountains green?
And was the holy Lamb of God
  On England's pleasant pastures seen?

And did the Countenance Divine
    Shine forth upon our clouded hills?
And was Jerusalem builded here
  Among those dark Satanic Mills?

Bring me my bow of burning gold!
  Bring me my arrows of desire!
Bring me my spear! O clouds, unfold!
  Bring me my chariot of fire!

I will not cease from mental fight,
  Nor shall my sword sleep in my hand
Till we have built Jerusalem
  In England's green and pleasant land.

from MILTON

TO THE MUSES

Whether on Ida's shady brow
  Or in the chambers of the East,
The chambers of the sun, that now
  From ancient melody have ceased;

Whether in Heaven ye wander fair,
  Or the green corners of the earth,
Or the blue regions of the air,
  Where the melodious winds have birth;

Whether on crystal rocks ye rove,
  Beneath the bosom of the sea

Wandering in many a coral grove;
    Fair Nine, forsaking Poetry!

How have you left the ancient love
    That bards of old enjoyed in you!
The languid strings do scarcely move!
    The sound is forced, the notes are few!

SONG

Memory, hither come,
    And tune your merry notes:
And, while upon the wind
    Your music floats,
I'll pore upon the stream
Where sighing lovers dream,
And fish for fancies as they pass
Within the watery glass.

I'll drink of the clear stream,
    And hear the linnet's song;
And there I'll lie and dream
    The day along:
And when night comes, I'll go
To places fit for woe,
Walking along the darkened valley
With silent Melancholy.

MAD SONG

The wild winds weep,
And the night is a-cold;
Come hither, Sleep,
And my griefs unfold:
But lo! the morning peeps
Over the eastern steeps,
And the rustling birds of
    dawn
The earth do scorn.

Lo! to the vault
Of pavèd heaven,
With sorrow fraught
My notes are driven:

They strike the ear of night,
Make weep the eyes of day;
They make mad the roaring
    winds,
And with tempests play.

Like a fiend in a cloud,
With howling woe
After night I do crowd,
And with night will go;
I turn my back to the east
From whence comforts have
    increased;
For light doth seize my brain
With frantic pain.

HOW SWEET I ROAMED FROM FIELD TO FIELD

How sweet I roamed from field to field,
And tasted all the summer's pride,
Till I the prince of love beheld,
Who in the sunny beams did glide!

He showed me lilies for my hair,
And blushing roses for my brow;
He led me through his gardens fair,
Where all his golden pleasures grow.

With sweet May dews my wings were wet,
And Phoebus fired my vocal rage;
He caught me in his silken net,
And shut me in his golden cage.

He loves to sit and hear me sing,
Then, laughing, sports and plays with me;
Then stretches out my golden wing,
And mocks my loss of liberty.

TO SPRING

O thou with dewy locks, who lookest down
Thro' the clear windows of the morning, turn
Thine angel eyes upon our western isle,
Which in full choir hails thy approach, O Spring!

The hills tell each other, and the list'ning
Valleys hear; all our longing eyes are turnèd
Up to thy bright pavilions: issue forth,
And let thy holy feet visit our clime.

Come o'er the eastern hills, and let our winds
Kiss thy perfumèd garments; let us taste
Thy morn and evening breath; scatter thy pearls
Upon our love-sick land that mourns for thee.

O deck her forth with thy fair fingers; pour
Thy soft kisses on her bosom; and put
Thy golden crown upon her languished head,
Whose modest tresses were bound up for thee!

Introduction to
SONGS OF INNOCENCE

Piping down the valleys wild,
Piping songs of pleasant glee,
On a cloud I saw a child,
And he laughing said to me:

'Pipe a song about a Lamb!'
So I piped with a merry cheer.
'Piper, pipe that song again;'
So I piped: he wept to hear.

'Drop thy pipe, thy happy pipe;
Sing thy songs of happy cheer:'
So I sung the same again,

While he wept with joy to
   hear.

'Piper, sit thee down and
   write
In a book, that all may read.'
So he vanished from my
   sight,
And I plucked a hollow reed,

And I made a rural pen,
And I stained the water clear,
And I wrote my happy songs
Every child may joy to hear.

THE LAMB

      Little Lamb, who made thee?
      Dost thou know who made thee?
   Gave thee life, and bid thee feed,
   By the stream and o'er the mead;
   Gave thee clothing of delight,
   Softest clothing, woolly, bright;
   Gave thee such a tender voice,
   Making all the vales rejoice?
      Little Lamb who made thee?
      Dost thou know who made thee?

      Little Lamb, I'll tell thee,
      Little Lamb, I'll tell thee:
   He is callèd by thy name,
   For he calls himself a Lamb.
   He is meek, and he is mild;
   He became a little child.
   I a child, and thou a lamb,
   We are callèd by his name.
      Little Lamb, God bless thee!
      Little Lamb, God bless thee!

THE DIVINE IMAGE

To Mercy, Pity, Peace, and Love
All pray in their distress;

And to these virtues of delight
Return their thankfulness.

For Mercy, Pity, Peace, and Love
Is God, our father dear,
And Mercy, Pity, Peace, and Love
Is Man, his child and care.

For Mercy has a human heart,
Pity, a human face,
And Love, the human form divine,
And Peace, the human dress.

Then every man, of every clime,
That prays in his distress,
Prays to the human form divine,
Love, Mercy, Pity, Peace.

And all must love the human form,
In heathen, Turk, or Jew;
Where Mercy, Love, and Pity dwell,
There God is dwelling too.

HOLY THURSDAY

'Twas on a Holy Thursday, their innocent faces clean,
The children walking two and two, in red and blue and
    green,
Grey-headed beadles walked before, with wands as white as
    snow,
Till into the high dome of Paul's they like Thames' waters
    flow.

O what a multitude they seemed, these flowers of London
    town!
Seated in companies they sit with radiance all their own.
The hum of multitudes was there, but multitudes of lambs,
Thousands of little boys and girls raising their innocent
    hands.

Now like a mighty wind they raise to Heaven the voice of
    song,
Or like harmonious thunderings the seats of Heavens among.
Beneath them sit the aged men, wise guardians of the poor;
Then cherish pity, lest you drive an angel from your door.

NIGHT

The sun descending in the west,
The evening star does shine;
The birds are silent in their nest,
And I must seek for mine.
The moon like a flower,
In heaven's high bower,
With silent delight
Sits and smiles on the night.

Farewell, green fields and happy groves,
Where flocks have took delight.
Where lambs have nibbled, silent moves
The feet of angels bright;
Unseen they pour blessing,
And joy without ceasing,
On each bud and blossom,
And each sleeping bosom.

They look in every thoughtless nest,
Where birds are covered warm;
They visit caves of every beast,
To keep them all from harm.
If they see any weeping
That should have been sleeping,
They pour sleep on their head,
And sit down by their bed.

When wolves and tigers howl for prey,
They pitying stand and weep;
Seeking to drive their thirst away,
And keep them from the sheep.
But if they rush dreadful,
The angels, most heedful,
Receive each mild spirit,
New worlds to inherit.

And there the lion's ruddy eyes
Shall flow with tears of gold,
And pitying the tender cries,
And walking round the fold,
Saying 'Wrath, by his meekness,
And, by his health, sickness
Is driven away
From our immortal day.

'And now beside thee, bleating lamb,
I can lie down and sleep;
Or think on him who bore thy name,
Graze after thee and weep.
For, washed in life's river,
My bright mane for ever
Shall shine like the gold
As I guard o'er the fold.'

THE SICK ROSE

O Rose, thou art sick!
The invisible worm
That flies in the night
In the howling storm,

Has found out thy bed
Of crimson joy:
And his dark secret love
Does thy life destroy.

THE FLY

Little Fly,
Thy summer's play
My thoughtless hand
Has brushed away.

Am not I
A fly like thee?
Or art not thou
A man like me?

For I dance,
And drink, and sing,

Till some blind hand
Shall brush my wing.

If thought is life
And strength and breath,
And the want
Of thought is death;

Then am I
A happy fly,
If I live
Or if I die.

THE TIGER

Tiger! Tiger! burning bright
In the forests of the night,
What immortal hand or eye,
Could frame thy fearful symmetry?

In what distant deeps or skies
Burnt the fire of thine eyes?
On what wings dare he aspire?
What the hand dare seize the fire?

And what shoulder, and what art,
Could twist the sinews of thy heart?
And when thy heart began to beat,
What dread hand? and what dread feet?

What the hammer? what the chain?
In what furnace was thy brain?
What the anvil? what dread grasp
Dare its deadly terrors clasp?

When the stars threw down their spears,
And watered heaven with their tears,
Did he smile his work to see?
Did he who made the Lamb make thee?

Tiger! Tiger! burning bright
In the forests of the night,
What immortal hand or eye,
Dare frame thy fearful symmetry?

AH SUN-FLOWER!

Ah, Sun-flower, weary of time,
Who countest the steps of the sun,
Seeking after that sweet golden clime
Where the traveller's journey is done;

Where the Youth pined away with desire,
And the pale Virgin shrouded in snow,
Arise from their graves, and aspire
Where my Sun-flower wishes to go.

LONDON

I wander thro' each chartered street,
Near where the chartered Thames does flow,
And mark in every face I meet
Marks of weakness, marks of woe.

In every cry of every Man,
In every Infant's cry of fear,
In every voice, in every ban,
The mind-forged manacles I hear.

How the chimney-sweeper's cry
Every black'ning church appals;
And the hapless soldier's sigh
Runs in blood down palace walls.

But most thro' midnight streets I hear
How the youthful Harlot's curse
Blasts the new born infant's tear,
And blights with plagues the Marriage hearse.

A POISON TREE

I was angry with my friend:
I told my wrath, my wrath did end.
I was angry with my foe:
I told it not, my wrath did grow.

And I watered it in fears,
Night and morning with my tears;
And I sunnèd it with smiles,
And with soft deceitful wiles.

And it grew both day and night,
Till it bore an apple bright;
And my foe beheld it shine,
And he knew that it was mine,

And into my garden stole
When the night had veiled the pole:
In the morning glad I see
My foe outstretched beneath the tree.

THE HUMAN ABSTRACT

Pity would be no more
If we did not make somebody poor;
And Mercy no more could be
If all were as happy as we.

And mutual fear brings peace,
Till the selfish loves increase:

Then Cruelty knits a snare,
And spreads his baits with care.

He sits down with holy fears,
And waters the ground with tears;
Then Humility takes its root
Underneath his foot.

Soon spreads the dismal shade
Of Mystery over his head;
And the caterpillar and fly
Feed on the Mystery.

And it bears the fruit of Deceit,
Ruddy and sweet to eat;
And the raven his nest has made
In its thickest shade.

The Gods of the earth and sea
Sought thro' Nature to find this tree;
But their search was all in vain:
There grows one in the Human Brain.

I SAW A CHAPEL ALL OF GOLD

I saw a Chapel all of gold
That none did dare to enter in,
And many weeping stood without,
Weeping, mourning, worshipping.

I saw a Serpent rise between
The white pillars of the door,
And he forced and forced and forced;
Down the golden hinges tore,

And along the pavement sweet,
Set with pearls and rubies bright,
All his slimy length he drew,
Till upon the altar white

Vomiting his poison out
On the Bread and on the Wine.
So I turned into a sty,
And laid me down among the swine.

THE ANGEL

I asked a thief to steal me a peach:
He turned up his eyes.
I asked a lithe lady to lie her down:
Holy and meek she cries.

As soon as I went
An angel came:
He winked at the thief
And smiled at the dame,

And without one word said
Had a peach from the tree,
And still as a maid
Enjoyed the lady.

THE IMMORTAL

The Immortal stood frozen amidst
The vast rock of eternity times
And times, a night of vast durance,
Impatient, stifled, stiffened, hardenèd;

Till impatience no longer could bear
The hard bondage: rent, rent, the vast solid,
With a crash from immense to immense,

Cracked across into numberless fragments.
The Prophetic wrath, struggling for vent,
Hurls apart, stamping furious to dust
And crumbling with bursting sobs, heaves
The black marble on high into fragments.

Hurled apart on all sides as a falling
Rock, the innumerable fragments away
Fell asunder; and horrible vacuum
Beneath him, and on all sides round,

Falling, falling, Los fell and fell,
Sunk precipitant, heavy, down, down,
Times on times, night on night, day on day—
Truth has bounds, Error none—falling, falling,
Years on years, and ages on ages
Still he fell thro' the void, still a void

Found for falling, day and night without end;
For tho' day or night was not, their spaces
Were measured by his incessant whirls
In the horrid vacuity bottomless.

The Immortal revolving, indignant,
First in wrath threw his limbs like the babe
New born into our world: wrath subsided,
And contemplative thoughts first arose;
Then aloft his head reared in the Abyss
And his downward-borne fall changed oblique

Many ages of groans, till there grew
Branchy forms organizing the Human
Into finite inflexible organs;

Till in process from falling he bore
Sidelong on the purple air, wafting
The weak breeze in efforts o'erwearied.

Incessant the falling Mind laboured,
Organizing itself, till the Vacuum
Became element, pliant to rise
Or to fall or to swim or to fly,
With ease searching the dire vacuity.

from THE BOOK OF LOS, CHAP. II

MOCK ON, MOCK ON, VOLTAIRE, ROUSSEAU

Mock on, mock on, Voltaire, Rousseau;
Mock on, mock on; 'tis all in vain!
You throw the sand against the wind,
And the wind blows it back again.

And every sand becomes a Gem
Reflected in the beams divine;
Blown back they blind the mocking eye,
But still in Israel's paths they shine.

The Atoms of Democritus
And Newton's Particles of light
Are sands upon the Red Sea shore,
Where Israel's tents do shine so bright.

THE MENTAL TRAVELLER

I travelled thro' a land of men,
A land of men and women too,
And heard and saw such dreadful things
As cold earth-wanderers never knew.

For there the Babe is born in joy
That was begotten in dire woe;
Just as we reap in joy the fruit
Which we in bitter tears did sow.

And if the Babe is born a boy
He's given to a Woman Old,
Who nails him down upon a rock,
Catches his shrieks in cups of gold.

She binds iron thorns around his head,
She pierces both his hands and feet,
She cuts his heart out at his side
To make it feel both cold and heat.

Her fingers number every nerve,
Just as a miser counts his gold;
She lives upon his shrieks and cries,
And she grows young as he grows old.

Till he becomes a bleeding Youth,
And she becomes a Virgin bright;
Then he rends up his manacles,
And binds her down for his delight.

He plants himself in all her nerves,
Just as a husbandman his mould;
And she becomes his dwelling-place
And Garden fruitful seventyfold.

An agèd Shadow, soon he fades,
Wandering round an earthly cot,
Full fillèd all with gems and gold
Which he by industry had got.

And these are the gems of the human soul,
The rubies and pearls of a love-sick eye,
The countless gold of the aching heart,
The martyr's groan and the lover's sigh.

They are his meat, they are his drink;
He feeds the beggar and the poor
And the wayfaring traveller:
For ever open is his door.

His grief is their eternal joy;
They make the roofs and walls to ring;
Till from the fire on the hearth
A little Female Babe does spring.

And she is all of solid fire
And gems and gold, that none his hand
Dares stretch to touch her baby form,
Or wrap her in his swaddling-band.

But she comes to the man she loves,
If young or old, or rich or poor;
They soon drive out the Agèd Host,
A beggar at another's door.

He wanders weeping far away,
Until some other take him in;
Oft blind and age-bent, sore distrest,
Until he can a Maiden win.

And to allay his freezing age,
The poor man takes her in his arms;
The cottage fades before his sight,
The garden and its lovely charms.

The guests are scattered thro' the land,
For the eye altering alters all;
The senses roll themselves in fear,
And the flat earth becomes a ball;

The stars, sun, Moon, all shrink away,
A desert vast without a bound,
And nothing left to eat or drink,
And a dark desert all around.

The honey of her Infant lips,
The bread and wine of her sweet smile,
The wild game of her roving eye,
Does him to infancy beguile;

For as he eats and drinks he grows
Younger and younger every day;
And on the desert wild they both
Wander in terror and dismay.

Like the wild stag she flees away,
Her fear plants many a thicket wild;
While he pursues her night and day,
By various arts of love beguiled,

By various arts of love and hate,
Till the wide desert planted o'er
With labyrinths of wayward love,
Where roam the lion, wolf, and boar,

Till he becomes a wayward Babe,
And she a weeping Woman Old.
Then many a lover wanders here;
The sun and stars are nearer rolled;

The trees bring forth sweet Ecstasy
To all who in the desert roam;
Till many a city there is built,
And many a pleasant shepherd's home.

But when they find the Frowning Babe,
Terror strikes thro' the region wide:
The cry 'The Babe! the Babe is Born!'
And flee away on every side.

For who dare touch the Frowning Form,
His arm is withered to its root;
Lions, boars, wolves, all howling flee,
And every Tree does shed its fruit.

And none can touch that frowning form,
Except it be a Woman Old;
She nails him down upon the rock,
And all is done as I have told.

THE CRYSTAL CABINET

The Maiden caught me in the Wild,
Where I was dancing merrily;
She put me into her Cabinet,
And locked me up with a golden key.

This Cabinet is formed of gold
And pearl and crystal shining bright,
And within it opens into a world
And a little lovely moony Night.

Another England there I saw,
Another London with its Tower,
Another Thames and other hills,
And another pleasant Surrey bower,

Another Maiden like herself,
Translucent, lovely, shining clear,
Threefold each in the other closed—
O, what a pleasant trembling fear!

O, what a smile! a threefold smile
Filled me, that like a flame I burned;
I bent to kiss the lovely Maid,
And found a threefold kiss returned.

I strove to seize the inmost form
With ardour fierce and hands of flame,
But burst the Crystal Cabinet,
And like a weeping Babe became—

A weeping Babe upon the wild,
And weeping Woman pale reclined,
And in the outward air again
I filled with woes the passing wind.

AUGURIES OF INNOCENCE

To see a World in a grain of sand,
And a Heaven in a wild flower,
Hold Infinity in the palm of your hand,
And Eternity in an hour.

A robin redbreast in a cage
Puts all Heaven in a rage.
A dove-house filled with doves and pigeons
Shudders Hell thro' all its regions.
A dog starved at his master's gate
Predicts the ruin of the State.
A horse misused upon the road
Calls to Heaven for human blood.

Each outcry of the hunted hare
A fibre from the brain does tear.
A skylark wounded in the wing,
A cherubim does cease to sing.
The game-cock clipped and armed for fight
Does the rising sun affright.
Every wolf's and lion's howl
Raises from Hell a Human soul.
The wild deer, wand'ring here and there,
Keeps the Human soul from care.
The lamb misused breeds public strife,
And yet forgives the butcher's knife.
The bat that flits at close of eve
Has left the brain that won't believe.
The owl that calls upon the night
Speaks the unbeliever's fright.
He who shall hurt the little wren
Shall never be beloved by men.
He who the ox to wrath has moved
Shall never be by woman loved.
The wanton boy that kills the fly
Shall feel the spider's enmity.
He who torments the chafer's sprite
Weaves a bower in endless night.
The caterpillar on the leaf
Repeats to thee thy mother's grief.
Kill not the moth nor butterfly,
For the Last Judgement draweth nigh.
He who shall train the horse to war
Shall never pass the polar bar.
The beggar's dog and widow's cat,
Feed them and thou wilt grow fat.
The gnat that sings his summer's song
Poison gets from slander's tongue.
The poison of the snake and newt
Is the sweat of Envy's foot.
The poison of the honey-bee
Is the artist's jealousy.
The prince's robes and beggar's rags
Are toadstools on the miser's bags.
A truth that's told with bad intent
Beats all the lies you can invent.
It is right it should be so;
Man was made for joy and woe;
And when this we rightly know,
Thro' the world we safely go.

Joy and woe are woven fine,
A clothing for the soul divine.
Under every grief and pine
Runs a joy with silken twine.
The babe is more than swaddling-bands;
Throughout all these human lands
Tools were made, and born were hands,
Every farmer understands.
Every tear from every eye
Becomes a babe in Eternity;
This is caught by Females bright,
And returned to its own delight.
The bleat, the bark, bellow and roar
Are waves that beat on Heaven's shore.
The babe that weeps the rod beneath
Writes revenge in realms of death.
The beggar's rags, fluttering in air,
Does to rags the heavens tear.
The soldier, armed with sword and gun,
Palsied strikes the summer's sun.
The poor man's farthing is worth more
Than all the gold on Afric's shore.
One mite wrung from the labourer's hands
Shall buy and sell the miser's lands:
Or, if protected from on high,
Does that whole nation sell and buy.
He who mocks the infant's faith
Shall be mocked in age and death.
He who shall teach the child to doubt
The rotting grave shall ne'er get out.
He who respects the infant's faith
Triumphs over Hell and Death.
The child's toys and the old man's reasons
Are the fruits of the two seasons.
The questioner, who sits so sly,
Shall never know how to reply.
He who replies to words of Doubt
Doth put the light of knowledge out.
The strongest poison ever known
Came from Caesar's laurel crown.
Naught can deform the human race
Like to the armour's iron brace.
When gold and gems adorn the plough
To peaceful arts shall Envy bow.
A riddle, or the cricket's cry,
Is to Doubt a fit reply.

The emmet's inch and eagle's mile
Make lame Philosophy to smile.
He who doubts from what he sees
Will ne'er believe, do what you please.
If the Sun and Moon should doubt,
They'd immediately go out.
To be in a passion you good may do,
But no good if a passion is in you.
The whore and gambler, by the state
Licenc'd, build that nation's fate.
The harlot's cry from street to street
Shall weave Old England's winding-sheet.
The winner's shout, the loser's curse,
Dance before dead England's hearse.
Every night and every morn
Some to misery are born.
Every morn and every night
Some are born to sweet delight.
Some are born to sweet delight,
Some are born to endless night.
We are led to believe a lie
When we see not thro' the eye,
Which was born in a night, to perish in a night,
When the soul slept in beams of light.
God appears and God is light,
To those poor souls who dwell in Night;
But does a Human Form display
To those who dwell in realms of Day.

FOR THE SEXES: THE GATES OF PARADISE

PROLOGUE

Mutual Forgiveness of each vice,
Such are the Gates of Paradise,
Against the Accuser's chief desire,
Who walked among the stones of fire.
Jehovah's Finger Wrote the Law;
Then wept! then rose in zeal and awe,
And the Dead Corpse, from Sinai's heat,
Buried beneath his Mercy-seat.
O Christians! Christians! tell me why
You rear it on your altars high?

THE KEYS

The Caterpillar on the leaf
Reminds thee of thy Mother's grief.

OF THE GATES

My Eternal Man set in repose,
The Female from his darkness rose;
And she found me beneath a Tree,
A Mandrake, and in her Veil hid me.
Serpent Reasonings us entice
Of good and evil, virtue and vice,
Doubt self-jealous, Wat'ry folly;
Struggling thro' Earth's melancholy;
Naked in Air, in shame and fear;
Blind in Fire, with shield and spear;
Two-horned Reasoning, cloven fiction,
In doubt, which is self-contradiction,
A dark Hermaphrodite we stood—
Rational truth, root of evil and good.
Round me flew the Flaming Sword;
Round her snowy Whirlwinds roared,
Freezing her Veil, the Mundane Shell.
I rent the Veil where the Dead dwell:
When weary Man enters his Cave,
He meets his Saviour in the grave.
Some find a Female Garment there,
And some a Male, woven with care;
Lest the Sexual Garments sweet
Should grow a devouring Winding-sheet.
One dies! Alas! the Living and Dead!
One is slain! and One is fled!
In Vain-glory hatcht and nurst,
By double Spectres, self-accurst.
My Son! my Son! thou treatest me
But as I have instructed thee.
On the shadows of the Moon,
Climbing thro' Night's highest noon;
In Time's Ocean falling drown'd;
In Agèd Ignorance profound,
Holy and cold, I clipped the wings
Of all sublunary things,
And in depths of my dungeons
Closed the Father and the Sons.

But when once I did descry
The Immortal Man that cannot die,
Thro' evening shades I haste away
To close the labours of my day.
The Door of Death I open found,
And the Worm weaving in the ground:
Thou'rt my Mother, from the womb;
Wife, Sister, Daughter, to the Tomb;
Weaving to Dreams the Sexual strife,
And weeping over the Web of Life.

EPILOGUE

TO THE ACCUSER WHO IS
THE GOD OF THIS WORLD

Truly, My Satan, thou art but a dunce,
And dost not know the garment from the man;
Every harlot was a virgin once,
Nor canst thou ever change Kate into Nan.

Tho' thou art Worshipped by the names divine
Of Jesus and Jehovah, thou art still
The Son of Morn in weary Night's decline,
The lost traveller's dream under the hill.

ABSTINENCE SOWS SAND ALL OVER

Abstinence sows sand all over
The ruddy limbs and flaming hair,
But Desire gratified
Plants fruits of life and beauty there.

IN A WIFE I WOULD DESIRE

In a wife I would desire
What in whores is always found—
The lineaments of Gratified desire.

ETERNITY

He who bends to himself a Joy
Does the wingèd life destroy;
But he who kisses the Joy as it flies
Lives in Eternity's sunrise.

THE QUESTION ANSWERED

What is it men in women do require?
The lineaments of gratified Desire.
What is it women do in men require?
The lineaments of gratified Desire.

LACEDEMONIAN INSTRUCTION

'Come hither, my boy, tell me what thou seest there.'
'A fool tangled in a religious snare.'

RICHES

The countless gold of a merry heart,
The rubies and pearls of a loving eye,
The indolent never can bring to the mart,
Nor the secret hoard up in his treasury.

AN ANSWER TO THE PARSON

'Why of the sheep do you not learn peace?'
'Because I don't want you to shear my fleece.'

PROVERBS OF HELL

In seed time learn, in harvest teach, in winter enjoy.
Drive your cart and your plough over the bones of the dead.
The road of excess leads to the palace of wisdom.
Prudence is a rich, ugly old maid courted by Incapacity.
He who desires but acts not, breeds pestilence.
The cut worm forgives the plough.
Dip him in the river who loves water.
A fool sees not the same tree that a wise man sees.
He whose face gives no light, shall never become a star.
Eternity is in love with the productions of time.
The busy bee has no time for sorrow.
The hours of folly are measured by the clock; but of wisdom,
    no clock can measure.
All wholesome food is caught without a net or a trap.
Bring out number, weight, and measure in a year of dearth.
No bird soars too high, if he soars with his own wings.

A dead body revenges not injuries.

The most sublime act is to set another before you.

If the fool would persist in his folly he would become wise.

Folly is the cloak of knavery.

Shame is Pride's cloak.

Prisons are built with stones of Law, brothels with bricks of Religion.

The pride of the peacock is the glory of God.

The lust of the goat is the bounty of God.

The wrath of the lion is the wisdom of God.

The nakedness of woman is the work of God.

Excess of sorrow laughs. Excess of joy weeps.

The roaring of lions, the howling of wolves, the raging of the stormy sea, and the destructive sword are portions of eternity too great for the eye of man.

The fox condemns the trap, not himself.

Joys impregnate. Sorrows bring forth.

Let man wear the fell of the lion, woman the fleece of the sheep.

The bird a nest, the spider a web, man friendship.

The selfish, smiling fool, and the sullen, frowning fool shall be both thought wise, that they may be a rod.

What is now proved was once only imagin'd.

The rat, the mouse, the fox, the rabbit watch the roots; the lion, the tiger, the horse, the elephant watch the fruits.

The cistern contains: the fountain overflows.

One thought fills immensity.

Always be ready to speak your mind, and a base man will avoid you.

Everything possible to be believed is an image of truth.

The eagle never lost so much time as when he submitted to learn of the crow.

The fox provides for himself; but God provides for the lion.

Think in the morning. Act in the noon. Eat in the evening. Sleep in the night.

He who has suffered you to impose on him, knows you.

As the plough follows words, so God rewards prayers.

The tigers of wrath are wiser than the horses of instruction.

Expect poison from the standing water.

You never know what is enough unless you know what is more than enough.

Listen to the fool's reproach! it is a kingly title!

The eyes of fire, the nostrils of air, the mouth of water, the beard of earth.

The weak in courage is strong in cunning.

The apple-tree never asks the beech how he shall grow; nor
    the lion, the horse, how he shall take his prey.
The thankful receiver bears a plentiful harvest.
If others had not been foolish, we should be so.
The soul of sweet delight can never be defiled.
When thou seest an eagle, thou seest a portion of Genius;
    lift up thy head!
As the caterpillar chooses the fairest leaves to lay her eggs on,
    so the priest lays his curse on the fairest joys.
To create a little flower is the labour of ages.
Damn braces. Bless relaxes.
The best wine is the oldest, the best water the newest.
Prayers plough not! Praises reap not!
Joys laugh not! Sorrows weep not!
The head Sublime, the heart Pathos, the genitals Beauty,
    the hands and feet Proportion.
As the air to a bird or the sea to a fish, so is contempt to the
    contemptible.
The crow wished every thing was black, the owl that every
    thing was white.
Exuberance is Beauty.
If the lion was advised by the fox, he would be cunning.
Improvement makes straight roads; but the crooked roads
    without Improvement are roads of Genius.
Sooner murder an infant in its cradle than nurse unacted
    desires.
Where man is not, nature is barren.
Truth can never be told so as to be understood, and not be
    believed.
Enough! or Too much.

from THE MARRIAGE OF HEAVEN AND HELL.

THE BOOK OF THEL

THEL'S MOTTO

Does the Eagle know what is in the pit?
Or wilt thou go ask the Mole?
Can Wisdom be put in a silver rod?
Or Love in a golden bowl?

I

The daughters of Mne Seraphim led round their sunny flocks,
All but the youngest: she in paleness sought the secret air,
To fade away like morning beauty from her mortal day:
Down by the river of Adona her soft voice is heard,
And thus her gentle lamentation falls like morning dew:

O life of this our spring! why fades the lotus of the water,
Why fade these children of the spring, born but to smile
and fall?
Ah! Thel is like a wat'ry bow, and like a parting cloud;
Like a reflection in a glass; like shadows in the water,
Like dreams of infants, like a smile upon an infant's face;
Like the dove's voice; like transient day; like music in the air.
Ah! gentle may I lay me down, and gentle rest my head,
And gentle sleep the sleep of death, and gentle hear the
voice
Of him that walketh in the garden in the evening time.'

The Lilly of the valley, breathing in the humble grass
Answer'd the lovely maid and said: 'I am a wat'ry weed,
And I am very small and love to dwell in lowly vales;
So weak, the gilded butterfly scarce perches on my head.
Yet I am visited from heaven, and he that smiles on all
Walks in the valley, and each morn over me spreads his
hand,
Saying, "Rejoice, thou humble grass, thou new-born lilly
flower,
Thou gentle maid of silent valleys and of modest brooks;
For thou shalt be clothed in light, and fed with morning
manna,
Till summer's heat melts thee beside the fountains and the
springs
To flourish in eternal vales:" Then why should Thel
complain?
Why should the mistress of the vales of Har utter a sigh?'

She ceased and smiled in tears, then sat down in her silver
shrine.

Thel answered: 'O thou little virgin of the peaceful valley,
Giving to those that cannot crave, the voiceless, the o'ertired;
Thy breath doth nourish the innocent lamb, he smells thy
milky garments;
He crops thy flowers while thou sittest smiling in his face,
Wiping his mild and meekin mouth from all contagious taints.
Thy wine doth purify the golden honey; thy perfume,
Which thou dost scatter on every little blade of grass that
springs,
Revives the milked cow, and tames the fire-breathing steed.
But Thel is like a faint cloud kindled at the rising sun:
I vanish from my pearly throne, and who shall find my
place?'

'Queen of the vales,' the Lilly answered, 'ask the tender cloud,
And it shall tell thee why it glitters in the morning sky,
And why it scatters its bright beauty thro' the humid air,
Descend, O little Cloud, and hover before the eyes of Thel.'
The Cloud descended, and the Lilly bowed her modest head
And went to mind her numerous charge among the verdant
    grass.

II

'O little Cloud,' the virgin said, 'I charge thee tell to me
Why thou complainest not when in one hour thou fade away:
Then we shall seek thee, but not find. Ah! Thel is like to thee:
I pass away: yet I complain, and no one hears my voice.'

The Cloud then shewed his golden head and his bright form
    emerged,
Hovering and glittering on the air before the face of Thel.

'O virgin, know'st thou not our steeds drink of the golden
    springs
Where Luvah doth renew his horses? Look'st thou on my
    youth,
And fearest thou, because I vanish and am seen no more,
Nothing remains? O maid, I tell thee, when I pass away
It is to tenfold life, to love, to peace and raptures holy:
Unseen descending, weigh my light wings upon balmy flowers,
And court the fair-eyed dew to take me to her shining tent:
The weeping virgin, trembling kneels before the risen sun,
Till we arise linked in a golden band and never part,
But walk united, bearing food to all our tender flowers.'

'Dost thou, O little Cloud? I fear that I am not like thee,
For I walk thro' the vales of Har, and smell the sweetest
    flowers,
But I feed not the little flowers; I hear the warbling birds,
But I feed not the warbling birds; they fly and seek their
    food:
But Thel delights in these no more, because I fade away;
And all shall say: "Without a use this shining woman lived,
Or did she only live to be at death the food of worms?" '

The Cloud reclined upon his airy throne and answered thus:
'Then if thou art the food of worms, O virgin of the skies,
How great thy use, how great thy blessing! Every thing that
    lives

Lives not alone nor for itself. Fear not, and I will call
The weak worm from its lowly bed, and thou shalt hear its
          voice.
Come forth, worm of the silent valley, to thy pensive queen.'

The helpless worm arose, and sat upon the Lilly's leaf,
And the bright Cloud sailed on, to find his partner in the
          vale.

III

Then Thel astonished viewed the Worm upon its dewy bed.
'Art thou a Worm? Image of weakness, art thou but a Worm?
I see thee like an infant wrappèd in the Lilly's leaf.
Ah! weep not, little voice, thou canst not speak, but thou
          canst weep.
Is this a Worm? I see thee lay helpless and naked, weeping,
And none to answer, none to cherish thee with mother's
          smiles.'

The Clod of Clay heard the Worm's voice and raised her
          pitying head:
She bowed over the weeping infant, and her life exhaled
In milky fondness: then on Thel she fixed her humble eyes.

'O beauty of the vales of Har, we live not for ourselves.
Thou seest me the meanest thing, and so I am indeed.
My bosom of itself is cold, and of itself is dark;
But he, that loves the lowly, pours his oil upon my head,
And kisses me, and binds his nuptial bands around my
          breast,
And says: "Thou mother of my children, I have lovèd thee,
And I have given thee a crown that none can take away."
But how this is, sweet maid, I know not, and I cannot
          know;
I ponder, and I cannot ponder; yet I live and love.'

The daughter of beauty wiped her pitying tears with her
          white veil,
And said: 'Alas! I knew not this, and therefore did I weep.
That God would love a Worm I knew, and punish the evil
          foot
That wilful bruised its helpless form; but that he cherished it
With milk and oil I never knew, and therefore did I weep;

And I complained in the mild air, because I fade away,
And lay me down in thy cold bed, and leave my shining
    lot.'

'Queen of the vales,' the matron Clay answered, 'I heard
    thy sighs,
And all thy moans flew o'er my roof, but I have called them
    down.
Wilt thou, O Queen, enter my house? 'Tis given thee to
    enter
And to return: fear nothing, enter with thy virgin feet.'

IV

The eternal gates' terrific porter lifted the northern bar.
Thel entered in and saw the secrets of the land unknown.
She saw the couches of the dead, and where the fibrous roots
Of every heart on earth infixes deep its restless twists:
A land of sorrows and tears where never smile was seen.

She wandered in the land of clouds thro' valleys dark,
    list'ning
Dolours and lamentations; waiting oft beside a dewy grave
She stood in silence, list'ning to the voices of the ground,
Till to her own grave plot she came, and there she sat down,
And heard this voice of sorrow breathèd from the hollow pit.

'Why cannot the Ear be closed to its own destruction?
Or the glist'ning Eye to the poison of a smile?
Why are Eyelids stored with arrows ready drawn,
Where a thousand fighting men in ambush lie?
Or an Eye of gifts and graces show'ring fruits and coined
    gold?
Why a Tongue impressed with honey from every wind?
Why an Ear, a whirlpool fierce to draw creations in?
Why a Nostril wide inhaling terror, trembling, and affright?
Why a tender curb upon the youthful burning boy?
Why a little curtain of flesh on the bed of our desire?'

The Virgin started from her seat, and with a shriek
Fled back unhindered till she came into the vales of Har.

WILLIAM WORDSWORTH

(1770-1850)

DAFFODILS

I wandered lonely as a cloud
  That floats on high o'er vales and hills,
When all at once I saw a crowd,
  A host, of golden daffodils;
Beside the lake, beneath the trees,
Fluttering and dancing in the breeze.

Continuous as the stars that shine
  And twinkle on the milky way,
They stretched in never-ending line
  Along the margin of a bay:
Ten thousand saw I at a glance,
Tossing their heads in sprightly dance.

The waves beside them danced; but they
  Out-did the sparkling waves in glee:
A poet could not but be gay,
  In such a jocund company:
I gazed—and gazed—but little thought
What wealth the show to me had brought:

For oft, when on my couch I lie
  In vacant or in pensive mood,
They flash upon that inward eye
  Which is the bliss of solitude;
And then my heart with pleasure fills,
And dances with the daffodils.

RESOLUTION AND INDEPENDENCE

There was a roaring in the wind all night;
The rain came heavily and fell in floods;
But now the sun is rising calm and bright;
The birds are singing in the distant woods;
Over his own sweet voice the Stock-dove broods;
The Jay makes answer as the Magpie chatters;
And all the air is filled with pleasant noise of waters.

All things that love the sun are out of doors;
The sky rejoices in the morning's birth;
The grass is bright with rain-drops;—on the moors
The hare is running races in her mirth;
And with her feet she from the plashy earth
Raises a mist, that, glittering in the sun,
Runs with her all the way, wherever she doth run.

I was a Traveller then upon the moor;
I saw the hare that raced about with joy;
I heard the woods and distant waters roar;
Or heard them not, as happy as a boy:
The pleasant season did my heart employ:
My old remembrances went from me wholly;
And all the ways of men, so vain and melancholy.

But, as it sometimes chanceth, from the might
Of joy in minds that can no further go,
As high as we have mounted in delight
In our dejection do we sink as low;
To me that morning did it happen so;
And fears and fancies thick upon me came;
Dim sadness—and blind thoughts, I knew not, nor could
    name.

I heard the sky-lark warbling in the sky;
And I bethought me of the playful hare:
Even such a happy Child of earth am I;
Even as these blissful creatures do I fare;
Far from the world I walk, and from all care;
But there may come another day to me—
Solitude, pain of heart, distress, and poverty.

My whole life I have lived in pleasant thought,
As if life's business were a summer mood;
As if all needful things would come unsought

To genial faith, still rich in genial good;
But how can He expect that others should
Build for him, sow for him, and at his call
Love him, who for himself will take no heed at all?

I thought of Chatterton, the marvellous Boy,
The sleepless Soul that perished in his pride;
Of Him who walked in glory and in joy
Following his plough, along the mountain-side:
By our own spirits are we deified:
We Poets in our youth begin in gladness;
But thereof come in the end despondency and madness.

Now, whether it were by peculiar grace,
A leading from above, a something given,
Yet it befell that, in this lonely place,
When I with these untoward thoughts had striven,
Beside a pool bare to the eye of heaven
I saw a Man before me unawares:
The oldest man he seemed that ever wore grey hairs.

As a huge stone is sometimes seen to lie
Couched on the bald top of an eminence;
Wonder to all who do the same espy,
By what means it could thither come, and whence;
So that it seems a thing endued with sense:
Like a sea-beast crawled forth, that on a shelf
Of rock or sand reposeth, there to sun itself;

Such seemed this man, not all alive nor dead,
Nor all asleep—in his extreme old age:
His body was bent double, feet and head
Coming together in life's pilgrimage;
As if some dire constraint of pain, or rage
Of sickness felt by him in times long past,
A more than human weight upon his frame had cast.

Himself he propped, limbs, body, and pale face,
Upon a long grey staff of shaven wood:
And, still as I drew near with gentle pace,
Upon the margin of that moorish flood
Motionless as a cloud the old Man stood,
That heareth not the loud winds when they call;
And moveth all together, if it move at all.

At length, himself unsettling, he the pond

Stirred with his staff, and fixedly did look
Upon the muddy water, which he conned,
As if he had been reading in a book:
And now a stranger's privilege I took;
And, drawing to his side, to him did say,
'This morning gives us promise of a glorious day.'

A gentle answer did the old Man make,
In courteous speech which forth he slowly drew:
And him with further words I thus bespake,
'What occupation do you there pursue?
This is a lonesome place for one like you.'
Ere he replied, a flash of mild surprise
Broke from the sable orbs of his yet-vivid eyes.

His words came feebly, from a feeble chest,
But each in solemn order followed each,
With something of a lofty utterance drest—
Choice word and measured phrase, above the reach
Of ordinary men; a stately speech;
Such as grave Livers do in Scotland use,
Religious men, who give to God and man their dues.

He told that to these waters he had come
To gather leeches, being old and poor:
Employment hazardous and wearisome!
And he had many hardships to endure:
From pond to pond he roamed, from moor to moor;
Housing, with God's good help, by choice or chance;
And in this way he gained an honest maintenance.

The old Man still stood talking by my side;
But now his voice to me was like a stream
Scarce heard; nor word from word could I divide;
And the whole body of the Man did seem
Like one whom I had met with in a dream;
Or like a man from some far region sent,
To give me human strength, by apt admonishment.

My former thoughts returned: the fear that kills;
And hope that is unwilling to be fed;
Cold, pain, and labour, and all fleshly ills;
And mighty Poets in their misery dead.
—Perplexed, and longing to be comforted,
My question eagerly did I renew,
'How is it that you live, and what is it you do?'

He with a smile did then his words repeat;
And said that, gathering leeches, far and wide
He travelled; stirring thus about his feet
The waters of the pools where they abide.
'Once I could meet with them on every side;
But they have dwindled long by slow decay;
Yet still I persevere, and find them where I may.'

While he was talking thus, the lonely place,
The old Man's shape, and speech—all troubled me:
In my mind's eye I seemed to see him pace
About the weary moors continually,
Wandering about alone and silently.
While I these thoughts within myself pursued,
He, having made a pause, the same discourse renewed.

And soon with this he other matter blended,
Cheerfully uttered, with demeanour kind,
But stately in the main; and, when he ended,
I could have laughed myself to scorn to find
In that decrepit Man so firm a mind.
'God,' said I, 'be my help and stay secure;
I'll think of the Leech-gatherer on the lonely moor!'

CHARACTER OF THE HAPPY WARRIOR

Who is the happy Warrior? Who is he
That every man in arms should wish to be?
—It is the generous Spirit, who, when brought
Among the tasks of real life, hath wrought
Upon the plan that pleased his boyish thought:
Whose high endeavours are an inward light
That makes the path before him always bright:
Who, with a natural instinct to discern
What knowledge can perform, is diligent to learn;
Abides by this resolve, and stops not there,
But makes his moral being his prime care;
Who, doomed to go in company with Pain,
And Fear, and Bloodshed, miserable train!
Turns his necessity to glorious gain;
In face of these doth exercise a power
Which is our human nature's highest dower;
Controls them and subdues, transmutes, bereaves
Of their bad influence, and their good receives:
By objects, which might force the soul to abate

Her feeling, rendered more compassionate;
Is placable—because occasions rise
So often that demand such sacrifice;
More skilful in self-knowledge, even more pure,
As tempted more; more able to endure,
As more exposed to suffering and distress;
Thence, also, more alive to tenderness.
—'Tis he whose law is reason; who depends
Upon that law as on the best of friends;
Whence, in a stage where men are tempted still
To evil for a guard against worse ill,
And what in quality or act is best
Doth seldom on a right foundation rest,
He labours good on good to fix, and owes
To virtue every triumph that he knows:
—Who, if he rises to station of command,
Rises by open means; and there will stand
On honourable terms, or else retire,
And in himself possess his own desire;
Who comprehends his trust, and to the same
Keeps faithful with a singleness of aim;
And therefore does not stoop, nor lie in wait
For wealth, or honours, or for worldly state;
Whom they must follow; on whose head must fall,
Like showers of manna, if they come at all:
Whose power shed round him in the common strife,
Or mild concerns of ordinary life,
A constant influence, a peculiar grace;
But who, if he be called upon to face
Some awful moment to which Heaven has joined
Great issues, good or bad for human kind,
Is happy as a Lover; and attired
With sudden brightness, like a Man inspired;
And, through the heat of conflict, keeps the law
In calmness made, and sees what he foresaw;
Or if an unexpected call succeed,
Come when it will, is equal to the need:
—He who, though thus endued as with a sense
And faculty for storm and turbulence,
Is yet a Soul whose master-bias leans
To homefelt pleasures and to gentle scenes;
Sweet images! which, wheresoe'er he be,
Are at his heart; and such fidelity
It is his darling passion to approve;
More brave for this, that he hath much to love:—
'Tis, finally, the Man, who, lifted high,

Conspicuous object in a Nation's eye,
Or left unthought-of in obscurity,—
Who, with a toward or untoward lot,
Prosperous or adverse, to his wish or not—
Plays, in the many games of life, that one
Where what he most doth value must be won:
Whom neither shape of danger can dismay,
Nor thought of tender happiness betray;
Who, not content that former worth stand fast,
Looks forward, persevering to the last,
From well to better, daily self-surpast:
Who, whether praise of him must walk the earth
For ever, and to noble deeds give birth,
Or he must fall, to sleep without his fame,
And leave a dead unprofitable name—
Finds comfort in himself and in his cause;
And, while the mortal mist is gathering, draws
His breath in confidence of Heaven's applause:
This is the happy Warrior; this is He
That every Man in arms should wish to be.

A SLUMBER DID MY SPIRIT SEAL

A slumber did my spirit seal;
    I had no human fears:
She seemed a thing that could not feel
    The touch of earthly years.

No motion has she now, no force;
    She neither hears nor sees,
Rolled round in earth's diurnal course,
    With rocks, and stones, and trees.

SHE DWELT AMONG THE UNTRODDEN WAYS

She dwelt among the untrodden ways
    Beside the springs of Dove,
A maid whom there were none to praise
    And very few to love:

A violet by a mossy stone
    Half hidden from the eye!
—Fair as a star, when only one
    Is shining in the sky.

She lived unknown, and few could know
    When Lucy ceased to be;
But she is in her grave, and, oh,
    The difference to me!

THE RAINBOW

My heart leaps up when I behold
A rainbow in the sky:
So was it when my life began;
So is it now I am a man;
So be it when I shall grow old,
        Or let me die!
The Child is father of the Man;
And I could wish my days to be
Bound each to each by natural piety.

THE SOLITARY REAPER

Behold her, single in the field,
Yon solitary Highland Lass!
Reaping and singing by herself;
Stop here, or gently pass!
Alone she cuts and binds the grain,
And sings a melancholy strain;
O listen! for the Vale profound
Is overflowing with the sound.

No nightingale did ever chaunt
More welcome notes to weary bands
Of travellers in some shady haunt,
Among Arabian sands:
A voice so thrilling ne'er was heard
In spring-time from the Cuckoo-bird,
Breaking the silence of the seas
Among the farthest Hebrides.

Will no one tell me what she sings?—
Perhaps the plaintive numbers flow
For old, unhappy, far-off things,
And battles long ago:
Or is it some more humble lay,
Familiar matter of to-day?
Some natural sorrow, loss, or pain,
That has been, and may be again?

Whate'er the theme, the Maiden sang
As if her song could have no ending;
I saw her singing at her work,
And o'er the sickle bending;—
I listened, motionless and still;
And, as I mounted up the hill,
The music in my heart I bore,
Long after it was heard no more.

SHE WAS A PHANTOM OF DELIGHT

She was a Phantom of delight
When first she gleamed upon my sight;
A lovely Apparition, sent
To be a moment's ornament;
Her eyes as stars of Twilight fair;
Like Twilight's, too, her dusky hair;
But all things else about her drawn
From May-time and the cheerful Dawn;
A dancing Shape, an Image gay,
To haunt, to startle, and way-lay.

I saw her upon nearer view,
A Spirit, yet a Woman too!
Her household motions light and free,
And steps of virgin-liberty;
A countenance in which did meet
Sweet records, promises as sweet;
A Creature not too bright or good
For human nature's daily food;
For transient sorrows, simple wiles,
Praise, blame, love, kisses, tears, and smiles.

And now I see with eye serene
The very pulse of the machine;
A Being breathing thoughtful breath,
A Traveller between life and death;
The reason firm, the temperate will,
Endurance, foresight, strength, and skill;
A perfect Woman, nobly planned,
To warn, to comfort, and command;
And yet a Spirit still, and bright
With something of angelic light.

IN ONE OF THOSE EXCURSIONS

In one of those excursions (may they ne'er
Fade from remembrance!) through the Northern tracts
Of Cambria ranging with a youthful friend,
I left Bethgelert's huts at couching-time,
And westward took my way, to see the sun
Rise from the top of Snowdon. To the door
Of a rude cottage at the mountain's base
We came, and roused the shepherd who attends
The adventurous stranger's steps, a trusty guide;
Then, cheered by short refreshment, sallied forth.

    It was a close, warm, breezeless summer night,
Wan, dull, and glaring, with a dripping fog
Low-hung and thick that covered all the sky;
But, undiscouraged, we began to climb
The mountain-side. The mist soon girt us round,
And, after ordinary travellers' talk
With our conductor, pensively we sank
Each into commerce with his private thoughts:
Thus did we breast the ascent, and by myself
Was nothing either seen or heard that checked
Those musings or diverted, save that once
The shepherd's lurcher, who, among the crags,
Had to his joy unearthed a hedgehog, teased
His coiled-up prey with barkings turbulent.
This small adventure, for even such it seemed
In that wild place and at the dead of night,
Being over and forgotten, on we wound
In silence as before. With forehead bent
Earthward, as if in opposition set
Against an enemy, I panted up
With eager pace, and no less eager thoughts.
Thus might we wear a midnight hour away
Ascending at loose distance each from each,
And I, as chanced, the foremost of the band;
When at my feet the ground appeared to brighten,
And with a step or two seemed brighter still;
Nor was time given to ask or learn the cause,
For instantly a light upon the turf
Fell like a flash, and lo! as I looked up,
The Moon hung naked in a firmament
Of azure without cloud, and at my feet
Rested a silent sea of hoary mist.
A hundred hills their dusky backs upheaved

All over this still ocean; and beyond,
Far, far beyond, the solid vapors stretched,
In headlands, tongues, and promontory shapes,
Into the main Atlantic, that appeared
To dwindle, and give up his majesty,
Usurped upon far as the sight could reach.
Not so the ethereal vault; encroachment none
Was there, nor loss; only the inferior stars
Had disappeared, or shed a fainter light
In the clear presence of the full-orbed Moon,
Who, from her sovereign elevation, gazed
Upon the billowy ocean, as it lay
All meek and silent, save that through a rift—
Not distant from the shore whereon we stood,
A fixed, abysmal, gloomy, breathing-place—
Mounted the roar of waters, torrents, streams
Innumerable, roaring with one voice!
Heard over earth and sea, and, in that hour,
For so it seemed, felt by the starry heavens.

    When into air had partially dissolved
That vision, given to spirits of the night
And three chance human wanderers, in calm thought
Reflected, it appeared to me the type
Of a majestic intellect, its acts
And its possessions, what it has and craves,
What in itself it is, and would become.
There I beheld the emblem of a mind
That feeds upon infinity, that broods
Over the dark abyss, intent to hear
Its voices issuing forth to silent light
In one continuous stream; a mind sustained
By recognitions of transcendent power,
In sense conducting to ideal form,
In soul of more than mortal privilege.
One function, above all, of such a mind
Had Nature shadowed there, by putting forth,
'Mid circumstances awful and sublime,
That mutual domination which she loves
To exert upon the face of outward things,
So moulded, joined, abstracted, so endowed
With interchangeable supremacy,
That men, least sensitive, see, hear, perceive,
And cannot choose but feel.

                              from THE PRELUDE

THERE WAS A BOY

There was a Boy; ye knew him well, ye cliffs
And islands of Winander!—many a time,
At evening, when the earliest stars began
To move along the edges of the hills,
Rising or setting, would he stand alone,
Beneath the trees, or by the glimmering lake;
And there, with fingers interwoven, both hands
Pressed closely palm to palm and to his mouth
Uplifted, he, as through an instrument,
Blew mimic hootings to the silent owls,
That they might answer him.—And they would shout
Across the watery vale, and shout again,
Responsive to his call,—with quivering peals,
And long halloos, and screams, and echoes loud
Redoubled and redoubled; concourse wild
Of jocund din! And, when there came a pause
Of silence such as baffled his best skill:
Then, sometimes, in that silence, while he hung
Listening, a gentle shock of mild surprise
Has carried far into his heart the voice
Of mountain-torrents; or the visible scene
Would enter unawares into his mind
With all its solemn imagery, its rocks,
Its woods, and that uncertain heaven received
Into the bosom of the steady lake.

   This boy was taken from his mates, and died
In childhood, ere he was full twelve years old.
Pre-eminent in beauty is the vale
Where he was born and bred: the church-yard hangs
Upon a slope above the village-school;
And, through that church-yard when my way has led
On summer-evenings, I believe that there
A long half-hour together I have stood
Mute—looking at the grave in which he lies!

from THE PRELUDE

TO H. C.

SIX YEARS OLD

O Thou! whose fancies from afar are brought;
Who of thy words dost make a mock apparel,
And fittest to unutterable thought
The breeze-like motion and the self-born carol:

Thou faery voyager! that dost float
In such clear water, that thy boat
May rather seem
To brood on air than on an earthly stream;
Suspended in a stream as clear as sky,
Where earth and heaven do make one imagery;
O blessed vision! happy child!
Thou art so exquisitely wild,
I think of thee with many fears
For what may be thy lot in future years.
    I thought of times when Pain might be thy guest,
Lord of thy house and hospitality;
And Grief, uneasy lover! never rest
But when she sate within the touch of thee.
O too industrious folly!
O vain and causeless melancholy!
Nature will either end thee quite;
Or, lengthening out thy season of delight,
Preserve for thee, by individual right,
A young lamb's heart among the full-grown flocks.
What hast thou to do with sorrow,
Or the injuries of to-morrow?
Thou art a dew-drop, which the morn brings forth,
Ill fitted to sustain unkindly shocks,
Or to be trailed along the soiling earth;
A gem that glitters while it lives,
And no forewarning gives;
But, at the touch of wrong, without a strife
Slips in a moment out of life.

LONDON, 1802

Milton! thou shouldst be living at this hour:
England hath need of thee: she is a fen
Of stagnant waters: altar, sword, and pen,
Fireside, the heroic wealth of hall and bower,
Have forfeited their ancient English dower
Of inward happiness. We are selfish men;
Oh! raise us up, return to us again;
And give us manners, virtue, freedom, power.
Thy soul was like a Star, and dwelt apart;
Thou hadst a voice whose sound was like the sea:
Pure as the naked heavens, majestic, free,
So didst thou travel on life's common way,

In cheerful godliness; and yet thy heart
The lowliest duties on herself did lay.

WHEN I HAVE BORNE IN MEMORY

When I have borne in memory what has tamed
Great Nations, how ennobling thoughts depart
When men change swords for ledgers, and desert
The student's bower for gold, some fears unnamed
I had, my Country!—am I to be blamed?
Now, when I think of thee, and what thou art,
Verily, in the bottom of my heart,
Of those unfilial fears I am ashamed.
For dearly must we prize thee; we who find
In thee a bulwark for the cause of men;
And I by my affection was beguiled:
What wonder if a Poet now and then,
Among the many movements of his mind,
Felt for thee as a lover or a child!

WHERE LIES THE LAND

Where lies the Land to which yon Ship must go?
Fresh as a lark mounting at break of day,
Festively she puts forth in trim array;
Is she for tropic suns, or polar snow?
What boots the enquiry?—Neither friend nor foe
She cares for; let her travel where she may,
She finds familiar names, a beaten way
Ever before her, and a wind to blow.
Yet still I ask, what haven is her mark?
And, almost as it was when ships were rare,
(From time to time, like Pilgrims, here and there
Crossing the waters) doubt, and something dark,
Of the old Sea some reverential fear,
Is with me at thy farewell, joyous Bark!

MUTABILITY

From low to high doth dissolution climb,
And sink from high to low, along a scale
Of awful notes, whose concord shall not fail;
A musical but melancholy chime,

Which they can hear who meddle not with crime,
Nor avarice, nor over-anxious care.
Truth fails not; but her outward forms that bear
The longest date do melt like frosty rime
That in the morning whitened hill and plain
And is no more; drop like the tower sublime
Of yesterday, which royally did wear
His crown of weeds, but could not even sustain
Some casual shout that broke the silent air,
Or the unimaginable touch of Time.

SURPRISED BY JOY—IMPATIENT AS THE WIND

Surprised by joy—impatient as the wind
I turned to share the transport—Oh! with whom
But Thee, deep buried in the silent tomb,
That spot which no vicissitude can find?
Love, faithful love, recalled thee to my mind—
But how could I forget thee? Through what power,
Even for the least division of an hour,
Have I been so beguiled as to be blind
To my most grievous loss?—That thought's return
Was the worst pang that sorrow ever bore,
Save one, one only, when I stood forlorn,
Knowing my heart's best treasure was no more;
That neither present time, nor years unborn
Could to my sight that heavenly face restore.

GREAT MEN HAVE BEEN AMONG US

Great men have been among us; hands that penned
And tongues that uttered wisdom—better none:
The later Sidney, Marvel, Harrington,
Young Vane, and others who called Milton friend.
These moralists could act and comprehend:
They knew how genuine glory was put on;
Taught us how rightfully a nation shone
In splendour: what strength was, that would not bend
But in magnanimous meekness. France, 'tis strange,
Hath brought forth no such souls as we had then.
Perpetual emptiness! unceasing change!
No single volume paramount, no code,
No master spirit, no determined road;
But equally a want of books and men!

IT IS A BEAUTEOUS EVENING

It is a beauteous evening, calm and free,
The holy time is quiet as a Nun
Breathless with adoration; the broad sun
Is sinking down in its tranquillity;
The gentleness of heaven broods o'er the Sea:
Listen! the mighty Being is awake,
And doth with his eternal motion make
A sound like thunder—everlastingly.
Dear Child! dear Girl! that walkest with me here,
If thou appear untouched by solemn thought,
Thy nature is not therefore less divine:
Thou liest in Abraham's bosom all the year;
And worship'st at the Temple's inner shrine,
God being with thee when we know it not.

THE WORLD IS TOO MUCH WITH US

The world is too much with us; late and soon,
Getting and spending, we lay waste our powers:
Little we see in Nature that is ours;
We have given our hearts away, a sordid boon!
This Sea that bares her bosom to the moon;
The winds that will be howling at all hours,
And are up-gathered now like sleeping flowers;
For this, for everything, we are out of tune;
It moves us not.—Great God! I'd rather be
A Pagan suckled in a creed outworn;
So might I, standing on this pleasant lea,
Have glimpses that would make me less forlorn;
Have sight of Proteus rising from the sea;
Or hear old Triton blow his wreathèd horn.

COMPOSED UPON WESTMINSTER BRIDGE

Earth has not anything to show more fair:
Dull would he be of soul who could pass by
A sight so touching in its majesty:
This City now doth, like a garment, wear
The beauty of the morning; silent, bare,
Ships, towers, domes, theatres, and temples lie
Open unto the fields, and to the sky;
All bright and glittering in the smokeless air.
Never did sun more beautifully steep

In his first splendour, valley, rock, or hill;
Ne'er saw I, never felt, a calm so deep!
The river glideth at his own sweet will:
Dear God! the very houses seem asleep;
And all that mighty heart is lying still!

SEPTEMBER, 1802: NEAR DOVER

Inland, within a hollow vale, I stood;
And saw, while sea was calm and air was clear,
The coast of France—the coast of France how near!
Drawn almost into frightful neighbourhood.
I shrunk; for verily the barrier flood
Was like a lake, or river bright and fair,
A span of waters; yet what power is there!
What mightiness for evil and for good!
Even so doth God protect us if we be
Virtuous and wise. Winds blow, and waters roll,
Strength to the brave, and Power, and Deity;
Yet in themselves are nothing! One decree
Spake laws to *them*, and said that by the soul
Only, the Nations shall be great and free.

ODE

INTIMATIONS OF IMMORTALITY FROM RECOLLECTIONS OF EARLY CHILDHOOD

The Child is father of the Man;
And I could wish my days to be
Bound each to each by natural piety.

There was a time when meadow, grove, and stream,
The earth, and every common sight,
    To me did seem
    Apparelled in celestial light,
The glory and the freshness of a dream.
It is not now as it hath been of yore;—
    Turn wheresoe'er I may,
    By night or day,
The things which I have seen I now can see no more.

    The Rainbow comes and goes,
    And lovely is the Rose,
    The Moon doth with delight

Look round her when the heavens are bare;
        Waters on a starry night
        Are beautiful and fair;
    The sunshine is a glorious birth;
    But yet I know, where'er I go,
That there hath past away a glory from the earth.

Now, while the birds thus sing a joyous song,
    And while the young lambs bound
        As to the tabor's sound,
To me alone there came a thought of grief:
A timely utterance gave that thought relief,
        And I again am strong:
The cataracts blow their trumpets from the steep;
No more shall grief of mine the season wrong;
I hear the Echoes through the mountains throng,
The Winds come to me from the fields of sleep,
        And all the earth is gay;
            Land and sea
        Give themselves up to jollity,
        And with the heart of May
    Doth every Beast keep holiday;—
        Thou Child of Joy,
Shout round me, let me hear thy shouts, thou happy
            Shepherd-boy!

Ye blessèd Creatures, I have heard the call
    Ye to each other make; I see
The heavens laugh with you in your jubilee;
    My heart is at your festival,
    My head hath its coronal,
The fulness of your bliss, I feel—I feel it all.
        Oh evil day! if I were sullen
        While Earth herself is adorning,
            This sweet May-morning,
        And the Children are culling
            On every side,
    In a thousand valleys far and wide,
    Fresh flowers; while the sun shines warm,
And the Babe leaps up on his Mother's arm:—
        I hear, I hear, with joy I hear!
        —But there's a Tree, of many, one,
A single Field which I have looked upon,
Both of them speak of something that is gone:
        The Pansy at my feet
        Doth the same tale repeat:

Whither is fled the visionary gleam?
Where is it now, the glory and the dream?

Our birth is but a sleep and a forgetting:
The Soul that rises with us, our life's Star,
          Hath had elsewhere its setting,
              And cometh from afar:
          Not in entire forgetfulness,
          And not in utter nakedness,
But trailing clouds of glory do we come
          From God, who is our home:
Heaven lies about us in our infancy!
Shades of the prison-house begin to close
          Upon the growing Boy,
But He beholds the light, and whence it flows,
          He sees it in his joy;
The Youth, who daily farther from the east
          Must travel, still is Nature's Priest,
          And by the vision splendid
          Is on his way attended;
At length the Man perceives it die away,
And fade into the light of common day.

Earth fills her lap with pleasures of her own;
Yearnings she hath in her own natural kind,
And, even with something of a Mother's mind,
          And no unworthy aim,
          The homely Nurse doth all she can
To make her Foster-child, her Inmate Man,
          Forget the glories he hath known,
And that imperial palace whence he came.

Behold the Child among his new-born blisses,
A six years' Darling of a pigmy size!
See, where 'mid work of his own hand he lies,
Fretted by sallies of his mother's kisses,
With light upon him from his father's eyes!
See, at his feet, some little plan or chart,
Some fragment from his dream of human life,
Shaped by himself with newly-learned art;
          A wedding or a festival,
          A mourning or a funeral;
              And this hath now his heart,
          And unto this he frames his song:
              Then will he fit his tongue
To dialogues of business, love, or strife;

But it will not be long
Ere this be thrown aside,
And with new joy and pride
The little Actor cons another part;
Filling from time to time his 'humorous stage'
With all the Persons, down to palsied Age,
That Life brings with her in her equipage;
As if his whole vocation
Were endless imitation.

Thou, whose exterior semblance doth belie
Thy Soul's immensity;
Thou best Philosopher, who yet dost keep
Thy heritage, thou Eye among the blind,
That, deaf and silent, read'st the eternal deep,
Haunted forever by the eternal mind,—
Mighty Prophet! Seer blest!
On whom those truths do rest,
Which we are toiling all our lives to find,
In darkness lost, the darkness of the grave;
Thou, over whom thy Immortality
Broods like the Day, a Master o'er a Slave,
A Presence which is not to be put by;
Thou little Child, yet glorious in the might
Of heaven-born freedom on thy being's height,
Why with such earnest pains dost thou provoke
The years to bring the inevitable yoke,
Thus blindly with thy blessedness at strife?
Full soon thy Soul shall have her earthly freight,
And custom lie upon thee with a weight,
Heavy as frost, and deep almost as life!

O joy! that is our embers
Is something that doth live,
That Nature yet remembers
What was so fugitive!
The thought of our past years in me doth breed
Perpetual benediction: not indeed
For that which is most worthy to be blest;
Delight and liberty, the simple creed
Of Childhood, whether busy or at rest,
With new-fledged hope still fluttering in his breast:—
Not for these I raise
The song of thanks and praise;
But for those obstinate questionings
Of sense and outward things,

Fallings from us, vanishings;
    Blank misgivings of a Creature
Moving about in worlds not realized,
High instincts before which our mortal Nature
Did tremble like a guilty Thing surprised:
        But for those first affections,
        Those shadowy recollections,
      Which, be they what they may,
Are yet the fountain light of all our day,
Are yet a master light of all our seeing;
      Uphold us, cherish, and have power to make
Our noisy years seem moments in the being
Of the eternal Silence: truths that wake,
        To perish never;
Which neither listlessness, nor mad endeavour,
        Nor Man nor Boy,
Nor all that is at enmity with joy.
Can utterly abolish or destroy!
        Hence in a season of calm weather
        Though inland far we be,
Our Souls have sight of that immortal sea
        Which brought us hither,
        Can in a moment travel thither,
And see the Children sport upon the shore,
And hear the mighty waters rolling evermore.

Then sing, ye Birds, sing, sing a joyous song!
        And let the young Lambs bound
        As to the tabor's sound!
We in thought will join your throng,
        Ye that pipe and ye that play,
        Ye that through your hearts to-day
        Feel the gladness of the May!
What though the radiance which was once so bright
Be now for ever taken from my sight,
      Though nothing can bring back the hour
Of splendour in the grass, of glory in the flower;
        We will grieve not, rather find
        Strength in what remains behind;
        In the primal sympathy
        Which having been must ever be;
        In the soothing thoughts that spring
        Out of human suffering;
        In the faith that looks through death,
In years that bring the philosophic mind.

And O, ye Fountains, Meadows, Hills, and Groves,

Forbode not any severing of our loves!
Yet in my heart of hearts I feel your might;
I only have relinquished one delight
To live beneath your more habitual sway.
I love the Brooks which down their channels fret,
Even more than when I tripped lightly as they;
The innocent brightness of a new-born Day
                    Is lovely yet;
The Clouds that gather round the setting sun
Do take a sober colouring from an eye
That hath kept watch o'er man's mortality;
Another race hath been, and other palms are won.
Thanks to the human heart by which we live,
Thanks to its tenderness, its joys, and fears,
To me the meanest flower that blows can give
Thoughts that do often lie too deep for tears.

LINES COMPOSED A FEW MILES ABOVE

TINTERN ABBEY

ON REVISITING THE BANKS OF THE WYE DURING A TOUR

Five years have past; five summers, with the length
Of five long winters! and again I hear
These waters, rolling from their mountain-springs
With a soft inland murmur.—Once again
Do I behold these steep and lofty cliffs,
That on a wild secluded scene impress
Thoughts of more deep seclusion; and connect
The landscape with the quiet of the sky.
The day is come when I again repose
Here, under this dark sycamore, and view
These plots of cottage-ground, these orchard-tufts,
Which at this season, with their unripe fruits,
Are clad in one green hue, and lose themselves
'Mid groves and copses. Once again I see
These hedge-rows, hardly hedge-rows, little lines
Of sportive wood run wild: these pastoral farms,
Green to the very door; and wreaths of smoke
Sent up, in silence, from among the trees!
With some uncertain notice, as might seem
Of vagrant dwellers in the houseless woods,
Or of some Hermit's cave, where by his fire
The Hermit sits alone.
                        These beauteous forms,
Through a long absence, have not been to me

As is a landscape to a blind man's eye:
But oft, in lonely rooms, and 'mid the din
Of towns and cities, I have owed to them
In hours of weariness, sensations sweet,
Felt in the blood, and felt along the heart;
And passing even into my purer mind,
With tranquil restoration:—feelings too
Of unremembered pleasure: such, perhaps,
As have no slight or trivial influence
On that best portion of a good man's life,
His little, nameless, unremembered, acts
Of kindness and of love. Nor less, I trust,
To them I may have owed another gift,
Of aspect more sublime; that blessed mood,
In which the burthen of the mystery,
In which the heavy and the weary weight
Of all this unintelligible world,
Is lightened:—that serene and blessed mood,
In which the affections gently lead us on,—
Until, the breath of this corporeal frame
And even the motion of our human blood
Almost suspended, we are laid asleep
In body, and become a living soul:
While with an eye made quiet by the power
Of harmony, and the deep power of joy,
We see into the life of things.

                                   If   this
Be but a vain belief, yet, oh!—how oft—
In darkness and amid the many shapes
Of joyless daylight; when the fretful stir
Unprofitable, and the fever of the world,
Have hung upon the beatings of my heart—
How oft, in spirit, have I turned to thee,
O sylvan Wye! thou wanderer thro' the woods,
How often has my spirit turned to thee!

   And now, with gleams of half-extinguished thought,
With many recognitions dim and faint,
And somewhat of a sad perplexity,
The picture of the mind revives again:
While here I stand, not only with the sense
Of present pleasure, but with pleasing thoughts
That in this moment there is life and food
For future years. And so I dare to hope,
Though changed, no doubt, from what I was when first
I came among these hills; when like a roe
I bounded o'er the mountains, by the sides

Of the deep rivers, and the lonely streams,
Wherever nature led: more like a man
Flying from something that he dreads, than one
Who sought the thing he loved. For nature then
(The coarser pleasures of my boyish days,
And their glad animal movements all gone by)
To me was all in all.—I cannot paint
What then I was. The sounding cataract
Haunted me like a passion: the tall rock,
The mountain, and the deep and gloomy wood,
Their colours and their forms, were then to me
An appetite; a feeling and a love,
That had no need of a remoter charm,
By thought supplied, nor any interest
Unborrowed from the eye.—That time is past,
And all its aching joys are now no more,
And all its dizzy raptures. Not for this
Faint I, nor mourn nor murmur; other gifts
Have followed; for such loss, I would believe,
Abundant recompense. For I have learned
To look on nature, not as in the hour
Of thoughtless youth; but hearing oftentimes
The still, sad music of humanity,
Nor harsh nor grating, though of ample power
To chasten and subdue. And I have felt
A presence that disturbs me with the joy
Of elevated thoughts; a sense sublime
Of something far more deeply interfused,
Whose dwelling is the light of setting suns,
And the round ocean and the living air,
And the blue sky, and in the mind of man;
A motion and a spirit, that impels
All thinking things, all objects of all thought,
And rolls through all things. Therefore am I still
A lover of the meadows and the woods,
And mountains; and of all that we behold
From this green earth; of all the mighty world
Of eye, and ear,—both what they half create,
And what perceive; well pleased to recognise
In nature and the language of the sense,
The anchor of my purest thoughts, the nurse,
The guide, the guardian of my heart, and soul
Of all my moral being.

                    Nor perchance,
If I were not thus taught, should I the more
Suffer my genial spirits to decay:

For thou art with me here upon the banks
Of this fair river; thou my dearest Friend,
My dear, dear Friend; and in thy voice I catch
The language of my former heart, and read
My former pleasures in the shooting lights
Of thy wild eyes. Oh! yet a little while
May I behold in thee what I was once,
My dear, dear Sister! and this prayer I make,
Knowing that Nature never did betray
The heart that loved her; 'tis her privilege,
Through all the years of this our life, to lead
From joy to joy: for she can so inform
The mind that is within us, so impress
With quietness and beauty, and so feed
With lofty thoughts, that neither evil tongues,
Rash judgments, nor the sneers of selfish men,
Nor greetings where no kindness is, nor all
The dreary intercourse of daily life,
Shall e'er prevail against us, or disturb
Our cheerful faith that all which we behold
Is full of blessings. Therefore let the moon
Shine on thee in thy solitary walk;
And let the misty mountain-winds be free
To blow against thee: and, in after years,
When these wild ecstasies shall be matured
Into a sober pleasure; when thy mind
Shall be a mansion for all lovely forms,
Thy memory be as a dwelling-place
For all sweet sounds and harmonies; oh! then,
If solitude, or fear, or pain, or grief,
Should be thy portion, with what healing thoughts
Of tender joy wilt thou remember me,
And these my exhortations! Nor, perchance—
If I should be where I no more can hear
Thy voice, nor catch from thy wild eyes these gleams
Of past existence—wilt thou then forget
That on the banks of this delightful stream
We stood together; and that I, so long
A worshipper of Nature, hither came
Unwearied in that service: rather say
With warmer love—oh! with far deeper zeal
Of holier love. Nor wilt thou then forget,
That after many wanderings, many years
Of absence, these steep woods and lofty cliffs,
And this green pastoral landscape, were to me
More dear, both for themselves and for thy sake!

SAMUEL TAYLOR COLERIDGE

(1772-1834)

KUBLA KHAN: OR, A VISION IN A DREAM

A FRAGMENT

The following fragment is here published at the request of a poet of great and deserved celebrity [Lord Byron]; and, as far as the author's own opinions are concerned, rather as a psychological curiosity, than on the ground of any supposed *poetic* merits.

In the summer of the year 1797, the Author, then in ill health, had retired to a lonely farm-house between Porlock and Linton, on the Exmoor confines of Somerset and Devonshire. In consequence of a slight indisposition, an anodyne had been prescribed, from the effects of which he fell asleep in his chair at the moment he was reading the following sentence, or words of the same substance, in Purchas's Pilgrimage: 'Here the Khan Kubla commanded a palace to be built, and a stately garden thereunto. And thus ten miles of fertile ground were inclosed with a wall.' The Author continued for about three hours in a profound sleep, at least of the external senses, during which time he has the most vivid confidence, that he could not have composed less than from two to three hundred lines; if that indeed can be called composition in which all the images rose up before him as things, with a parallel production of the correspondent expressions, without any sensation or consciousness of effort. On awaking he appeared to himself to have a distinct recollection of the whole, and taking his pen, ink, and paper, instantly and eagerly wrote down the lines that are here preserved. At this moment he was unfortunately called out by a person on business from Porlock, and detained by him above an hour, and on his return to his room, found, to his no small surprise and mortification, that though he still retained some vague and dim recollecton of the general purport of the vision, yet, with the exception of some eight or ten scattered lines and images, all the rest had passed away like the images on the surface of a stream into which a stone had been cast, but, alas! without the after restoration of the latter:

> *Then all the charm*
> *Is broken—all that phantom-world so fair*
> *Vanishes, and a thousand circlets spread,*
> *And each mis-shape[s] the other. Stay awhile,*
> *Poor youth! who scarcely dar'st lift up thine eyes—*
> *The stream will soon renew its smoothness, soon*
> *The visions will return! And lo, he stays,*
> *And soon the fragments dim of lovely forms*
> *Come trembling back, unite, and now once more*
> *The pool becomes a mirror.*

[From 'The Picture']

Yet from the still surviving recollections in his mind, the Author has frequently purposed to finish for himself what had been originally, as it were, given to him Σαμερον αδιον ασω but the to-morrow is yet to come.

In Xanadu did Kubla Khan
A stately pleasure-dome decree:
Where Alph, the sacred river, ran
Through caverns measureless to man
   Down to a sunless sea.
So twice five miles of fertile ground
With walls and towers were girdled round:
And there were gardens bright with sinuous rills,
Where blossomed many an incense-bearing tree;
And here were forests ancient as the hills,
Enfolding sunny spots of greenery.

But oh! that deep romantic chasm which slanted
Down the green hill athwart a cedarn cover!
A savage place! as holy and enchanted
As e'er beneath a waning moon was haunted
By woman wailing for her demon-lover!
And from this chasm, with ceaseless turmoil seething,
As if this earth in fast thick pants were breathing,
A mighty fountain momently was forced:
Amid whose swift half-intermitted burst
Huge fragments vaulted like rebounding hail,
Or chaffy grain beneath the thresher's flail:
And 'mid these dancing rocks at once and ever
It flung up momently the sacred river.
Five miles meandering with a mazy motion
Through wood and dale the sacred river ran,
Then reached the caverns measureless to man,
And sank in tumult to a lifeless ocean:
And 'mid this tumult Kubla heard from far
Ancestral voices prophesying war!

The shadow of the dome of pleasure
Floated midway on the waves;
Where was heard the mingled measure
From the fountain and the caves.
It was a miracle of rare device,
A sunny pleasure-dome with caves of ice!

A damsel with a dulcimer
In a vision once I saw:
It was an Abyssinian maid,
And on her dulcimer she played,
Singing of Mount Abora.
Could I revive within me
Her symphony and song,
To such a deep delight 'twould win me,
That with music loud and long,
I would build that dome in air,
That sunny dome! those caves of ice!
And all who heard should see them there,
And all should cry, Beware! Beware!
His flashing eyes, his floating hair!
Weave a circle round him thrice,
And close your eyes with holy dread,
For he on honey-dew hath fed,
And drunk the milk of Paradise.

FROST AT MIDNIGHT

The frost performs its secret ministry,
Unhelped by any wind. The owlet's cry
Came loud—and hark, again! loud as before.
The inmates of my cottage, all at rest,
Have left me to that solitude, which suits
Abstruser musings: save that at my side
My cradled infant slumbers peacefully.
'Tis calm indeed! so calm, that it disturbs
And vexes meditation with its strange
And extreme silentness. Sea, hill, and wood,
This populous village! Sea, and hill, and wood,
With all the numberless goings-on of life,
Inaudible as dreams! the thin blue flame
Lies on my low-burnt fire, and quivers not;
Only that film, which fluttered on the grate,
Still flutters there, the sole unquiet thing.
Methinks, its motion in this hush of nature

Gives it dim sympathies with me who live,
Making it a companionable form,
Whose puny flaps and freaks the idling spirit
By its own moods interprets, everywhere
Echo or mirror seeking of itself,
And makes a toy of thought.

                              But O! how oft,
How oft, at school, with most believing mind,
Presageful, have I gazed upon the bars,
To watch that fluttering *stranger!* and as oft
With unclosed lids, already had I dreamt
Of my sweet birth-place, and the old church-tower,
Whose bells, the poor man's only music, rang
From morn to evening, all the hot Fair-day,
So sweetly, that they stirred and haunted me
With a wild pleasure, falling on mine ear
Most like articulate sounds of things to come!
So gazed I, till the soothing things, I dreamt,
Lulled me to sleep, and sleep prolonged my dreams!
And so I brooded all the following morn,
Awed by the stern preceptor's face, mine eye
Fixed with mock study on my swimming book:
Save if the door half opened, and I snatched
A hasty glance, and still my heart leaped up,
For still I hoped to see the *stranger's* face,
Townsman, or aunt, or sister more beloved,
My playmate when we both were clothed alike!

    Dear babe, that sleepest cradled by my side,
Whose gentle breathings, heard in this deep calm,
Fill up the interspersèd vacancies
And momentary pauses of the thought!
My babe so beautiful! it thrills my heart
With tender gladness, thus to look at thee,
And think that thou shalt learn far other lore,
And in far other scenes! For I was reared
In the great city, pent 'mid cloisters dim,
And saw naught lovely but the sky and stars.
But *thou,* my babe! shalt wander like a breeze
By lakes and sandy shores, beneath the crags
Of ancient mountain, and beneath the clouds,
Which image in their bulk both lakes and shores
And mountain crags: so shalt thou see and hear
The lovely shapes and sounds intelligible
Of that eternal language, which thy God

Utters, who from eternity doth teach
Himself in all, and all things in himself.
Great universal Teacher! He shall mould
Thy spirit, and by giving make it ask.

Therefore all seasons shall be sweet to thee,
Whether the summer clothes the general earth
With greenness, or the redbreast sit and sing
Betwixt the tufts of snow on the bare branch
Of mossy apple-tree, while the nigh thatch
Smokes in the sun-thaw; whether the eave-drops fall
Heard only in the trances of the blast,
Or if the secret ministry of frost
Shall hang them up in silent icicles,
Quietly shining to the quiet moon.

DEJECTION: AN ODE

Late, late yestreen I saw the new Moon,
With the old Moon in her arms;
And I fear, I fear, my Master dear!
We shall have a deadly storm.
Ballad of Sir Patrick Spence

Well! If the bard was weather-wise, who made
    The grand old ballad of *Sir Patrick Spence,*
    This night, so tranquil now, will not go hence
Unroused by winds, that ply a busier trade
Than those which mould yon cloud in lazy flakes,
Or the dull sobbing draft, that moans and rakes
Upon the strings of this Æolian lute,
    Which better far were mute.
For lo! the New-moon winter-bright!
And overspread with phantom light,
    (With swimming phantom light o'erspread
    But rimmed and circled by a silver thread)
I see the old Moon in her lap, foretelling
    The coming-on of rain and squally blast.
And oh! that even now the gust were swelling,
    And the slant night-shower driving loud and fast!
Those sounds which oft have raised me, whilst they awed,
        And sent my soul abroad,
Might now perhaps their wonted impulse give,
Might startle this dull pain, and make it move and live!

A grief without a pang, void, dark, and drear,
    A stifled, drowsy, unimpassioned grief,
    Which finds no natural outlet, no relief,

In word, or sigh, or tear—
O Lady! in this wan and heartless mood,
To other thoughts by yonder throstle wooed,
    All this long eve, so balmy and serene,
Have I been gazing on the western sky,
    And its peculiar tint of yellow green:
And still I gaze—and with how blank an eye!
And those thin clouds above, in flakes and bars,
That give away their motion to the stars;
Those stars, that glide behind them or between,
Now sparkling, now bedimmed, but always seen:
Yon crescent Moon, as fixed as if it grew
In its own cloudless, starless lake of blue;
I see them all so excellently fair,
I see, not feel, how beautiful they are!

        My genial spirits fail;
        And what can these avail
To lift the smothering weight from off my breast?
        It were a vain endeavour,
        Though I should gaze for ever
On that green light that lingers in the west:
I may not hope from outward forms to win
The passion and the life, whose fountains are within.

O Lady! we receive but what we give,
And in our life alone does Nature live:
Ours is her wedding garment, ours her shroud!
    And would we aught behold, of higher worth,
Than that inanimate cold world allowed
To the poor loveless ever-anxious crowd,
    Ah! from the soul itself must issue forth
A light, a glory, a fair luminous cloud
    Enveloping the Earth—
And from the soul itself must there be sent
    A sweet and potent voice, of its own birth,
Of all sweet sounds the life and element!

O pure of heart! thou need'st not ask of me
What this strong music in the soul may be!
What, and wherein it doth exist,
This light, this glory, this fair luminous mist,
This beautiful and beauty-making power.
    Joy, virtuous lady! Joy that ne'er was given,
Save to the pure, and in their purest hour,
Life, and Life's effluence, cloud at once and shower,

Joy, Lady! is the spirit and the power,
Which wedding Nature to us gives in dower
   A new Earth and new Heaven,
Undreamt of by the sensual and the proud—
Joy is the sweet voice, Joy the luminous cloud—
     We in ourselves rejoice!
And thence flows all that charms or ear or sight,
   All melodies the echoes of that voice,
All colors a suffusion from that light.

There was a time when, though my path was rough,
   This joy within me dallied with distress,
And all misfortunes were but as the stuff
   Whence Fancy made me dreams of happiness:
For hope grew round me, like the twining vine,
And fruits, and foliage, not my own, seemed mine.
But now afflictions bow me down to earth:
Nor care I that they rob me of my mirth;
   But oh! each visitation
Suspends what nature gave me at my birth,
   My shaping spirit of Imagination.
For not to think of what I needs must feel,
   But to be still and patient, all I can;
And haply by abstruse research to steal
   From my own nature all the natural man—
This was my sole resource, my only plan:
Till that which suits a part infects the whole,
And now is almost grown the habit of my soul.

Hence, viper thoughts, that coil around my mind,
    Reality's dark dream!
I turn from you, and listen to the wind,
   Which long has raved unnoticed. What a scream
Of agony by torture lengthened out
That lute sent forth! Thou Wind, that rav'st without,
   Bare crag, or mountain-tairn, or blasted tree,
Or pine-grove whither woodman never clomb,
Or lonely house, long held the witches' home,
   Methinks were fitter instruments for thee,
Mad Lutanist! who in this month of showers,
Of dark-brown gardens, and of peeping flowers,
Mak'st Devils' yule, with worse than wintry song,
The blossoms, buds, and timorous leaves among.
   Thou Actor, perfect in all tragic sounds!
Thou mighty Poet, e'en to frenzy bold!
    What tell'st thou now about?
    'Tis of the rushing of an host in rout,

With groans, of trampled men, with smarting wounds—
At once they groan with pain, and shudder with the cold!
But hush! there is a pause of deepest silence!
And all that noise, as of a rushing crowd,
With groans, and tremulous shudderings—all is over—
It tells another tale, with sounds less deep and loud!
    A tale of less affright,
    And tempered with delight,
As Otway's self had framed the tender lay,—
    'Tis of a little child
    Upon a lonesome wild,
Not far from home, but she hath lost her way:
And now moans low in bitter grief and fear,
And now screams loud, and hopes to make her mother hear.

'Tis midnight, but small thoughts have I of sleep:
Full seldom may my friend such vigils keep!
Visit her, gentle Sleep! with wings of healing,
    And may this storm be but a mountain-birth,
May all the stars hang bright above her dwelling,
    Silent as though they watched the sleeping Earth!
        With light heart may she rise,
        Gay fancy, cheerful eyes,
    Joy lift her spirit, joy attune her voice;
To her may all things live, from pole to pole,
Their life the eddying of her living soul!
    O simple spirit, guided from above,
Dear Lady! friend devoutest of my choice,
Thus mayest thou ever, evermore rejoice.

THIS LIME-TREE BOWER MY PRISON

ADDRESSED TO CHARLES LAMB
OF THE INDIA HOUSE, LONDON

*In the June of 1797 some long-expected friends paid a visit to
the author's cottage; and on the morning of their arrival, he
met with an accident, which disabled him from walking during the
whole time of their stay. One evening, when they had left him
for a few hours, he composed the following lines in the garden-
bower.*

Well, they are gone, and here must I remain,
This lime-tree bower my prison! I have lost
Beauties and feelings, such as would have been
Most sweet to my remembrance even when age

Had dimmed mine eyes to blindness! They, meanwhile,
Friends, whom I never more may meet again,
On springy heath, along the hill-top edge,
Wander in gladness, and wind down, perchance,
To that still roaring dell, of which I told;
The roaring dell, o'erwooded, narrow, deep,
And only speckled by the mid-day sun;
Where its slim trunk the ash from rock to rock
Flings arching like a bridge;—that branchless ash,
Unsunned and damp, whose few poor yellow leaves
Ne'er tremble in the gale, yet tremble still,
Fanned by the water-fall! and there my friends
Behold the dark green file of long lank weeds,
That all at once (a most fantastic sight!)
Still nod and drip beneath the dripping edge
Of the blue clay-stone.

           Now, my friends emerge
Beneath the wide wide Heaven—and view again
The many-steepled tract magnificent
Of hilly fields and meadows, and the sea,
With some fair bark, perhaps, whose sails light up
The slip of smooth clear blue betwixt two Isles
Of purple shadow! Yes! they wander on
In gladness all; but thou, methinks, most glad,
My gentle-hearted Charles! for thou hast pined
And hungered after Nature, many a year,
In the great City pent, winning thy way
With sad yet patient soul, through evil and pain
And strange calamity! Ah! slowly sink
Behind the western ridge, thou glorious Sun!
Shine in the slant beams of the sinking orb,
Ye purple heath-flowers! richlier burn, ye clouds!
Live in the yellow light, ye distant groves!
And kindle, thou blue Ocean! So my friend
Struck with deep joy may stand, as I have stood,
Silent with swimming sense; yea, gazing round
On the wide landscape, gaze till all doth seem
Less gross than bodily; and of such hues
As veil the Almighty Spirit, when yet he makes
Spirits perceive his presence.

           A delight
Comes sudden on my heart, and I am glad
As I myself were there! Nor in this bower,
This little lime-tree bower, have I not marked

Much that has soothed me. Pale beneath the blaze
Hung the transparent foliage; and I watched
Some broad and sunny leaf, and loved to see
The shadow of the leaf and stem above
Dappling its sunshine! And that walnut-tree
Was richly tinged, and a deep radiance lay
Full on the ancient ivy, which usurps
Those fronting elms, and now, with blackest mass
Makes their dark branches gleam a lighter hue
Through the late twilight: and though now the bat
Wheels silent by, and not a swallow twitters,
Yet still the solitary humble-bee
Sings in the bean-flower! Henceforth I shall know
That Nature ne'er deserts the wise and pure;
No plot so narrow, be but Nature there,
No waste so vacant, but may well employ
Each faculty of sense, and keep the heart
Awake to Love and Beauty! and sometimes
'Tis well to be bereft of promised good,
That we may lift the soul, and contemplate
With lively joy the joys we cannot share.
My gentle-hearted Charles! when the last rook
Beat its straight path along the dusky air
Homewards, I blest it! deeming its black wing
(Now a dim speck, now vanishing in light)
Had crossed the mighty Orb's dilated glory,
While thou stood'st gazing; or, when all was still,
Flew creeking o'er thy head, and had a charm
For thee, my gentle-hearted Charles, to whom
No sound is dissonant which tells of Life.

CHRISTABEL

PREFACE

*The first part of the following poem was written in the year 1797,
at Stowey, in the county of Somerset. The second part, after my re-
turn from Germany, in the year 1800, at Keswick, Cumberland.
It is probable that if the poem had been finished at either of the
former periods, or if even the first and second part had been pub-
lished in the year 1800, the impression of its originality would have
been much greater than I dare at present expect. But for this I
have only my own indolence to blame. The dates are mentioned
for the exclusive purpose of precluding charges of plagiarism or
servile imitation from myself. For there is amongst us a set of
critics, who seem to hold, that every possible thought and image*

is traditional; who have no notion that there are such things as fountains in the world, small as well as great; and who would therefore charitably derive every rill they behold flowing, from a perforation made in some other man's tank. I am confident, however, that as far as the present poem is concerned, the celebrated poets [Scott and Byron] whose writings I might be suspected of having imitated, either in particular passages, or in the tone and the spirit of the whole, would be among the first to vindicate me from the charge, and who, on any striking coincidence, would permit me to address them in this doggerel version of two monkish Latin hexameters.

> 'Tis mine and it is likewise yours;
> But an if this will not do;
> Let it be mine, good friend! for I
> Am the poorer of the two.

I have only to add that the metre of Christabel is not, properly speaking, irregular, though it may seem so from its being founded on a new principle: namely, that of counting in each line the accents, not the syllables. Though the latter may vary from seven to twelve, yet in each line the accents will be found to be only four. Nevertheless, this occasional variation in number of syllables is not introduced wantonly, or for the mere ends of convenience, but in correspondence with some transition in the nature of the imagery or passion.

PART I

'Tis the middle of night by the castle clock,
And the owls have awakened the crowing cock;
Tu—whit!——Tu—whoo!
And hark, again! the crowing cock,
How drowsily it crew.

Sir Leoline, the Baron rich,
Hath a toothless mastiff bitch;
From her kennel beneath the rock
She maketh answer to the clock,
Four for the quarters, and twelve for the hour;
Ever and aye, by shine and shower,
Sixteen short howls, not over loud;
Some say, she sees my lady's shroud.

Is the night chilly and dark?
The night is chilly, but not dark.
The thin grey cloud is spread on high,
It covers but not hides the sky.
The moon is behind, and at the full;
And yet she looks both small and dull.
The night is chill, the cloud is grey:
'Tis a month before the month of May,
And the Spring comes slowly up this way.

The lovely lady, Christabel,
Whom her father loves so well,
What makes her in the wood so late,
A furlong from the castle gate?
She had dreams all yesternight
Of her own bethrothèd knight;
And she in the midnight wood will pray
For the weal of her lover that's far away.

She stole along, she nothing spoke,
The sighs she heaved were soft and low,
And naught was green upon the oak
But moss and rarest mistletoe:
She kneels beneath the huge oak tree,
And in silence prayeth she.

The lady sprang up suddenly,
The lovely lady, Christabel!
It moaned as near, as near can be,
But what it is she cannot tell.—
On the other side it seems to be,
Of the huge, broad-breasted, old oak-tree.

The night is chill; the forest bare;
Is it the wind that moaneth bleak?
There is not wind enough in the air
To move away the ringlet curl
From the lovely lady's cheek—
There is not wind enough to twirl
The one red leaf, the last of its clan,
That dances as often as dance it can,
Hanging so light, and hanging so high,
On the topmost twig that looks up at the sky.

Hush, beating heart of Christabel!
Jesu, Maria, shield her well!
She folded her arms beneath her cloak,
And stole to the other side of the oak.
        What sees she there?

There she sees a damsel bright,
Drest in a silken robe of white,
That shadowy in the moonlight shone:
The neck that made that white robe wan,
Her stately neck, and arms were bare;
Her blue-veined feet unsandal'd were,

And wildly glittered here and there
The gems entangled in her hair.
I guess, 'twas frightful there to see
A lady so richly clad as she—
Beautiful exceedingly!

Mary mother, save me now!
(Said Christabel,) And who art thou?

The lady strange made answer meet,
And her voice was faint and sweet:—
Have pity on my sore distress,
I scarce can speak for weariness:
Stretch forth thy hand, and have no fear!
Said Christabel, How camest thou here?
And the lady, whose voice was faint and sweet,
Did thus pursue her answer meet:—

My sire is of a noble line,
And my name is Geraldine:
Five warriors seized me yestermorn,
Me, even me, a maid forlorn:
They choked my cries with force and fright,
And tied me on a palfrey white.
The palfrey was as fleet as wind,
And they rode furiously behind.

They spurred amain, their steeds were white:
And once we crossed the shade of night.
As sure as Heaven shall rescue me,
I have no thought what men they be;
Nor do I know how long it is
(For I have lain entranced I wis)
Since one, the tallest of the five,
Took me from the palfrey's back,
A weary woman, scarce alive.
Some muttered words his comrades spoke:
He placed me underneath this oak;
He swore they would return with haste;
Whither they went I cannot tell—
I thought I heard, some minutes past,
Sounds as of a castle bell.
Stretch forth thy hand (thus ended she),
And help a wretched maid to flee.

Then Christabel stretched forth her hand,
And comforted fair Geraldine:

O well, bright dame! may you command
The service of Sir Leoline;
And gladly our stout chivalry
Will he send forth and friends withal
To guide and guard you safe and free
Home to your noble father's hall.

She rose: and forth with steps they passed
That strove to be, and were not, fast.
Her gracious stars the lady blest,
And thus spake on sweet Christabel:
All our household are at rest,
The hall as silent as the cell;
Sir Leoline is weak in health,
And may not well awakened be,
But we will move as if in stealth,
And I beseech your courtesy,
This night, to share your couch with me.

They crossed the moat, and Christabel
Took the key that fitted well;
A little door she opened straight,
All in the middle of the gate;
The gate that was ironed within and without,
Where an army in battle array had marched out.
The lady sank, belike through pain,
And Christabel with might and main
Lifted her up, a weary weight,
Over the threshold of the gate:
Then the lady rose again,
And moved, as she were not in pain.

So free from danger, free from fear,
They crossed the court: right glad they were.
And Christabel devoutedly cried
To the lady by her side,
Praise we the Virgin all divine
Who hath rescued thee from thy distress!
Alas, alas! said Geraldine,
I cannot speak for weariness.
So free from danger, free from fear,
They crossed the court: right glad they were.

Outside her kennel, the mastiff old
Lay fast asleep, in moonshine cold.
The mastiff old did not awake,
Yet she an angry moan did make!

And what can ail the mastiff bitch?
Never till now she uttered yell
Beneath the eye of Christabel.
Perhaps it is the owlet's scritch:
For what can ail the mastiff bitch?

They passed the hall, that echoes still,
Pass as lightly as you will!
The brands were flat, the brands were dying,
Amid their own white ashes lying;
But when the lady passed, there came
A tongue of light, a fit of flame;
And Christabel saw the lady's eye,
And nothing else saw she thereby,
Save the boss of the shield of Sir Leoline tall,
Which hung in a murky old niche in the wall.
O softly tread, said Christabel,
My father seldom sleepeth well.

Sweet Christabel her feet doth bare,
And jealous of the listening air
They steal their way from stair to stair,
Now in glimmer, and now in gloom,
And now they pass the Baron's room,
As still as death, with stifled breath!
And now have reached her chamber door;
And now doth Geraldine press down
The rushes of the chamber floor.

The moon shines dim in the open air,
And not a moonbeam enters here.
But they without its light can see
The chamber carved so curiously,
Carved with figures strange and sweet,
All made out of the carver's brain,
For a lady's chamber meet:
The lamp with twofold silver chain
Is fastened to an angel's feet.

The silver lamp burns dead and dim;
But Christabel the lamp will trim.
She trimmed the lamp, and made it bright,
And left it swinging to and fro,
While Geraldine, in wretched plight,
Sank down upon the floor below.

O weary lady, Geraldine,
I pray you, drink this cordial wine!

It is a wine of virtuous powers;
My mother made it of wild flowers.

And will your mother pity me,
Who am a maiden most forlorn?
Christabel answered—Woe is me!
She died the hour that I was born.
I have heard the grey-haired friar tell
How on her death-bed she did say,
That she should hear the castle-bell
Strike twelve upon my wedding-day.
O mother dear! that thou wert here!
I would, said Geraldine, she were!

But soon with altered voice, said she—
'Off, wandering mother! Peak and pine!
I have power to bid thee flee.'
Alas! What ails poor Geraldine?
Why stares she with unsettled eye?
Can she the bodiless dead espy?
And why with hollow voice cries she,
'Off, woman, off! this hour is mine—
Though thou her guardian spirit be,
Off, woman, off! 'tis given to me.'

Then Christabel knelt by the lady's side,
And raised to heaven her eyes so blue—
Alas! said she, this ghastly ride—
Dear lady! it hath wildered you!
The lady wiped her moist cold brow,
And faintly said, ' 'tis over now!'

Again the wild-flower wine she drank:
Her fair large eyes 'gan glitter bright,
And from the floor whereon she sank,
The lofty lady stood upright:
She was most beautiful to see,
Like a lady of a far countrée.

And thus the lofty lady spake—
'All they who live in the upper sky,
Do love you, holy Christabel!
And you love them, and for their sake
And for the good which me befel,
Even I in my degree will try,
Fair maiden, to requite you well.

But now unrobe yourself; for I
Must pray, ere yet in bed I lie.'

Quoth Christabel, So let it be!
And as the lady bade, did she.
Her gentle limbs did she undress,
And lay down in her loveliness.

But through her brain of weal and woe
So many thoughts moved to and fro,
That vain it were her lids to close;
So half-way from the bed she rose,
And on her elbow did recline
To look at the lady Geraldine.

Beneath the lamp the lady bowed,
And slowly rolled her eyes around;
Then drawing in her breath aloud,
Like one that shuddered, she unbound
The cincture from beneath her breast:
Her silken robe, and inner vest,
Dropt to her feet, and full in view,
Behold! her bosom and half her side——
A sight to dream of, not to tell!
O shield her! shield sweet Christabel!

Yet Geraldine nor speaks nor stirs;
Ah! what a stricken look was hers!
Deep from within she seems half-way
To lift some weight with sick assay,
And eyes the maid and seeks delay;
Then suddenly, as one defied,
Collects herself in scorn and pride,
And lay down by the Maiden's side!—
And in her arms the maid she took,
        Ah wel-a-day!
And with low voice and doleful look
These words did say:
'In the touch of this bosom there worketh a spell,
Which is lord of thy utterance, Christabel!
Thou knowest to-night, and wilt know to-morrow,
This mark of my shame, this seal of my sorrow;
        But vainly thou warrest,
            For this is alone in
        Thy power to declare,
            That in the dim forest

Thou heard'st a low moaning,
And found'st a bright lady, surpassingly fair;
And didst bring her home with thee in love and in charity,
To shield her and shelter her from the damp air.'

THE CONCLUSION TO PART I

It was a lovely sight to see
The lady Christabel, when she
Was praying at the old oak-tree.
    Amid the jaggèd shadows
    Of mossy leafless boughs,
    Kneeling in the moonlight,
    To make her gentle vows;
Her slender palms together prest,
Heaving sometimes on her breast;
Her face resigned to bliss or bale—
Her face, oh call it fair not pale,
And both blue eyes more bright than clear,
Each about to have a tear.

With open eyes (ah woe is me!)
Asleep, and dreaming fearfully,
Fearfully dreaming, yet, I wis,
Dreaming that alone, which is—
O sorrow and shame! Can this be she,
The lady, who knelt at the old oak tree?
And lo! the worker of these harms,
That holds the maiden in her arms,
Seems to slumber still and mild,
As a mother with her child.

A star hath set, a star hath risen,
O Geraldine! since arms of thine
Have been the lovely lady's prison.
O Geraldine! one hour was thine—
Thou'st had thy will! By tairn and rill,
The night-birds all that hour were still.
But now they are jubilant anew,
From cliff and tower, tu—whoo! tu—whoo!
Tu—whoo! tu—whoo! from wood and fell!

And see! the lady Christabel
Gathers herself from out her trance;
Her limbs relax, her countenance
Grows sad and soft; the smooth thin lids

Close o'er her eyes; and tears she sheds—
Large tears that leave the lashes bright!
And oft the while she seems to smile
As infants at a sudden light!

Yea, she doth smile, and she doth weep,
Like a youthful hermitess,
Beauteous in a wilderness,
Who, praying always, prays in sleep.
And, if she move unquietly,
Perchance, 'tis but the blood so free
Comes back and tingles in her feet.
No doubt, she hath a vision sweet.
What if her guardian spirit 'twere,
What if she knew her mother near?
But this she knows, in joys and woes,
That saints will aid if men will call:
For the blue sky bends over all!

PART II

Each matin bell, the Baron saith,
Knells us back to a world of death.
These words Sir Leoline first said,
When he rose and found his lady dead:
These words Sir Leoline will say
Many a morn to his dying day!

And hence the custom and law began
That still at dawn the sacristan,
Who duly pulls the heavy bell,
Five and forty beads must tell
Between each stroke—a warning knell,
Which not a soul can choose but hear
From Bratha Head to Wyndermere.

Saith Bracy the bard, So let it knell!
And let the drowsy sacristan
Still count as slowly as he can!
There is no lack of such, I ween,
As well fill up the space between.
In Langdale Pike and Witch's Lair,
And Dungeon-ghyll so foully rent,
With ropes of rock and bells of air,
Three sinful sextons' ghosts are pent,
Who all give back, one after t'other,

SAMUEL TAYLOR COLERIDGE 97

The death-note to their living brother;
And oft too, by the knell offended,
Just as their one! two! three! is ended,
The devil mocks the doleful tale
With a merry peal from Borodale.

The air is still! through mist and cloud
That merry peal comes ringing loud;
And Geraldine shakes off her dread,
And rises lightly from the bed;
Puts on her silken vestments white,
And tricks her hair in lovely plight,
And nothing doubting of her spell
Awakens the lady Christabel.
'Sleep you, sweet lady Christabel?
I trust that you have rested well.'

And Christabel awoke and spied
The same who lay down by her side—
O rather say, the same whom she
Raised up beneath the old oak-tree!
Nay, fairer yet! and yet more fair!
For she belike hath drunken deep
Of all the blessedness of sleep!
And while she spake, her looks, her air
Such gentle thankfulness declare,
That (so it seemed) her girded vests
Grew tight beneath her heaving breasts.
'Sure I have sinn'd!' said Christabel,
'Now heaven be praised if all be well!'
And in low faltering tones, yet sweet,
Did she the lofty lady greet
With such perplexity of mind
As dreams too lively leave behind.

So quickly she rose, and quickly arrayed
Her maiden limbs, and having prayed
That He, who on the cross did groan,
Might wash away her sins unknown,
She forthwith led fair Geraldine
To meet her sire, Sir Leoline.

The lovely maid and the lady tall
Are pacing both into the hall,
And pacing on through page and groom,
Enter the Baron's presence-room.

The Baron rose, and while he prest
His gentle daughter to his breast,
With cheerful wonder in his eyes
The lady Geraldine espies,
And gave such welcome to the same,
As might beseem so bright a dame!

But when he heard the lady's tale,
And when she told her father's name,
Why waxed Sir Leoline so pale,
Murmuring o'er the name again,
Lord Roland de Vaux of Tryermaine?

Alas! they had been friends in youth;
But whispering tongues can poison truth;
And constancy lives in realms above;
And life is thorny; and youth is vain;
And to be wroth with one we love
Doth work like madness in the brain.
And thus it chanced, as I divine,
With Roland and Sir Leoline.
Each spake words of high disdain
And insult to his heart's best brother:
They parted—ne'er to meet again!
But never either found another
To free the hollow heart from paining—
They stood aloof, the scars remaining,
Like cliffs which had been rent asunder;
A dready sea now flows between;—
But neither heat, nor frost, nor thunder,
Shall wholly do away, I ween,
The marks of that which once hath been.

Sir Leoline, a moment's space,
Stood gazing on the damsel's face:
And the youthful Lord of Tryermaine
Came back upon his heart again.

O then the Baron forgot his age,
His noble heart swelled high with rage;
He swore by the wounds in Jesu's side
He would proclaim it far and wide,
With trump and solemn heraldry,
That they, who thus had wronged the dame,
Were base as spotted infamy!
'And if they dare deny the same,

My herald shall appoint a week,
And let the recreant traitors seek
My tourney court—that there and then
I may dislodge their reptile souls
From the bodies and forms of men!'
He spake: his eye in lightning rolls!
For the lady was ruthlessly seized; and he kenned
In the beautiful lady the child of his friend!
And now the tears were on his face,
And fondly in his arms he took
Fair Geraldine, who met the embrace,
Prolonging it with joyous look.
Which when she viewed, a vision fell
Upon the soul of Christabel,
The vision of fear, the touch and pain!
She shrunk and shuddered, and saw again—
(Ah, woe is me! Was it for thee,
Thou gentle maid! such sights to see?)

Again she saw that bosom old,
Again she felt that bosom cold,
And drew in her breath with a hissing sound:
Whereat the Knight turned wildly round,
And nothing saw, but his own sweet maid
With eyes upraised, as one that prayed.

The touch, the sight, had passed away,
And in its stead that vision blest,
Which comforted her after-rest
While in the lady's arms she lay,
Had put a rapture in her breast,
And on her lips and o'er her eyes
Spread smiles like light!
                           With new surprise,
'What ails then my beloved child?'
The Baron said—His daughter mild
Made answer, 'All will yet be well!'
I ween, she had no power to tell
Aught else: so mighty was the spell.

Yet he, who saw this Geraldine,
Had deemed her sure a thing divine:
Such sorrow with such grace she blended,
As if she feared she had offended
Sweet Christabel, that gentle maid!
And with such lowly tones she prayed
She might be sent without delay

Home to her father's mansion.
                              'Nay!
Nay, by my soul!' said Leoline.
'Ho! Bracy the bard, the charge be thine!
Go thou, with music sweet and loud,
And take two steeds with trappings proud,
And take the youth whom thou lov'st best
To bear thy harp, and learn thy song,
And clothe you both in solemn vest,
And over the mountains haste along,
Lest wandering folk, that are abroad,
Detain you on the valley road.

'And when he has crossed the Irthing flood,
My merry bard! he hastes, he hastes
Up Knorren Moor, through Halegarth Wood,
And reaches soon that castle good
Which stands and threatens Scotland's wastes.

'Bard Bracy! bard Bracy! your horses are fleet,
Ye must ride up the hall, your music so sweet,
More loud than your horses' echoing feet!
And loud and loud to Lord Roland call,
Thy daughter is safe in Langdale hall!
Thy beautiful daughter is safe and free—
Sir Leoline greets thee thus through me!
He bids thee come without delay
With all thy numerous array
And take thy lovely daughter home:
And he will meet thee on the way
With all his numerous array
White with their panting palfreys' foam:
And, by mine honour! I will say,
That I repent me of the day
When I spake words of fierce disdain
To Roland de Vaux of Tryermaine!—
—For since that evil hour hath flown,
Many a summer's sun hath shone;
Yet ne'er found I a friend again
Like Roland de Vaux of Tryermaine.'

The lady fell, and clasped his knees,
Her face upraised, her eyes o'erflowing;
And Bracy replied, with faltering voice,
His gracious Hail on all bestowing!—
'Thy words, thou sire of Christabel,
Are sweeter than my harp can tell;
Yet might I gain a boon of thee,

This day my journey should not be,
So strange a dream hath come to me,
That I had vowed with music loud
To clear yon wood from thing unblest,
Warned by a vision in my rest!
For in my sleep I saw that dove,
That gentle bird, whom thou dost love,
And call'st by thy own daughter's name—
Sir Leoline! I saw the same
Fluttering, and uttering fearful moan,
Among the green herbs in the forest alone.
Which when I saw and when I heard,
I wonder'd what might ail the bird;
For nothing near it could I see,
Save the grass and green herbs underneath the old tree.

'And in my dream methought I went
To search out what might there be found;
And what the sweet bird's trouble meant,
That thus lay fluttering on the ground.
I went and peered, and could descry
No cause for her distressful cry;
But yet for her dear lady's sake
I stooped, methought, the dove to take,
When lo! I saw a bright green snake
Coiled around its wings and neck.
Green as the herbs on which it couched,
Close by the dove's its head it crouched;
And with the dove it heaves and stirs,
Swelling its neck as she swelled hers!
I woke; it was the midnight hour,
The clock was echoing in the tower;
But though my slumber was gone by,
This dream it would not pass away—
It seems to live upon my eye!
And thence I vowed this self-same day
With music strong and saintly song
To wander through the forest bare,
Lest aught unholy loiter there.'

Thus Bracy said: the Baron, the while,
Half-listening heard him with a smile;
Then turned to Lady Geraldine,
His eyes made up of wonder and love;
And said in courtly accents fine,
'Sweet maid, Lord Roland's beauteous dove,
With arms more strong than harp or song,

Thy sire and I will crush the snake!'
He kissed her forehead as he spake,
And Geraldine in maiden wise
Casting down her large bright eyes,
With blushing cheek and courtesy fine
She turned her from Sir Leoline;
Softly gathering up her train,
That o'er her right arm fell again;
And folded her arms across her chest,
And couched her head upon her breast,
And looked askance at Christabel——
Jesu, Maria, shield her well!

A snake's small eye blinks dull and shy;
And the lady's eyes they shrunk in her head,
Each shrunk up to a serpent's eye,
And with somewhat of malice, and more of dread,
At Christabel she looked askance!—
One moment—and the sight was fled!
But Christabel in dizzy trance
Stumbling on the unsteady ground
Shuddered aloud, with a hissing sound;
And Geraldine again turned round,
And like a thing, that sought relief,
Full of wonder and full of grief,
She rolled her large bright eyes divine
Wildly on Sir Leoline.

The maid, alas! her thoughts are gone,
She nothing sees—no sight but one!
The maid, devoid of guile and sin,
I know not how, in fearful wise,
So deeply had she drunken in
That look, those shrunken serpent eyes,
That all her features were resigned
To this sole image in her mind:
And passively did imitate
That look of dull and treacherous hate!
And thus she stood, in dizzy trance,
Still picturing that look askance
With forced unconscious sympathy
Full before her father's view——
As far as such a look could be
In eyes so innocent and blue!

And when the trance was o'er, the maid
Paused awhile, and inly prayed:

Then falling at the Baron's feet,
'By my mother's soul do I entreat
That thou this woman send away!'
She said: and more she could not say:
For what she knew she could not tell,
O'er-mastered by the mighty spell.

Why is thy cheek so wan and wild,
Sir Leoline? Thy only child
Lies at thy feet, thy joy, thy pride,
So fair, so innocent, so mild;
The same, for whom thy lady died!
O by the pangs of her dear mother
Think thou no evil of thy child!
For her, and thee, and for no other,
She prayed the moment ere she died:
Prayed that the babe for whom she died,
Might prove her dear lord's joy and pride!
     That prayer her deadly pangs beguiled,
               Sir Leoline!
     And wouldst thou wrong thy only child,
               Her child and thine?

Within the Baron's heart and brain
If thoughts, like these, had any share,
They only swelled his rage and pain,
And did but work confusion there.
His heart was cleft with pain and rage,
His cheeks they quivered, his eyes were wild,
Dishonoured thus in his old age;
Dishonoured by his only child,
And all his hospitality
To the wronged daughter of his friend
By more than woman's jealousy
Brought thus to a disgraceful end—
He rolled his eye with stern regard
Upon the gentle minstrel bard,
And said in tones abrupt, austere—
'Why, Bracy! dost thou loiter here?
I bade thee hence!' The bard obeyed;
And turning from his own sweet maid,
The agèd knight, Sir Leoline,
Led forth the lady Geraldine!

THE CONCLUSION TO PART II

A little child, a limber elf,
Singing, dancing to itself,

A fairy thing with red round cheeks,
That always finds, and never seeks,
Makes such a vision to the sight
As fills a father's eyes with light;
And pleasures flow in so thick and fast
Upon his heart, that he at last
Must needs express his love's excess
With words of unmeant bitterness.
Perhaps 'tis pretty to force together
Thoughts so all unlike each other;
To mutter and mock a broken charm,
To dally with wrong that does no harm.
Perhaps 'tis tender too and pretty
At each wild word to feel within
A sweet recoil of love and pity.
And what, if in a world of sin
(O sorrow and shame should this be true!)
Such giddiness of heart and brain
Comes seldom save from rage and pain,
So talks as it's most used to do.

TIME, REAL AND IMAGINARY

AN ALLEGORY

On the wide level of a mountain's head,
(I knew not where, but 'twas some faery place)
Their pinions, ostrich-like, for sails out-spread,
Two lovely children run an endless race,
      A sister and a brother!
      This far outstripped the other;
Yet ever runs she with reverted face,
And looks and listens for the boy behind:
      For he, alas! is blind!
O'er rough and smooth with even step he passed,
And knows not whether he be first or last.

SONG

A sunny shaft did I behold,
    From sky to earth it slanted:
    And poised therein a bird so bold—
Sweet bird, thou wert enchanted!

He sank, he rose, he twinkled, he trolled
   Within that shaft of sunny mist;
His eyes of fire, his beak of gold,
   All else of amethyst!

And thus he sang: 'Adieu! adieu!
Love's dreams prove seldom true.
The blossoms they make no delay:
The sparkling dew-drops will not stay.
   Sweet month of May,
     We must away;
       Far, far away
         To-day! to-day!'

from ZAPOLYA

CONSTANCY TO AN IDEAL OBJECT

Since all that beat about in Nature's range,
Or veer or vanish; why should'st thou remain
The only constant in a world of change,
O yearning Thought! that liv'st but in the brain?
Call to the Hours, that in the distance play,
The faery people of the future day——
Fond Thought! not one of all that shining swarm
Will breathe on thee with life-enkindling breath,
Till when, like strangers shelt'ring from a storm,
Hope and Despair meet in the porch of Death!
Yet still thou haunt'st me; and though well I see,
She is not thou, and only thou art she,
Still, still as though some dear embodied Good,
Some living Love before my eyes there stood
With answering look a ready ear to lend,
I mourn to thee and say—'Ah! loveliest friend!
That this the meed of all my toils might be,
To have a home, an English home, and thee!'
Vain repetition! Home and Thou are one.
The peacefull'st cot, the moon shall shine upon,
Lulled by the thrush and wakened by the lark,
Without thee were but a becalmèd bark,
Whose Helmsman on an ocean waste and wide
Sits mute and pale his mouldering helm beside.

And art thou nothing? Such thou art, as when
The woodman winding westward up the glen
At wintry dawn, where o'er the sheep-track's maze

The viewless snow-mist weaves a glist'ning haze,
Sees full before him, gliding without tread,
An image with a glory round its head;
The enamoured rustic worships its fair hues,
Nor knows he makes the shadow, he pursues!

WORK WITHOUT HOPE

LINES COMPOSED 21ST FEBRUARY 1825

All Nature seems at work. Slugs leave their lair—
The bees are stirring—birds are on the wing—
And Winter slumbering in the open air,
Wears on his smiling face a dream of Spring!
And I the while, the sole unbusy thing,
Nor honey make, nor pair, nor build, nor sing.

Yet well I ken the banks where amaranths blow,
Have traced the fount whence streams of nectar flow.
Bloom, O ye amaranths! bloom for whom ye may,
For me ye bloom not! Glide, rich streams, away!
With lips unbrightened, wreathless brow, I stroll:
And would you learn the spells that drowse my soul?
Work without Hope draws nectar in a sieve,
And Hope without an object cannot live.

PHANTOM

All look and likeness caught from earth,
All accident of kin and birth,
Had passed away. There was no trace
Of aught on that illumined face,
Uprais'd beneath the rifted stone
But of one spirit all her own;—
She, she herself, and only she,
Shone through her body visibly.

PSYCHE

The butterfly the ancient Grecians made
The soul's fair emblem, and its only name—
But of the soul, escaped the slavish trade
Of mortal life!—For in this earthly frame

Ours is the reptile's lot, much toil, much blame,
Manifold motions making little speed,
And to deform and kill the things whereon we feed.

THE KNIGHT'S TOMB

Where is the grave of Sir Arthur O'Kellyn?
Where may the grave of that good man be?—
By the side of a spring, on the breast of Helvellyn,
Under the twigs of a young birch tree!
The oak that in summer was sweet to hear,
And rustled its leaves in the fall of the year,
And whistled and roared in the winter alone,
Is gone,—and the birch in its stead is grown.—
The Knight's bones are dust,
And his good sword rust;—
His soul is with the saints, I trust.

ON DONNE'S POETRY

With Donne, whose muse on dromedary trots,
Wreathe iron pokers into true-love knots;
Rhyme's sturdy cripple, fancy's maze and clue,
Wit's forge and fire-blast, meaning's press and screw.

THE RIME OF THE ANCIENT MARINER

PART I

An ancient Mar-   It is an ancient Mariner
iner meeteth   And he stoppeth one of three.
three Gallants   'By thy long grey beard and glittering eye,
bidden to a   Now wherefore stopp'st thou me?
wedding-feast,
and detaineth
one.

The Bridegroom's doors are opened wide,
And I am next of kin;
The guests are met, the feast is set:
May'st hear the merry din.'

He holds him with his skinny hand,
There was a ship, quoth he.
'Hold off! unhand me, grey-beard loon!'
Eftsoons his hand dropt he.

The Wedding-Guest is spellbound by the eye of the old seafaring man, and constrained to hear his tale.

He holds him with his glittering eye—
The Wedding-Guest stood still,
And listens like a three years' child:
The Mariner hath his will.

The Wedding-Guest sat on a stone:
He cannot choose but hear;
And thus spake on that ancient man,
The bright-eyed Mariner.

The ship was cheered, the harbour cleared,
Merrily did we drop
Below the kirk, below the hill,
Below the lighthouse top.

The Mariner tells how the ship sailed southward with a good wind and fair weather, till it reached the Line.

The Sun came up upon the left,
Out of the sea came he!
And he shone bright, and on the right
Went down into the sea.

Higher and higher every day,
Till over the mast at noon—
The Wedding-Guest here beat his breast,
For he heard the loud bassoon.

The Wedding-Guest heareth the bridal music; but the Mariner continueth his tale.

The bride hath paced into the hall,
Red as a rose is she;
Nodding their heads before her goes
The merry minstrelsy.

The Wedding-Guest he beat his breast,
Yet he cannot choose but hear;
And thus spake on that ancient man,
The bright-eyed Mariner.

The ship driven by a storm towards the south pole.

And now the STORM-BLAST came, and he
Was tyrannous and strong:
He struck with his o'ertaking wings,
And chased us south along.

With sloping masts and dipping prow,
As who pursued with yell and blow
Still treads the shadow of his foe,
And forward bends his head,
The ship drove fast, loud roared the blast,
And southward aye we fled.

And now there came both mist and snow,
And it grew wondrous cold:
And ice, mast-high, came floating by,
As green as emerald.

*The land of ice,
and of fearful
sounds, where no
living thing was
to be seen.*

And through the drifts the snowy clifts
Did send a dismal sheen:
Nor shapes of men nor beasts we ken—
The ice was all between.

The ice was here, the ice was there,
The ice was all around:
It cracked and growled, and roared and
    howled,
Like noises in a swound!

*Till a great sea-
bird, called the
Albatross, came
through the
snow-fog, and
was received
with great joy
and hospitality.*

At length did cross an Albatross,
Through the fog it came;
As if it had been a Christian soul,
We hailed it in God's name.

It ate the food it ne'er had eat,
And round and round it flew.
The ice did split with a thunder-fit;
The helmsman steered us through!

*And lo! the Al-
batross proveth
a bird of good
omen, and fol-
loweth the ship
as it returned
northward
through fog and
floating ice.*

And a good south wind sprung up behind;
The Albatross did follow,
And every day, for food or play,
Came to the mariners' hollo!

In mist or cloud, on mast or shroud,
It perched for vespers nine;
Whiles all the night, through fog-smoke
    white,
Glimmered the white Moon-shine.

*The ancient
Mariner inhospi-
tably killeth the
pious bird of
good omen.*

'God save thee, ancient Mariner!
From the fiends, that plague thee thus!—
Why look'st thou so?'—With my cross-bow
I shot the ALBATROSS.

PART II

The Sun now rose upon the right:
Out of the sea came he,

Still hid in mist, and on the left
Went down into the sea.

And the good south wind still blew behind,
But no sweet bird did follow,
Nor any day for food or play
Came to the mariners' hollo!

*His shipmates
cry out against
the ancient Mar-
iner, for killing
the bird of good
luck.*

And I had done a hellish thing,
And it would work 'em woe:
For all averred, I had killed the bird
That made the breeze to blow.
Ah, wretch! said they, the bird to slay,
That made the breeze to blow!

*But when the
fog cleared off,
they justify the
same, and thus
make themselves
accomplices in
the crime.*

Nor dim nor red, like God's own head,
The glorious Sun uprist:
Then all averred, I had killed the bird
That brought the fog and mist.
'Twas right, said they, such birds to slay,
That bring the fog and mist.

*The fair breeze
continues; the
ship enters the
Pacific Ocean,
and sails north-
ward, even till it
reaches the Line.*

The fair breeze blew, the white foam flew,
The furrow followed free;
We were the first that ever burst
Into that silent sea.

*The ship hath
been suddenly
becalmed.*

Down dropt the breeze, the sails dropt down,
'Twas sad as sad could be;
And we did speak only to break
The silence of the sea!

All in a hot and copper sky,
The bloody Sun, at noon,
Right up above the mast did stand,
No bigger than the Moon.

Day after day, day after day,
We stuck, nor breath nor motion;
As idle as a painted ship
Upon a painted ocean.

*And the Alba-
tross begins to
be avenged.*

Water, water, every where,
And all the boards did shrink;
Water, water, every where,
Nor any drop to drink.

The very deep did rot: O Christ!
That ever this should be!
Yea, slimy things did crawl with legs
Upon the slimy sea.

About, about, in reel and rout
The death-fires danced at night;
The water, like a witch's oils,
Burnt green, and blue and white.

*A Spirit had
followed them;
one of the invis-
ible inhabitants
of this planet,
neither departed
souls nor angels;
concerning
whom the
learned Jew, Jo-
sephus, and the
Platonic Con-*

And some in dreams assurèd were
Of the Spirit that plagued us so;
Nine fathom deep he had followed us
From the land of mist and snow.

And every tongue, through utter drought,
Was withered at the root;
We could not speak, no more than if
We had been choked with soot.

*stantinopolitan, Michael Psellus, may be consulted. They are very
numerous, and there is no climate or element without one or more.*

*The shipmates,
in their sore dis-
tress, would fain
throw the whole
guilt on the an-
cient Mariner: in*

Ah! well-a-day! what evil looks
Had I from old and young!
Instead of the cross, the Albatross
About my neck was hung.

sign whereof they hang the dead sea-bird round his neck.

PART III

There passed a weary time. Each throat
Was parched, and glazed each eye.
A weary time! a weary time!

*The ancient
Mariner behold-
eth a sign in the
element afar off.*

How glazed each weary eye,
When looking westward, I beheld
A something in the sky.

At first it seemed a little speck,
And then it seemed a mist;
It moved and moved, and took at last
A certain shape, I wist.

A speck, a mist, a shape, I wist!
And still it neared and neared:

As if it dodged a water-sprite,
It plunged and tacked and veered.

At its nearer approach, it seemeth him to be a ship; and at a dear ransom he freeth his speech from the bonds of thirst.

With throats unslaked, with black lips baked,
We could nor laugh nor wail;
Through utter drought all dumb we stood!
I bit my arm, I sucked the blood,
And cried, A sail! a sail!

A flash of joy;

With throats unslaked, with black lips baked,
Agape they heard me call:
Gramercy! they for joy did grin,
And all at once their breath drew in,
As they were drinking all.

And horror follows. For can it be a ship that comes onward without wind or tide?

See! see! (I cried) she tacks no more!
Hither to work us weal;
Without a breeze, without a tide,
She steadies with upright keel!

The western wave was all a-flame.
The day was well nigh done!
Almost upon the western wave
Rested the broad bright Sun;
When that strange shape drove suddenly
Betwixt us and the Sun.

It seemeth him but the skeleton of a ship.

And straight the Sun was flecked with bars,
(Heaven's Mother send us grace!)
As if through a dungeon-grate he peered
With broad and burning face.

Alas! (thought I, and my heart beat loud)
How fast she nears and nears!
Are those *her* sails that glance in the Sun,
Like restless gossameres?

And its ribs are seen as bars on the face of the setting Sun. The Spectre-Woman and her Deathmate, and no other on the skeleton ship.

Are those *her* ribs through which the Sun
Did peer, as through a grate?
And is that Woman all her crew?
Is that a DEATH? and are there two?
Is DEATH that woman's mate?

Like vessel, like crew!

Her lips were red, *her* looks were free,
Her locks were yellow as gold:
Her skin was as white as leprosy,

The Night-mare LIFE-IN-DEATH was she,
Who thicks man's blood with cold.

*Death and Life-
in-Death have
diced for the
ship's crew, and
she (the latter)
winneth the an-
cient Mariner.*

The naked hulk alongside came,
And the twain were casting dice;
'The game is done! I've won! I've won!'
Quoth she, and whistles thrice.

*No twilight
within the courts
of the Sun.*

The Sun's rim dips; the stars rush out:
At one stride comes the dark;
With far-heard whisper, o'er the sea,
Off shot the spectre-bark.

*At the rising of
the Moon,*

We listened and looked sideways up!
Fear at my heart, as at a cup,
My life-blood seemed to sip!
The stars were dim, and thick the night,
The steersman's face by his lamp gleamed
        white;
From the sails the dew did drip—
Till clomb above the eastern bar
The hornèd Moon, with one bright star
Within the nether tip.

*One after an-
other,*

One after one, by the star-dogged Moon,
Too quick for groan or sigh,
Each turned his face with a ghastly pang,
And cursed me with his eye.

*His shipmates
drop down dead.*

Four times fifty living men,
(And I heard nor sigh nor groan)
With heavy thump, a lifeless lump,
They dropped down one by one.

*But Life-in-
Death begins her
work on the an-
cient Mariner.*

The souls did from their bodies fly,—
They fled to bliss or woe!
And every soul, it passed me by,
Like the whizz of my cross-bow!

PART IV

*The Wedding-
Guest feareth
that a Spirit is
talking to him;*

'I fear thee, ancient Mariner!
I fear thy skinny hand!
And thou art long, and lank, and brown,
As is the ribbed sea-sand.

'I fear thee and thy glittering eye,
And thy skinny hand, so brown.'—

But the ancient Mariner assureth him of his bodily life, and proceedeth to relate his horrible penance.

Fear not, fear not, thou Wedding-Guest!
This body dropt not down.

Alone, alone, all, all alone,
Alone on a wide wide sea!
And never a saint took pity on
My soul in agony.

He despiseth the creatures of the calm,

The many men, so beautiful!
And they all dead did lie:
And a thousand thousand slimy things
Lived on; and so did I.

And envieth that they should live, and so many lie dead.

I looked upon the rotting sea,
And drew my eyes away;
I looked upon the rotting deck,
And there the dead men lay.

I looked to heaven, and tried to pray;
But or ever a prayer had gusht,
A wicked whisper came, and made
My heart as dry as dust.

I closed my lids, and kept them close,
And the balls like pulses beat;
For the sky and the sea, and the sea and the
 sky
Lay like a load on my weary eye,
And the dead were at my feet.

But the curse liveth for him in the eye of the dead men.

The cold sweat melted from their limbs,
Nor rot nor reek did they:
The look with which they looked on me
Had never passed away.

An orphan's curse would drag to hell
A spirit from on high;
But oh! more horrible than that
Is the curse in a dead man's eye!
Seven days, seven nights, I saw that curse,
And yet I could not die.

In his loneliness and fixedness he yearneth towards the journeying Moon, and the

The moving Moon went up the sky,
And no where did abide:
Softly she was going up,
And a star or two beside—

stars that still sojourn, yet still move onward; and every where the blue sky belongs to them, and is their appointed rest, and their native country and their own natural homes, which they enter unannounced, as lords that are certainly expected and yet there is a silent joy at their arrival.

Her beams bemocked the sultry main,
Like April hoar-frost spread;
But where the ship's huge shadow lay,
The charmèd water burnt alway
A still and awful red.

By the light of the Moon he beholdeth God's creatures of the great calm.

Beyond the shadow of the ship,
I watched the water-snakes:
They moved in tracks of shining white,
And when they reared, the elfish light
Fell off in hoary flakes.

Within the shadow of the ship
I watched their rich attire:
Blue, glossy green, and velvet black,
They coiled and swam; and every track
Was a flash of golden fire.

Their beauty and their happiness.

O happy living things! no tongue
Their beauty might declare:
A spring of love gushed from my heart,

He blesseth them in his heart.

And I blessed them unaware:
Sure my kind saint took pity on me,
And I blessed them unaware.

The spell begins to break.

The self-same moment I could pray;
And from my neck so free
The Albatross fell off, and sank
Like lead into the sea.

PART V

Oh sleep! it is a gentle thing,
Beloved from pole to pole!
To Mary Queen the praise be given!
She sent the gentle sleep from Heaven,
That slid into my soul.

By grace of the holy Mother, the ancient Mariner is refreshed with rain.

The silly buckets on the deck,
That had so long remained,
I dreamt that they were filled with dew;
And when I awoke, it rained.

My lips were wet, my throat was cold,
My garments all were dank;

Sure I had drunken in my dreams,
And still my body drank.

I moved, and could not feel my limbs:
I was so light—almost
I thought that I had died in sleep,
And was a blessèd ghost.

*He heareth
sounds and seeth
strange sights
and commotions
in the sky and
the element.*

And soon I heard a roaring wind:
It did not come anear;
But with its sound it shook the sails,
That were so thin and sere.

The upper air burst into life!
And a hundred fire-flags sheen,
To and fro they were hurried about!
And to and fro, and in and out,
The wan stars danced between.

And the coming wind did roar more loud,
And the sails did sigh like sedge;
And the rain poured down from one black
     cloud;
The Moon was at its edge.

The thick black cloud was cleft, and still
The Moon was at its side:
Like waters shot from some high crag,
The lightning fell with never a jag,
A river steep and wide.

*The bodies of
the ship's crew
are inspired and
the ship moves
on;*

The loud wind never reached the ship,
Yet now the ship moved on!
Beneath the lightning and the Moon
The dead men gave a groan.

They groaned, they stirred, they all up-rose,
Nor spake, nor moved their eyes;
It had been strange, even in a dream,
To have seen those dead men rise.

The helmsman steered, the ship moved on;
Yet never a breeze up-blew;
The mariners all 'gan work the ropes,
Where they were wont to do;
The raised their limbs like lifeless tools—
We were a ghastly crew.

The body of my brother's son
Stood by me, knee to knee:
The body and I pulled at one rope,
But he said naught to me.

'I fear thee, ancient Mariner!'
Be calm, thou Wedding-Guest!

But not by the
souls of the men,
nor by daemons
of earth or mid-
dle air, but by a
blessed troop of
angelic spirits,
sent down by
the invocation of
the guardian
saint.

'Twas not those souls that fled in pain,
Which to their corses came again,
But a troop of spirits blest:

For when it dawned—they dropped their
     arms,
And clustered round the mast;
Sweet sounds rose slowly through their
     mouths,
And from their bodies passed.

Around, around, flew each sweet sound,
Then darted to the Sun;
Slowly the sounds came back again,
Now mixed, now one by one.

Sometimes a-dropping from the sky
I heard the sky-lark sing;
Sometimes all little birds that are,
How they seemed to fill the sea and air
With their sweet jargoning!

And now 'twas like all instruments,
Now like a lonely flute;
And now it is an angel's song,
That makes the heavens be mute.

It ceased; yet still the sails made on
A pleasant noise till noon,
A noise like of a hidden brook
In the leafy month of June,
That to the sleeping woods all night
Singeth a quiet tune.

Till noon we quietly sailed on,
Yet never a breeze did breathe:
Slowly and smoothly went the ship,
Moved onward from beneath.

The lonesome Spirit from the south pole carries on the ship as far as the Line, in obedience to the angelic troop, but still requireth vengeance.

Under the keel nine fathom deep,
From the land of mist and snow,
The spirit slid: and it was he
That made the ship to go.
The sails at noon left off their tune,
And the ship stood still also.

The Sun, right up above the mast,
Had fixed her to the ocean:
But in a minute she 'gan stir,
With a shorty uneasy motion—
Backwards and forwards half her length
With a short uneasy motion.

Then like a pawing horse let go,
She made a sudden bound:
It flung the blood into my head,
And I fell down in a swound.

The Polar Spirit's fellow-daemons, the invisible inhabitants of the element, take part in his wrong; and two of them relate, one to the other, that penance long and heavy for the ancient Mariner hath been accorded to the Polar Spirit, who returneth southward.

How long in that same fit I lay,
I have not to declare;
But ere my living life returned,
I heard and in my soul discerned
Two voices in the air.

'Is it he?' quoth one, 'Is this the man?
By him who died on cross,
With his cruel bow he laid full low
The harmless Albatross.

The spirit who bideth by himself
In the land of mist and snow,
He loved the bird that loved the man
Who shot him with his bow.'

The other was a softer voice,
As soft as honey-dew:
Quoth he, 'The man hath penance done,
And penance more will do.'

PART VI

FIRST VOICE

'But tell me, tell me! speak again,
Thy soft response renewing—

What makes that ship drive on so fast?
What is the ocean doing?'

SECOND VOICE

'Still as a slave before his lord,
The ocean hath no blast;
His great bright eye most silently
Up to the Moon is cast—

If he may know which way to go;
For she guides him smooth or grim.
See, brother, see! how graciously
She looketh down on him.'

FIRST VOICE

The Mariner
hath been cast
into a trance; for
the angelic
power causeth
the vessel to
drive northward
faster than hu-
man life could
endure.

'But why drives on that ship so fast,
Without or wave or wind?'

SECOND VOICE

'The air is cut away before,
And closes from behind.

Fly, brother, fly! more high, more high!
Or we shall be belated:
For slow and slow that ship will go,
When the Mariner's trance is abated.'

The supernatural
motion is re-
tarded; the
Mariner awakes,
and his penance
begins anew.

I woke, and we were sailing on
As in a gentle weather:
'Twas night, calm night, the Moon was high;
The dead men stood together.

All stood together on the deck,
For a charnel-dungeon fitter:
All fixed on me their stony eyes,
That in the Moon did glitter.

The pang, the curse, with which they died,
Had never passed away:
I could not draw my eyes from theirs,
Nor turn them up to pray.

The curse is
finally expiated.

And now this spell was snapt: once more
I viewed the ocean green,
And looked far forth, yet little saw
Of what had else been seen—

Like one, that on a lonesome road
Doth walk in fear and dread,
And having once turned round walks on,
And turns no more his head;
Because he knows, a frightful fiend
Doth close behind him tread.

But soon there breathed a wind on me,
Nor sound nor motion made:
Its path was not upon the sea,
In ripple or in shade.

It raised my hair, it fanned my cheek
Like a meadow-gale of spring—
It mingled strangely with my fears,
Yet it felt like a welcoming.

Swiftly, swiftly flew the ship,
Yet she sailed softly too:
Sweetly, sweetly blew the breeze—
On me alone it blew.

*And the ancient
Mariner behold-
eth his native
country.*

Oh! dream of joy! is this indeed
The light-house top I see?
Is this the hill? is this the kirk?
Is this mine own countree?

We drifted o'er the harbour-bar,
And I with sobs did pray—
O let me be awake, my God!
Or let me sleep alway.

The harbour-bay was clear as glass,
So smoothly it was strewn!
And on the bay the moonlight lay,
And the shadow of the Moon.

The rock shone bright, the kirk no less,
That stands above the rock:
The moonlight steeped in silentness
The steady weathercock.

*The angelic
spirits leave the
dead bodies,*

And the bay was white with silent light,
Till rising from the same,
Full many shapes, that shadows were,
In crimson colours came.

*And appear in
their own forms
of light.*

A little distance from the prow
Those crimson shadows were:
I turned my eyes upon the deck—
Oh, Christ! what saw I there!

Each corse lay flat, lifeless and flat,
And, by the holy rood!
A man all light, a seraph-man,
On every corse there stood.

This seraph-band, each waved his hand:
It was a heavenly sight!
They stood as signals to the land,
Each one a lovely light;

This seraph-band, each waved his hand,
No voice did they impart—
No voice; but oh! the silence sank
Like music on my heart.

But soon I heard the dash of oars,
I heard the Pilot's cheer;
My head was turned perforce away,
And I saw a boat appear.

The Pilot, and the Pilot's boy.
I heard them coming fast:
Dear Lord in Heaven! it was a joy
The dead men could not blast.

I saw a third—I heard his voice:
It is the Hermit good!
He singeth loud his godly hymns
That he makes in the wood.
He'll shrieve my soul, he'll wash away
The Albatross's blood.

PART VII

*The Hermit of
the Wood,*

This Hermit good lives in that wood
Which slopes down to the sea.
How loudly his sweet voice he rears!
He loves to talk with marineres
That come from a far countree.

He kneels at morn, and noon, and eve—
He hath a cushion plump:

It is the moss that wholly hides
The rotted old oak-stump.

The skiff-boat neared: I heard them talk,
'Why this is strange, I trow!
Where are those lights so many and fair,
That signal made but now?'

*Approacheth the
ship with won-
der.*

'Strange, by my faith!' the Hermit said—
'And they answered not our cheer!
The planks looked warped! and see those
    sails,
How thin they are and sere!
I never saw aught like to them,
Unless perchance it were

Brown skeletons of leaves that lag
My forest-brook along;
When the ivy-tod is heavy with snow,
And the owlet whoops to the wolf below,
That eats the she-wolf's young.'

'Dear Lord! it hath a fiendish look—
(The Pilot made reply)
I am a-feared'—'Push on, push on!'
Said the Hermit cheerily.

The boat came closer to the ship,
But I nor spake nor stirred;
The boat came close beneath the ship,
And straight a sound was heard.

*The ship sud-
denly sinketh.*

Under the water it rumbled on,
Still louder and more dread:
It reached the ship, it split the bay;
The ship went down like lead.

*The ancient
Mariner is saved
in the Pilot's
boat.*

Stunned by that loud and dreadful sound,
Which sky and ocean smote,
Like one that hath been seven days drowned
My body lay afloat;
But swift as dreams, myself I found
Within the Pilot's boat.

Upon the whirl, where sank the ship,
The boat spun round and round;

And all was still, save that the hill
Was telling of the sound.

I moved my lips—the Pilot shrieked
And fell down in a fit;
The holy Hermit raised his eyes,
And prayed where he did sit.

I took the oars: the Pilot's boy,
Who now doth crazy go,
Laughed loud and long, and all the while
His eyes went to and fro.
'Ha! ha!' quoth he, 'full plain I see,
The Devil knows how to row.'

And now, all in my own countree,
I stood on the firm land!
The Hermit stepped forth from the boat,
And scarcely he could stand.

*The ancient
Mariner earn-
estly entreateth
the Hermit to
shrieve him; and
the penance of
life falls on him.*

'O shrieve me, shrieve me, holy man!'
The Hermit crossed his brow.
'Say quick,' quoth he, 'I bid thee say—
What manner of man art thou?'

Forthwith this frame of mine was wrenched
With a woful agony,
Which forced me to begin my tale;
And then it left me free.

*And ever and
anon throughout
his future life an
agony constrain-
eth him to travel
from land to
land;*

Since then, at an uncertain hour,
That agony returns:
And till my ghastly tale is told,
This heart within me burns.

I pass, like night, from land to land;
I have strange power of speech;
That moment that his face I see,
I know the man that must hear me:
To him my tale I teach.

What loud uproar bursts from that door!
The wedding-guests are there:
But in the garden-bower the bride
And bride-maids singing are:
And hark the little vesper bell,
Which biddeth me to prayer!

O Wedding-Guest! this soul hath been
Alone on a wide, wide sea:
So lonely 'twas, that God Himself
Scarce seemed there to be.

O sweeter than the marriage-feast,
'Tis sweeter far to me,
To walk together to the kirk
With a goodly company!—

To walk together to the kirk,
And all together pray,
While each to his great Father bends,
Old men, and babes, and loving friends,
And youths and maidens gay!

Farewell, farewell! but this I tell
To thee, thou Wedding-Guest!
He prayeth well, who loveth well
Both man and bird and beast.

*And to teach,
by his own
example, love
and reverence
to all things
that God
made and
loveth.*

He prayeth best, who loveth best
All things both great and small;
For the dear God who loveth us,
He made and loveth all.

The Mariner, whose eye is bright,
Whose beard with age is hoar,
Is gone: and now the Wedding-Guest
Turned from the bridegroom's door.

He went like one that hath been stunned,
And is of sense forlorn:
A sadder and a wiser man
He rose the morrow morn.

EPITAPH

Stop, Christian passer-by!—Stop, child of God,
And read with gentle breast. Beneath this sod
A poet lies, or that which once seemed he.—
O, lift one thought in prayer for S. T. C.;
That he who many a year with toil of breath
Found death in life, may here find life in death!
Mercy for praise—to be forgiven for fame
He asked, and hoped, through Christ. Do thou the same!

GEORGE GORDON, LORD BYRON

(1788-1824)

SHE WALKS IN BEAUTY

She walks in Beauty, like the night
    Of cloudless climes and starry skies;
And all that's best of dark and bright
    Meet in her aspect and her eyes:
Thus mellowed to that tender light
    Which heaven to gaudy day denies.

One shade the more, one ray the less,
    Had half impaired the nameless grace
Which waves in every raven tress,
    Or softly lightness o'er her face;
Where thoughts serenely sweet express
    How pure, how dear their dwelling-place.

And on that cheek, and o'er that brow,
    So soft, so calm, yet eloquent,
The smiles that win, the tints that glow,
    But tell of days in goodness spent,
A mind at peace with all below,
    A heart whose love is innocent!

THERE'S NOT A JOY

There's not a joy the world can give like that it takes away,
When the glow of early thought declines in feeling's dull
    decay;
'Tis not on youth's smooth cheek the blush alone, which fades
    so fast,
But the tender bloom of heart is gone, ere youth itself be
    past.

Then the few whose spirits float above the wreck of happiness
Are driven o'er the shoals of guilt or ocean of excess:
The magnet of their course is gone, or only points in vain
The shore to which their shivered sail shall never stretch
      again.

Then the mortal coldness of the soul like death itself comes
      down;
It cannot feel for others' woes, it dare not dream its own;
That heavy chill has frozen o'er the fountain of our tears,
And though the eye may sparkle still, 'tis where the ice
      appears.

Though wit may flash from fluent lips, and mirth distract
      the breast,
Through midnight hours that yield no more their former
      hope of rest;
'Tis but ivy-leaves around the ruined turret wreath,
All green and wildly fresh without, but worn and grey
      beneath.

Oh could I feel as I have felt,—or be what I have been,
Or weep as I could once have wept o'er many a vanish'd
      scene;
As springs in deserts found seem sweet, all brackish though
      they be,
So, midst the withered waste of life, those tears would flow to
      me.

SO, WE'LL GO NO MORE A-ROVING

So, we'll go no more a-roving
    So late into the night,
Though the heart be still as loving,
    And the moon be still as bright.

For the sword outwears its sheath,
    And the soul wears out the breast,
And the heart must pause to breathe,
    And Love itself have rest.

Though the night was made for loving,
    And the day returns too soon,
Yet we'll go no more a-roving
    By the light of the moon.

THERE BE NONE OF BEAUTY'S DAUGHTERS

There be none of Beauty's daughters
 With a magic like thee;
And like music on the waters
 Is thy sweet voice to me:
When, as if its sound were causing
The charmèd ocean's pausing,
The waves lie still and gleaming,
And the lulled winds seem dreaming:

And the midnight moon is weaving
 Her bright chain o'er the deep;
Whose breast is gently heaving
 As an infant's asleep:
So the spirit bows before thee,
To listen and adore thee;
With a full but soft emotion,
Like the swell of Summer's ocean.

SONNET ON CHILLON

Eternal Spirit of the chainless Mind!
 Brightest in dungeons, Liberty! thou art,
 For thee thy habitation is the heart—
The heart which love of thee alone can bind;
And when thy sons to fetters are consigned—
 To fetters, and the damp vault's dayless gloom,
 Their country conquers with their martyrdom,
And Freedom's fame finds wings on every wind.
Chillon! thy prison is a holy place,
 And thy sad floor an altar—for 'twas trod,
Until his very steps have left a trace
 Worn, as if thy cold pavement were a sod,
By Bonnivard! May none those marks efface!
 For they appeal from tyranny to God.

AND THOU ART DEAD

"Heu, quanto minus est cum reliquis versari quam tui meminisse!"

And thou art dead, as young and fair
 As aught of mortal birth;
And form so soft, and charms so rare,
 Too soon returned to Earth!

Though Earth received them in her bed
And o'er the spot the crowd may tread
   In carelessness or mirth,
There is an eye which could not brook
A moment on that grave to look.

I will not ask where thou liest low,
   Nor gaze upon the spot;
There flowers or weeds at will may grow,
   So I behold them not:
It is enough for me to prove
That what I loved, and long must love,
   Like common earth can rot;
To me there needs no stone to tell,
'Tis nothing that I loved so well.

Yet did I love thee to the last
   As fervently as thou,
Who didst not change through all the past,
   And canst not alter now.
The love where Death has set his seal,
Nor age can chill, nor rival steal,
   Nor falsehood disavow:
And, what were worse, thou canst not see
Or wrong, or change, or fault in me.

The better days of life were ours;
   The worst can be but mine:
The sun that cheers, the storm that lowers,
   Shall never more be thine.
The silence of that dreamless sleep
I envy now too much to weep;
   Nor need I to repine,
That all those charms have passed away;
I might have watched through long decay.

The flower in ripened bloom unmatched
   Must fall the earliest prey;
Though by no hand untimely snatched,
   The leaves must drop away:
And yet it were a greater grief
To watch it withering, leaf by leaf,
   Than see it plucked to-day;
Since earthly eye but ill can bear
To trace the change to foul from fair.

I know not if I could have borne
    To see thy beauties fade;
The night that followed such a morn
    Had worn a deeper shade:
The day without a cloud hath passed,
And thou wert lovely to the last;
    Extinguished, not decayed;
As stars that shoot along the sky
Shine brightest as they fall from high.

As once I wept, if I could weep,
    My tears might well be shed,
To think I was not near to keep
    One vigil o'er thy bed;
To gaze, how fondly! on thy face,
To fold thee in a faint embrace,
    Uphold thy drooping head;
And show that love, however vain,
Nor thou nor I can feel again.

Yet how much less it were to gain,
    Though thou hast left me free,
The loveliest things that still remain,
    Than thus remember thee!
The all of thine that cannot die
Through dark and dread Eternity
    Returns again to me,
And more thy buried love endears
Than aught except its living years.

FARE THEE WELL

Fare thee well! and if for ever,
    Still for ever, fare thee well:
Even though unforgiving, never
    'Gainst thee shall my heart rebel.

Would that breast were bared before thee
    Where thy head so oft hath lain.
While that placid sleep came o'er thee
    Which thou ne'er canst know again:

Would that breast, by thee glanced over,
    Every inmost thought could show!
Then thou wouldst at last discover
    'Twas not well to spurn it so.

Though the world for this commend thee—
 Though it smile upon the blow,
Even its praises must offend thee,
 Founded on another's woe:

Though my many faults defaced me,
 Could no other arm be found,
Than the one which once embraced me,
 To inflict a cureless wound?

Yet, oh yet, thyself deceive not;
 Love may sink by slow decay,
But by sudden wrench, believe not
 Hearts can thus be torn away:

Still thine own its life retaineth,
 Still must mine, though bleeding, beat;
And the undying thought which paineth
 Is—that we no more may meet.

These are words of deeper sorrow
 Than the wail above the dead;
Both shall live, but every morrow
 Wake us from a widow'd bed.

And when thou wouldst solace gather,
 When our child's first accents flow,
Wilt thou teach her to say 'Father!'
 Though his care she must forego?

When her little hands shall press thee,
 When her lip to thine is pressed,
Think of him whose prayer shall bless thee,
 Think of him thy love had blessed!

Should her lineaments resemble
 Those thou never more may'st see,
Then thy heart will softly tremble
 With a pulse yet true to me.

All my faults perchance thou knowest,
 All my madness none can know;
All my hopes, where'er thou goest,
 Wither, yet with *thee* they go.

Every feeling hath been shaken;
 Pride, which not a world could bow,

Bows to thee—by thee forsaken,
  Even my soul forsakes me now:

But 'tis done—all words are idle—
  Words from me are vainer still;
But the thoughts we cannot bridle
  Force their way without the will.

Fare thee well!—thus disunited,
  Torn from every nearer tie,
Sear'd in heart, and lone, and blighted,
  More than this I scarce can die.

DARKNESS

I had a dream, which was not all a dream.
The bright sun was extinguished, and the stars
Did wander darkling in the eternal space,
Rayless, and pathless, and the icy earth
Swung blind and blackening in the moonless air;
Morn came and went—and came, and brought no day,
And men forgot their passions in the dread
Of this their desolation; and all hearts
Were chilled into a selfish prayer for light:
And they did live by watchfires—and the thrones,
The palaces of crowned kings—the huts,
The habitations of all things which dwell,
Were burnt for beacons; cities were consumed,
And men were gathered round their blazing homes
To look once more into each other's face;
Happy were those who dwelt within the eye
Of the volcanos, and their mountain-torch:
A fearful hope was all the world contained;
Forests were set on fire—but hour by hour
They fell and faded—and the crackling trunks
Extinguished with a crash—and all was black.
The brows of men by the despairing light
Wore an unearthly aspect, as by fits
The flashes fell upon them; some lay down
And hid their eyes and wept; and some did rest
Their chins upon their clenchèd hands, and smiled;
And others hurried to and fro, and fed
Their funeral piles with fuel, and looked up
With mad disquietude on the dull sky,
The pall of a past world; and then again

With curses cast them down upon the dust,
And gnashed their teeth and howled: the wild birds shrieked
And, terrified, did flutter on the ground,
And flap their useless wings; the wildest brutes
Came tame and tremulous; and vipers crawled
And twined themselves among the multitude,
Hissing, but stingless—they were slain for food.
And War, which for a moment was no more,
Did glut himself again:—a meal was bought
With blood, and each sate sullenly apart
Gorging himself in gloom: no love was left;
All earth was but one thought—and that was death
Immediate and inglorious; and the pang
Of famine fed upon all entrails—men
Died, and their bones were tombless as their flesh;
The meagre by the meagre were devoured,
Even dogs assailed their masters, all save one,
And he was faithful to a corse, and kept
The birds and beasts and famished men at bay,
Till hunger clung them, or the dropping dead
Lured their lank jaws; himself sought out no food,
But with a piteous and perpetual moan,
And a quick desolate cry, licking the hand
Which answer'd not with a caress—he died.
The crowd was famished by degrees; but two
Of an enormous city did survive,
And they were enemies: they met beside
The dying embers of an altar-place
Where had been heaped a mass of holy things
For an unholy usage; they raked up,
And shivering scraped with their cold skeleton hands
The feeble ashes, and their feeble breath
Blew for a little life, and made a flame
Which was a mockery; then they lifted up
Their eyes as it grew lighter, and beheld
Each other's aspects—saw, and shrieked, and died—
Even of their mutual hideousness they died,
Unknowing who he was upon whose brow
Famine had written Fiend. The world was void,
The populous and the powerful was a lump
Seasonless, herbless, treeless, manless, lifeless,
A lump of death—a chaos of hard clay.
The rivers, lakes, and ocean all stood still,
And nothing stirred within their silent depths;
Ships sailorless lay rotting on the sea,
And their masts fell down piecemeal: as they dropped

They slept on the abyss without a surge—
The waves were dead; the tides were in their grave,
The moon, their mistress, had expired before;
The winds were withered in the stagnant air,
And the clouds perished; Darkness had no need
Of aid from them—She was the Universe.

THE OCEAN

There is a pleasure in the pathless woods,
There is a rapture on the lonely shore,
There is society, where none intrudes,
By the deep Sea, and music in its roar:
I love not Man the less, but Nature more,
From these our interviews, in which I steal
From all I may be, or have been before,
To mingle with the Universe, and feel
What I can ne'er express, yet cannot all conceal.

Roll on, thou deep and dark blue Ocean—roll!
Ten thousand fleets sweep over thee in vain;
Man marks the earth with ruin—his control
Stops with the shore; upon the watery plain
The wrecks are all thy deed, nor doth remain
A shadow of man's ravage, save his own,
When, for a moment, like a drop of rain,
He sinks into thy depths with bubbling groan,
Without a grave, unknelled, uncoffined, and unknown.

His steps are not upon thy paths,—thy fields
Are not a spoil for him,—thou dost arise
And shake him from thee; the vile strength he wields
For earth's destruction thou dost all despise,
Spurning him from thy bosom to the skies,
And send'st him, shivering in thy playful spray
And howling, to his Gods, where haply lies
His petty hope in some near port or bay,
And dashest him again to earth:—there let him lay.

The armaments which thunderstrike the walls
Of rock-built cities, bidding nations quake,
And monarchs tremble in their capitals,
The oak leviathans, whose huge ribs make
Their clay creator the vain title take
Of lord of thee, and arbiter of war—

These are thy toys, and, as the snowy flake,
They melt into thy yeast of waves, which mar
Alike the Armada's pride or spoils of Trafalgar.

Thy shores are empires, changed in all save thee—
Assyria, Greece, Rome, Carthage, what are they?
Thy waters washed them power while they were free,
And many a tyrant since; their shores obey
The stranger, slave, or savage; their decay
Has dried up realms to deserts:—not so thou;—
Unchangeable, save to thy wild waves' play,
Time writes no wrinkle on thine azure brow:
Such as creation's dawn beheld, thou rollest now.

Thou glorious mirror, where the Almighty's form
Glasses itself in tempests; in all time,—
Calm or convulsed, in breeze, or gale, or storm,
Icing the pole, or in the torrid clime
Dark-heaving—boundless, endless, and sublime,
The image of eternity, the throne
Of the Invisible; even from out thy slime
The monsters of the deep are made; each zone
Obeys thee; thou goest forth, dread, fathomless, alone.

And I have loved thee, Ocean! and my joy
Of youthful sports was on thy breast to be
Borne, like thy bubbles, onward: from a boy
I wantoned with thy breakers—they to me
Were a delight; and if the freshening sea
Made them a terror—'twas a pleasing fear,
For I was as it were a child of thee,
And trusted to thy billows far and near,
And laid my hand upon thy mane—as I do here.

from CHILDE HAROLD'S PILGRIMAGE, *Canto IV*

IT IS THE HUSH OF NIGHT

It is the hush of night, and all between
Thy margin and the mountains, dusk, yet clear,
Mellowed and mingling, yet distinctly seen,
Save darken'd Jura, whose capt heights appear
Precipitously steep; and drawing near,
There breathes a living fragrance from the shore,
Of flowers yet fresh with childhood; on the ear

Drops the light drip of the suspended oar,
Or chirps the grasshopper one good-night carol more;

He is an evening reveller, who makes
His life an infancy, and sings his fill;
At intervals, some bird from out the brakes
Starts into voice a moment, then is still.
There seems a floating whisper on the hill,
But that is fancy, for the starlight dews
All silently their tears of love instil,
Weeping themselves away, till they infuse
Deep into Nature's breast the spirit of her hues.

Ye stars! which are the poetry of heaven!
If in your bright leaves we would read the fate
Of men and empires,—'tis to be forgiven,
That in our aspirations to be great,
Our destinies o'erleap their mortal state,
And claim a kindred with you; for ye are
A beauty and a mystery, and create
In us such love and reverence from afar,
That fortune, fame, power, life, have named themselves a
        star.

All heaven and earth are still—though not in sleep,
But breathless, as we grow when feeling most;
And silent, as we stand in thoughts too deep:—
All heaven and earth are still: From the high host
Of stars, to the lulled lake and mountain-coast,
All is concentred in a life intense,
Where not a beam, nor air, nor leaf is lost,
But hath a part of being, and a sense
Of that which is of all Creator and defence.

Then stirs the feeling infinite, so felt
In solitude, where we are *least* alone;
A truth, which through our being then doth melt,
And purifies from self: it is a tone,
The soul and source of music, which makes known
Eternal harmony, and sheds a charm
Like to the fabled Cytherea's zone,
Binding all things with beauty;—'twould disarm
The spectre Death, had he substantial power to harm.

Not vainly did the early Persian make
His altar the high places, and the peak

Of earth-o'ergazing mountains, and thus take
A fit and unwalled temple, there to seek
The Spirit, in whose honour shrines are weak,
Uprear'd of human hands. Come, and compare
Columns and idol-dwellings, Goth or Greek,
With Nature's realms of worship, earth and air,
Nor fix on fond abodes to circumscribe thy pray'r!

Thy sky is changed!—and such a change! Oh night,
And storm, and darkness, ye are wondrous strong,
Yet lovely in your strength, as is the light
Of a dark eye in woman! Far along,
From peak to peak, the rattling crags among
Leaps the live thunder! Not from one lone cloud,
But every mountain now hath found a tongue,
And Jura answers, through her misty shroud,
Back to the joyous Alps, who call to her aloud!

And this is in the night:—Most glorious night!
Thou wert not sent for slumber! let me be
A sharer in thy fierce and far delight,—
A portion of the tempest and of thee!
How the lit lake shines, a phosphoric sea,
And the big rain comes dancing to the earth!
And now again 'tis black,—and now, the glee
Of the loud hills shakes with its mountain-mirth,
As if they did rejoice o'er a young earthquake's birth.

from CHILDE HAROLD'S PILGRIMAGE, *Canto III.*

'TIS SWEET

'Tis sweet to see the evening star appear;
  'Tis sweet to listen as the night-winds creep
From leaf to leaf; 'tis sweet to view on high
The rainbow, based on ocean, span the sky.

'Tis sweet to hear the watch-dog's honest bark
  Bay deep-mouthed welcome as we draw near home;
'Tis sweet to know there is an eye will mark
  Our coming, and look brighter when we come;
'Tis sweet to be awakened by the lark,
  Or lulled by falling waters; sweet the hum
Of bees, the voice of girls, the song of birds,
The lisp of children, and their earliest words.

Sweet is the vintage, when the showering grapes
   In Bacchanal profusion reel to earth,
Purple and gushing: sweet are our escapes
   From civic revelry to rural mirth;
Sweet to the miser are his glittering heaps,
   Sweet to the father is his first-born's birth,
Sweet is revenge—especially to women,
Pillage to soldiers, prize-money to seamen.

Sweet is a legacy, and passing sweet
   The unexpected death of some old lady
Or gentleman of seventy years complete,
   Who've made 'us youth' wait too—too long already,
For an estate, or cash, or country seat,
   Still breaking, but with stamina so steady
That all the Israelites are fit to mob its
Next owner for their double-damned post-obits.

'Tis sweet to win, no matter how, one's laurels,
   By blood or ink; 'tis sweet to put an end
To strife; 'tis sometimes sweet to have our quarrels,
   Particularly with a tiresome friend:
Sweet is old wine in bottles, ale in barrels;
   Dear is the helpless creature we defend
Against the world; and dear the schoolboy spot
We ne'er forget, though there we are forgot.

But sweeter still than this, than these, than all,
   Is first and passionate love—it stands alone,
Like Adam's recollection of his fall;
   The Tree of Knowledge has been pluc'ked—all's known—
And life yields nothing further to recal'
   Worthy of this ambrosial sin, so shown,
No doubt in fable, as the unforgiven
Fire which Prometheus filched for us from heaven.

from DON JUAN, *Canto I.*

DON JUAN, CANTO XIII

I now mean to be serious;—it is time,
   Since laughter now-a-days is deemed too serious;
A jest at Vice by Virtue's called a crime,
   And critically held as deleterious:
Besides, the sad's a source of the sublime,

Although when long a little apt to weary us;
And therefore shall my lay soar high and solemn,
As an old temple dwindled to a column.

The Lady Adeline Amundeville
    ('Tis an old Norman name, and to be found
In pedigrees, by those who wander still
    Along the last fields of that Gothic ground)
Was high-born, wealthy by her father's will,
    And beauteous, even where beauties most abound,
In Britain—which of course true patriots find
The goodliest soil of body and of mind.

I'll not gainsay them; it is not my cue;
    I'll leave them to their taste, no doubt the best:
An eye's an eye, and whether black or blue,
    Is no great matter, so 'tis in request;
'Tis nonsense to dispute about a hue—
    The kindest may be taken as a test.
The fair sex should be always fair; and no man
Till thirty, should perceive there's a plain woman.

And after that serene and somewhat dull
    Epoch, that awkward corner turned for days
More quiet, when our moon's no more at full,
    We may presume to criticise or praise;
Because indifference begins to lull
    Our passions, and we walk in wisdom's ways;
Also because the figure and the face
Hint, that 'tis time to give the younger place.

I know that some would fain postpone this era,
    Reluctant as all placemen to resign
Their post; but theirs is merely a chimera,
    For they have passed life's equinoctial line:
But then they have their claret and Madeira
    To irrigate the dryness of decline;
And county meetings, and the parliament,
And debt, and what not, for their solace sent.

And is there not religion, and reform,
    Peace, war, the taxes, and what's called the 'Nation'?
The struggle to be pilots in a storm?
    The landed and the monied speculation?
The joys of mutual hate to keep them warm,
    Instead of love, that mere hallucination?

Now hatred is by far the longest pleasure;
Men love in haste, but they detest at leisure.

Rough Johnson, the great moralist, professed,
    Right honestly, 'he liked an honest hater!'—
The only truth that yet has been confest
    Within these latest thousand years or later.
Perhaps the fine old fellow spoke in jest:—
    For my part, I am but a mere spectator,
And gaze where'er the palace or the hovel is,
Much in the mode of Goethe's Mephistopheles;

But neither love nor hate in much excess;
    Though 'twas not once so. If I sneer sometimes,
It is because I cannot well do less,
    And now and then it also suits my rhymes.
I should be very willing to redress
    Men's wrongs, and rather check than punish crimes,
Had not Cervantes, in that too true tale
Of Quixote, shown how all such efforts fail.

Of all tales 'tis the saddest—and more sad,
    Because it makes us smile: his hero's right,
And still pursues the right;—to curb the bad
    His only object, and 'gainst odds to fight
His guerdon: 'tis his virtue makes him mad!
    But his adventures form a sorry sight;—
A sorrier still is the great moral taught
By that real epic unto all who have thought.

Redressing injury, revenging wrong,
    To aid the damsel and destroy the caitiff;
Opposing singly the united strong,
    From foreign yoke to free the helpless native:—
Alas! must noblest views, like an old song,
    Be for mere fancy's sport a theme creative,
A jest, a riddle, Fame through thick and thin sought!
And Socrates himself but Wisdom's Quixote?

Cervantes smiled Spain's chivalry away;
    A single laugh demolished the right arm
Of his own country;—seldom since that day
    Has Spain had heroes. While Romance could charm,
The world gave ground before her bright array;
    And therefore have his volumes done such harm,
That all their glory, as a composition,
Was dearly purchased by his land's perdition.

I'm 'at my old lunes'—digression, and forget
  The Lady Adeline Amundeville;
The fair most fatal Juan ever met,
  Although she was not evil nor meant ill;
But Destiny and Passion spread the net
  (Fate is a good excuse for our own will),
And caught them;—what do they *not* catch, methinks?
But I'm not Œdipus, and life's a Sphinx.

I tell the tale as it is told, nor dare
  To venture a solution: *'Davus sum!'*
And now I will proceed upon the pair.
  Sweet Adeline, amidst the gay world's hum,
Was the Queen-Bee, the glass of all that's fair;
  Whose charms made all men speak, and women
    dumb.
The last's a miracle, and such was reckoned,
And since that time there has not been a second.

Chaste was she, to detraction's desperation,
  And wedded unto one she had loved well—
A man known in the councils of the nation,
  Cool, and quite English, imperturbable,
Though apt to act with fire upon occasion,
  Proud of himself and her: the world could tell
Nought against either, and both seemed secure—
She in her virtue, he in his hauteur.

It chanced some diplomatical relations,
  Arising out of business, often brought
Himself and Juan in their mutual stations
  Into close contact. Though reserved, nor caught
By specious seeming, Juan's youth, and patience,
  And talent, on his haughty spirit wrought,
And form'd a basis of esteem, which ends
In making men what courtesy calls friends.

And thus Lord Henry, who was cautious as
  Reserve and pride could make him, and full slow
In judging men—when once his judgment was
  Determined, right or wrong, on friend or foe,
Had all the pertinacity pride has,
  Which knows no ebb to its imperious flow,
And loves or hates, disdaining to be guided,
Because its own good pleasure hath decided.

His friendships, therefore, and no less aversions,
    Though oft well founded, which confirmed but more
His prepossessions, like the laws of Persians
    And Medes, would ne'er revoke what went before.
His feelings had not those strange fits, like tertians,
    Of common likings, which make some deplore
What they should laugh at—the mere ague still
Of men's regard, the fever or the chill.

' 'Tis not in mortals to command success:
    But *do you more*, Sempronius—*don't* deserve it,'
And take my word, you won't have any less.
    Be wary, watch the time, and always serve it;
Give gently way, when there's too great a press;
    And for your conscience only learn to nerve it,
For, like a racer, or a boxer training,
'Twill make, if proved, vast efforts without paining.

Lord Henry also liked to be superior,
    As most men do, the little or the great;
The very lowest find out an inferior,
    At least they think so, to exert their state
Upon: for there are very few things wearier
    Than solitary Pride's oppressive weight,
Which mortals generously would divide,
By bidding others carry while they ride.

In birth, in rank, in fortune likewise equal,
    O'er Juan he could no distinction claim;
In years he had the advantage of time's sequel;
    And, as he thought, in country much the same—
Because bold Britons have a tongue and free quill,
    At which all modern nations vainly aim;
And the Lord Henry was a great debater,
So that few members kept the House up later.

These were advantages: and then he thought—
    It was his foible, but by no means sinister—
That few or none more than himself had caught
    Court mysteries, having been himself a minister:
He liked to teach that which he had been taught,
    And greatly shone whenever there had been a stir;
And reconciled all qualities which grace man,
Always a patriot, and sometimes a placeman.

He liked the gentle Spaniard for his gravity;
    He almost honoured him for his docility;

Because, though young, he acquiesced with suavity,
    Or contradicted but with proud humility.
He knew the world, and would not see depravity
    In faults which sometimes show the soil's fertility,
If that the weeds o'erlive not the first crop—
For then they are very difficult to stop.

And then he talked with him about Madrid,
    Constantinople, and such distant places;
Where people always did as they were bid,
    Or did what they should not with foreign graces.
Of coursers also spake they: Henry rid
    Well, like most Englishmen, and loved the races;
And Juan, like a true-born Andalusian,
Could back a horse, as despots ride a Russian.

And thus acquaintance grew, at noble routs,
    And diplomatic dinners, or at other—
For Juan stood well both with Ins and Outs,
    As in freemasonry a higher brother.
Upon his talent Henry had no doubts;
    His manner showed him sprung from a high mother;
And all men like to show their hospitality
To him whose breeding matches with his quality.

At Blank-Blank Square;—for we will break no squares
    By naming streets: since men are so censorious,
And apt to sow an author's wheat with tares,
    Reaping allusions private and inglorious,
Where none were dreamt of, unto love's affairs,
    Which were, or are, or are to be notorious,
That therefore do I previously declare,
Lord Henry's mansion was in Blank-Blank Square.

Also there bin another pious reason
    For making squares and streets anonymous;
Which is, that there is scarce a single season
    Which doth not shake some very splendid house
With some slight heart-quake of domestic treason—
    A topic scandal doth delight to rouse:
Such I might stumble over unawares,
Unless I knew the very chastest squares.

'Tis true, I might have chosen Piccadilly,
    A place where peccadillos are unknown;
But I have motives, whether wise or silly,

For letting that pure sanctuary alone.
Therefore I name not square, street, place, until I
   Find one where nothing naughty can be shown,
A vestal shrine of innocence of heart:
Such are—but I have lost the London Chart.

At Henry's mansion then, in Blank-Blank Square,
   Was Juan a *recherché*, welcome guest,
As many other noble scions were;
   And some who had but talent for their crest;
Or wealth, which is a passport everywhere;
   Or even mere fashion, which indeed's the best
Recommendation; and to be well drest
Will very often supersede the rest.

And since 'there's safety in a multitude
   Of counsellors,' as Solomon has said,
Or some one for him, in some sage, grave mood;—
   Indeed we see the daily proof displayed
In senates, at the bar, in wordy feud,
   Where'er collective wisdom can parade,
Which is the only cause that we can guess
Of Britain's present wealth and happiness;—

But as 'there's safety' grafted in the number
   'Of counsellors' for men,—thus for the sex
A large acquaintance lets not Virtue slumber;
   Or should it shake, the choice will more perplex—
Variety itself will more encumber.
   'Midst many rocks we guard more against wrecks;
And thus with women: howsoe'er it shocks some's
Self-love, there's safety in a crowd of coxcombs.

But Adeline had not the least occasion
   For such a shield, which leaves but little merit
To virtue proper, or good education.
   Her chief resource was in her own high spirit,
Which judged mankind at their due estimation;
   And for coquetry, she disdained to wear it:
Secure of admiration, its impression
Was faint as of an every-day possession.

To all she was polite without parade;
   To some she showed attention of that kind
Which flatters, but is flattery conveyed
   In such a sort as cannot leave behind
A trace unworthy either wife or maid;—

A gentle, genial courtesy of mind,
To those who were, or passed for meritorious,
Just to console sad glory for being glorious;

Which is in all respects, save now and then,
  A dull and desolate appendage. Gaze
Upon the shades of those distinguished men
  Who were or are the puppet-shows of praise,
The praise of persecution. Gaze again
  On the most favoured; and amidst the blaze
Of sunset halos o'er the laurel-browed,
What can ye recognize?—a gilded cloud.

There also was of course in Adeline
  That calm patrician polish in the address,
Which ne'er can pass the equinoctial line
  Of anything which nature would express;
Just as a mandarin finds nothing fine,—
  At least his manner suffers not to guess,
That anything he views can greatly please.
Perhaps we have borrowed this from the Chinese—

Perhaps from Horace: his *'Nil admirari'*
  Was what he call'd the 'Art of Happiness'—
An art on which the artists greatly vary,
  And have not yet attained to much success.
However, 'tis expedient to be wary:
  Indifference certes don't produce distress;
And rash enthusiasm in good society
Were nothing but a moral inebriety.

But Adeline was not indifferent: for
  (*Now* for a common-place!) beneath the snow,
As a volcano holds the lava more
  Within—*et cætera*. Shall I go on?—No
I hate to hunt down a tired metaphor,
  So let the often-used volcano go.
Poor thing! How frequently, by me and others,
It hath been stirred up till its smoke quite smothers!

I'll have another figure in a trice:—
  What say you to a bottle of champagne?
Frozen into a very vinous ice,
  Which leaves few drops of that immortal rain,
Yet in the very centre, past all price,

About a liquid glassful will remain;
And this is stronger than the strongest grape
Could e'er express in its expanded shape:

'Tis the whole spirit brought to a quintessence;
   And thus the chilliest aspects may concentre
A hidden nectar under a cold presence.
   And such are many—though I only meant her
From whom I now deduce these moral lessons,
   On which the Muse has always sought to enter.
And your cold people are beyond all price,
When once you've broken their confounded ice.

But after all they are a North-West Passage
   Unto the glowing India of the soul;
And as the good ships sent upon that message
   Have not exactly ascertained the Pole
(Though Parry's efforts look a lucky presage),
   Thus gentlemen may run upon a shoal;
For if the Pole's not open, but all frost
(A chance still), 'tis a voyage or vessel lost.

And young beginners may as well commence
   With quiet cruising o'er the ocean Woman;
While those who are not beginners should have sense
   Enough to make for port, ere Time shall summon
With his grey signal-flag; and the past tense,
   The dreary *'Fuimus'* of all things human,
Must be declined, while life's thin thread's spun out
Between the gaping heir and gnawing gout.

But heaven must be diverted; its diversion
   Is sometimes truculent—but never mind;
The world upon the whole is worth the assertion
   (If but for comfort) that all things are kind:
And that same devilish doctrine of the Persian,
   Of the 'Two Principles,' but leaves behind
As many doubts as any other doctrine
Has ever puzzled Faith withal, or yoked her in.

The English winter—ending in July,
   To recommence in August—now was done.
'Tis the postilion's paradise: wheels fly;
   On roads, east, south, north, west, there is a run.
But for post-horses who finds sympathy?
   Man's pity for himself, or for his son,

Always premising that said son at college
Has not contracted much more debt than knowledge.

The London winter's ended in July—
    Sometimes a little later. I don't err
In this: whatever other blunders lie
    Upon my shoulders, here I must aver
My Muse a glass of weatherology;
    For parliament is our barometer:
Let radicals its other acts attack,
Its sessions form our only almanack.

When its quicksilver's down at zero,—lo!
    Coach, chariot, luggage, baggage, equipage!
Wheels whirl from Carlton palace to Soho,
    And happiest they who horses can engage;
The turnpikes glow with dust; and Rotten Row
    Sleeps from the chivalry of this bright age;
And tradesmen, with long bills and longer faces,
Sigh—as the postboys fasten on the traces.

They and their bills, 'Arcadians both,' are left
    To the Greek kalends of another session.
Alas! to them of ready cash bereft,
    What hope remains? Of *hope* the full possession
Or generous draft, conceded as a gift,
    At a long date—till they can get a fresh one—
Hawked about at a discount, small or large;
Also the solace of an overcharge.

But these are trifles. Downward flies my lord,
    Nodding beside my lady in his carriage.
Away! away! 'Fresh horses!' are the word,
    And changed as quickly as hearts after marriage;
The obsequious landlord hath the change restored;
    The postboys have no reason to disparage
Their fee; but ere the watered wheels may hiss hence,
The ostler pleads too for a reminiscence.

'Tis granted; and the valet mounts the dickey—
    That gentleman of lords and gentlemen;
Also my lady's gentlewoman, tricky,
    Tricked out, but modest more than poet's pen
Can paint,—'*Cosi viaggino i Ricchi!*'
    (Excuse a foreign slipslop now and then,
If but to show I've travelled: and what's travel,
Unless it teaches one to quote and cavil?)

The London winter and the country summer
    Were well nigh over. 'Tis perhaps a pity,
When nature wears the gown that doth become her.
    To lose those best months in a sweaty city,
And wait until the nightingale grows dumber,
    Listening debates not very wise or witty,
Ere patriots their true *country* can remember;—
But there's no shooting (save grouse) till September.

I've done with my tirade. The world was gone;
    The twice two thousand, for whom earth was made,
Were vanished to be what they call alone—
    That is, with thirty servants for parade,
As many guests, or more; before whom groan
    As many covers, duly, daily laid.
Let none accuse old England's hospitality—
Its quantity is but condensed to quality.

Lord Henry and the Lady Adeline
    Departed like the rest of their compeers,
The peerage, to a mansion very fine;
    The Gothic Babel of a thousand years.
None than themselves could boast a longer line,
    Where time through heroes and through beauties
       steers;
And oaks as olden as their pedigree
Told of their sires, a tomb in every tree.

A paragraph in every paper told
    Of their departure: such is modern fame:
'Tis pity that it takes no further hold
    Than an advertisement, or much the same;
When, ere the ink be dry, the sound grows cold.
    The Morning Post was foremost to proclaim—
'Departure, for his country seat, to-day,
Lord H. Amundeville and Lady A.

'We understand the splendid host intends
    To entertain, this autumn, a select
And numerous party of his noble friends;
    'Midst whom we have heard, from sources quite
       correct,
The Duke of D—— the shooting season spends,
    With many more by rank and fashion decked;
Also a foreigner of high condition,
The envoy of the secret Russian mission.'

And thus we see—who doubts the Morning Post?
    (Whose articles are like the 'Thirty-nine,'
Which those most swear to who believe them most)—
    Our gay Russ Spaniard was ordained to shine,
Decked by the rays reflected from his host,
    With those who, Pope says, 'greatly daring dine.'—
'Tis odd, but true,—last war the News abounded
More with these dinners than the killed or wounded;—

As thus: 'On Thursday there was a grand dinner;
    Present, Lords A.B.C.'—Earls, dukes, by name
Announced with no less pomp than victory's winner:
    Then underneath, and in the very same
Column: date, 'Falmouth. There has lately been here
    The Slap-dash regiment, so well known to fame,
Whose loss in the late action we regret:
The vacancies are filled up—see Gazette.'

To Norman Abbey whirled the noble pair,—
    An old, old monastery once, and now
Still older mansion,—of a rich and rare
    Mixed Gothic, such as artists all allow
Few specimens yet left us can compare
    Withal: it lies perhaps a little low,
Because the monks preferred a hill behind,
To shelter their devotion from the wind.

It stood embosomed in a happy valley,
    Crowned by high woodlands, where the Druid oak
Stood, like Caractacus, in act to rally
    His host, with broad arms 'gainst the thunderstroke,
And from beneath his boughs were seen to sally
    The dappled foresters; as day awoke,
The branching stag swept down with all his herd,
To quaff a brook which murmured like a bird.

Before the mansion lay a lucid lake,
    Broad as transparent, deep, and freshly fed
By a river, which its softened way did take
    In currents through the calmer water spread
Around: the wildfowl nestled in the brake
    And sedges, brooding in their liquid bed:
The woods sloped downwards to its brink, and stood
With their green faces fixed upon the flood.

Its outlet dashed into a deep cascade,
    Sparkling with foam, until again subsiding,

Its shriller echoes—like an infant made
    Quiet—sank into softer ripples, gliding
Into a rivulet; and thus allayed,
    Pursued its course, now gleaming, and now hiding
Its windings through the woods; now clear, now blue,
According as the skies their shadows threw.

A glorious remnant of the Gothic pile
    (While yet the church was Rome's) stood half apart
In a grand arch, which once screened many an aisle.
    These last had disappeared—a loss to art:
The first yet frowned superbly o'er the soil,
    And kindled feelings in the roughest heart,
Which mourned the power of time's or tempest's march,
In gazing on that venerable arch.

Within a niche, nigh to its pinnacle,
    Twelve saints had once stood sanctified in stone;
But these had fallen, not when the friars fell,
    But in the war which struck Charles from his throne,
When each house was a fortalice—as tell
    The annals of full many a line undone,—
The gallant cavaliers, who fought in vain
For those who knew not to resign or reign.

But in a higher niche, alone, but crowned,
    The Virgin-Mother of the God-born Child,
With her Son in her blessed arms, looked round,
    Spared by some chance when all beside was spoiled;
She made the earth below seem holy ground.
    This may be superstition, weak or wild,
But even the faintest relics of a shrine
Of any worship wake some thoughts divine.

A mighty window, hollow in the centre,
    Shorn of its glass of thousand colourings,
Through which the deepened glories once could enter,
    Streaming from off the sun like seraph's wings,
Now yawns all desolate: now loud, now fainter,
    The gale sweeps through its fretwork, and oft sings
The owl his anthem, where the silenced quire
Lie with their hallelujahs quench'd like fire.

But in the noontide of the moon, and when
    The wind is wingèd from one point of heaven,
There moans a strange unearthly sound, which then

Is musical—a dying accent driven
Through the huge arch, which soars and sinks again.
    Some deem it but the distant echo given
Back to the night wind by the waterfall,
And harmonised by the old choral wall:

Others, that some original shape, or form
    Shaped by decay perchance, hath given the power
(Though less than that of Memnon's statue, warm
    In Egypt's rays, to harp at a fixed hour)
To this grey ruin, with a voice to charm
    Sad, but serene, it sweeps o'er tree or tower;
The cause I know not, nor can solve; but such
The fact:—I've heard it,—once perhaps too much.

Amidst the court a Gothic fountain played,
    Symmetrical, but decked with carvings quaint—
Strange faces, like to men in masquerade,
    And here perhaps a monster, there a saint:
The spring gushed through grim mouths of granite made,
    And sparkled into basins, where it spent
Its little torrent in a thousand bubbles,
Like man's vain glory, and his vainer troubles.

The mansion's self was vast and venerable,
    With more of the monastic than has been
Elsewhere preserved: the cloisters still were stable,
    The cells, too, and refectory, I ween:
An exquisite small chapel had been able,
    Still unimpaired, to decorate the scene;
The rest had been reformed, replaced, or sunk,
And spoke more of the baron than the monk.

Huge halls, long galleries, spacious chambers, joined
    By no quite lawful marriage of the arts,
Might shock a connoisseur; but when combined,
    Formed a whole which, irregular in parts,
Yet left a grand impression on the mind,
    At least of those whose eyes are in their hearts:
We gaze upon a giant for his stature,
Nor judge at first if all be true to nature.

Steel barons, molten the next generation
    To silken rows of gay and gartered earls,
Glanced from the walls in goodly preservation:
    And Lady Marys blooming into girls,

With fair long locks, had also kept their station:
   And countesses mature in robes and pearls:
Also some beauties of Sir Peter Lely,
Whose drapery hints we may admire them freely.

Judges in very formidable ermine
   Were there, with brows that did not much invite
The accused to think their lordships would determine
   His cause by leaning much from might to right;
Bishops, who had not left a single sermon;
   Attorneys-general, awful to the sight,
As hinting more (unless our judgments warp us)
Of the 'Star Chamber' than of 'Habeas Corpus.'

Generals, some all in armour, of the old
   And iron time, ere lead had ta'en the lead;
Others in wigs of Marlborough's martial fold,
   Huger than twelve of our degenerate breed:
Lordlings, with staves of white or keys of gold:
   Nimrods, whose canvas scarce contained the steed;
And here and there some stern high patriot stood,
Who could not get the place for which he sued.

But ever and anon, to soothe your vision,
   Fatigued with these hereditary glories,
There rose a Carlo Dolce or a Titian,
   Or wilder group of savage Salvatore's:
Here danced Albano's boys, and here the sea shone
   In Vernet's ocean lights; and there the stories
Of martyrs awed, as Spagnoletto tainted
His brush with all the blood of all the sainted.

Here sweetly spread a landscape of Lorraine;
   There Rembrandt made his darkness equal light,
Or gloomy Caravaggio's gloomier stain
   Bronzed o'er some lean and stoic anchorite:—
But, lo! a Teniers woos, and not in vain,
   Your eyes to revel in a livelier sight:
His bell-mouthed goblet makes me feel quite Danish
Or Dutch with thirst—What, ho! a flask of Rhenish.

O reader! if that thou canst read,—and know,
   'Tis not enough to spell, or even to read,
To constitute a reader; there must go
   Virtues of which both you and I have need.
Firstly, begin with the beginning—(though

That clause is hard); and secondly, proceed;
Thirdly, commence not with the end—or, sinning
In this sort, end at last with the beginning.

But reader, thou hast patient been of late,
   While I, without remorse of rhyme, or fear,
Have built and laid out ground at such a rate,
   Dan Phœbus takes me for an auctioneer.
That poets were so from their earliest date,
   By Homer's 'Catalogue of ships' is clear;
But a mere modern must be moderate—
I spare you then the furniture and plate.

The mellow autumn came, and with it came
   The promised party, to enjoy its sweets.
The corn is cut, the manor full of game;
   The pointer ranges, and the sportsman beats
In russet jacket:—lynx-like is his aim;
   Full grows his bag, and wonder*ful* his feats.
Ah, nutbrown partridges! Ah, brilliant pheasants!
And ah, ye poachers!—'Tis no sport for peasants.

An English autumn, though it hath no vines,
   Blushing with Bacchant coronals along
The paths, o'er which the far festoon entwines
   The red grape in the sunny lands of song,
Hath yet a purchased choice of choicest wines;
   The claret light, and the Madeira strong.
If Britain mourn her bleakness, we can tell her,
The very best of vineyards is the cellar.

Then, if she hath not that serene decline
   Which makes the southern autumn's day appear
As if 'twould to a second spring resign
   The season, rather than to winter drear,—
Of in-door comforts still she hath a mine,—
   The sea-coal fires, the 'earliest of the year';
Without doors, too, she may compete in mellow,
As what is lost in green is gained in yellow.

And for the effeminate *villiggiatura*—
   Rife with more horns than hounds—she hath the
      chase,
So animated that it might allure a
   Saint from his beads to join the jocund race;
Even Nimrod's self might leave the plains of Dura,

And wear the Melton jacket for a space:
If she hath no wild boars, she hath a tame
Preserve of bores, who ought to be made game.

The noble guests, assembled at the Abbey,
   Consisted of—we give the sex the *pas*—
The Duchess of Fitz-Fulke; the Countess Crabby;
   The Ladies Scilly, Busey;—Miss Eclat,
Miss Bombazeen, Miss Mackstay, Miss O'Tabby,
   And Mrs. Rabbi, the rich banker's squaw;
Also the honourable Mrs. Sleep,
Who look'd a white lamb, yet was a black sheep;

With other Countesses of Blank—but rank;
   At once the 'lie' and the *élite* of crowds;
Who passed like water filtered in a tank,
   All purged and pious from their native clouds;
Or paper turned to money by the Bank:
   No matter how or why, the passport shrouds
The *passée* and past; for good society
Is no less famed for tolerance than piety,—

That is, up to a certain point; which point
   Forms the most difficult in punctuation.
Appearances appear to form the joint
   On which it hinges in a higher station;
And so that no explosion cry 'Aroint
   Thee, witch!' or each Medea has her Jason;
Or (to the point with Horace and with Pulci)
'Omne tulit punctum, quæ miscuit utile dulci.'

I can't exactly trace their rule of right,
   Which hath a little leaning to a lottery.
I've seen a virtuous woman put down quite
   By the mere combination of a coterie;
Also a so-so matron boldly fight
   Her way back to the world by dint of plottery,
And shine the very *Siria* of the spheres,
Escaping with a few slight, scarless sneers.

I have seen more than I'll say:—but we will see
   How our *villeggiatura* will get on.
The party might consist of thirty-three
   Of highest caste—the Brahmins of the *ton*.
I have named a few, not foremost in degree,
   But ta'en at hazard as the rhyme may run.

By way of sprinkling, scattered amongst these
There also were some Irish absentees.

There was Parolles, too, the legal bully,
  Who limits all his battles to the bar
And senate: when invited elsewhere, truly,
  He shows more appetite for words than war.
There was the young bard Rackrhyme, who had newly
  Come out and glimmer'd as a six weeks' star.
There was Lord Pyrrho, too, the great freethinker;
And Sir John Pottledeep, the mighty drinker.

There was the Duke of Dash, who was a—duke,
  'Ay, every inch a' duke; there were twelve peers
Like Charlemagne's—and all such peers in *look*
  And *intellect,* that neither eyes nor ears
For commoners had ever them mistook.
  There were the six Miss Rawbolds—pretty dears!
All song and sentiment; whose hearts were set
Less on a convent than a coronet.

There were four Honourable Misters, whose
  Honour was more before their names than after;
There was the *preux Chevalier de la Ruse,*
  Whom France and Fortune lately deigned to waft
    here,
Whose chiefly harmless talent was to amuse;
  But the clubs found it rather serious laughter,
Because—such was his magic power to please—
The dice seem'd charmed, too, with his repartees.

There was Dick Dubious, the metaphysician,
  Who loved philosophy and a good dinner;
Angle, the *soi-disant* mathematician;
  Sir Henry Silvercup, the great race-winner.
There was the Reverend Rodomont Precisian,
  Who did not hate so much the sin as sinner;
And Lord Augustus Fitz-Plantagenet,
Good at all things, but better at a bet.

There was Jack Jargon, the gigantic guardsman;
  And General Fireface, famous in the field,
A great tactician, and no less a swordsman,
  Who ate, last war, more Yankees than he kill'd.
There was the waggish Welsh Judge, Jefferies Hards-
    man,

In his grave office so completely skilled,
That when a culprit came for condemnation,
He had his judge's joke for consolation.

Good company's a chess-board—there are kings,
    Queens, bishops, knights, rooks, pawns; the world's a
        game;
Save that the puppets pull at their own strings,
    Methinks gay Punch hath something of the same.
My Muse, the butterfly hath but her wings,
    Not stings, and flits through ether without aim,
Alighting rarely:—were she but a hornet,
Perhaps there might be vices which would mourn it.

I had forgotten—but must not forget—
    An orator, the latest of the session,
Who had deliver'd well a very set
    Smooth speech, his first and maidenly transgression
Upon debate: the papers echoed yet
    With his *début*, which made a strong impression,
And rank'd with what is every day displayed—
'The best first speech that ever yet was made.'

Proud of his 'Hear hims!' proud, too, of his vote
    And lost virginity of oratory,
Proud of his learning (just enough to quote),
    He revelled in his Ciceronian glory:
With memory excellent to get by rote,
    With wit to hatch a pun or tell a story,
Graced with some merit, and with more effrontery,
'His country's pride,' he came down to the country.

There also were two wits by acclamation,
    Longbow from Ireland, Strongbow from the Tweed,
Both lawyers and both men of education;
    But Strongbow's wit was of more polished breed;
Longbow was rich in an imagination
    As beautiful and bounding as a steed,
But sometimes stumbling over a potato,—
While Strongbow's best things might have come from
    Cato.

Strongbow was like a new-tuned harpsichord;
    But Longbow wild as an Æolian harp,
With which the winds of heaven can claim accord,
    And make a music, whether flat or sharp.

Of Strongbow's talk you would not change a word:
   At Longbow's phrases you might sometimes carp:
Both wits—one born so, and the other bred,
This by his heart—his rival by his head.

If all these seem an heterogeneous mass
   To be assembled at a country seat,
Yet think, a specimen of every class
   Is better than a humdrum tête-à-tête.
The days of Comedy are gone, alas!
   When Congreve's fool could vie with Molière's *bête:*
Society is smoothed to that excess,
That manners hardly differ more than dress.

Our ridicules are kept in the back ground—
   Ridiculous enough, but also dull;
Professions, too, are no more to be found
   Professional; and there is naught to cull
Of folly's fruit: for though your fools abound,
   They're barren, and not worth the pains to pull.
Society is now one polished horde,
Formed of two mighty tribes, the *Bores* and *Bored.*

But from being farmers, we turn gleaners, gleaning
   The scanty but right-well threshed ears of truth;
And, gentle reader! when you gather meaning,
   You may be Boaz, and I—modest Ruth.
Further I'd quote, but Scripture intervening
   Forbids. A great impression in my youth
Was made by Mrs. Adams, where she cries
'That Scriptures out of church are blasphemies.'

But what we can we glean in this vile age
   Of chaff, although our gleanings be not grist.
I must not quite omit the talking sage,
   Kit-Cat, the famous Conversationist,
Who, in his common-place book, had a page
   Prepared each morn for evenings. 'List, oh list!'
'Alas, poor ghost!'—What unexpected woes
Await those who have studied their *bons-mots!*

Firstly, they must allure the conversation
   By many windings to their clever clinch;
And secondly, must let slip no occasion,
   Nor *bate* (abate) their hearers of an *inch,*
But take an ell—and make a great sensation,

If possible; and thirdly, never flinch
When some smart talker puts them to the test,
But seize the last word, which no doubt's the best.

Lord Henry and his lady were the hosts;
   The party we have touched on were the guests.
Their table was a board to tempt even ghosts
   To pass the Styx for more substantial feasts.
I will not dwell upon *ragoûts* or roasts,
   Albeit all human history attests
That happiness for man—the hungry sinner!—
Since Eve ate apples, much depends on dinner.

Witness the lands which 'flowed with milk and honey,'
   Held out unto the hungry Israelites:
To this we have added since, the love of money,
   The only sort of pleasure which requites.
Youth fades, and leaves our days no longer sunny;
   We tire of mistresses and parasites;
But oh, ambrosial cash! Ah! who would lose thee?
When we no more can use, or even abuse thee!

The gentlemen got up betimes to shoot,
   Or hunt: the young, because they liked the sport—
The first thing boys like after play and fruit;
   The middle-aged, to make the day more short;
For *ennui* is a growth of English root,
   Though nameless in our language:—we retort
The fact for words, and let the French translate
That awful yawn which sleep cannot abate.

The elderly walked through the library,
   And tumbled books, or criticised the pictures,
Or sauntered through the gardens piteously,
   And made upon the hot-house several strictures,
Or rode a nag which trotted not too high,
   Or on the morning papers read their lectures,
Or on the watch their longing eyes would fix,
Longing at sixty for the hour of six.

But none were *gêné*: the great hour of union
   Was rung by dinner's knell; till then all were
Masters of their own time—or in communion,
   Or solitary, as they chose to bear
The hours, which how to pass is but to few known.
   Each rose up at his own, and had to spare

What time he chose for dress, and broke his fast
When, where, and how he chose for that repast.

The ladies—some rouged, some a little pale—
    Met the morn as they might. If fine, they rode,
Or walked; if foul, they read, or told a tale,
    Sung, or rehearsed the last dance from abroad;
Discussed the fashion which might next prevail,
    And settled bonnets by the newest code,
Or crammed twelve sheets into one little letter,
To make each correspondent a new debtor.

For some had absent lovers, all had friends.
    The earth has nothing like a she epistle,
And hardly heaven—because it never ends.
    I love the mystery of a female missal,
Which, like a creed, ne'er says all it intends,
    But full of cunning as Ulysses' whistle,
When he allured poor Dolon:—you had better
Take care what you reply to such a letter.

Then there were billiards; cards, too, but *no* dice;—
    Save in the clubs no man of honour plays;—
Boats when 'twas water, skating when 'twas ice,
    And the hard frost destroyed the scenting days:
And angling, too, that solitary vice,
    Whatever Izaak Walton sings or says:
The quaint, old, cruel coxcomb, in his gullet
Should have a hook, and a small trout to pull it.

With evening came the banquet and the wine;
    The conversazione; the duet,
Attuned by voices more or less divine
    (My heart or head aches with the memory yet).
The four Miss Rawbolds in a glee would shine;
    But the two youngest loved more to be set
Down to the harp—because to music's charms
They added graceful necks, white hands and arms.

Sometimes a dance (though rarely on field days,
    For then the gentlemen were rather tired)
Displayed some sylph-like figures in its maze;
    Then there was small-talk ready when required;
Flirtation—but decorous; the mere praise
    Of charms that should or should not be admired.

The hunters fought their fox-hunt o'er again,
And then retreated soberly—at ten.

The politicians, in a nook apart,
     Discussed the world, and settled all the spheres;
The wits watched every loophole for their art,
     To introduce a *bon-mot* head and ears;
Small is the rest of those who would be smart,
     A moment's good thing may have cost them years
Before they find an hour to introduce it;
And then, even *then*, some bore may make them lose it.

But all was gentle and aristocratic
     In this our party; polished, smooth, and cold,
As Phidian forms cut out of marble Attic,
     There now are no Squire Westerns as of old;
And our Sophias are not so emphatic,
     But fair as then, or fairer to behold.
We have no accomplished blackguards, like Tom Jones,
But gentlemen in stays, as stiff as stones.

They separated at an early hour;
     That is, ere midnight—which is London's noon:
But in the country ladies seek their bower
     A little earlier than the waning moon.
Peace to the slumbers of each folded flower—
     May the rose call back its true colour soon!
Good hours of fair cheeks are the fairest tinters,
And lower the price of rouge—at least some winters.

ON THIS DAY I COMPLETE MY THIRTY-SIXTH YEAR

     'Tis time this heart should be unmoved,
          Since others it hath ceased to move:
     Yet, though I cannot be beloved,
          Still let me love!

     My days are in the yellow leaf;
          The flowers and fruits of love are gone;
     The worm, the canker, and the grief
          Are mine alone!

     The fire that on my bosom preys
          Is lone as some volcanic isle;

No torch is kindled at its blaze—
    A funeral pile.

The hope, the fear, the jealous care,
    The exalted portion of the pain
And power of love, I cannot share,
    But wear the chain.

But 'tis not *thus*—and 'tis not *here*—
    Such thoughts should shake my soul, nor *now*,
Where glory decks the hero's bier,
    Or binds his brow.

The sword, the banner, and the field,
    Glory and Greece, around me see!
The Spartan, borne upon his shield,
    Was not more free.

Awake! (not Greece—she *is* awake!)
    Awake, my spirit! Think through *whom*
Thy life-blood tracks its parent lake,
    And then strike home!

Tread those reviving passions down,
    Unworthy manhood!—unto thee
Indifferent should the smile or frown
    Of beauty be.

If thou regret'st thy youth, *why live?*
    The land of the honourable death
Is here:—up to the field, and give
    Away thy breath!

Seek out—less often sought than found—
    A soldier's grave, for thee the best;
Then look around, and choose thy ground,
    And take thy rest.

PERCY BYSSHE SHELLEY

(1792-1822)

ONE WORD IS TOO OFTEN PROFANED

One word is too often profaned
    For me to profane it,
One feeling too falsely disdained
    For thee to disdain it;
One hope is too like despair
    For prudence to smother,
And pity from thee more dear
    Than that from another.

I can give not what men call love,
    But wilt thou accept not
The worship the heart lifts above
    And the heavens reject not,—
The desire of the moth for the star,
    Of the night for the morrow,
The devotion to something afar
    From the sphere of our sorrow?

MUSIC, WHEN SOFT VOICES DIE

Music, when soft voices die,
Vibrates in the memory—
Odours, when sweet violets sicken,
Live within the sense they quicken.

Rose leaves, when the rose is dead,
Are heap'd for the belovèd's bed;
And so thy thoughts, when thou art gone,
Love itself shall slumber on.

SONG

A widow bird sate mourning for her love
  Upon a wintry bough;
The frozen wind crept on above,
  The freezing stream below.

There was no leaf upon the forest bare,
  No flower upon the ground,
And little motion in the air
  Except the mill-wheel's sound.

from CHARLES THE FIRST

LIFE OF LIFE

Life of life! thy lips enkindle
  With their love the breath between them;
And thy smiles before they dwindle
  Make the cold air fire; then screen them
In those looks, where whoso gazes
Faints, entangled in their mazes.

Child of Light! thy limbs are burning
  Through the vest which seems to hide them;
As the radiant lines of morning
  Through the clouds ere they divide them;
And this atmosphere divinest
Shrouds thee wheresoe'er thou shinest.

Fair are others; none beholds thee,
  But thy voice sounds low and tender
Like the fairest, for it folds thee
  From the sight, that liquid splendour,
And all feel, yet see thee never,
As I feel now, lost for ever!

Lamp of Earth! where'er thou movest
  Its dim shapes are clad with brightness,
And the souls of whom thou lovest
  Walk upon the winds with lightness,
Till they fail, as I am failing,
Dizzy, lost, yet unbewailing!

from PROMETHEUS UNBOUND

HYMN OF PAN

From the forests and highlands
  We come, we come;
From the river-girt islands,
  Where loud waves are dumb
    Listening to my sweet pipings.
The wind in the reeds and the rushes,
  The bees on the bells of thyme,
The birds on the myrtle bushes,
  The cicale above in the lime,
And the lizards below in the grass,
Were as silent as ever old Temolus was,
    Listening to my sweet pipings.

Liquid Peneus was flowing,
  And all dark Tempe lay
In Pelion's shadow, outgrowing
  The light of the dying day,
    Speeded by my sweet pipings.
The Sileni, and Sylvans, and Fauns,
  And the Nymphs of the woods and the waves,
To the edge of the moist river-lawns,
  And the brink of the dewy caves,
And all that did then attend and follow,
Were silent with love, as you now, Apollo,
    With envy of my sweet pipings.

I sang of the dancing stars,
  I sang of the daedal Earth,
And of Heaven—and the giant wars,
  And Love, and Death, and Birth,—
    And then I changed my pipings,—
Singing how down the vale of Maenalus
  I pursued a maiden and clasped a reed.
Gods and men, we are all deluded thus!
  It breaks in our bosom and then we bleed:
All wept, as I think both ye now would,
If envy or age had not frozen your blood,
    At the sorrow of my sweet pipings.

THE WORLD'S GREAT AGE

The world's great age begins anew,
  The golden years return,
The earth doth like a snake renew
  Her winter weeds outworn;

Heaven smiles, and faiths and empires gleam,
Like wrecks of a dissolving dream.

A brighter Hellas rears its mountains
    From waves serener far;
A new Peneus rolls his fountains
    Against the morning-star.
Where fairer Tempes bloom, there sleep
Young Cyclads on a sunnier deep.

A loftier Argo cleaves the main,
    Fraught with a later prize;
Another Orpheus sings again,
    And loves, and weeps, and dies.
A new Ulysses leaves once more
Calypso for his native shore.

Oh, write no more the tale of Troy,
    If earth Death's scroll must be!
Nor mix with Laian rage the joy
    Which dawns upon the free;
Although a subtler Sphinx renew
Riddles of death Thebes never knew.

Another Athens shall arise,
    And to remoter time
Bequeath, like sunset to the skies,
    The splendour of its prime;
And leave, if nought so bright may live,
All earth can take or Heaven can give.

Saturn and Love their long repose
    Shall burst, more bright and good
Than all who fell, than One who rose,
    Then many unsubdued;
Not gold, not blood, their altar dowers,
But votive tears and symbol flowers.

Oh, cease! must hate and death return?
    Cease! must men kill and die?
Cease! drain not to its dregs the urn
    Of bitter prophecy.
The world is weary of the past,
Oh, might it die or rest at last!

from HELLAS

TO NIGHT

Swiftly walk o'er the western wave,
        Spirit of Night!
Out of the misty eastern cave,
Where all the long and lone daylight,
Thou wovest dreams of joy and fear,
Which make thee terrible and dear,—
        Swift be thy flight!

Wrap thy form in a mantle grey,
        Star-inwrought!
Blind with thine hair the eyes of Day;
Kiss her until she be wearied out,
Then wander o'er city, and sea, and land,
Touching all with thine opiate wand—
        Come, long-sought!

When I arose and saw the dawn,
        I sighed for thee;
When light rode high, and the dew was gone,
And noon lay heavy on flower and tree,
And the weary Day turned to his rest,
Lingering like an unloved guest,
        I sighed for thee.

Thy brother Death came, and cried,
        Wouldst thou me?
Thy sweet child Sleep, the filmy-eyed,
Murmured like a noon-tide bee,
Shall I nestle near thy side?
Wouldst thou me?—And I replied,
        No, not thee!

Death will come when thou art dead,
        Soon, too soon—
Sleep will come when thou art fled;
Of neither would I ask the boon
I ask of thee, belovèd Night—
Swift be thine approaching flight,
        Come soon, soon!

LINES: WHEN THE LAMP IS SHATTERED

  When the lamp is shattered,
The light in the dust lies dead;
  When the cloud is scattered,
The rainbow's glory is shed;

When the lute is broken,
Sweet tones are remembered not;
    When the lips have spoken,
Love accents are soon forgot.

    As music and splendour
Survive not the lamp and the lute,
    The heart's echoes render
No song when the spirit is mute:—
    No song but sad dirges,
Like the wind through a ruined cell,
    Or the mournful surges
That ring the dead seaman's knell.

    When hearts have once mingled,
Love first leaves the well-built nest;
    The weak one is singled
To endure what it once possessed.
    O, Love! who bewailest
The frailty of all things here,
    Why choose you the frailest
For your cradle, your home, and your bier?

    Its passions will rock thee,
As the storms rock the ravens on high;
    Bright reason will mock thee,
Like the sun from a wintry sky.
    From thy nest every rafter
Will rot, and thine eagle home
    Leave thee naked to laughter,
When leaves fall and cold winds come.

OZYMANDIAS

I met a traveller from an antique land
Who said: 'Two vast and trunkless legs of stone
Stand in the desert. Near them, on the sand,
Half sunk, a shattered visage lies, whose frown,
And wrinkled lip, and sneer of cold command,
Tell that its sculptor well those passions read
Which yet survive, stamped on these lifeless things,
The hand that mocked them and the heart that fed.
And on the pedestal these words appear—
"My name is Ozymandias, king of kings:
Look on my works, ye Mighty, and despair!"

Nothing beside remains. Round the decay
Of that colossal wreck, boundless and bare
The lone and level sands stretch far away.'

LOVE'S PHILOSOPHY

The fountains mingle with the river
    And the rivers with the Ocean,
The winds of Heaven mix for ever
    With a sweet emotion;
Nothing in the world is single;
    All things by a law divine
In one spirit meet and mingle.
    Why not I with thine?—

See the mountains kiss high Heaven
    And the waves clasp one another;
No sister-flower would be forgiven
    If it disdained its brother;
And the sunlight clasps the earth
    And the moonbeams kiss the sea:
What is all this sweet work worth
    If thou kiss not me?

HYMN TO INTELLECTUAL BEAUTY

The awful shadow of some unseen Power
    Floats though unseen among us,—visiting
    This various world with as inconstant wing
As summer winds that creep from flower to flower,—
Like moonbeams that behind some piny mountain shower,
    It visits with inconstant glance
    Each human heart and countenance;
Like hues and harmonies of evening,—
    Like clouds in starlight widely spread,—
    Like memory of music fled,—
    Like aught that for its grace may be
Dear, and yet dearer for its mystery.

Spirit of B E A U T Y, that dost consecrate
    With thine own hues all thou dost shine upon
    Of human thought or form,—where art thou gone?
Why dost thou pass away and leave our state,
This dim vast vale of tears, vacant and desolate?

Ask why the sunlight not for ever
Weaves rainbows o'er yon mountain-river,
Why aught should fail and fade that once is shown,
Why fear and dream and death and birth
Cast on the daylight of this earth
Such gloom,—why man has such a scope
For love and hate, despondency and hope?

No voice from some sublimer world hath ever
To sage or poet these responses given—
Therefore the names of Demon, Ghost, and Heaven,
Remain the records of their vain endeavour,
Frail spells—whose uttered charm might not avail to sever,
From all we hear and all we see,
Doubt, chance, and mutability.
Thy light alone—like mist o'er mountains driven,
Or music by the night-wind sent
Through strings of some still instrument,
Or moonlight on a midnight stream,
Gives grace and truth to life's unquiet dream.

Love, Hope, and Self-esteem, like clouds depart
And come, for some uncertain moments lent.
Man were immortal, and omnipotent,
Didst thou, unknown and awful as thou art,
Keep with thy glorious train firm state within his heart.
Thou messenger of sympathies,
That wax and wane in lovers' eyes—
Thou—that to human thought art nourishment,
Like darkness to a dying flame!
Depart not as thy shadow came,
Depart not—lest the grave should be,
Like life and fear, a dark reality.

While yet a boy I sought for ghosts, and sped
Through many a listening chamber, cave and ruin,
And starlight wood, with fearful steps pursuing
Hopes of high talk with the departed dead.
I called on poisonous names with which our youth is fed:
I was not heard—I saw them not—
When musing deeply on the lot
Of life, at that sweet time when winds are wooing
All vital things that wake to bring
News of birds and blossoming,—
Sudden, thy shadow fell on me;
I shrieked, and clasped my hands in ecstasy!

I vowed that I would dedicate my powers

To thee and thine—have I not kept the vow?
With beating heart and streaming eyes, even now
I call the phantoms of a thousand hours
Each from his voiceless grave: they have in visioned bowers
    Of studious zeal or love's delight
    Outwatched with me the envious night—
They know that never joy illumed my brow
    Unlinked with hope that thou wouldst free
    This world from its dark slavery,
    That Thou—O awful L O V E L I N E S S,
Wouldst give whate'er these words cannot express.

The day becomes more solemn and serene
  When noon is past—there is a harmony
  In autumn, and a lustre in its sky,
Which through the summer is not heard or seen,
As if it could not be, as if it had not been!
    Thus let thy power, which like the truth
    Of nature on my passive youth
Descended, to my onward life supply
    Its calm—to one who worships thee,
    And every form containing thee,
    Whom, S P I R I T fair, thy spells did bind
To fear himself, and love all human kind.

ODE TO THE WEST WIND

O wild West Wind, thou breath of Autumn's being,
Thou, from whose unseen presence the leaves dead
Are driven, like ghosts from an enchanter fleeing,
Yellow, and black, and pale, and hectic red,
Pestilence-stricken multitudes: O thou,
Who chariotest to their dark wintry bed
The wingèd seeds, where they lie cold and low,
Each like a corpse within its grave, until
Thine azure sister of the Spring shall blow
Her clarion o'er the dreaming earth, and fill
(Driving sweet buds like flocks to feed in air)
With living hues and odours plain and hill:
Wild Spirit, which art moving everywhere;
Destroyer and preserver; hear, oh, hear!

Thou on whose stream, mid the steep sky's commotion,
Loose clouds like earth's decaying leaves are shed,
Shook from the tangled boughs of Heaven and Ocean,
Angels of rain and lightning: there are spread
On the blue surface of thine aëry surge,

Like the bright hair uplifted from the head
Of some fierce Maenad, even from the dim verge
Of the horizon to the zenith's height,
The locks of the approaching storm. Thou dirge
Of the dying year, to which this closing night
Will be the dome of a vast sepulchre,
Vaulted with all thy congregated might
Of vapours, from whose solid atmosphere
Black rain, and fire, and hail, will burst: oh hear!

Thou who didst waken from his summer dreams
The blue Mediterranean, where he lay,
Lulled by the coil of his crystàlline streams,
Beside a pumice isle in Baiæ's bay,
And saw in sleep old palaces and towers
Quivering within the wave's intenser day,
All overgrown with azure moss and flowers
So sweet, the sense faints picturing them! Thou
For whose path the Atlantic's level powers
Cleave themselves into chasms, while far below
The sea-blooms and the oozy woods which wear
The sapless foliage of the ocean, know
Thy voice, and suddenly grow grey with fear,
And tremble and despoil themselves: oh hear!

If I were a dead leaf thou mightest bear;
If I were a swift cloud to fly with thee;
A wave to pant beneath thy power, and share
The impulse of thy strength, only less free
Than thou, O uncontrollable! if even
I were as in my boyhood, and could be
The comrade of thy wanderings over heaven,
As then, when to outstrip thy skiey speed
Scarce seem'd a vision—I would ne'er have striven
As thus with thee in prayer in my sore need.
Oh, lift me as a wave, a leaf, a cloud!
I fall upon the thorns of life! I bleed!
A heavy weight of hours has chained and bowed
One too like thee: tameless, and swift, and proud.

Make me thy lyre, even as the forest is;
What if my leaves are falling like its own!
The tumult of thy mighty harmonies
Will take from both a deep, autumnal tone,
Sweet though in sadness. Be thou, spirit fierce,
My spirit! Be thou me, impetuous one!
Drive my dead thoughts over the universe

Like withered leaves to quicken a new birth!
And, by the incantation of this verse,
Scatter, as from an unextinguished hearth
Ashes and sparks, my words among mankind!
Be through my lips to unawakened earth
The trumpet of a prophecy! O Wind,
If Winter comes, can Spring be far behind?

THE CLOUD

I bring fresh showers for the thirsting flowers,
    From the seas and the streams;
I bear light shade for the leaves when laid
    In their noonday dreams.
From my wings are shaken the dews that waken
    The sweet buds every one,
When rocked to rest on their mother's breast,
    As she dances about the sun.
I wield the flail of the lashing hail,
    And whiten the green plains under,
And then again I dissolve it in rain,
    And laugh as I pass in thunder.

I sift the snow on the mountains below,
    And their great pines groan aghast;
And all the night 'tis my pillow white,
    While I sleep in the arms of the blast.
Sublime on the towers of my skiey bowers,
    Lightning my pilots sits;
In a cavern under is fettered the thunder,
    Its struggles and howls at fits;
Over earth and ocean, with gentle motion,
    This pilot is guiding me,
Lured by the love of the genii that move
    In the depths of the purple sea;
Over the rills, and the crags, and the hills,
    Over the lakes and the plains,
Wherever he dream, under mountain or stream,
    The Spirit he loves remains;
And I all the while bask in Heaven's blue smile,
    Whilst he is dissolving in rains.

The sanguine Sunrise, with his meteor eyes,
    And his burning plumes outspread,
Leaps on the back of my sailing rack,
    When the morning star shines dead;
As on the jag of a mountain crag,

Which an earthquake rocks and swings,
An eagle alit one moment may sit
   In the light of its golden wings.
And when Sunset may breathe, from the lit sea beneath,
   Its ardours of rest and of love,
And the crimson pall of eve may fall
   From the depth of Heaven above,
With wings folded I rest, on mine aëry nest,
   As still as a brooding dove.

That orbèd maiden with white fire laden,
   Whom mortals call the Moon,
Glides glimmering o'er my fleece-like floor,
   By the midnight breezes strewn;
And wherever the beat of her unseen feet,
   Which only the angels hear,
May have broken the woof of my tent's thin roof,
   The stars peep behind her and peer;
And I laugh to see them whirl and flee,
   Like a swarm of golden bees,
When I widen the rent in my wind-built tent,
   Till the calm rivers, lakes, and seas,
Like strips of the sky fallen through me on high,
   Are each paved with the moon and these.

I bind the Sun's throne with a burning zone,
   And the Moon's with a girdle of pearl;
The volcanoes are dim, and the stars reel and swim,
   When the whirlwinds my banner unfurl.
From cape to cape, with a bridge-like shape,
   Over a torrent sea,
Sunbeam-proof, I hang like a roof,—
   The mountains its columns be.
The triumphal arch through which I march
   With hurricane, fire, and snow,
When the Powers of the air are chained to my chair,
   Is the million-coloured bow;
The sphere-fire above its soft colours wove,
   While the moist Earth was laughing below.

I am the daughter of Earth and Water,
   And the nursling of the Sky;
I pass through the pores of the ocean and shores:
   I change, but I cannot die.
For after the rain when with never a stain
   The pavilion of Heaven is bare,
And the winds and sunbeams with their convex gleams
   Build up the blue dome of air,

I silently laugh at my own cenotaph,
  And out of the caverns of rain,
Like a child from the womb, like a ghost from the tomb,
  I arise and unbuild it again.

THE INDIAN SERENADE

I arise from dreams thee
In the first sweet sleep of
  night,
When the winds are
  breathing low,
And the stars are shining
  bright;
I arise from dreams of thee,
And a spirit in my feet
Hath led me—who knows
  how?
To thy chamber window,
  Sweet!

The wandering airs they faint
On the dark, the silent
  stream—
And the Champak's odours
  fail

Like sweet thoughts in a
  dream;
The nightingale's complaint,
It dies upon her heart,
As I must on thine,
Oh, belovèd as thou art!

Oh, lift me from the grass!
I die! I faint! I fail!
Let thy love in kisses rain
On my lips and eyelids pale.
My cheek is cold and white,
  alas!
My heart beats loud and
  fast,
Oh, press it to thine own
  again,
Where it will break at last.

TO A SKYLARK

Hail to thee, blithe spirit!
  Bird thou never wert,
That from heaven, or near it,
  Pourest thy full heart
In profuse strains of unpremeditated art.

Higher still and higher
  From the earth thou springest
Like a cloud of fire;
  The blue deep thou wingest,
And singing still dost soar, and soaring ever singest.

In the golden lightning
  Of the sunken sun,
O'er which clouds are bright'ning,
  Thou dost float and run;
Like an unbodied joy whose race is just begun.

The pale purple even
  Melts around thy flight;
Like a star of heaven,

In the broad daylight
Thou art unseen, but yet I hear thy shrill delight,

Keen as are the arrows
Of that silver sphere
Whose intense lamp narrows
In the white dawn clear
Until we hardly see—we feel that it is there.

All the earth and air
With thy voice is loud,
As, when night is bare,
From one lonely cloud
The moon rains out her beams, and Heaven is overflowed.

What thou art we know not;
What is most like thee?
From rainbow clouds there flow not
Drops so bright to see
As from thy presence showers a rain of melody.

Like a Poet hidden
In the light of thought,
Singing hymns unbidden,
Till the world is wrought
To sympathy with hopes and fears it heeded not:

Like a high-born maiden
In a palace-tower,
Soothing her love-laden
Soul in secret hour
With music sweet as love, which overflows her bower:

Like a glow-worm golden
In a dell of dew,
Scattering unbeholden
Its aërial hue
Among the flowers and grass, which screen it from the view!

Like a rose embowered
In its own green leaves,
By warm winds deflowered,
Till the scent it gives
Makes faint with too much sweet these heavy-wingèd thieves:

Sound of vernal showers
On the twinkling grass,
Rain-awakened flowers,

All that ever was
Joyous, and clear, and fresh, thy music doth surpass.

Teach us, Sprite or Bird,
What sweet thoughts are thine:
I have never heard
Praise of love or wine
That panted forth a flood of rapture so divine.

Chorus Hymeneal,
Or triumphal chant,
Matched with thine, would be all
But an empty vaunt,
A thing wherein we feel there is some hidden want.

What objects are the fountains
Of thy happy strain?
What fields, or waves, or mountains?
What shapes of sky or plain?
What love of thine own kind? what ignorance of pain?

With thy clear keen joyance
Languor cannot be:
Shadow of annoyance
Never came near thee:
Thou lovest—but ne'er knew love's sad satiety.

Waking or asleep,
Thou of death must deem
Things more true and deep
Than we mortals dream,
Or how could thy notes flow in such a crystal stream?

We look before and after,
And pine for what is not:
Our sincerest laughter
With some pain is fraught;
Our sweetest songs are those that tell of saddest thought.

Yet if we could scorn
Hate, and pride, and fear;
If we were things born
Not to shed a tear,
I know not how thy joy we ever should come near.

Better than all measures
Of delightful sound,

Better than all treasures
That in books are found,
Thy skill to poet were, thou scorner of the ground!

Teach me half the gladness
That thy brain must know,
Such harmonious madness
From my lips would flow
The world should listen then, as I am listening now.

ADONAIS

AN ELEGY ON THE DEATH OF JOHN KEATS

I weep for Adonais—he is dead!
Oh, weep for Adonais! though our tears
Thaw not the frost which binds so dear a head!
And thou, sad Hour, selected from all years
To mourn our loss, rouse thy obscure compeers,
And teach them thine own sorrow, say: 'With me
Died Adonais; till the Future dares
Forget the Past, his fate and fame shall be
An echo and a light unto eternity!'

Where wert thou, mighty Mother, when he lay,
When thy Son lay, pierced by the shaft which flies
In darkness? where was lorn Urania
When Adonais died? With veilèd eyes,
'Mid listening Echoes, in her Paradise
She sate, while one, with soft enamored breath,
Rekindled all the fading melodies,
With which, like flowers that mock the corse beneath,
He had adorned and hid the coming bulk of Death.

Oh, weep for Adonais—he is dead!
Wake, melancholy Mother, wake and weep!
Yet wherefore? Quench within their burning bed
Thy fiery tears, and let thy loud heart keep
Like his, a mute and uncomplaining sleep;
For he is gone, where all things wise and fair
Descend;—oh, dream not that the amorous Deep
Will yet restore him to the vital air;
Death feeds on his mute voice, and laughs at our despair.

Most musical of mourners, weep again!
Lament anew, Urania!—He died,

Who was the Sire of an immortal strain,
Blind, old, and lonely, when his country's pride,
The priest, the slave, and the liberticide,
Trampled and mocked with many a loathèd rite
Of lust and blood; he went, unterrified,
Into the gulf of death; but his clear Sprite
Yet reigns o'er earth; the third among the sons of light.

Most musical of mourners, weep anew!
Not all to that bright station dared to climb;
And happier they their happiness who knew,
Whose tapers yet burn through that night of time
In which suns perished; others more sublime,
Struck by the envious wrath of man or God,
Have sunk, extinct in their refulgent prime;
And some yet live, treading the thorny road,
Which leads, through toil and hate, to Fame's serene abode.

But now, thy youngest, dearest one, has perished—
The nursling of thy widowhood, who grew,
Like a pale flower by some sad maiden cherished,
And fed with true-love tears, instead of dew;
Most musical of mourners, weep anew!
Thy extreme hope, the lovliest and last,
The bloom, whose petals, nipped before they blew,
Died on the promise of the fruit, is waste;
The broken lily lies—the storm is overpast.

To that high Capital, where kingly Death
Keeps his pale court in beauty and decay,
He came; and bought, with price of purest breath,
A grave among the eternal.—Come away!
Haste, while the vault of blue Italian day
Is yet his fitting charnel-roof! while still
He lies, as if in dewy sleep he lay;
Awake him not! surely he takes his fill
Of deep and liquid rest, forgetful of all ill.

He will awake no more, oh, never more!—
Within the twilight chamber spreads apace,
The shadow of white Death, and at the door
Invisible Corruption waits to trace
His extreme way to her dim dwelling-place;
The eternal Hunger sits, but pity and awe
Soothe her pale rage, nor dares she to deface
So fair a prey, till darkness, and the law
Of change, shall o'er his sleep the mortal curtain draw.

Oh, weep for Adonais!—The quick Dreams,
The passion-wingèd Ministers of thought,
Who were his flocks, whom near the living streams
Of his young spirit he fed, and whom he taught
The love which was its music, wander not,—
Wander no more, from kindling brain to brain,
But droop there, whence they sprung; and mourn their lot
Round the cold heart, where, after their sweet pain,
They ne'er will gather strength, or find a home again.

And one with trembling hands clasps his cold head,
And fans him with her moonlight wings, and cries;
'Our love, our hope, our sorrow, is not dead;
See, on the silken fringe of his faint eyes,
Like dew upon a sleeping flower, there lies
A tear some Dream has loosened from his brain.'
Lost Angel of a ruined Paradise!
She knew not 'twas her own; as with no stain
She faded, like a cloud which had outwept its rain.

One from a lucid urn of starry dew
Washed his light limbs as if embalming them;
Another clipped her profuse locks, and threw
The wreath upon him, like an anadem,
Which frozen tears instead of pearls begem;
Another in her wilful grief would break
Her bow and wingèd reeds, as if to stem
A greater loss with one which was more weak;
And dull the barbèd fire against his frozen cheek.

Another Splendour on his mouth alit,
That mouth, whence it was wont to draw the breath
Which gave it strength to pierce the guarded wit,
And pass into the panting heart beneath
With lightning and with music: the damp death
Quenched its caress upon his icy lips;
And, as a dying meteor stains a wreath
Of moonlight vapour, which the cold night clips,
It flushed through his pale limbs, and passed to its eclipse.

And others came . . . Desires and Adorations,
Wingèd Persuasions and veiled Destinies,
Splendours, and Glooms, and glimmering Incarnations
Of hopes and fears, and twilight Phantasies;
And Sorrow, with her family of Sighs,
And Pleasure, blind with tears, led by the gleam
Of her own dying smile instead of eyes,

Came in slow pomp;—the moving pomp might seem
Like pageantry of mist on an autumnal stream.

All he had loved, and moulded into thought,
From shape, and hue, and odour, and sweet sound,
Lamented Adonais. Morning sought
Her eastern watch-tower, and her hair unbound,
Wet with the tears which should adorn the ground,
Dimmed the aërial eyes that kindle day;
Afar the melancholy thunder moaned,
Pale Ocean in unquiet slumber lay,
And the wild Winds flew round, sobbing in their dismay.

Lost Echo sits amid the voiceless mountains,
And feeds her grief with his remembered lay,
And will no more reply to winds or fountains,
Or amorous birds perched on the young green spray,
Or herdsman's horn, or bell at closing day;
Since she can mimic not his lips, more dear
Than those for whose disdain she pined away
Into a shadow of all sounds:—a drear
Murmur, between their songs, is all the woodmen hear.

Grief made the young Spring wild, and she drew down
Her kindling buds, as if she Autumn were,
Or they dead leaves; since her delight is flown,
For whom should she have waked the sullen year?
To Phoebus was not Hyacinth so dear
Nor to himself Narcissus, as to both
Thou, Adonais: wan they stand and sere
Amid the faint companions of their youth,
With dew all turned to tears; odour, to sighing ruth.

Thy spirit's sister, the lorn nightingale
Mourns not her mate with such melodious pain;
Not so the eagle, who like thee could scale
Heaven, and could nourish in the sun's domain
Her mighty youth with morning, doth complain,
Soaring and screaming round her empty nest,
As Albion wails for thee: the curse of Cain
Light on his head who pierced thy innocent breast,
And scared the angel soul that was its earthly guest!

Ah, woe is me! Winter is come and gone,
But grief returns with the revolving year;
The airs and streams renew their joyous tone;
The ants, the bees, the swallows reappear;

Fresh leaves and flowers deck the dead Seasons' bier;
The amorous birds now pair in every brake,
And build their mossy homes in field and brere;
And the green lizard, and the golden snake,
Like unimprisoned flames, out of their trance awake.

Through wood and stream and field and hill and Ocean
A quickening life from the Earth's heart has burst
As it has ever done, with change and motion,
From the great morning of the world when first
God dawned on Chaos; in its stream immersed,
The lamps of Heaven flash with a softer light;
All baser things pant with life's sacred thirst;
Diffuse themselves; and spend in love's delight,
The beauty and the joy of their renewèd might.

The leprous corpse, touched by this spirit tender,
Exhales itself in flowers of gentle breath;
Like incarnations of the stars, when splendour
Is changed to fragrance, they illumine death
And mock the merry worm that wakes beneath;
Nought we know, dies. Shall that alone which knows
Be as a sword consumed before the sheath
By sightless lightning?—the intense atom glows
A moment, then is quenched in a most cold repose.

Alas! that all we loved of him should be,
But for our grief, as if it had not been,
And grief itself be mortal! Woe is me!
Whence are we, and why are we? of what scene
The actors or spectators? Great and mean
Meet massed in death, who lends what life must borrow.
As long as skies are blue, and fields are green,
Evening must usher night, night urge the morrow,
Month follow month with woe, and year wake year to sorrow.

He will awake no more, oh, never more!
'Wake thou,' cried Misery, 'childless Mother, rise
Out of thy sleep, and slake, in thy heart's core,
A wound more fierce than his with tears and sighs.'
And all the Dreams that watched Urania's eyes,
And all the Echoes whom their sister's song
Had held in holy silence, cried: 'Arise!'
Swift as a Thought by the snake Memory stung,
From her ambrosial rest the fading Splendour sprung.

She rose like an autumnal Night, that springs

Out of the East, and follows wild and drear
The golden Day, which, on eternal wings,
Even as a ghost abandoning a bier,
Had left the Earth a corpse. Sorrow and fear
So struck, so roused, so rapt Urania;
So saddened round her like an atmosphere
Of stormy mist; so swept her on her way
Even to the mournful place where Adonais lay.

Out of her secret Paradise she sped,
  Through camps and cities rough with stone, and steel,
  And human hearts, which to her aery tread
Yielding not, wounded the invisible
Palms of her tender feet where'er they fell:
And barbèd tongues, and thoughts more sharp than they,
  Rent the soft Form they never could repel,
  Whose sacred blood, like the young tears of May,
Paved with eternal flowers that undeserving way.

In the death-chamber for a moment Death,
Shamed by the presence of that living Might,
Blushed to annihilation, and the breath
Revisited those lips, and Life's pale light
Flashed through those limbs, so late her dear delight.
'Leave me not wild and drear and comfortless,
As silent lightning leaves the starless night!
Leave me not!' cried Urania: her distress
Roused Death: Death rose and smiled, and met her vain
      caress.

'Stay yet awhile! Speak to me once again;
Kiss me, so long but as a kiss may live;
And in my heartless breast and burning brain
That word, that kiss, shall all thoughts else survive,
With food of saddest memory kept alive,
Now thou art dead, as if it were a part
Of thee, my Adonais! I would give
All that I am to be as thou now art!
But I am chained to Time, and cannot thence depart!

'O gentle child, beautiful as thou wert,
Why didst thou leave the trodden paths of men
Too soon, and with weak hands though mighty heart
Dare the unpastured dragon in his den?
Defenceless as thou wert, oh, where was then
Wisdom the mirrored shield, or scorn the spear?
Or hadst thou waited the full cycle, when

Thy spirit should have filled its crescent sphere,
The monsters of life's waste had fled from thee like deer.

'The herded wolves, bold only to pursue;
The obscene ravens, clamorous o'er the dead;
The vultures to the conqueror's banner true
Who feed where Desolation first has fed,
And whose wings rain contagion;—how they fled,
When, like Apollo, from his golden bow
The Pythian of the age one arrow sped
And smiled!—The spoilers tempt no second blow,
They fawn on the proud feet that spurn them lying low.

'The sun comes forth, and many reptiles spawn;
He sets, and each ephemeral insect then
Is gathered into death without a dawn,
And the immortal stars awake again;
So is it in the world of living men:
A godlike mind soars forth, in its delight
Making earth bare and veiling heaven, and when
It sinks, the swarms that dimmed or shared its light
Leave to its kindred lamps the spirit's awful night.'

Thus ceased she: and the mountain shepherds came,
Their garlands sere, their magic mantles rent;
The Pilgrim of Eternity, whose fame
Over his living head like Heaven is bent,
An early but enduring monument,
Came, veiling all the lightnings of his song
In sorrow; from her wilds Ierne sent
The sweetest lyrist of her saddest wrong,
And Love taught Grief to fall like music from his tongue.

Midst others of less note, came one frail Form,
A phantom among men; companionless
As the last cloud of an expiring storm
Whose thunder is its knell; he, as I guess,
Had gazed on Nature's naked loveliness,
Actaeon-like, and now he fled astray
With feeble steps o'er the world's wilderness,
And his own thoughts, along that rugged way,
Pursued, like raging hounds, their father and their prey.

A pardlike Spirit beautiful and swift—
A Love in desolation masked;—a Power
Girt round with weakness;—it can scarce uplift
The weight of the superincumbent hour;

It is a dying lamp, a falling shower,
  A breaking billow;—even whilst we speak
Is it not broken? On the withering flower
  The killing sun smiles brightly: on a cheek
The life can burn in blood, even while the heart may break.

  His head was bound with pansies overblown,
  And faded violets, white, and pied, and blue;
  And a light spear topped with a cypress cone,
  Round whose rude shaft dark ivy-tresses grew
  Yet dripping with the forest's noonday dew,
  Vibrated, as the ever-beating heart
  Shook the weak hand that grasped it; of that crew
  He came the last, neglected and apart;
A herd-abandoned deer struck by the hunter's dart.

  All stood aloof, and at his partial moan
  Smiled through their tears; well knew that gentle band
  Who in another's fate now wept his own,
  As in the accents of an unknown land
  He sung new sorrow; sad Urania scanned
  The Stranger's mien, and murmured: 'Who art thou?'
  He answered not, but with a sudden hand
  Made bare his branded and ensanguined brow,
Which was like Cain's or Christ's—oh! that it should be so!

  What softer voice is hushed over the dead?
  Athwart what brow is that dark mantle thrown?
  What form leans sadly o'er the white death-bed,
  In mockery of monumental stone,
  The heavy heart heaving without a moan?
  If it be He, who, gentlest of the wise,
  Taught, soothed, loved, honoured the departed one,
  Let me not vex, with inharmonious sighs,
The silence of that heart's accepted sacrifice.

  Our Adonais has drunk poison—oh!
  What deaf and viperous murderer could crown
  Life's early cup with such a draught of woe?
  The nameless worm would now itself disown:
  It felt, yet could escape, the magic tone
  Whose prelude held all envy, hate, and wrong,
  But what was howling in one breast alone,
  Silence with expectation of the song,
Whose master's hand is cold, whose silver lyre unstrung.

  Live thou, whose infamy is not thy fame!

Live! fear no heavier chastisement from me,
Thou noteless blot on a remembered name!
But be thyself, and know thyself to be!
And ever at thy season be thou free
To spill the venom when thy fangs o'erflow;
Remorse and Self-contempt shall cling to thee;
Hot Shame shall burn upon thy secret brow,
And like a beaten hound tremble thou shalt—as now.

Nor let us weep that our delight is fled
Far from these carrion kites that scream below;
He wakes or sleeps with the enduring dead;
Thou canst not soar where he is sitting now.—
Dust to the dust! but the pure spirit shall flow
Back to the burning fountain whence it came,
A portion of the Eternal, which must glow
Through time and change, unquenchably the same,
Whilst thy cold embers choke the sordid hearth of shame.

Peace, peace he is not dead, he doth not sleep,—
He hath awakened from the dream of life—
'Tis we, who lost in stormy visions, keep
With phantoms an unprofitable strife,
And in mad trance, strike with our spirit's knife
Invulnerable nothings.—*We* decay
Like corpses in a charnel; fear and grief
Convulse us and consume us day by day,
And cold hopes swarm like worms within our living clay.

He has outsoared the shadow of our night;
Envy and calumny and hate and pain,
And that unrest which men miscall delight,
Can touch him not and torture not again;
From the contagion of the world's slow stain
He is secure, and now can never mourn
A heart grown cold, a head grown grey in vain;
Nor, when the spirit's self has ceased to burn,
With sparkless ashes load an unlamented urn.

He lives, he wakes—'tis Death is dead, not he;
Mourn not for Adonais.—Thou young Dawn,
Turn all thy dew to splendour, for from thee
The spirit thou lamentest is not gone;
Ye caverns and ye forests, cease to moan!
Cease, ye faint flowers and fountains, and thou Air,
Which like a mourning veil thy scarf hadst thrown
O'er the abandoned Earth, now leave it bare
Even to the joyous stars which smile on its despair!

He is made one with Nature: there is heard
His voice in all her music, from the moan
Of thunder, to the song of night's sweet bird;
He is a presence to be felt and known
In darkness and in light, from herb and stone,
Spreading itself where'er that Power may move
Which has withdrawn his being to its own;
Which wields the world with never-wearied love,
Sustains it from beneath, and kindles it above.

He is a portion of the loveliness
Which once he made more lovely: he doth bear
His part, while the one Spirit's plastic stress
Sweeps through the dull dense world, compelling there,
All new successions to the forms they wear;
Torturing th' unwilling dross that checks its flight
To its own likeness, as each mass may bear;
And bursting in its beauty and its might
From trees and beasts and men into the Heaven's light.

The splendours of the firmament of time
May be eclipsed, but are extinguished not;
Like stars to their appointed height they climb,
And death is a low mist which cannot blot
The brightness it may veil. When lofty thought
Lifts a young heart above its mortal lair,
And love and life contend in it, for what
Shall be its earthly doom, the dead live there
And move like winds of light on dark and stormy air.

The inheritors of unfulfilled renown
Rose from their thrones, built beyond mortal thought,
Far in the Unapparent. Chatterton
Rose pale,—his solemn agony had not
Yet faded from him; Sidney, as he fought
And as he fell and as he lived and loved
Sublimely mild, a Spirit without spot,
Arose; and Lucan, by his death approved:
Oblivion as they rose shrank like a thing reproved.

And many more, whose names on Earth are dark,
But whose transmitted effluence cannot die
So long as fire outlives the parent spark,
Rose, robed in dazzling immortality.
'Thou art become as one of us,' they cry,

'It was for thee yon kingless sphere has long
Swung blind in unascended majesty,
Silent alone amid an Heaven of song.
Assume thy wingèd throne, thou Vesper of our throng!'

Who mourns for Adonais? Oh, come forth,
Fond wretch! and know thyself and him aright.
Clasp with thy panting soul the pendulous Earth;
As from a centre, dart thy spirit's light
Beyond all worlds, until its spacious might
Satiate the void circumference: then shrink
Even to a point within our day and night;
And keep thy heart light lest it make thee sink
When hope has kindled hope, and lured thee to the brink.

Or go to Rome, which is the sepulchre,
Oh, not of him, but of our joy: 'tis nought
That ages, empires, and religions there
Lie buried in the ravage they have wrought;
For such as he can lend,—they borrow not
Glory from those who made the world their prey;
And he is gathered to the kings of thought
Who waged contention with their time's decay,
And of the past are all that cannot pass away.

Go thou to Rome,—at once the Paradise,
The grave, the city, and the wilderness;
And where its wrecks like shattered mountains rise,
And flowering weeds, and fragrant copses dress
The bones of Desolation's nakedness
Pass, till the spirit of the spot shall lead
Thy footsteps to a slope of green access
Where, like an infant's smile, over the dead
A light of laughing flowers along the grass is spread;

And grey walls moulder round, on which dull Time
Feeds, like slow fire upon a hoary brand;
And one keen pyramid with wedge sublime,
Pavilioning the dust of him who planned
This refuge for his memory, doth stand
Like flame transformed to marble; and beneath,
A field is spread, on which a newer band
Have pitched in Heaven's smile their camp of death,
Welcoming him we lose with scarce extinguished breath.

Here pause: these graves are all too young as yet
To have outgrown the sorrow which consigned

Its charge to each; and if the seal is set,
Here, on one fountain of a mourning mind,
Break it not thou! too surely shalt thou find
Thine own well full, if thou returnest home,
Of tears and gall. From the world's bitter wind
Seek shelter in the shadow of the tomb.
What Adonais is, why fear we to become?

The One remains, the many change and pass;
Heaven's light forever shines, Earth's shadows fly;
Life, like a dome of many-coloured glass,
Stains the white radiance of Eternity,
Until Death tramples it to fragments.—Die,
If thou wouldst be with that which thou dost seek!
Follow where all is fled!—Rome's azure sky,
Flowers, ruins, statues, music, words, are weak
The glory they transfuse with fitting truth to speak.

Why linger, why turn back, why shrink, my Heart?
Thy hopes are gone before: from all things here
They have departed; thou shouldst now depart!
A light is past from the revolving year,
And man, and woman; and what still is dear
Attracts to crush, repels to make thee wither.
The soft sky smiles,—the low wind whispers near:
'Tis Adonais calls! oh, hasten thither,
No more let Life divide what Death can join together.

That Light whose smile kindles the Universe,
That Beauty in which all things work and move,
That Benediction which the eclipsing Curse
Of birth can quench not, that sustaining Love
Which through the web of being blindly wove
By man and beast and earth and air and sea,
Burns bright or dim, as each are mirrors of
The fire for which all thirst; now beams on me,
Consuming the last clouds of cold mortality.

The breath whose might I have invoked in song
Descends on me; my spirit's bark is driven,
Far from the shore, far from the trembling throng
Whose sails were never to the tempest given;
The massy earth and spherèd skies are riven!
I am borne darkly, fearfully, afar;
Whilst, burning through the inmost veil of Heaven,
The soul of Adonais, like a star,
Beacons from the abode where the Eternal are.

JOHN KEATS

(1795-1821)

LA BELLE DAME SANS MERCI

O what can ail thee, Knight-at-arms,
  Alone and palely loitering?
The sedge has withered from the lake,
  And no birds sing.

O what can ail thee, Knight-at-arms,
  So haggard and so woe-begone?
The squirrel's granary is full,
  And the harvest's done.

I see a lily on thy brow
  With anguish moist and fever dew,
And on thy cheeks a fading rose
  Fast withereth too.

I met a lady in the meads,
  Full beautiful—a faery's child,
Her hair was long, her foot was light,
  And her eyes were wild.

I made a garland for her head,
  And bracelets too, and fragrant zone;
She looked at me as she did love,
  And made sweet moan.

I set her on my pacing steed,
  And nothing else saw all day long;
For sidelong would she bend, and sing
  A faery's song.

She found me roots of relish sweet,
  And honey wild, and manna dew;
And sure in language strange she said,
  'I love thee true!'

She took me to her elfin grot,
   And there she wept and sighed full sore,
And there I shut her wild wild eyes
   With kisses four.

And there she lullèd me asleep,
   And there I dreamed—ah, woe betide!
The latest dream I ever dreamed
   On the cold hill-side.

I saw pale kings, and princes too,
   Pale warriors, death-pale were they all;
They cried—'La Belle Dame sans Merci
   Hath thee in thrall!'

I saw their starved lips in the gloam,
   With horrid warning gapèd wide,
And I awoke and found me here,
   On the cold hill-side.

And this is why I sojourn here,
   Alone and palely loitering,
Though the sedge is withered from the lake,
   And no birds sing.

TO SLEEP

O soft embalmer of the still midnight,
   Shutting, with careful fingers and benign,
Our gloom-pleased eyes, embowered from the light,
   Enshaded in forgetfulness divine:
O soothest Sleep! if so it please thee, close,
   In midst of this thine hymn, my willing eyes,
Or wait the amen, ere thy poppy throws
   Around my bed its lulling charities.
Then save me, or the passed day will shine
Upon my pillow, breeding many woes,—
   Save me from curious conscience, that still lords
Its strength for darkness, burrowing like a mole;
   Turn the key deftly in the oilèd wards,
And seal the hushèd casket of my soul.

ON THE GRASSHOPPER AND THE CRICKET

The poetry of earth is never dead:
   When all the birds are faint with the hot sun,
   And hide in cooling trees, a voice will run
From hedge to hedge about the new-mown mead;
That is the Grasshopper's—he takes the lead
   In summer luxury,—he has never done
   With his delights; for when tired out with fun
He rests at ease beneath some pleasant weed.
The poetry of earth is ceasing never:
   On a long winter evening, when the frost
     Has wrought a silence, from the stove there shrills
The Cricket's song, in warmth increasing ever,
   And seems to one in drowsiness half lost,
     The Grasshopper's among some grassy hills.

TO ONE WHO HAS BEEN LONG IN CITY PENT

To one who has been long in city pent,
   'Tis very sweet to look into the fair
   And open face of heaven,—to breathe a prayer
Full in the smile of the blue firmament.
Who is more happy, when, with heart's content,
   Fatigued he sinks into some pleasant lair
   Of wavy grass, and reads a debonair
And gentle tale of love and languishment?
Returning home at evening, with an ear
   Catching the notes of Philomel,—an eye
Watching the sailing cloudlet's bright career,
   He mourns that day so soon as glided by:
E'en like the passage of an angel's tear
   That falls through the clear ether silently.

ON SEEING THE ELGIN MARBLES

My spirit is too weak—mortality
   Weighs heavily on me like unwilling sleep,
   And each imagined pinnacle and steep
Of godlike hardship, tells me I must die
Like a sick Eagle looking at the sky.
   Yet 'tis a gentle luxury to weep
   That I have not the cloudy winds to keep,
Fresh for the opening of the morning's eye.

Such dim-conceivèd glories of the brain
 Bring round the heart an undescribable feud;
So do these wonders a most dizzy pain,
 That mingles Grecian grandeur with the rude
Wasting of old Time—with a billowy main—
 A sun—a shadow of a magnitude.

ON FIRST LOOKING INTO CHAPMAN'S HOMER

Much have I travelled in the realms of gold,
 And many goodly states and kingdoms seen;
 Round many western islands have I been
Which bards in fealty to Apollo hold.
Oft of one wide expanse had I been told
 That deep-browed Homer ruled as his demesne:
 Yet did I never breathe its pure serene
Till I heard Chapman speak out loud and bold:
Then felt I like some watcher of the skies
 When a new planet swims into his ken;
Or like stout Cortez when with eagle eyes
 He stared at the Pacific—and all his men
Looked at each other with a wild surmise—
 Silent, upon a peak in Darien.

KEEN, FITFUL GUSTS ARE WHISP'RING

Keen, fitful gusts are whisp'ring here and there
 Among the bushes half leafless, and dry;
 The stars look very cold about the sky,
And I have many miles on foot to fare.
Yet feel I little of the cool bleak air,
 Or of the dead leaves rustling drearily,
 Or of those silver lamps that burn on high,
Or of the distance from home's pleasant lair:
For I am brimful of the friendliness
 That in a little cottage I have found;
Of fair-haired Milton's eloquent distress,
 And all his love for gentle Lycid drowned;
Of lovely Laura in her light green dress,
 And faithful Petrarch gloriously crowned.

ON THE SEA

It keeps eternal whisperings around
   Desolate shores, and with its mighty swell
   Gluts twice ten thousand caverns, till the spell
Of Hecate leaves them their old shadowy sound.
Often 'tis in such gentle temper found
    That scarcely will the very smallest shell
    Be moved for days from where it sometime fell,
When last the winds of heaven were unbound.
Oh, ye who have your eye-balls vexed and tired,
    Feast them upon the wideness of the Sea;
      Oh, ye whose ears are dinned with uproar rude,
   Or fed too much with cloying melody,
      Sit ye near some old cavern's mouth, and brood
Until ye start, as if the sea-nymphs quired.

WHEN I HAVE FEARS THAT I MAY CEASE TO BE

When I have fears that I may cease to be
   Before my pen has gleaned my teeming brain,
Before high-piled books, in charactery,
   Hold like rich garners the full-ripened grain;
When I behold, upon the night's starred face,
   Huge cloudy symbols of a high romance,
And think that I may never live to trace
   Their shadows, with the magic hand of chance;
And when I feel, fair creature of an hour!
   That I shall never look upon thee more,
Never have relish in the faery power
   Of unreflecting love; then on the shore
Of the wide world I stand alone, and think
Till love and fame to nothingness do sink.

BRIGHT STAR, WOULD I WERE STEADFAST AS THOU ART

Bright star, would I were steadfast as thou art—
   Not in lone splendour hung aloft the night
And watching, with eternal lids apart,
   Like nature's patient, sleepless Eremite,
The moving waters at their priestlike task,
   Of pure ablution round earth's human shores,
Or gazing on the new soft-fallen mask

Of snow upon the mountains and the moors.
No—yet still steadfast, still unchangeable,
　　Pillowed upon my fair love's ripening breast,
To feel for ever its soft fall and swell,
　　Awake for ever in a sweet unrest,
Still, still to hear her tender-taken breath,
And so live ever—or else swoon to death.

ODE ON MELANCHOLY

No, no, go not to Lethe, neither twist
　　Wolf's-bane, tight-rooted, for its poisonous wine;
Nor suffer thy pale forehead to be kissed
　　By nightshade, ruby grape of Proserpine;
Make not your rosary of yew-berries,
　　Nor let the beetle, nor the death-moth be
　　　　Your mournful Psyche, nor the downy owl
A partner in your sorrow's mysteries;
　　For shade to shade will come too drowsily,
　　　　And drown the wakeful anguish of the soul.

But when the melancholy fit shall fall
　　Sudden from heaven like a weeping cloud,
That fosters the droop-headed flowers all,
　　And hides the green hill in an April shroud;
Then glut thy sorrow on a morning rose,
　　Or on the rainbow of the salt sand-wave,
　　　　Or on the wealth of globed peonies;
Of if thy mistress some rich anger shows,
　　Emprison her soft hand, and let her rave,
　　　　And feed deep, deep upon her peerless eyes.

She dwells with Beauty—Beauty that must die;
　　And Joy, whose hand is ever at his lips
Bidding adieu; and aching Pleasure nigh,
　　Turning to poison while the bee-mouth sips:
Ay, in the very temple of Delight
　　Veiled Melancholy has her sovran shrine,
　　　　Though seen of none save him whose strenuous tongue
　　Can burst Joy's grape against his palate fine;
His soul shall taste the sadness of her might,
　　And be among her cloudy trophies hung.

ODE TO A NIGHTINGALE

My heart aches, and a drowsy numbness pains
  My sense, as though of hemlock I had drunk,
Or emptied some dull opiate to the drains
  One minute past, and Lethe-wards had sunk:
'Tis not through envy of thy happy lot,
  But being too happy in thine happiness,—
    That thou, light-winged Dryad of the trees,
      In some melodious plot
Of beechen green, and shadows numberless,
  Singest of summer in full-throated ease.

O, for a draught of vintage! that hath been
  Cool'd a long age in the deep-delved earth,
Tasting of Flora and the country green,
  Dance, and Provençal song, and sunburnt mirth!
O for a beaker full of the warm South,
  Full of the true, the blushful Hippocrene,
    With beaded bubbles winking at the brim,
      And purple-stained mouth;
That I might drink, and leave the world unseen,
  And with thee fade away into the forest dim:

Fade far away, dissolve, and quite forget
  What thou among the leaves hast never known,
The weariness, the fever, and the fret
  Here, where men sit and hear each other groan;
Where palsy shakes a few, sad, last grey hairs,
  Where youth grows pale, and specter-thin, and dies;
    Where but to think is to be full of sorrow
      And leaden-eyed despairs,
  Where Beauty cannot keep her lustrous eyes,
    Or new Love pine at them beyond to-morrow.

Away! away! for I will fly to thee,
  Not charioted by Bacchus and his pards,
But on the viewless wings of Poesy,
  Though the dull brain perplexes and retards:
Already with thee! tender is the night,
  And haply the Queen-Moon is on her throne,
    Cluster'd around by all her starry Fays;
      But here there is no light,
Save what from heaven is with the breezes blown
  Through verdurous glooms and winding mossy ways.

I cannot see what flowers are at my feet,
  Nor what soft incense hangs upon the boughs,
But, in embalmed darkness, guess each sweet
  Wherewith the seasonable month endows
The grass, the thicket, and the fruit-tree wild;
  White hawthorn, and the pastoral eglantine;
    Fast fading violets covered up in leaves;
      And mid-May's eldest child,
The coming musk-rose, full of dewy wine,
  The murmurous haunt of flies on summer eves.

Darkling I listen; and, for many a time
  I have been half in love with easeful Death,
Called him soft names in many a mused rhyme,
  To take into the air my quiet breath;
Now more than ever seems it rich to die,
  To cease upon the midnight with no pain,
    While thou art pouring forth thy soul abroad
      In such an ecstasy!
Still wouldst thou sing, and I have ears in vain—
  To thy high requiem become a sod.

Thou wast not born for death, immortal Bird!
  No hungry generations tread thee down;
The voice I hear this passing night was heard
  In ancient days by emperor and clown:
Perhaps the self-same song that found a path
  Through the sad heart of Ruth, when, sick for home,
    She stood in tears amid the alien corn;
      The same that oft-times hath
Charmed magic casements, opening on the foam
  Of perilous seas, in faery lands forlorn.

Forlorn! the very word is like a bell
  To toll me back from thee to my sole self!
Adieu! the fancy cannot cheat so well
  As she is fam'd to do, deceiving elf.
Adieu! adieu! thy plaintive anthem fades
  Past the near meadows, over the still stream,
    Up the hill-side; and now 'tis buried deep
      In the next valley-glades:
Was it a vision, or a waking dream?
  Fled is that music:—Do I wake or sleep?

ODE ON A GRECIAN URN

Thou still unravished bride of quietness,
    Thou foster-child of silence and slow time,
Sylvan historian, who canst thus express
    A flowery tale more sweetly than our rhyme:
What leaf-fringed legend haunts about thy shape
      Of deities or mortals, or of both,
        In Tempe or the dales of Arcady?
What men or gods are these? What maidens loth?
What mad pursuit? What struggle to escape?
    What pipes and timbrels? What wild ecstasy?

Heard melodies are sweet, but those unheard
    Are sweeter; therefore, ye soft pipes, play on;
Not to the sensual ear, but, more endeared,
    Pipe to the spirit ditties of no tone:
Fair youth, beneath the trees, thou canst not leave
      Thy song, nor ever can those trees be bare;
        Bold Lover, never, never canst thou kiss,
Though winning near the goal—yet, do not grieve;
      She cannot fade, though thou hast not thy bliss,
    For ever wilt thou love, and she be fair!

Ah, happy, happy boughs! that cannot shed
    Your leaves, nor ever bid the Spring adieu;
And, happy melodist, unwearied,
    For ever piping songs for ever new;
More happy love! more happy, happy love!
      For ever warm and still to be enjoyed,
        For ever panting, and for ever young;
All breathing human passion far above,
      That leaves a heart high-sorrowful and cloyed,
    A burning forehead, and a parching tongue.

Who are these coming to the sacrifice?
    To what green altar, O mysterious priest,
Lead'st thou that heifer lowing at the skies,
    And all her silken flanks with garlands drest?
What little town by river or sea shore,
    Or mountain-built with peaceful citadel,
      Is emptied of this folk, this pious morn?
And, little town, thy streets for evermore
    Will silent be; and not a soul to tell
    Why thou art desolate, can e'er return.

O Attic shape! Fair attitude! with brede
    Of marble men and maidens overwrought,
        With forest branches and the trodden weed;
            Thou, silent form, dost tease us out of thought
        As doth eternity: Cold Pastoral!
            When old age shall this generation waste,
                Thou shalt remain, in midst of other woe
            Than ours, a friend to man, to whom thou say'st,
        'Beauty is truth, truth beauty,'—that is all
            Ye know on earth, and all ye need to know.

ODE TO PSYCHE

O Goddess! hear these tuneless numbers, wrung
    By sweet enforcement and remembrance dear,
And pardon that thy secrets should be sung
    Even into thine own soft-conched ear:
Surely I dreamt to-day, or did I see
    The winged Psyche with awakened eyes?
I wander'd in a forest thoughtlessly,
    And, on the suden, fainting with surprise,
Saw two fair creatures, couched side by side
    In deepest grass, beneath the whisp'ring roof
    Of leaves and trembled blossoms, where there ran
        A brooklet, scarce espied:

'Mid hush'd, cool-rooted flowers, fragrant-eyed,
    Blue, silver-white, and budded Tyrian,
They lay calm-breathing, on the bedded grass;
    Their arms embraced, and their pinions too;
    Their lips touch'd not, but had not bade adieu,
As if disjoined by soft-handed slumber,
And ready still past kisses to outnumber
    At tender eye-dawn of aurorean love:
        The winged boy I knew;
    But who wast thou, O happy, happy dove?
        His Psyche true!

O latest born and loveliest vision far
    Of all Olympus' faded hierarchy!
Fairer than Phoebe's sapphire-regioned star,
    Or Vesper, amorous glow-worm of the sky;
Fairer than these, though temple thou hast none,
        Nor altar heaped with flowers;
Nor virgin-choir to make delicious moan

Upon the midnight hours;
No voice, no lute, no pipe, no incense sweet
    From chain-swung censer teeming;
No shrine, no grove, no oracle, no heat
    Of pale-mouth'd prophet dreaming.

O brightest! though too late for antique vows,
    Too, too late for the fond believing lyre,
When holy were the haunted forest boughs,
    Holy the air, the water, and the fire;
Yet even in these days so far retired
    From happy pieties, thy lucent fans,
    Fluttering among the faint Olympians,
I see, and sing, by my own eyes inspired.
So let me be thy choir, and make a moan
            Upon the midnight hours;
Thy voice, thy lute, thy pipe, thy incense sweet
    From swinged censer teeming;
Thy shrine, thy grove, thy oracle, thy heat
    Of pale-mouth'd prophet dreaming.

Yes, I will be thy priest, and build a fane
    In some untrodden region of my mind,
Where branched thoughts, new grown with pleasant pain,
    Instead of pines shall murmur in the wind:
Far, far around shall those dark-clustered trees
    Fledge the wild-ridged mountains steep by steep;
And there by zephyrs, streams, and birds, and bees,
    The moss-lain Dryads shall be lulled to sleep;
And in the midst of this wide quietness
A rosy sanctuary will I dress
With the wreathed trellis of a working brain,
    With buds, and bells, and stars without a name,
With all the gardener Fancy e'er could feign,
    Who breeding flowers, will never breed the same.
And there shall be for thee all soft delight
    That shadowy thought can win,
A bright torch, and a casement ope at night,
    To let the warm Love in!

ODE ON INDOLENCE

They toil not, neither do they spin.

One morn before me were three figures seen,
    With bowed necks, and joined hands, side-faced;
And one behind the other stepp'd serene,
    In placid sandals, and in white robes graced;

They passed, like figures on a marble urn,
    When shifted round to see the other side;
    They came again; as when the urn once more
Is shifted round, the first seen shades return;
    And they were strange to me, as may betide
    With vases, to one deep in Phidian lore.

How is it, Shadows! that I knew ye not?
    How came ye muffled in so hush a mask?
Was it a silent deep-disguisèd plot
    To steal away, and leave without a task
My idle days? Ripe was the drowsy hour;
    The blissful cloud of summer-indolence
    Benumbed my eyes; my pulse grew less and less;
Pain had no sting, and pleasure's wreath no flower:
    O, why did ye not melt, and leave my sense
    Unhaunted quite of all but—nothingness?

A third time passed they by, and, passing, turned
    Each one the face a moment whiles to me;
Then faded, and to follow them I burned
    And ached for wings, because I knew the three;
The first was a fair maid, and Love her name;
    The second was Ambition, pale of cheek,
    And ever watchful with fatiguèd eye;
The last, whom I love more, the more of blame
    Is heaped upon her, maiden most unmeek,—
    I knew to be my demon Poesy.

They faded, and, forsooth! I wanted wings:
    O folly! What is Love? And where is it?
And for that poor Ambition! it springs
    From a man's little heart's short fever-fit;
For Poesy!—no,—she has not a joy,—
    At least for me,—so sweet as drowsy noons,
    And evenings steeped in honied indolence;
O, for an age so sheltered from annoy,
    That I may never know how change the moons,
    Or hear the voice of busy common-sense!

And once more came they by;—alas! wherefore?
    My sleep had been embroidered with dim dreams;
My soul had been a lawn besprinkled o'er
    With flowers, and stirring shades, and baffled beams:
The morn was clouded, but no shower fell,
    Tho' in her lids hung the sweet tears of May;

The open casement pressed a new-leaved vine,
  Let in the budding warmth and throstle's lay;
O shadows! 'twas a time to bid farewell!
  Upon your skirts had fallen no tears of mine.

So, ye three ghosts, adieu! Ye cannot raise
  My head cool-bedded in the flowery grass;
For I would not be dieted with praise,
  A pet-lamb in a sentimental farce!
Fade softly from my eyes, and be once more
  In masque-like figures on the dreamy urn;
    Farewell! I yet have visions for the night,
And for the day faint visions there is store;
  Vanish, ye Phantoms! from my idle spright,
Into the clouds, and nevermore return!

TO AUTUMN

Season of mists and mellow fruitfulness,
  Close bosom-friend of the maturing sun;
Conspiring with him how to load and bless
  With fruit the vines that round the thatch-eaves run;
To bend with apples the mossed cottage-trees,
  And fill all fruit with ripeness to the core;
    To swell the gourd, and plump the hazel shells
With a sweet kernel; to set budding more,
And still more, later flowers for the bees,
Until they think warm days will never cease,
    For Summer has o'er-brimmed their clammy cells.

Who hath not seen thee oft amid thy store?
  Sometimes whoever seeks abroad may find
Thee sitting careless on a granary floor,
  Thy hair soft-lifted by the winnowing wind;
Or on a half-reap'd furrow sound asleep,
  Drows'd with the fume of poppies, while thy hook
    Spares the next swath and all its twined flowers:
And sometimes like a gleaner thou dost keep
  Steady thy laden head across a brook;
    Or by a cider-press, with patient look,
      Thou watchest the last oozings, hours by hours.

Where are the songs of Spring? Ay, where are they?
  Think not of them, thou hast thy music too,—
While barred clouds bloom the soft-dying day,

And touch the stubble-plains with rosy hue;
Then in a wailful choir the small gnats mourn
    Among the river sallows, borne aloft
        Or sinking as the light wind lives or dies;
And full-grown lambs loud bleat from hilly bourn;
    Hedge-crickets sing; and now with treble soft
    The redbreast whistles from a garden-croft;
        And gathering swallows twitter in the skies.

A THING OF BEAUTY

A thing of beauty is a joy for ever:
Its loveliness increases; it will never
Pass into nothingness; but still will keep
A bower quiet for us, and a sleep
Full of sweet dreams, and health, and quiet breathing.
Therefore, on every morrow, are we wreathing
A flowery band to bind us to the earth,
Spite of despondence, of the inhuman dearth
Of noble natures, of the gloomy days,
Of all the unhealthy and o'er-darkened ways
Made for our searching: yes, in spite of all,
Some shape of beauty moves away the pall
From our dark spirits. Such the sun, the moon,
Trees old and young, sprouting a shady boon
For simple sheep; and such are daffodils
With the green world they live in; and clear rills
That for themselves a cooling covert make
'Gainst the hot season; the mid-forest brake,
Rich with a sprinkling of fair musk-rose blooms:
And such too is the grandeur of the dooms
We have imagined for the mighty dead;
All lovely tales that we have heard or read:
An endless fountain of immortal drink,
Pouring unto us from the heaven's brink.

Nor do we merely feel these essences
For one short hour; no, even as the trees
That whisper round a temple become soon
Dear as the temple's self, so does the moon,
The passion poesy, glories infinite,
Haunt us till they become a cheering light
Unto our souls, and bound to us so fast,
That, whether there be shine, or gloom o'ercast,
They always must be with us, or we die.

from ENDYMION

A SONG ABOUT MYSELF

From a letter to Fanny Keats

There was a naughty Boy,
  A naughty boy was he,
He would not stop at home,
  He could not quiet be—
    He took
    In his Knapsack
    A Book
    Full of vowels;
    And a shirt
    With some towels—
    A slight cap
    For night cap—
    A hair brush,
    Comb ditto,
    New Stockings
    For old ones
    Would split O!
    This Knapsack
    Tight at's back
    He rivetted close
And followed his Nose
    To the North,
    To the North,
And follow'd his nose
    To the North.

There was a naughty boy
  And a naughty boy was
    he,
For nothing would he do
  But scribble poetry—
    He took
    An ink stand
    In his hand
    And a Pen
    Big as ten
    In the other.
    And away
    In a Pother

    He ran
    To the mountains
    And fountains
    And ghostes
    And Postes
    And witches
    And ditches
    And wrote
    In his coat
When the weather
    Was cool,
Fear of gout,
And without
When the weather
    Was warm—
Och the charm
When we choose
To follow one's nose
    To the North,
    To the North,
To follow one's nose
    To the North!

There was a naughty boy
  And a naughty boy was
    he,
He kept little fishes
In washing tubs three
    In spite
    Of the might
    Of the Maid
    Nor affraid
    Of his Granny-good—
    He often would
    Hurly burly
    Get up early
    And go
    By hook or crook
    To the brook

And bring home
Miller's thumb,
Tittlebat

Not over fat,
Minnows small
As the stall
Of a glove,
Not above
The size
Of a nice
Little Baby's
Little fingers—
O he made
'Twas his trade
Of Fish a pretty Kettle
    A Kettle—
    A Kettle
Of Fish a pretty Kettle
    A Kettle!

There was a naughty Boy,
    And a naughty boy was
        he,

He ran away to Scotland
    The people for to see—
        Then he found
        That the ground
        Was as hard,
        That a yard
        Was as long,
        That a song
        Was as merry,
        That a cherry
        Was as red—
        That lead
        Was as weighty,
        That fourscore
        Was as eighty,
        That a door
        Was as wooden
        As in England—
So he stood in his shoes
    And he wonder'd,
        He wonder'd,
He stood in his shoes
    And he wonder'd.

HYMN TO PAN

'O thou, whose mighty palace roof doth hang
From jagged trunks, and overshadoweth
Eternal whispers, glooms, the birth, life, death
Of unseen flowers in heavy peacefulness;
Who lov'st to see the hamadryads dress
Their ruffled locks where meeting hazels darken;
And through whole solemn hours dost sit, and hearken
The dreary melody of bedded reeds—
In desolate places, where dank moisture breeds
The pipy hemlock to strange overgrowth;
Bethinking thee, how melancholy loth
Thou wast to lose fair Syrinx—do thou now,
By thy love's milky brow!
By all the trembling mazes that she ran,
Hear us, great Pan!

'O thou, for whose soul-soothing quiet, turtles
Passion their voices cooingly 'mong myrtles,

What time thou wanderest at eventide
Through sunny meadows, that outskirt the side
Of thine enmossed realms; O thou, to whom
Broad-leaved fig-trees even now foredoom
Their ripened fruitage; yellow-girted bees
Their golden honeycombs; our village leas
Their fairest blossomed beans and poppied corn;
The chuckling linnet its five young unborn,
To sing for thee; low-creeping strawberries
Their summer coolness; pent-up butterflies
Their freckled wings; yea, the fresh-budding year
All its completions—be quickly near,
By every wind that nods the mountain pine,
O forester divine!

'Thou, to whom every faun and satyr flies
For willing service; whether to surprise
The squatted hare while in half sleeping fit;
Or upward ragged precipices flit
To save poor lambkins from the eagle's maw;
Or by mysterious enticement draw
Bewildered shepherds to their path again;
Or to tread breathless round the frothy main,
And gather up all fancifullest shells
For thee to tumble into Naiad's cells
And, being hidden, laugh at their out-peeping;
Or to delight thee with fantastic leaping,
The while they pelt each other on the crown
With silvery oak-apples, and fir-cones brown—
By all the echoes that about thee ring,
Hear us, O satyr king!

'O Hearkener to the loud-clapping shears,
While ever and anon to his shorn peers
A ram goes bleating: Winder of the horn,
When snouted wild-boars routing tender corn
Anger our huntsmen: Breather round our farms,
To keep off mildews, and all weather harms:
Strange ministrant of undescribed sounds,
That comes a swooning over hollow grounds,
And wither drearily on barren moors:
Dread opener of the mysterious doors
Leading to universal knowledge—see,
Great son of Dryope,
The many that are come to pay their vows
With leaves about their brows!

'Be still the unimaginable lodge
For solitary thinkings; such as dodge
Conception to the very bourne of heaven,
Then leave the naked brain: be still the leaven,
That spreading in this dull and clodded earth
Gives it a touch ethereal—a new birth:
Be still a symbol of immensity;
A firmament reflected in a sea;
An element filling the space between;
An unknown—but no more: we humbly screen
With uplift hands our foreheads, lowly bending,
And giving out a shout most heaven-rending,
Conjure thee to receive our humble Pæan,
Upon thy Mount Lycean!'

from ENDYMION

THE EVE OF ST. AGNES

St. Agnes' Eve—Ah, bitter chill it was!
The owl, for all his feathers, was a-cold;
The hare limped trembling through the frozen grass,
And silent was the flock in woolly fold:
Numb were the Beadsman's fingers, while he told
His rosary, and while his frosted breath,
Like pious incense from a censer old,
Seem'd taking flight for heaven, without a death,
Past the sweet Virgin's picture, while his prayer he saith.

His prayer he saith, this patient, holy man;
Then takes his lamp, and riseth from his knees,
And back returneth, meagre, barefoot, wan,
Along the chapel aisle by slow degrees:
The sculptur'd dead, on each side, seem to freeze,
Emprison'd in black, purgatorial rails:
Knights, ladies, praying in dumb orat'ries,
He passeth by; and his weak spirit fails
To think how they may ache in icy hoods and mails.

Northward he turneth through a little door,
And scarce three steps, ere Music's golden tongue
Flattered to tears this agèd man and poor;
But no—already had his deathbell rung;
The joys of all his life were said and sung:
His was harsh penance on St. Agnes' Eve:

Another way he went, and soon among
Rough ashes sat he for his soul's reprieve,
And all night kept awake, for sinners' sake to grieve.

That ancient Beadsman heard the prelude soft;
And so it chanced, for many a door was wide,
From hurry to and fro. Soon, up aloft,
The silver, snarling trumpets 'gan to chide:
The level chambers, ready with their pride,
Were glowing to receive a thousand guests:
The carvèd angels, ever eager-eyed,
Stared, where upon their heads the cornice rests,
With hair blown back, and wings put cross-wise on their
   breasts.

At length burst in the argent revelry,
With plume, tiara, and all rich array,
Numerous as shadows haunting fairly
The brain, new stuffed, in youth, with triumphs gay
Of old romance. These let us wish away,
And turn, sole-thoughted, to one Lady there,
Whose heart had brooded, all that wintry day,
On love, and winged St. Agnes' saintly care,
As she had heard old dames full many times declare.

They told her how, upon St. Agnes' Eve,
Young virgins might have visions of delight,
And soft adorings from their loves receive
Upon the honeyed middle of the night,
If ceremonies due they did aright;
As, supperless to bed they must retire,
And couch supine their beauties, lily white;
Nor look behind, nor sideways, but require
Of Heaven with upward eyes for all that they desire.

Full of this whim was thoughtful Madeline:
The music, yearning like a God in pain,
She scarcely heard: her maiden eyes divine,
Fixed on the floor, saw many a sweeping train
Pass by—she heeded not at all: in vain
Came many a tiptoe, amorous cavalier,
And back retired: not cooled by high disdain,
But she saw not: her heart was otherwhere:
She sighed for Agnes' dreams, the sweetest of the year.

She danced along with vague, regardless eyes,
Anxious her lips, her breathing quick and short:
The hallowed hour was near at hand: she sighs
Amid the timbrels, and the thronged resort
Of whisperers in anger, or in sport;
'Mid looks of love, defiance, hate, and scorn,
Hoodwinked with faery fancy; all amort,
Save to St. Agnes and her lambs unshorn,
And all the bliss to be before to-morrow morn.

So, purposing each moment to retire,
She lingered still. Meantime, across the moors,
Had come young Porphyro, with heart on fire
For Madeline. Beside the portal doors,
Buttressed from moonlight, stands he, and implores
All saints to give him sight of Madeline,
But for one moment in the tedious hours,
That he might gaze and worship all unseen;
Perchance speak, kneel, touch, kiss—in sooth such things
        have been.

He ventures in: let no buzzed whisper tell:
All eyes be muffled, or a hundred swords
Will storm his heart, Love's fev'rous citadel:
For him, those chambers held barbarian hordes,
Hyena foemen, and hot-blooded lords,
Whose very dogs would execrations howl
Against his lineage: not one breast affords
Him any mercy, in that mansion foul,
Save one old beldame, weak in body and in soul.

Ah, happy chance! the agèd creature came,
Shuffling along with ivory-headed wand,
To where he stood, hid from the torch's flame,
Being a broad hall-pillar, far beyond
The sound of merriment and chorus bland:
He startled her; but soon she knew his face,
And grasped his fingers in her palsied hand,
Saying, 'Mercy, Porphyro! hie thee from this place;
They are all here to-night, the whole blood-thirsty race!

'Get hence! get hence! there's dwarfish Hildebrand;
He had a fever late, and in the fit
He cursèd thee and thine, both house and land:
Then there's that old Lord Maurice, not a whit
More tame for his grey hairs—Alas me! flit!

Flit like a ghost away.'—'Ah, Gossip dear,
We're safe enough; here in this arm-chair sit,
And tell me how'—'Good Saints! not here, not here;
Follow me, child, or else these stones will be thy bier.'

He followed through a lowly archèd way,
Brushing the cobwebs with his lofty plume,
And as she muttered 'Well-a—well-a-day!'
He found him in a little moonlight room,
Pale, latticed, chill, and silent as a tomb.
'Now tell me where is Madeline,' said he,
'O tell me, Angela, by the holy loom
Which none but secret sisterhood may see,
When they St. Agnes' wool are weaving piously.'

'St. Agnes! Ah! it is St. Agnes' Eve—
Yet men will murder upon holy days:
Thou must hold water in a witch's sieve,
And be liege-lord of all the Elves and Fays,
To venture so: it fills me with amaze
To see thee, Porphyro!—St. Agnes' Eve!
God's help! my lady fair the conjuror plays
This very night: good angels her deceive!
But let me laugh awhile, I've mickle time to grieve.'

Feebly she laugheth in the languid moon,
While Porphyro upon her face doth look,
Like puzzled urchin on an agèd crone
Who keepeth closed a wond'rous riddle-book,
As spectacled she sits in chimney nook.
But soon his eyes grew brilliant, when she told
His lady's purpose; and he scarce could brook
Tears, at the thought of those enchantments cold,
And Madeline asleep in lap of legends old.

Sudden a thought came like a full-blown rose,
Flushing his brow, and in his painèd heart
Made purple riot: then doth he propose
A stratagem, that makes the beldame start:
'A cruel man and impious thou art:
Sweet lady, let her pray, and sleep, and dream
Alone with her good angels, far apart
From wicked men like thee. Go, go!—I deem
Thou canst not surely be the same that thou didst seem.'

'I will not harm her, by all saints I swear,'

Quoth Porphyro: 'O may I ne'er find grace
When my weak voice shall whisper its last prayer,
If one of her soft ringlets I displace,
Or look with ruffian passion in her face:
Good Angela, believe me by these tears;
Or I will, even in a moment's space,
Awake, with horrid shout, my foemen's ears,
And beard them, though they be more fang'd than
    wolves and bears.'

'Ah! why wilt thou affright a feeble soul?
A poor, weak, palsy-stricken, churchyard thing,
Whose passing-bell may ere the midnight toll;
Whose prayers for thee, each morn and evening,
Were never miss'd.'—Thus plaining, doth she bring
A gentler speech from burning Porphyro;
So woful, and of such deep sorrowing,
That Angela gives promise she will do
Whatever he shall wish, betide her weal or woe.

Which was, to lead him, in close secrecy,
Even to Madeline's chamber, and there hide
Him in a closet, of such privacy
That he might see her beauty unespied,
And win perhaps that night a peerless bride,
While legioned fairies paced the coverlet,
And pale enchantment held her sleepy-eyed.
Never on such a night have lovers met,
Since Merlin paid his Demon all the monstrous debt.

'It shall be as thou wishest,' said the Dame:
'All cates and dainties shall be storèd there
Quickly on this feast-night: by the tambour frame
Her own lute thou wilt see: no time to spare,
For I am slow and feeble, and scarce dare
On such a catering trust my dizzy head.
Wait here, my child, with patience; kneel in prayer
The while: Ah! thou must needs the lady wed,
Or may I never leave my grave among the dead.'

So saying, she hobbled off with busy fear.
The lover's endless minutes slowly passed;
The Dame returned, and whispered in his ear
To follow her; with agèd eyes aghast
From fright of dim espial. Safe at last,
Through many a dusky gallery, they gain

The maiden's chamber, silken, hushed, and chaste;
Where Porphyro took covert, pleased amain.
His poor guide hurried back with agues in her brain.

Her falt'ring hand upon the balustrade,
Old Angela was feeling for the stair,
When Madeline, St. Agnes' charmèd maid,
Rose, like a mission'd spirit, unaware:
With silver taper's light, and pious care,
She turned, and down the agèd gossip led
To a safe level matting. Now prepare,
Young Porphyro, for gazing on that bed;
She comes, she comes again, like ring-dove frayed and fled.

Out went the taper as she hurried in;
Its little smoke, in pallid moonshine, died:
She closed the door, she panted, all akin
To spirits of the air, and visions wide:
No uttered syllable, or, woe betide!
But to her heart, her heart was voluble,
Paining with eloquence her balmy side;
As though a tongueless nightingale should swell
Her throat in vain, and die, heart-stifled, in her dell.

A casement high and triple-arched there was,
All garlanded with carven imag'ries
Of fruits, and flowers, and bunches of knot-grass,
And diamonded with panes of quaint device,
Innumerable of stains and splendid dyes,
As are the tiger-moth's deep-damasked wings;
And in the midst, 'mong thousand heraldries,
And twilight saints, and dim emblazonings,
A shielded scutcheon blush'd with blood of queens and kings.

Full on this casement shone the wintry moon,
And threw warm gules on Madeline's fair breast,
As down she knelt for heaven's grace and boon;
Rose-bloom fell on her hands, together prest,
And on her silver cross soft amethyst,
And on her hair a glory, like a saint:
She seemed a splendid angel, newly drest,
Save wings, for heaven:—Porphyro grew faint:
She knelt, so pure a thing, so free from mortal taint.

Anon his heart revives: her vespers done,
Of all its wreathèd pearls her hair she frees;

Unclasps her warmèd jewels one by one;
Loosens her fragrant boddice; by degrees
Her rich attire creeps rustling to her knees:
Half-hidden, like a mermaid in sea-weed,
Pensive awhile she dreams awake, and sees,
In fancy, fair St. Agnes in her bed,
But dares not look behind, or all the charm is fled.

Soon, trembling in her soft and chilly nest,
In sort of wakeful swoon, perplexed she lay,
Until the poppied warmth of sleep oppressed
Her soothèd limbs, and soul fatigued away;
Flown, like a thought, until the morrow-day;
Blissfully havened both from joy and pain;
Clasped like a missal where swart Paynims pray;
Blinded alike from sunshine and from rain,
As though a rose should shut, and be a bud again.

Stol'n to this paradise, and so entranced,
Porphyro gazed upon her empty dress,
And listened to her breathing, if it chanced
To wake into a slumberous tenderness:
Which when he heard, that minute did he bless,
And breathed himself: then from the closet crept,
Noiseless as fear in a wide wilderness,
And over the hushed carpet, silent, stept,
And 'tween the curtains peep'd, where, lo!—how fast she
    slept.

Then by the bed-side, where the faded moon
Made a dim, silver twilight, soft he set
A table, and, half anguish'd, threw thereon
A cloth of woven crimson, gold, and jet:—
O for some drowsy Morphean amulet!
The boisterous, midnight, festive clarion,
The kettledrum, and far-heard clarionet,
Affray his ears, though but in dying tone:—
The hall door shuts again, and all the noise is gone.

And still she slept an azure-lidded sleep,
In blanchèd linen, smooth, and lavendered,
While he from forth the closet brought a heap
Of candid apple, quince, and plum, and gourd;
With jellies soother than the creamy curd,
And lucent syrops, tinct and cinnamon;
Manna and dates, in argosy transferred

From Fez; and spicèd dainties, every one,
From silken Samarkand to cedared Lebanon.

These delicates he heaped with glowing hand
On golden dishes and in baskets bright
Of wreathèd silver: sumptuous they stand
In the retired quiet of the night,
Filling the chilly room with perfume light.—
'And now, my love, my seraph fair, awake!
Thou art my heaven, and I thine eremite:
Open thine eyes, for meek St. Agnes' sake,
Or I shall drowse beside thee, so my soul doth ache.'

Thus whispering, his warm, unnervèd arm
Sank in her pillow. Shaded was her dream
By the dusk curtains:—'twas a midnight charm
Impossible to melt as icèd stream:
The lustrous salvers in the moonlight gleam;
Broad golden fringe upon the carpet lies:
It seem'd he never, never could redeem
From such a steadfast spell his lady's eyes;
So mused awhile, entoil'd in woofèd phantasies.

Awakening up, he took her hollow lute,—
Tumultuous,—and, in chords that tenderest be,
He play'd an ancient ditty, long since mute,
In Provence called, 'La belle dame sans merci:'
Close to her ear touching the melody;—
Wherewith disturbed, she uttered a soft moan:
He ceased—she panted quick—and suddenly
Her blue affrayèd eyes wide open shone:
Upon his knees he sank, pale as smooth-sculptured stone.

Her eyes were open, but she still beheld,
Now wide awake, the vision of her sleep:
There was a painful change, that nigh expelled
The blisses of her dream so pure and deep,
At which fair Madeline began to weep,
And moan forth witless words with many a sigh;
While still her gaze on Porphyro would keep;
Who knelt, with joinèd hands and piteous eye,
Fearing to move or speak, she looked so dreamingly.

'Ah, Porphyro!' said she, 'but even now
Thy voice was at sweet tremble in mine ear,
Made tuneable with every sweetest vow;

And those sad eyes were spiritual and clear:
How changed thou art! how pallid, chill, and drear!
Give me that voice again, my Porphyro,
Those looks immortal, those complainings dear!
Oh leave me not in this eternal woe,
For if thou diest, my Love, I know not where to go.'

Beyond a mortal man impassion'd far
At these voluptuous accents, he arose,
Ethereal, flushed, and like a throbbing star
Seen mid the sapphire heaven's deep repose;
Into her dream he melted, as the rose
Blendeth its odour with the violet,—
Solution sweet: meantime the frost-wind blows
Like Love's alarum pattering the sharp sleet
Against the window-panes; St. Agnes' moon hath set.

'Tis dark: quick pattereth the flaw-blown sleet:
'This is no dream, my bride, my Madeline!'
'Tis dark: the icèd gusts still rave and beat:
'No dream, alas! alas! and woe is mine!
Porphyro will leave me here to fade and pine.—
Cruel! what traitor could thee hither bring?
I curse not, for my heart is lost in thine,
Though thou forsakest a deceivèd thing;—
A dove forlorn and lost with sick unprunèd wing.'

'My Madeline! sweet dreamer! lovely bride!
Say, may I be for aye thy vassal blest?
Thy beauty's shield, heart-shaped and vermeil dyed?
Ah, silver shrine, here will I take my rest
After so many hours of toil and quest,
A famished pilgrim,—saved by miracle.
Though I have found, I will not rob thy nest
Saving of thy sweet self; if thou think'st well
To trust, fair Madeline, to no rude infidel.

'Hark! 'tis an elfin-storm from faery land
Of haggard seeming, but a boon indeed:
Arise—arise! the morning is at hand;—
The bloated wassaillers will never heed:—
Let us away, my love, with happy speed;
There are no ears to hear, or eyes to see,—
Drowned all in Rhenish and the sleepy mead:
Awake! arise! my love, and fearless be,
For o'er the southern moors I have a home for thee.'

She hurried at his words, beset with fears,
For there were sleeping dragons all around,
At glaring watch, perhaps, with ready spears—
Down the wide stairs a darkling way they found.—
In all the house was heard no human sound.
A chain-drooped lamp was flickering by each door;
The arras, rich with horseman, hawk, and hound,
Fluttered in the besieging wind's uproar;
And the long carpets rose along the gusty floor.

They glide, like phantoms, into the wide hall;
Like phantoms, to the iron porch, they glide;
Where lay the Porter, in uneasy sprawl,
With a huge empty flaggon by his side:
The wakeful bloodhound rose, and shook his hide,
But his sagacious eye an inmate owns:
By one, and one, the bolts full easy slide:—
The chains lie silent on the footworn stones;—
The key turns, and the door upon its hinges groans.

And they are gone: ay, ages long ago
These lovers fled away into the storm.
That night the Baron dreamt of many a woe,
And all his warrior-guests, with shade and form
Of witch, and demon, and large coffin-worm,
Were long be-nightmared. Angela the old
Died palsy-twitched, with meagre face deform;
The Beadsman, after a thousand aves told,
For aye unsought-for slept among his ashes cold.

ALFRED, LORD TENNYSON

(1809-1892)

MARIANA

"Mariana in the moated grange."

MEASURE FOR MEASURE

With blackest moss the flower-plots
    Were thickly crusted, one and all;
The rusted nails fell from the knots
    That held the pear to the gable-wall.
The broken sheds looked sad and strange:
    Unlifted was the clinking latch;
    Weeded and worn the ancient thatch
Upon the lonely moated grange.
        She only said, 'My life is dreary,
            He cometh not,' she said;
        She said, 'I am aweary, aweary,
            I would that I were dead!'

Her tears fell with the dews at even;
    Her tears fell ere the dews were dried;
She could not look on the sweet heaven,
    Either at morn or eventide.
After the flitting of the bats,
    When thickest dark did trance the sky,
    She drew her casement-curtain by,
And glanced athwart the glooming flats.
        She only said, 'The night is dreary,
            He cometh not,' she said;
        She said, 'I am aweary, aweary,
            I would that I were dead!'

Upon the middle of the night,
    Waking she heard the night-fowl crow:
The cock sung out an hour ere light:

From the dark fen the oxen's low
Came to her: without hope of change,
   In sleep she seemed to walk forlorn,
   Till cold winds woke the grey-eyed morn
About the lonely moated grange.
      She only said, 'The day is dreary,
         He cometh not,' she said;
      She said, 'I am aweary, aweary,
         I would that I were dead!'

About a stone-cast from the wall
   A sluice with blackened waters slept,
And o'er it many, round and small,
   The clustered marish-mosses crept.
Hard by a poplar shook alway,
   All silver-green with gnarled bark:
   For leagues no other tree did mark
The level waste, the rounding grey.
      She only said, 'My life is dreary,
         He cometh not,' she said;
      She said, 'I am aweary, aweary,
         I would that I were dead!'

And ever when the moon was low,
   And the shrill winds were up and away,
In the white curtain, to and fro,
   She saw the gusty shadow sway.
But when the moon was very low,
   And wild winds bound within their cell,
   The shadow of the poplar fell
Upon her bed, across her brow.
      She only said, 'The night is dreary,
         He cometh not,' she said;
      She said, 'I am aweary, aweary,
         I would that I were dead!'

All day within the dreamy house,
   The doors upon their hinges creaked;
The blue fly sung in the pane; the mouse
   Behind the mouldering wainscot shrieked,
Or from the crevice peered about.
   Old faces glimmered thro' the doors,
   Old footsteps trod the upper floors,
Old voices called her from without.
      She only said, 'My life is dreary,
         He cometh not,' she said;

She said, 'I am aweary, aweary,
    I would that I were dead!'

The sparrow's chirrup on the roof,
    The slow clock ticking, and the sound
Which to the wooing wind aloof
    The poplar made, did all confound
Her sense; but most she loathed the hour
    When the thick-moted sunbeam lay
    Athwart the chambers, and the day
Was sloping toward his western bower.
        Then, said she, 'I am very dreary,
            He will not come,' she said;
        She wept, 'I am aweary, aweary,
            Oh God, that I were dead!'

A SPIRIT HAUNTS THE YEAR'S LAST HOURS

A spirit haunts the year's last hours
Dwelling amid these yellowing bowers:
        To himself he talks:
For at eventide, listening earnestly,
At his work you may hear him sob and sigh
        In the walks;
        Earthward he boweth the heavy stalks
Of the mouldering flowers:
    Heavily hangs the broad sunflower
        Over its grave i' the earth so chilly;
    Heavily hangs the hollyhock,
        Heavily hangs the tiger-lily.

The air is damp, and hushed, and close,
As a sick man's room when he taketh repose
        An hour before death;
My very heart faints and my whole soul grieves
At the moist rich smell of the rotting leaves,
        And the breath
        Of the fading edges of box beneath,
And the year's last rose.
    Heavily hangs the broad sunflower
        Over its grave i' the earth so chilly;
    Heavily hangs the hollyhock,
        Heavily hangs the tiger-lily.

TITHONUS

The woods decay, the woods decay and fall,
The vapours weep their burthen to the ground,
Man comes and tills the field and lies beneath,
And after many a summer dies the swan.
Me only cruel immortality
Consumes; I wither slowly in thine arms,
Here at the quiet limit of the world,
A white-haired shadow roaming like a dream
The ever-silent spaces of the East,
Far-folded mists, and gleaming halls of morn.

Alas! for this grey shadow, once a man—
So glorious in his beauty and thy choice,
Who madest him thy chosen, that he seem'd
To his great heart none other than a God!
I ask'd thee, 'Give me immortality.'
Then didst thou grant mine asking with a smile,
Like wealthy men who care not how they give.
But thy strong Hours indignant worked their wills,
And beat me down and marred and wasted me,
And tho' they could not end me, left me maim'd
To dwell in presence of immortal youth,
Immortal age beside immortal youth,
And all I was, in ashes. Can thy love,
Thy beauty, make amends, tho' even now,
Close over us, the silver star, thy guide,
Shines in those tremulous eyes that fill with tears
To hear me? Let me go: take back thy gift:
Why should a man desire in any way
To vary from the kindly race of men,
Or pass beyond the goal of ordinance
Where all should pause, as is most meet for all?

A soft air fans the cloud apart; there comes
A glimpse of that dark world where I was born.
Once more the old mysterious glimmer steals
From thy pure brows, and from thy shoulders pure,
And bosom beating with a heart renewed.
Thy cheek begins to redden thro' the gloom,
Thy sweet eyes brighten slowly close to mine,
Ere yet they blind the stars, and the wild team
Which love thee, yearning for thy yoke, arise,
And shake the darkness from their loosened manes,
And beat the twilight into flakes of fire.

Lo! ever thus thou growest beautiful
In silence, then before thine answer given
Departest, and thy tears are on my cheek.

Why wilt thou ever scare me with thy tears,
And make me tremble lest a saying learnt,
In days far-off, on that dark earth, be true?
'The Gods themselves cannot recall their gifts.'

Ay me! ay me! with what another heart
In days far-off, and with what other eyes
I used to watch—if I be he that watched—
The lucid outline forming round thee; saw
The dim curls kindle into sunny rings;
Changed with thy mystic change, and felt my blood
Glow with the glow that slowly crimsoned all
Thy presence and thy portals, while I lay,
Mouth, forehead, eyelids, growing dewy-warm
With kisses balmier than half-opening buds
Of April, and could hear the lips that kissed
Whispering I knew not what of wild and sweet,
Like that strange song I heard Apollo sing,
While Ilion like a mist rose into towers.

Yet hold me not for ever in thine East;
How can my nature longer mix with thine?
Coldly thy rosy shadows bathe me, cold
Are all thy lights, and cold my wrinkled feet
Upon thy glimmering thresholds, when the steam
Floats up from those dim fields about the homes
Of happy men that have the power to die,
And grassy barrows of the happier dead.
Release me, and restore me to the ground;
Thou seëst all things, thou wilt see my grave;
Thou wilt renew thy beauty morn by morn;
I earth in earth forget these empty courts,
And thee returning on thy silver wheels.

OF OLD SAT FREEDOM ON THE HEIGHTS

Of old sat Freedom on the heights,
  The thunders breaking at her feet;
Above her shook the starry lights;
  She heard the torrents meet.

There in her place she did rejoice,
   Self-gathered in her prophet-mind,
But fragments of her mighty voice
   Came rolling on the wind.

Then stept she down thro' town and field
   To mingle with the human race,
And part by part to men revealed
   The fullness of her face—

Grave mother of majestic works,
   From her isle-altar gazing down,
Who, God-like, grasps the triple forks,
   And, King-like, wears the crown:

Her open eyes desire the truth.
   The wisdom of a thousand years
Is in them. May perpetuate youth
   Keep dry their light from tears;

That her fair form may stand and shine,
   Make bright our days and light our dreams,
Turning to scorn with lips divine
   The falsehood of extremes!

ST. AGNES' EVE

Deep on the convent-roof the snows
   Are sparkling to the moon;
My breath to heaven like vapour goes;
   May my soul follow soon!
The shadows of the convent-towers
    Slant down the snowy sward,
Still creeping with the creeping hours
   That lead me to my Lord:
Make Thou my spirit pure and clear
   As are the frosty skies,
Or this first snowdrop of the year
   That in my bosom lies.

As these white robes are soiled and dark,
   To yonder shining ground;
As this pale taper's earthly spark,
   To yonder argent round;
So shows my soul before the Lamb,

My spirit before Thee;
So in mine earthly house I am,
   To that I hope to be.
Break up the heavens, O Lord! and far,
   Thro' all yon starlight keen,
Draw me, thy bride, a glittering star,
   In raiment white and clean.

He lifts me to the golden doors;
   The flashes come and go;
All heaven bursts her starry floors,
   And strows her lights below,
And deepens on and up! the gates
   Roll back, and far within
For me the Heavenly Bridegroom waits,
   To make me pure of sin.
The Sabbaths of Eternity,
   One Sabbath deep and wide—
A light upon the shining sea—
   The Bridegroom with his bride!

THE LOTOS-EATERS

'Courage!' he said, and pointed toward the land,
'This mounting wave will roll us shoreward soon.'
In the afternoon they came unto a land,
In which it seemed always afternoon.
All round the coast the languid air did swoon,
Breathing like one that hath a weary dream.
Full-faced above the valley stood the moon;
And like a downward smoke, the slender stream
Along the cliff to fall and pause and fall did seem.

A land of streams! some, like a downward smoke,
Slow-dropping veils of thinnest lawn, did go;
And some thro' wavering lights and shadows broke,
Rolling a slumbrous sheet of foam below.
They saw the gleaming river seaward flow
From the inner land; far off, three mountain-tops,
Three silent pinnacles of aged snow,
Stood sunset-flushed: and, dewed with showery drops,
Up-clomb the shadowy pine above the woven copse.

The charmed sunset lingered low adown
In the red West: thro' mountain clefts the dale

Was seen far inland, and the yellow down
Bordered with palm, and many a winding vale
And meadow, set with slender galingale;
A land where all things always seemed the same!
And round about the keel with faces pale,
Dark faces pale against that rosy flame,
The mild-eyed melancholy Lotos-eaters came.

Branches they bore of that enchanted stem,
Laden with flower and fruit, whereof they gave
To each, but whoso did receive of them,
And taste, to him the gushing of the wave
Far far away did seem to morn and rave
On alien shores; and if his fellow spake,
His voice was thin, as voices from the grave;
And deep-asleep he seemed, yet all awake,
And music in his ears his beating heart did make.

They sat them down upon the yellow sand,
Between the sun and moon upon the shore;
And sweet it was to dream of Fatherland,
Of child, and wife, and slave; but evermore
Most weary seem'd the sea, weary the oar,
Weary the wandering fields of barren foam.
Then some one said, 'We will return no more;'
And all at once they sang, 'Our island home
Is far beyond the wave; we will no longer roam.'

CHORIC SONG

There is sweet music here that softer falls
Than petals from blown roses on the grass,
Or night-dews on still waters between walls
Of shadowy granite, in a gleaming pass;
Music that gentlier on the spirit lies,
Than tired eyelids upon tired eyes;
Music that brings sweet sleep down from the blissful skies.
Here are cool mosses deep,
And thro' the moss the ivies creep,
And in the stream the long-leaved flowers weep,
And from the craggy ledge the poppy hangs in sleep.

Why are we weighed upon with heaviness,
And utterly consumed with sharp distress,
While all things else have rest from weariness?

All things have rest: why should we toil alone,
We only toil, who are the first of things,
And make perpetual moan,
Still from one sorrow to another thrown:
Nor ever fold our wings,
And cease from wanderings,
Nor steep our brows in slumber's holy balm;
Nor hearken what the inner spirit sings,
'There is no joy but calm!'
Why should we only toil, the roof and crown of things?

Lo! in the middle of the wood,
The folded leaf is wooed from out the bud
With winds upon the branch, and there
Grows green and broad, and takes no care,
Sun-steeped at noon, and in the moon
Nightly dew-fed; and turning yellow
Falls, and floats adown the air.
Lo! sweetened with the summer light,
The full-juiced apple, waxing over-mellow,
Drops in a silent autumn night.
All its allotted length of days
The flower ripens in its place,
Ripens and fades, and falls, and hath no toil,
Fast-rooted in the fruitful soil.

Hateful is the dark-blue sky,
Vaulted o'er the dark-blue sea.
Death is the end of life; ah, why
Should life all labour be?
Let us alone. Time driveth onward fast,
And in a little while our lips are dumb.
Let us alone. What is it that will last?
All things are taken from us, and become
Portions and parcels of the dreadful Past.
Let us alone. What pleasure can we have
To war with evil? Is there any peace
In ever climbing up the climbing wave?
All things have rest, and ripen toward the grave
In silence; ripen, fall, and cease:
Give us long rest or death, dark death, or dreamful ease.

How sweet it were, hearing the downward stream,
With half-shut eyes ever to seem
Falling asleep in a half-dream!
To dream and dream, like yonder amber light,

Which will not leave the myrrh-bush on the height;
To hear each other's whisper'd speech;
Eating the Lotos day by day,
To watch the crisping ripples on the beach,
And tender curving lines of creamy spray;
To lend our hearts and spirits wholly
To the influence of mild-minded melancholy;
To muse and brood and live again in memory,
With those old faces of our infancy
Heaped over with a mound of grass,
Two handfuls of white dust, shut in an urn of brass!

Dear is the memory of our wedded lives,
And dear the last embraces of our wives
And their warm tears: but all hath suffered change:
For surely now our household hearths are cold:
Our sons inherit us: our looks are strange:
And we should come like ghosts to trouble joy.
Or else the island princes over-bold
Have eat our substance, and the minstrel sings
Before them of the ten years' war in Troy,
And our great deeds, as half-forgotten things.
Is there confusion in the little isle?
Let what is broken so remain.
The Gods are hard to reconcile:
'Tis hard to settle order once again.
There *is* confusion worse than death,
Trouble on trouble, pain on pain,
Long labour unto aged breath,
Sore task to hearts worn out by many wars
And eyes grown dim with gazing on the pilot-stars.

But, propt on beds of amaranth and moly,
How sweet (while warm airs lull us, blowing lowly)
With half-dropt eyelid still,
Beneath a heaven dark and holy,
To watch the long bright river drawing slowly
His waters from the purple hill—
To hear the dewy echoes calling
From cave to cave through the thick-twined vine—
To watch the emerald-colour'd water falling
Through many a woven acanthus-wreath divine!
Only to hear and see the far-off sparkling brine,
Only to hear were sweet, stretch'd out beneath the pine.

The Lotos blooms below the barren peak:

The Lotos blows by every winding creek:
All day the wind breathes low with mellower tone:
Thro' every hollow cave and alley lone
Round and round the spicy downs the yellow Lotos-dust is
      blown.
We have had enough of action, and of motion we,
Rolled to starboard, rolled to larboard, when the surge was
      seething free,
Where the wallowing monster spouted his foam-fountains in
      the sea.
Let us swear an oath, and keep it with an equal mind,
In the hollow Lotos-land to live and lie reclined
On the hills like Gods together, careless of mankind.
For they lie beside their nectar, and the bolts are hurled
Far below them in the valleys, and the clouds are lightly
      curled
Round their golden houses, girdled with the gleaming world:
Where they smile in secret, looking over wasted lands,
Blight and famine, plague and earthquake, roaring deeps and
      fiery sands,
Clanging fights, and flaming towns, and sinking ships, and
      praying hands.
But they smile, they find a music centred in a doleful song
Steaming up, a lamentation and an ancient tale of wrong,
Like a tale of little meaning tho' the words are strong;
Chanted from an ill-used race of men that cleave the soil,
Sow the seed, and reap the harvest with enduring toil,
Storing yearly little dues of wheat, and wine and oil;
Till they perish and they suffer—some, 'tis whispered—
      down in hell
Suffer endless anguish, others in Elysian valleys dwell,
Resting weary limbs at last on beds of asphodel.
Surely, surely, slumber is more sweet than toil, the shore
Than labour in the deep mid-ocean, wind and wave and oar;
Oh rest ye, brother mariners, we will not wander more.

ULYSSES

It little profits that an idle king,
By this still hearth, among these barren crags,
Matched with an aged wife, I mete and dole
Unequal laws unto a savage race,
That hoard, and sleep, and feed, and know not me.
I cannot rest from travel: I will drink
Life to the lees: all times I have enjoyed

Greatly, have suffered greatly, both with those
That loved me, and alone; on shore, and when
Thro' scudding drifts the rainy Hyades
Vext the dim sea: I am become a name;
For always roaming with a hungry heart
Much have I seen and known; cities of men
And manners, climates, councils, governments,
Myself not least, but honoured of them all;—
And drunk delight of battle with my peers,
Far on the ringing plains of windy Troy.
I am a part of all that I have met;
Yet all experience is an arch wherethro'
Gleams that untravelled world, whose margin fades
For ever and for ever when I move.
How dull it is to pause, to make an end,
To rust unburnished, not to shine in use!
As tho' to breathe were life! Life piled on life
Were all too little, and of one to me
Little remains; but every hour is saved
From that eternal silence, something more,
A bringer of new things; and vile it were
For some three suns to store and hoard myself,
And this grey spirit yearning in desire
To follow knowledge, like a sinking star,
Beyond the utmost bound of human thought.

   This is my son, mine own Telemachus,
To whom I leave the scepter and the isle,—
Well-loved of me, discerning to fulfil
This labour, by slow prudence to make mild
A rugged people, and thro' soft degrees
Subdue them to the useful and the good.
Most blameless is he, centred in the sphere
Of common duties, decent not to fail
In offices of tenderness, and pay
Meet adoration to my household gods,
When I am gone. He works his work, I mine.

   There lies the port: the vessel puffs her sail:
There gloom the dark broad seas. My mariners,
Souls that have toiled, and wrought, and thought with me—
That ever with a frolic welcome took
The thunder and the sunshine, and opposed
Free hearts, free foreheads—you and I are old;
Old age hath yet his honour and his toil.
Death closes all: but something ere the end,
Some work of noble note, may yet be done,
Not unbecoming men that strove with Gods.

The lights begin to twinkle from the rocks:
The long day wanes: the slow moon climbs: the deep
Moans round with many voices. Come, my friends,
'Tis not too late to seek a newer world.
Push off, and sitting well in order smite
The sounding furrows; for my purpose holds
To sail beyond the sunset, and the baths
Of all the western stars, until I die.
It may be that the gulfs will wash us down:
It may be we shall touch the Happy Isles,
And see the great Achilles, whom we knew.
Tho' much is taken, much abides; and though
We are not now that strength which in old days
Moved earth and heaven, that which we are, we are;
One equal temper of heroic hearts,
Made weak by time and fate, but strong in will
To strive, to seek, to find, and not to yield.

TEARS, IDLE TEARS

'Tears, idle tears, I know not what they mean,
Tears from the depth of some divine despair
Rise in the heart, and gather to the eyes,
In looking on the happy Autumn fields,
And thinking of the days that are no more.

'Fresh as the first beam glittering on a sail,
That brings our friends up from the underworld,
Sad as the last which reddens over one
That sinks with all we love below the verge;
So sad, so fresh, the days that are no more.

'Ah, sad and strange as in dark summer dawns
The earliest pipe of half-awakened birds
To dying ears, when unto dying eyes
The casement slowly grows a glimmering square;
So sad, so strange, the days that are no more.

'Dear as remember'd kisses after death,
And sweet as those by hopeless fancy feign'd
On lips that are for others; deep as love,
Deep as first love, and wild with all regret;
O Death in Life, the days that are no more.'

from THE PRINCESS

ASK ME NO MORE

Ask me no more: the moon may draw the sea;
  The cloud may stoop from heaven and take the shape
  With fold to fold, of mountain or of cape;
But O too fond, when have I answered thee?
           Ask me no more.

Ask me no more: what answer should I give?
  I love not hollow cheek or faded eye;
  Yet, O my friend, I will not have thee die!
Ask me no more, lest I should bid thee live;
           Ask me no more.

Ask me no more: they fate and mine are sealed:
  I strove against the stream and all in vain;
  Let the great river take me to the main;
No more, dear love, for at a touch I yield;
           Ask me no more.

from THE PRINCESS

NOW SLEEPS THE CRIMSON PETAL

  'Now sleeps the crimson petal, now the white;
Nor waves the cypress in the palace walk;
Nor winks the gold fin in the porphyry font.
The fire-fly wakens: waken thou with me.

  'Now droops the milk-white peacock like a ghost,
And like a ghost she glimmers on to me.
  Now lies the Earth all Danaë to the stars,
And all thy heart lies open unto me.
  Now slides the silent meteor on, and leaves
A shining furrow, as thy thoughts in me.

  'Now folds the lily all her sweetness up,
And slips into the bosom of the lake.
So fold thyself, my dearest, thou, and slip
Into my bosom and be lost in me.

from THE PRINCESS

COME DOWN, O MAID, FROM YONDER MOUNTAIN HEIGHT

Come down, O maid, from yonder mountain height:
What pleasure lives in height (the shepherd sang)
In height and cold, the splendor of the hills?
But cease to move so near the Heavens, and cease
To glide a sunbeam by the blasted Pine,
To sit a star upon the sparkling spire;
And come, for Love is of the valley, come,
For Love is of the valley, come thou down
And find him; by the happy threshold, he,
Or hand in hand with Plenty in the maize,
Or red with spirted purple of the vats,
Or foxlike in the vine; nor cares to walk
With Death and Morning on the silver horns,
Nor wilt thou snare him in the white ravine,
Nor find him dropt upon the firths of ice,
That huddling slant in furrow-cloven falls
To roll the torrent out of dusky doors;
But follow; let the torrent dance thee down
To find him in the valley; let the wild
Lean-headed Eagles yelp alone, and leave
The monstrous ledges there to slope, and spill
Their thousand wreaths of dangling water-smoke,
That like a broken purpose waste in air:
So waste not thou; but come; for all the vales
Await thee; azure pillars of the hearth
Arise to thee; the children call, and I
Thy shepherd pipe, and sweet is every sound,
Sweeter thy voice, but every sound is sweet;
Myriads of rivulets hurrying thro' the lawn,
The moan of doves in immemorial elms,
And murmuring of innumerable bees.

from THE PRINCESS

THE SPLENDOUR FALLS

The splendour falls on castle walls
    And snowy summits old in story;
The long light shakes across the lakes,
    And the wild cataract leaps in glory.
Blow, bugle, blow, set the wild echoes flying,
Blow, bugle; answer, echoes, dying, dying, dying.

O hark, O hear! how thin and clear,
    And thinner, clearer, farther going!
O sweet and far from cliff and scar
    The horns of Elfland faintly blowing!
Blow, let us hear the purple glens replying;
Blow, bugle; answer, echoes, dying, dying, dying.

O love, they die in yon rich sky,
    They faint on hill or field or river;
Our echoes roll from soul to soul,
    And grow for ever and for ever.
Blow, bugle, blow, set the wild echoes flying,
And answer, echoes, answer, dying, dying, dying.

THE EAGLE: (A FRAGMENT)

He clasps the crag with crooked hands;
Close to the sun in lonely lands,
Ring'd with the azure world, he stands.

The wrinkled sea beneath him crawls;
He watches from his mountain walls,
And like a thunderbolt he falls.

From IN MEMORIAM A.H.H.

STRONG SON OF GOD, IMMORTAL LOVE

Strong Son of God, immortal Love,
    Whom we, that have not seen thy face,
    By faith, and faith alone, embrace,
Believing where we cannot prove;

Thine are these orbs of light and shade;
    Thou madest Life in man and brute;
    Thou madest Death; and lo, thy foot
Is on the skull which thou hast made.

Thou wilt not leave us in the dust:
    Thou madest man, he knows not why,
    He thinks he was not made to die;
And thou has made him: thou art just.

Thou seemest human and divine,
   The highest, holiest manhood, thou:
   Our wills are ours, we know not how;
Our wills are ours, to make them thine.

Our little systems have their day;
   They have their day and cease to be:
   They are but broken lights of thee,
And thou, O Lord, art more than they.

We have but faith: we cannot know;
   For knowledge is of things we see;
   And yet we trust it comes from thee,
A beam in darkness: let it grow.

Let knowledge grow from more to more,
   But more of reverence in us dwell;
   That mind and soul according well,
May make one music as before,

But vaster. We are fools and slight;
   We mock thee when we do not fear:
   But help thy foolish ones to bear;
Help thy vain worlds to bear thy light.

Forgive what seemed my sin in me,
   What seemed my worth since I began;
   For merit lives from man to man,
And not from man, O Lord, to thee.

Forgive my grief for one removed,
   Thy creature, whom I found so fair.
   I trust he lives in thee, and there
I find him worthier to be loved.

Forgive these wild and wandering cries,
   Confusions of a wasted youth;
   Forgive them where they fail in truth,
And in thy wisdom make me wise.

I HELD IT TRUTH, WITH HIM WHO SINGS

I held it truth, with him who sings
   To one clear harp in divers tones,
   That men may rise on stepping-stones
Of their dead selves to higher things.

But who shall so forecast the years
   And find in loss a gain to match?
   Or reach a hand thro' time to catch
The far-off interest of tears?

Let Love clasp Grief lest both be drowned,
   Let darkness keep her raven gloss:
   Ah, sweeter to be drunk with loss,
To dance with Death, to beat the ground,

Than that the victor Hours should scorn
   The long result of love, and boast,
   'Behold the man that loved and lost,
But all he was is overworn.'

DARK HOUSE, BY WHICH ONCE MORE I STAND

Dark house, by which once more I stand
   Here in the long unlovely street,
   Doors, where my heart was used to beat
So quickly, waiting for a hand,

A hand that can be clasped no more—
   Behold me, for I cannot sleep,
   And like a guilty thing I creep
At earliest morning to the door.

He is not here; but far away
   The noise of life begins again,
   And ghastly thro' the drizzling rain
On the bald street breaks the blank day.

IF ONE SHOULD BRING ME THIS REPORT

If one should bring me this report,
   That thou hadst touched the land to-day,
   And I went down unto the quay,
And found thee lying in the port;

And standing, muffled round with woe,
   Should see thy passengers in rank
   Come stepping lightly down the plank,
And beckoning unto those they know;

And if along with these should come
 The man I held as half-divine;
 Should strike a sudden hand in mine,
And ask a thousand things of home;

And I should tell him all my pain,
 And how my life had drooped of late,
 And he should sorrow o'er my state
And marvel what possessed my brain;

And I perceived no touch of change,
 No hint of death in all his frame,
 But found him all in all the same,
I should not feel it to be strange.

I ENVY NOT IN ANY MOODS

I envy not in any moods
 The captive void of noble rage,
 The linnet born within the cage,
That never knew the summer woods:

I envy not the beast that takes
 His license in the field of time,
 Unfetter'd by the sense of crime,
To whom a conscience never wakes;

Nor, what may count itself as blest,
 The heart that never plighted troth,
 But stagnates in the weeds of sloth;
Nor any want-begotten rest.

I hold it true, whate'er befall;
 I feel it, when I sorrow most;
 'Tis better to have loved and lost
Than never to have loved at all.

IF SLEEP AND DEATH BE TRULY ONE

If Sleep and Death be truly one,
 And every spirit's folded bloom
 Thro' all its intervital gloom
In some long trance should slumber on;

Unconscious of the sliding hour,
  Bare of the body, might it last,
  And silent traces of the past
Be all the colour of the flower:

So then were nothing lost to man;
  So that still garden of the souls
  In many a figured leaf enrolls
The total world since life began;

And love will last as pure and whole
  As when he loved me here in Time,
  And at the spiritual prime
Reawaken with the dawning soul.

THE BABY NEW TO EARTH AND SKY

The baby new to earth and sky,
  What time his tender palm is prest
  Against the circle of the breast,
Has never thought that 'this is I;'

But as he grows he gathers much,
  And learns the use of 'I,' and 'me,'
  And finds 'I am not what I see,
And other than the things I touch.'

So rounds he to a separate mind
  From whence clear memory may begin,
  As thro' the frame that binds him in
His isolation grows defined.

This use may lie in blood and breath,
  Which else were fruitless of their due,
  Had man to learn himself anew
Beyond the second birth of Death.

BE NEAR ME WHEN MY LIGHT IS LOW

Be near me when my light is low,
  When the blood creeps, and the nerves prick
  And tingle; and the heart is sick,
And all the wheels of Being slow.

Be near me when the sensuous frame
    Is racked with pangs that conquer trust;
    And Time, a maniac scattering dust,
And Life, a Fury slinging flame.

Be near me when my faith is dry,
    And men the flies of latter spring,
    That lay their eggs, and sting and sing
And weave their petty cells and die.

Be near me when I fade away,
    To point the term of human strife,
    And on the low dark verge of life
The twilight of eternal day.

O YET WE TRUST THAT SOMEHOW GOOD

O yet we trust that somehow good
    Will be the final goal of ill,
    To pangs of nature, sins of will,
Defects of doubt, and taints of blood;

That nothing walks with aimless feet;
    That not one life shall be destroyed,
    Or cast as rubbish to the void,
When God hath made the pile complete;

That not a worm is cloven in vain;
    That not a moth with vain desire
    Is shrivelled in a fruitless fire,
Or but subserves another's gain.

Behold, we know not anything;
    I can but trust that good shall fall
    At last—far off—at last, to all,
And every winter change to spring.

So runs my dream; but what am I?
    An infant crying in the night;
    An infant crying for the light;
And with no language but a cry.

WHEN ON MY BED THE MOONLIGHT FALLS

When on my bed the moonlight falls,
  I know that in thy place of rest,
  By that broad water of the west,
There comes a glory on the walls:

Thy marble bright in dark appears,
  As slowly steals a silver flame
  Along the letters of thy name,
And o'er the number of thy years.

The mystic glory swims away;
  From off my bed the moonlight dies;
  And closing eaves of wearied eyes
I sleep till dusk is dipt in grey:

And then I know the mist is drawn
  A lucid veil from coast to coast
  And in the dark church like a ghost
Thy tablet glimmers to the dawn.

I CANNOT SEE THE FEATURES RIGHT

I cannot see the features right,
  When on the gloom I strive to paint
  The face I know; the hues are faint
And mix with hollow masks of night;

Cloud-towers by ghostly masons wrought,
  A gulf that ever shuts and gapes,
  A hand that points, and palled shapes
In shadowy thoroughfares of thought;

And crowds that stream from yawning doors,
  And shoals of puckered faces drive;
  Dark bulks that tumble half alive,
And lazy lengths on boundless shores;

Till all at once beyond the will
  I hear a wizard music roll,
  And thro' a lattice on the soul
Looks thy fair face and makes it still.

WHAT HOPE IS HERE FOR MODERN RHYME

What hope is here for modern rhyme
   To him, who turns a musing eye
   On songs, and deeds, and lives, that lie
Foreshortened in the tract of time?

These mortal lullabies of pain
   May bind a book, may line a box,
   May serve to curl a maiden's locks;
Or when a thousand moons shall wane

A man upon a stall may find,
   And, passing, turn the page that tells
   A grief, then changed to something else,
Sung by a long-forgotten mind.

But what of that? My darkened ways
   Shall ring with music all the same;
   To breathe my loss is more than fame,
To utter love more sweet than praise.

HOW PURE AT HEART AND SOUND IN HEAD

How pure at heart and sound in head,
   With what divine affections bold
   Should be the man whose thought would hold
An hour's communion with the dead.

In vain shalt thou, or any, call
   The spirits from their golden day,
   Except, like them, thou too canst say,
My spirit is at peace with all.

They haunt the silence of the breast,
   Imaginations calm and fair,
   The memory like a cloudless air,
The conscience as a sea at rest;

But when the heart is full of din,
   And doubt beside the portal waits,
   They can but listen at the gates,
And hear the household jar within.

RING OUT, WILD BELLS, TO THE WILD SKY

Ring out, wild bells, to the wild sky,
  The flying cloud, the frosty light:
  The year is dying in the night;
Ring out, wild bells, and let him die.

Ring out the old, ring in the new,
  Ring, happy bells, across the snow:
  The year is going, let him go;
Ring out the false, ring in the true.

Ring out the grief that saps the mind,
  For those that here we see no more;
  Ring out the feud of rich and poor,
Ring in redress to all mankind.

Ring out a slowly dying cause,
  And ancient forms of party strife;
  Ring in the nobler modes of life,
With sweeter manners, purer laws.

Ring out the want, the care, the sin,
  The faithless coldness of the times;
  Ring out, ring out my mournful rhymes,
But ring the fuller minstrel in.

Ring out false pride in place and blood,
  The civic slander and the spite;
  Ring in the love of truth and right,
Ring in the common love of good.

Ring out old shapes of foul disease;
  Ring out the narrowing lust of gold;
  Ring out the thousand wars of old,
Ring in the thousand years of peace.

Ring in the valiant man and free,
  The larger heart, the kindlier hand;
  Ring out the darkness of the land,
Ring in the Christ that is to be.

O, WAST THOU WITH ME, DEAREST, THEN

O, wast thou with me, dearest, then,
  While I rose up against my doom,
  And yearn'd to burst the folded gloom,
To bare the eternal heavens again,

To feel once more, in placid awe,
　　The strong imagination roll
　　A sphere of stars about my soul,
In all her motion one with law?

If thou wert with me, and the grave
　　Divide us not, be with me now,
　　And enter in at breast and brow,
Till all my blood, a fuller wave,

Be quickened with a livelier breath,
　　And like an inconsiderate boy,
　　As in the former flash of joy,
I slip the thoughts of life and death;

And all the breeze of Fancy blows,
　　And every dewdrop paints a bow,
　　The wizard lightnings deeply glow,
And every thought breaks out a rose.

O LIVING WILL THAT SHALT ENDURE

O living will that shalt endure
　　When all that seems shall suffer shock,
　　Rise in the spiritual rock,
Flow thro' our deeds and make them pure,

That we may lift from out of dust
　　A voice as unto him that hears,
　　A cry above the conquer'd years
To one that with us works, and trust,

With faith that comes of self-control,
　　The truths that never can be proved
　　Until we close with all we loved,
And all we flow from, soul in soul.

THE TWO VOICES

A still small voice spake unto me,
'Thou art so full of misery,
Were it not better not to be?'

Then to the still small voice I said:
'Let me not cast in endless shade
What is so wonderfully made.'

To which the voice did urge reply:
'To-day I saw the dragon-fly
Come from the wells where he did lie.

'An inner impulse rent the veil
Of his old husk; from head to tail
Came out clear plates of sapphire mail.

'He dried his wings; like gauze they grew;
Thro' crofts and pastures wet with dew
A living flash of light he flew.'

I said: 'When first the world began,
Young Nature thro' five cycles ran,
And in the sixth she moulded man.

'She gave him mind, the lordliest
Proportion, and, above the rest,
Dominion in the head and breast.'

Thereto the silent voice replied:
'Self-blinded are you by your pride;
Look up thro' night; the world is wide.

'This truth within thy mind rehearse,
That in a boundless universe
Is boundless better, boundless worse.

'Think you this mould of hopes and fears
Could find no statelier than his peers
In yonder hundred million spheres?'

It spake, moreover, in my mind:
'Tho' thou wert scattered to the wind,
Yet is there plenty of the kind.'

Then did my response clearer fall:
'No compound of this earthly ball
Is like another, all in all.'

To which he answered scoffingly:
'Good soul! suppose I grant it thee,
Who'll weep for thy deficiency?

'Or will one beam be less intense,
When thy peculiar difference
Is cancelled in the world of sense?'

I would have said, 'Thou canst not know,'
But my full heart, that worked below,
Rain'd thro' my sight its overflow.

Again the voice spake unto me:
'Thou art so steeped in misery,
Surely 't were better not to be.

'Thine anguish will not let thee sleep,
Nor any train of reason keep;
Thou canst not think, but thou wilt weep.'

I said: 'The years with change advance;
If I make dark my countenance,
I shut my life from happier chance.

'Some turn this sickness yet might take,
Ev'n yet.' But he: 'What drug can make
A withered palsy cease to shake?'

I wept: 'Tho' I should die, I know
That all about the thorn will blow
In tufts of rosy-tinted snow;

'And men, thro' novel spheres of thought
Still moving after truth long sought,
Will learn new things when I am not.'

'Yet,' said the secret voice, 'some time,
Sooner or later, will grey prime
Make thy grass hoar with early rime.

'Not less swift souls that yearn for light,
Rapt after heaven's starry flight,
Would sweep the tracts of day and night.

'Not less the bee would range her cells,
The furzy prickle fire the dells,
The foxgove cluster dappled bells.'

I said that 'all the years invent;
Each month is various to present
The world with some development.

'Were this not well, to bide mine hour,
Tho' watching from a ruined tower
How grows the day of human power?'

'The highest-mounted mind,' he said,
'Still sees the sacred morning spread
The silent summit overhead.

'Will thirty seasons render plain
Those lonely lights that still remain,
Just breaking over land and main?

'Or make that morn, from his cold crown
And crystal silence creeping down,
Flood with full daylight glebe and town?

'Forerun thy peers, thy time, and let
Thy feet, millenniums hence, be set
In midst of knowledge, dreamed not yet.

'Thou hast not gained a real height,
Nor art thou nearer to the light,
Because the scale is infinite.

' 'T were better not to breathe or speak,
Than cry for strength, remaining weak,
And seem to find, but still to seek.

'Moreover, but to seem to find
Asks what thou lackest, thought resigned,
A healthy frame, a quiet mind.'

I said, 'When I am gone away,
"He dared not tarry," men will say,
Doing dishonour to my clay.'

'This is more vile,' he made reply,
'To breathe and loathe, to live and sigh,
Than once from dread of pain to die.

'Sick art thou—a divided will
Still heaping on the fear of ill
The fear of men, a coward still.

'Do men love thee? Art thou so bound
To men, that how thy name may sound
Will vex thee lying underground?

'The memory of the withered leaf
In endless time is scarce more brief
Than of the garnered Autumn-sheaf.

'Go, vexed Spirit, sleep in trust;
The right ear, that is filled with dust,
Hears little of the false or just.'

'Hard task, to pluck resolve,' I cried,
'From emptiness and the waste wide
Of that abyss, or scornful pride!

'Nay—rather yet that I could raise
One hope that warmed me in the days
While still I yearned for human praise.

'When, wide in soul and bold of tongue,
Among the tents I paused and sung,
The distant battle flash'd and rung.

'I sung the joyful Pæan clear,
And, sitting, burnished without fear
The brand, the buckler, and the spear—

'Waiting to strive a happy strife,
To war with falsehood to the knife,
And not to lose the good of life—

'Some hidden principle to move,
To put together, part and prove,
And mete the bounds of hate and love—

'As far as might be, to carve out
Free space for every human doubt,
That the whole mind might orb about—

'To search thro' all I felt or saw,
The springs of life, the depths of awe,
And reach the law within the law;

'At least, not rotting like a weed,
But, having sown some generous seed,
Fruitful of further thought and deed,

'To pass, when Life her light withdraws,
Not void of righteous self-applause,
Nor in a merely selfish cause—

'In some good cause, not in mine own,
To perish, wept for, honour'd, known,
And like a warrior overthrown;

'Whose eyes are dim with glorious tears,
When, soiled with noble dust, he hears
His country's war-song thrill his ears:

'Then dying of a mortal stroke,
What time the foeman's line is broke,
And all the war is rolled in smoke.'

'Yea!' said the voice, 'thy dream was good,
While thou abodest in the bud.
It was the stirring of the blood.

'If Nature put not forth her power
About the opening of the flower,
Who is it that could live an hour?

'Then comes the check, the change, the fall,
Pain rises up, old pleasures pall.
There is one remedy for all.

'Yet hadst thou, thro' enduring pain,
Link'd month to month with such a chain
Of knitted purport, all were vain.

'Thou hadst not between death and birth
Dissolved the riddle of the earth.
So were thy labour little-worth.

'That men with knowledge merely played,
I told thee—hardly nigher made,
Tho' scaling slow from grade to grade;

'Much less this dreamer, deaf and blind,
Named man, may hope some truth to find,
That bears relation to the mind.

'For every worm beneath the moon
Draws different threads, and late and soon
Spins, toiling out his own cocoon.

'Cry, faint not; either Truth is born
Beyond the polar gleam forlorn,
Or in the gateways of the morn.

'Cry, faint not, climb: the summits slope
Beyond the furthest flights of hope,
Wrapt in dense cloud from base to cope.

'Sometimes a little corner shines,
As over rainy mist inclines
A gleaming crag with belts of pines.

'I will go forward, sayest thou,
I shall not fail to find her now.
Look up, the fold is on her brow.

'If straight thy track, or if oblique,
Thou know'st not. Shadows thou dost strike,
Embracing cloud, Ixion-like;

'And owning but a little more
Than beasts, abidest lame and poor,
Calling thyself a little lower

'Than angels. Cease to wail and brawl!
Why inch by inch to darkness crawl?
There is one remedy for all.'

'O dull, one-sided voice,' said I,
'Wilt thou make everything a lie,
To flatter me that I may die?

'I know that age to age succeeds,
Blowing a noise of tongues and deeds,
A dust of systems and of creeds.

'I cannot hide that some have striven,
Achieving calm, to whom was given
The joy that mixes man with Heaven:

'Who, rowing hard against the stream,
Saw distant gates of Eden gleam,
And did not dream it was a dream;

'But heard, by secret transport led,
Ev'n in the charnels of the dead,
The murmur of the fountain-head—

'Which did accomplish their desire,
Bore and forebore, and did not tire,
Like Stephen, an unquenched fire.

'He heeded not reviling tones,
Nor sold his heart to idle moans,
Tho' cursed and scorn'd, and bruised with stones;

'But looking upward, full of grace,
He prayed, and from a happy place
God's glory smote him on the face.'

The sullen answer slid betwixt:
'Not that the grounds of hope were fixed,
The elements were kindlier mixed.'

I said, 'I toil beneath the curse,
But, knowing not the universe,
I fear to slide from bad to worse.

'And that in seeking to undo
One riddle, and to find the true,
I knit a hundred others new.

'Or that this anguish fleeting hence,
Unmanacled from bonds of sense,
Be fixed and froz'n to permanence:

'For I go, weak from suffering here;
Naked I go, and void of cheer:
What is it that I may not fear?'

'Consider well,' the voice replied,
'His face, that two hours since hath died;
Wilt thou find passion, pain or pride?

'Will he obey when one commands?
Or answer should one press his hands?
He answers not, nor understands.

'His palms are folded on his breast:
There is no other thing expressed
But long disquiet merged in rest.

'His lips are very mild and meek:
Tho' one should smite him on the cheek,
And on the mouth, he will not speak.

'His little daughter, whose sweet face
He kissed, taking his last embrace,
Becomes dishonour to her race—

'His sons grow up that bear his name,
Some grow to honour, some to shame,—
But he is chill to praise or blame.

'He will not hear the north-wind rave,
Nor, moaning, household shelter crave
From winter rains that beat his grave.

'High up the vapours fold and swim;
About him broods the twilight dim;
The place he knew forgetteth him.'

'If all be dark, vague voice,' I said,
'These things are wrapt in doubt and dread,
Nor canst thou show the dead are dead.

'The sap dries up: the plant declines.
A deeper tale my heart divines.
Know I not Death? the outward signs?

'I found him when my years were few;
A shadow on the graves I knew,
And darkness in the village yew.

'From grave to grave the shadow crept;
In her still place the morning wept;
Touch'd by his feet the daisy slept.

'The simple senses crowned his head:
"Omega! thou art Lord," they said,
"We find no motion in the dead."

'Why, if man rot in dreamless ease,
Should that plain fact, as taught by these,
Not make him sure that he shall cease?

'Who forged that other influence,
That heat of inward evidence,
By which he doubts against the sense?

'He owns the fatal gift of eyes,
That read his spirit blindly wise,
Not simple as a thing that dies.

'Here sits he shaping wings to fly;
His heart forebodes a mystery;
He names the name Eternity.

'That type of Perfect in his mind
In Nature can he nowhere find.
He sows himself on every wind.

'He seems to hear a Heavenly Friend,
And thro' thick veils to apprehend
A labour working to an end.

'The end and the beginning vex
His reason: many things perplex,
With motions, checks, and counterchecks.

'He knows a baseness in his blood
At such strange war with something good,
He may not do the thing he would.

'Heaven opens inward, chasms yawn,
Vast images in glimmering dawn,
Half shown, are broken and withdrawn.

'Ah! sure within him and without,
Could his dark wisdom find it out,
There must be answer to his doubt,

'But thou canst answer not again.
With thine own weapon art thou slain,
Or thou wilt answer but in vain.

'The doubt would rest, I dare not solve,
In the same circle we revolve.
Assurance only breeds resolve.'

As when a billow, blown against,
Falls back, the voice with which I fenced
A little ceased, but recommenced.

'Where wert thou when thy father played
In this free field, and pastime made,
A merry boy in sun and shade?

'A merry boy they called him then,
He sat upon the knees of men
In days that never come again.

'Before the little ducts began
To feed thy bones with lime, and ran
Their course, till thou wert also man:

'Who took a wife, who reared his race,
Whose wrinkles gathered on his face,
Whose troubles number with his days.

'A life of nothings, nothing-worth,
From that first nothing ere his birth
To the last nothing under earth!'

'These words,' I said, 'are like the rest;
No certain clearness, but at best
A vague suspicion of the breast:

'But if I grant, thou might'st defend
The thesis which thy words intend—
That to begin implies to end;

'Yet how should I for certain hold,
Because my memory is so cold,
That I first was in human mould?

'I cannot make this matter plain,
But I would shoot, howe'er in vain,
A random arrow from the brain.

'It may be that no life is found,
Which only to one engine bound
Falls off, but cycles always round.

'As old mythologies relate,
Some draught of Lethe might await
The slipping thro' from state to state.

'As here we find in trances, men
Forget the dream that happens then,
Until they fall in trance again.

'So might we, if our state were such
As one before, remember much,
For those two likes might meet and touch.

'But, if I lapsed from nobler place,
Some legend of a fallen race
Alone might hint of my disgrace;

'Some vague emotion of delight
In gazing up an Alpine height,
Some yearning toward the lamps of night;

'Or if thro' lower lives I came—
Tho' all experience past became
Consolidate in mind and frame—

'I might forget my weaker lot;
For is not our first year forgot?
The haunts of memory echo not.

'And men, whose reason long was blind,
From cells of madness unconfined,
Oft lose whole years of darker mind.

'Much more, if first I floated free,
As naked essence, must I be
Incompetent of memory;

'For memory dealing but with time,
And he with matter, could she climb
Beyond her own material prime?

'Moreover, something is or seems,
That touches me with mystic gleams,
Like glimpses of forgotten dreams—

'Of something felt, like something here;
Of something done, I know not where;
Such as no language may declare.'

The still voice laughed, 'I talk,' said he,
'Not with thy dreams. Suffice it thee
Thy pain is a reality.'

'But thou,' said I, 'hast missed thy mark,
Who sought'st to wreck my mortal ark,
By making all the horizon dark.

'Why not set forth, if I should do
This rashness, that which might ensue
With this old soul in organs new?

'Whatever crazy sorrow saith,
No life that breathes with human breath
Has ever truly longed for death.

' 'Tis life, whereof our nerves are scant,
O life, not death, for which we pant;
More life, and fuller, that I want.'

I ceased, and sat as one forlorn.
Then said the voice, in quiet scorn,
'Behold, it is the Sabbath morn.'

And I arose, and I released
The casement, and the light increased
With freshness in the dawning east.

Like softened airs that blowing steal,
When meres begin to uncongeal,
The sweet church bells began to peal.

On to God's house the people prest;
Passing the place where each must rest,
Each enter'd like a welcome guest.

One walked between his wife and child,
With measured footfall firm and mild,
And now and then he gravely smiled.

The prudent partner of his blood
Leaned on him, faithful, gentle, good,
Wearing the rose of womanhood.

And in their double love secure,
The little maiden walked demure,
Pacing with downward eyelids pure.

These three made unity so sweet,
My frozen heart began to beat,
Remembering its ancient heat.

I blest them, and they wandered on;
I spoke, but answer came there none;
The dull and bitter voice was gone.

A second voice was at mine ear,
A little whisper silver-clear,
A murmur, 'Be of better cheer.'

As from some blissful neighbourhood,
A notice faintly understood,
'I see the end, and know the good.'

A little hint to solace woe,
A hint, a whisper breathing low,
'I may not speak of what I know.'

Like an Æolian harp that wakes
No certain air, but overtakes
Far thought with music that it makes;

Such seemed the whisper at my side:
'What is it thou knowest, sweet voice?' I cried.
'A hidden hope,' the voice replied;

So heavenly-toned, that in that hour
From out my sullen heart a power
Broke, like the rainbow from the shower,

To feel, altho' no tongue can prove,
That every cloud, that spreads above
And veileth love, itself is love.

And forth into the fields I went,
And Nature's living motion lent
The pulse of hope to discontent.

I wondered at the bounteous hours,
The slow result of winter showers;
You scarce could see the grass for flowers.

I wondered, while I paced along;
The woods were filled so full with song,
There seemed no room for sense of wrong.

So variously seemed all things wrought,
I marvelled how the mind was brought
To anchor by one gloomy thought;

And wherefore rather I made choice
To commune with that barren voice,
Than him that said, 'Rejoice! rejoice!'

SEE WHAT A LOVELY SHELL

See what a lovely shell,
Small and pure as a pearl,
Lying close to my foot,
Frail, but a work divine,
Made so fairly well
With delicate spire and whorl,
How exquisitely minute,
A miracle of design!

What is it? a learned man
Could give it a clumsy name.
Let him name it who can,
The beauty would be the same.

The tiny cell is forlorn,
Void of the little living will
That made it stir on the shore.
Did he stand at the diamond door
Of his house in a rainbow frill?
Did he push, when he was uncurled,
A golden foot or a fairy horn
Thro' his dim water-world?

Slight, to be crushed with a tap
Of my finger-nail on the sand,
Small, but a work divine,
Frail, but of force to withstand,
Year upon year, the shock
Of cataract seas that snap
The three-decker's oaken spine
Athwart the ledges of rock,
Here on the Breton strand!

from MAUD

I HAVE LED HER HOME, MY LOVE

I have led her home, my love, my only friend.
There is none like her, none.
And never yet so warmly ran my blood
And sweetly, on and on
Calming itself to the long-wished-for end,
Full to the banks, close on the promised good.

None like her, none.
Just now the dry-tongued laurels' pattering talk
Seem'd her light foot along the garden walk,
And shook my heart to think she comes once more;
But even then I heard her close the door,
The gates of Heaven are closed, and she is gone.

There is none like her, none.
Nor will be when our summers have deceased.
O, art thou sighing for Lebanon
In the long breeze that streams to thy delicious East,
Sighing for Lebanon,
Dark cedar, tho' thy limbs have here increased,
Upon a pastoral slope as fair,

And looking to the South, and fed
With honeyed rain and delicate air,
And haunted by the starry head
Of her whose gentle will has changed my fate,
And made my life a perfumed altar-flame;
And over whom thy darkness must have spread
With such delight as theirs of old, thy great
Forefathers of the thornless garden, there
Shadowing the snow-limbed Eve from whom she came.

Here will I lie, while these long branches sway,
And you fair stars that crown a happy day
Go in and out as if at merry play,
Who am no more so all forlorn,
As when it seemed far better to be born
To labour and the mattock-hardened hand
Than nursed at ease and brought to understand
A sad astrology, the boundless plan
That makes you tyrants in your iron skies,
Innumerable, pitiless, passionless eyes,
Cold fires, yet with power to burn and brand
His nothingness into man.

But now shine on, and what care I,
Who in this stormy gulf have found a pearl
The countercharm of space and hollow sky,
And do accept my madness, and would die
To save from some slight shame one simple girl.

Would die; for sullen-seeming Death may give
More life to Love than is or ever was
In our low world, where yet 'tis sweet to live.
Let no one ask me how it came to pass;
It seems that I am happy, that to me
A livelier emerald twinkles in the grass,
A purer sapphire melts into the sea.

Not die; but live a life of truest breath,
And teach true life to fight with mortal wrongs.
Oh, why should Love, like men in drinking-songs,
Spice his fair banquet with the dust of death?
Make answer, Maud my bliss,
Maud made my Maud by that long loving kiss,
Life of my life, wilt thou not answer this?
'The dusky strand of Death inwoven here
With dear Love's tie, makes Love himself more dear.'

Is that enchanted moan only the swell
Of the long waves that roll in yonder bay?
And hark the clock within, the silver knell
Of twelve sweet hours that past in bridal white,
And die to live, long as my pulses play;
But now by this my love has closed her sight
And given false death her hand, and stol'n away
To dreamful wastes where footless fancies dwell

Among the fragments of the golden day.
May nothing there her maiden grace affright!
Dear heart, I feel with thee the drowsy spell.
My bride to be, my evermore delight,
My own heart's heart, my ownest own, farewell;
It is but for a little space I go:
And ye meanwhile far over moor and fell
Beat to the noiseless music of the night!
Has our whole earth gone nearer to the glow
Of your soft splendour that you look so bright?
I have climbed nearer out of lonely Hell.
Beat, happy stars, timing with things below,
Beat with my heart more blest than heart can tell,
Blest, but for some dark undercurrent woe
That seems to draw—but it shall not be so:
Let all be well, be well.

from MAUD

FLOWER IN THE CRANNIED WALL

Flower in the crannied wall,
I pluck you out of the crannies;—
I hold you here, root and all, in my hand,
Little flower—but if I could understand
What you are, root and all, and all in all,
I should know what God and man is.

TO VIRGIL

*Written at the Request of the Mantuans for the Nineteenth
Centenary of Virgil's Death*

Roman Virgil, thou that singest
    Ilion's lofty temples robed in fire,
Ilion falling, Rome arising,
    wars, and filial faith, and Dido's pyre;

Landscape-lover, lord of language
    more than he that sang the 'Works and Days,'
All the chosen coin of fancy
    flashing out from many a golden phrase;

Thou that singest wheat and woodland,
    tilth and vineyard, hive and horse and herd;
All the charm of all the Muses
    often flowering in a lonely word;

Poet of the happy Tityrus
    piping underneath his breechen bowers;
Poet of the poet-satyr
    whom the laughing shepherd bound with flowers;

Chanter of the Pollio, glorying
    in the blissful years again to be,
Summers of the snakeless meadow,
    unlaborious earth and oarless sea;

Thou that seest Universal
    Nature moved by Universal Mind;
Thou majestic in thy sadness
    at the doubtful doom of human kind;

Light among the vanished ages;
    star that gildest yet this phantom shore;
Golden branch amid the shadows,
    kings and realms that pass to rise no more;

Now thy Forum roars no longer,
    fallen every purple Cæsar's dome—
Tho' thine ocean-roll of rhythm
    sound forever of Imperial Rome—

Now the Rome of slaves hath perished,
    and the Rome of freemen holds her place,
I, from out the Northern Island
    sundered once from all the human race,

I salute thee, Mantovano,
    I that loved thee since my day began,
Wielder of the stateliest measure
    ever moulded by the lips of men.

BREAK, BREAK, BREAK

Break, break, break,
   On thy cold grey stones, O Sea!
And I would that my tongue could utter
   The thoughts that arise in me.

O well for the fisherman's boy,
   That he shouts with his sister at play!
O well for the sailor lad,
   That he sings in his boat on the bay!

And the stately ships go on
   To their haven under the hill;
For O for the touch of a vanished hand,
   And the sound of a voice that is still!

Break, break, break,
   At the foot of thy crags, O Sea!
But the tender grace of a day that is dead
   Will never come back to me.

CROSSING THE BAR

Sunset and evening star,
   And one clear call for me!
And may there be no moaning of the bar,
   When I put out to sea,

But such a tide as moving seems asleep,
   Too full for sound and foam,
When that which drew from out the boundless deep
   Turns again home.

Twilight and evening bell,
   And after that the dark!
And may there be no sadness of farewell,
   When I embark;

For tho' from out our bourne of Time and Place
   The flood may bear me far,
I hope to see my Pilot face to face
   When I have crost the bar.

ROBERT BROWNING

(1812-1889)

HOME-THOUGHTS FROM ABROAD

Oh, to be in England
Now that April's there,
And whoever wakes in England
Sees, some morning, unaware,
That the lowest boughs and the brush-wood sheaf
Round the elm-tree bole are in tiny leaf,
While the chaffinch sings on the orchard bough
In England—now!

And after April, when May follows,
And the whitethroat builds, and all the swallows!
Hark, where my blossomed pear-tree in the hedge
Leans to the field and scatters on the clover
Blossoms and dewdrops—at the bent spray's edge—
That's the wise thrush; he sings each song twice over,
Lest you should think he never could recapture
The first fine careless rapture!
And though the fields look rough with hoary dew,
All will be gay when noontide wakes anew
The buttercups, the little children's dower,
—Far brighter than this gaudy melon-flower!

SONG

Nay but you, who do not love her,
    Is she not pure gold, my mistress?
Holds earth aught—speak truth—above her?
    Aught like this tress, see, and this tress,
And this last fairest tress of all,
So fair, see, ere I let it fall?

Because you spend your lives in praising;
    To praise, you search the wide world over:
Then why not witness, calmly gazing,

If earth holds aught—speak truth—above her?
Above this tress, and this, I touch
But cannot praise, I love so much!

EVELYN HOPE

Beautiful Evelyn Hope is dead!
   Sit and watch by her side an hour.
That is her book-shelf, this her bed;
   She plucked that piece of geranium-flower,
Beginning to die too, in the glass;
   Little has yet been changed, I think:
The shutters are shut, no light may pass
   Save two long rays through the hinge's chink.

Sixteen years old when she died!
   Perhaps she had scarcely heard my name;
It was not her time to love: beside,
   Her life had many a hope and aim,
Duties enough and little cares,
   And now was quiet, now astir,
Till God's hand beckoned unawares,—
   And the sweet white brow is all of her.

Is it too late then, Evelyn Hope?
   What, your soul was pure and true,
The good stars met in your horoscope,
   Made you of spirit, fire and dew—
And, just because I was thrice as old
   And our paths in the world diverged so wide,
Each was naught to each, must I be told?
   We were fellow mortals, naught beside?

No, indeed! for God above
   Is great to grant, as mighty to make,
And creates the love to reward the love:
   I claim you still, for my own love's sake!
Delayed it may be for more lives yet,
   Through worlds I shall traverse, not a few:
Much is to learn, much to forget
   Ere the time be come for taking you.

But the time will come,—at last it will,
   When, Evelyn Hope, what meant (I shall say)
In the lower earth, in the years long still,

That body and soul so pure and gay?
Why your hair was amber, I shall divine,
    And your mouth of your own geranium's red—
And what you would do with me, in fine,
    In the new life come in the old one's stead.

I have lived (I shall say) so much since then,
    Given up myself so many times,
Gained me the gains of various men,
    Ransacked the ages, spoiled the climes;
Yet one thing, one, in my soul's full scope,
    Either I missed or itself missed me:
And I want and find you, Evelyn Hope!
    What is the issue? let us see!

I loved you, Evelyn, all the while!
    My heart seemed full as it could hold;
There was place and to spare for the frank young
        smile,
    And the red young mouth, and the hair's young
        gold.
So, hush,—I will give you this leaf to keep:
    See, I shut it inside the sweet cold hand!
There, that is our secret: go to sleep!
    You will wake, and remember, and understand.

*

SOLILOQUY OF THE SPANISH CLOISTER

Gr-r-r—there go, my heart's abhorrence!
    Water your damned flower-pots, do!
If hate killed men, Brother Lawrence,
    God's blood, would not mine kill you!
What? your myrtle-bush wants trimming?
    Oh, that rose has prior claims—
Needs its leaden vase filled brimming?
    Hell dry you up with its flames!

At the meal we sit together:
    Salve tibi! I must hear
Wise talk of the kind of weather,
    Sort of season, time of year:
Not a plenteous cork-crop; scarcely
    Dare we hope oak-galls, I doubt:
What's the Latin name for 'parsley'?
    What's the Greek name for Swine's Snout?

Whew! We'll have our platter burnished,
    Laid with care on our own shelf!
With a fire-new spoon we're furnished,
    And a goblet for ourself,
Rinsed like something sacrificial
    Ere 'tis fit to touch our chaps—
Marked with L. for our initial!
    (He-he! There his lily snaps!)

Saint, forsooth! While brown Dolores
    Squats outside the Convent bank
With Sanchicha, telling stories,
    Steeping tresses in the tank,
Blue-black, lustrous, thick like horsehairs,
    —Can't I see his dead eye glow,
Bright as 'twere a Barbary corsair's?
    (That is, if he'd let it show!)

When he finishes refection,
    Knife and fork he never lays
Cross-wise, to my recollection,
    As do I, in Jesu's praise.
I the Trinity illustrate,
    Drinking watered orange-pulp—
In three sips the Arian frustrate;
    While he drains his at one gulp.

Oh, those melons! if he's able
    We're to have a feast! so nice!
One goes to the Abbot's table,
    All of us get each a slice.
How go on your flowers? None double?
    Not one fruit-sort can you spy?
Strange!—And I, too, at such trouble,
    Keep them close-nipped on the sly!

There's a great text in Galatians,
    Once you trip on it, entails
Twenty-nine distinct damnations,
    One sure, if another fails:
If I trip him just a-dying,
    Sure of heaven as sure can be,
Spin him round and send him flying
    Off to hell, a Manichee?

Or, my scrofulous French novel

On grey paper with blunt type!
    Simply glance at it, you grovel
        Hand and foot in Belial's gripe:
If I double dōwn its pages
        At the woeful sixteenth print,
When he gathers his greengages,
        Ope a sieve and slip it in't?

Or, there's Satan!——one might venture
    Pledge one's soul to him, yet leave
Such a flaw in the indenture
    As he'd miss till, past retrieve,
Blasted lay that rose-acacia
    We're so proud of! *Hy, Zy, Hine . . .*
'St, there's Vespers! *Plena gratiâ*
    Ave, Virgo! Gr-r-r——you swine!

LOVE AMONG THE RUINS

Where the quiet-coloured end of evening smiles,
    Miles and miles
On the solitary pastures where our sheep
    Half-asleep
Tinkle homeward thro' the twilight, stray or stop
    As they crop——
Was the site once of a city great and gay,
    (So they say)
Of our country's very capital, its prince
    Ages since
Held his court in, gathered councils, wielding far
    Peace or war.

Now,——the country does not even boast a tree,
    As you see,
To distinguish slopes of verdure, certain rills
    From the hills
Intersect and give a name to, (else they run
    Into one,)
Where the domed and daring palace shot its spires
    Up like fires
O'er the hundred-gated circuit of a wall
    Bounding all,
Made of marble, men might march on nor be pressed,
    Twelve abreast.

And such plenty and perfection, see, of grass
    Never was!
Such a carpet as, this summer-time, o'erspreads
    And embeds
Every vestige of the city, guessed alone,
    Stock or stone—
Where a multitude of men breathed joy and woe
    Long ago;
Lust of glory pricked their hearts up, dread of shame
    Struck them tame;
And that glory and that shame alike, the gold
    Bought and sold.

Now,—the single little turret that remains
    On the plains,
By the caper overrooted, by the gourd
    Overscored,
While the patching houseleek's head of blossom winks
    Through the chinks—
Marks the basement whence a tower in ancient time
    Sprang sublime,
And a burning ring, all round, the chariots traced
    As they raced,
And the monarch and his minions and his dames
    Viewed the games.

And I know, while thus the quiet-coloured eve
    Smiles to leave
To their folding, all our many-tinkling fleece
    In such peace,
And the slopes and rills in undistinguished grey
    Melt away—
That a girl with eager eyes and yellow hair
    Waits me there
In the turret whence the charioteers caught soul
    For the goal,
When the king looked, where she looks now, breathless, dumb
    Till I come.

But he looked upon the city, every side,
    Far and wide,
All the mountains topped with temples, all the glades'
    Colonnades,
All the causeys, bridges, aqueducts,—and then,
    All the men!
When I do come, she will speak not, she will stand,

Either hand
On my shoulder, give her eyes the first embrace
Of my face,
Ere we rush, ere we extinguish sight and speech
Each on each.

In one year they sent a million fighters forth
South and North,
And they built their gods a brazen pillar high
As the sky,
Yet reserved a thousand chariots in full force—
Gold, of course.
Oh, heart! oh, blood that freezes, blood that burns!
Earth's returns
For whole centuries of folly, noise and sin!
Shut them in,
With their triumphs and their glories and the rest!
Love is best.

TWO IN THE CAMPAGNA

I wonder do you feel to-day
As I have felt, since, hand in hand,
We sat down on the grass, to stray
In spirit better through the land,
This morn of Rome and May?

For me, I touched a thought, I know,
Has tantalized me many times,
(Like turns of thread the spiders throw
Mocking across our path) for rhymes
To catch at and let go.

Help me to hold it! First it left
The yellowing fennel, run to seed
There, branching from the brickwork's cleft,
Some old tomb's ruin: yonder weed
Took up the floating weft,

Where one small orange cup amassed
Five beetles,—blind and green they grope
Among the honey-meal: and last,
Everywhere on the grassy slope
I traced it. Hold it fast!

The champaign with its endless fleece
   Of feathery grasses everywhere!
Silence and passion, joy and peace,
   An everlasting wash of air—
Rome's ghost since her decease.

Such life here, through such lengths of hours,
   Such miracles performed in play,
Such primal naked forms of flowers,
   Such letting nature have her way
While heaven looks from its towers!

How say you? Let us, O my dove,
   Let us be unashamed of soul,
As earth lies bare to heaven above!
   How is it under our control
To love or not to love?

I would that you were all to me,
   You that are just so much, no more.
Nor yours, nor mine, nor slave nor free!
   Where does the fault lie? What the core
O' the wound, since wound must be?

I would I could adopt your will,
   See with your eyes, and set my heart
Beating by yours, and drink my fill
   At your soul's springs,—your part my part
In life, for good and ill.

No. I yearn upward, touch you close,
   Then stand away. I kiss your cheek,
Catch your soul's warmth,—I pluck the rose
   And love it more than tongue can speak—
Then the good minute goes.

Already how am I so far
   Out of that minute? Must I go
Still like the thistle-ball, no bar,
   Onward, whenever light winds blow,
Fixed by no friendly star?

Just when I seemed about to learn!
   Where is the thread now? Off again!
The old trick! Only I discern—
   Infinite passion, and the pain
Of finite hearts that yearn.

PORPHYRIA'S LOVER

The rain set early in to-night,
    The sullen wind was soon awake,
It tore the elm-tops down for spite,
    And did its worst to vex the lake:
I listened with heart fit to break;
When glided in Porphyria; straight
    She shut the cold out and the storm,
And kneeled and made the cheerless grate
    Blaze up, and all the cottage warm;
Which done, she rose, and from her form
Withdrew the dripping cloak and shawl,
    And laid her soiled gloves by, untied
Her hat, and let the damp hair fall,
    And, last, she sat down by my side
And called me. When no voice replied,
She put my arm about her waist,
    And made her smooth white shoulder bare,
And all her yellow hair displaced,
    And, stooping, made my cheek lie there,
And spread, o'er all, her yellow hair,
Murmuring how she loved me—she
    Too weak, for all her heart's endeavour,
To set its struggling passion free
    From pride, and vainer ties dissever,
And give herself to me for ever.
But passion sometimes would prevail,
    Nor could to-night's gay feast restrain
A sudden thought of one so pale
    For love of her, and all in vain:
So, she was come through wind and rain.
Be sure I looked up at her eyes
    Happy and proud; at last I knew
Porphyria worshipped me; surprise
    Made my heart swell, and still it grew
While I debated what to do.
That moment she was mine, mine, fair,
    Perfectly pure and good: I found
A thing to do, and all her hair
    In one long yellow string I wound
Three times her little throat around,
And strangled her. No pain felt she;
    I am quite sure she felt no pain.
As a shut bud that holds a bee,
    I warily oped her lids: again

Laughed the blue eyes without a stain.
And I untightened next the tress
   About her neck; her cheek once more
Blushed bright beneath my burning kiss:
   I propped her head up as before,
Only, this time my shoulder bore
Her head, which droops upon it still:
   The smiling rosy little head,
So glad it has its utmost will,
   That all it scorned at once is fled,
And I, its love, am gained instead!
Porphyria's love: she guessed not how
   Her darling one wish would be heard.
And thus we sit together now,
   And all night long we have not stirred,
And yet God has not said a word!

MY LAST DUCHESS

FERRARA

That's my last Duchess painted on the wall,
Looking as if she were alive. I call
That piece a wonder, now; Frà Pandolf's hands
Worked busily a day, and there she stands.
Will 't please you sit and look at her? I said
'Frà Pandolf' by design, for never read
Strangers like you that pictured countenance,
The depth and passion of its earnest glance,
But to myself they turned (since none puts by
The curtain I have drawn for you, but I)
And seemed as they would ask me, if they durst,
How such a glance came there; so, not the first
Are you to turn and ask thus. Sir, 'twas not
Her husband's presence only, called that spot
Of joy into the Duchess' cheek: perhaps
Frà Pandolf chanced to say, 'Her mantle laps
Over my lady's wrist too much,' or 'Paint
Must never hope to reproduce the faint
Half-flush that dies along her throat: 'such stuff
Was courtesy, she thought, and cause enough
For calling up that spot of joy. She had
A heart—how shall I say?—too soon made glad,
Too easily impressed; she liked whate'er
She looked on, and her looks went everywhere.

Sir, 'twas all one! My favour at her breast,
The dropping of the daylight in the West,
The bough of cherries some officious fool
Broke in the orchard for her, the white mule
She rode with round the terrace—all and each
Would draw from her alike the approving speech,
Or blush, at least. She thanked men,—good! but thanked
Somehow—I know not how—as if she ranked
My gift of a nine-hundred-years-old name
With anybody's gift. Who'd stoop to blame
This sort of trifling? Even had you skill
In speech—(which I have not)—to make your will
Quite clear to such an one, and say, 'Just this
Or that in you disgusts me; here you miss,
Or there exceed the mark'—and if she let
Herself be lessoned so, nor plainly set
Her wits to yours, forsooth, and made excuse,
—E'en then would be some stooping; and I choose
Never to stoop. Oh sir, she smiled, no doubt,
Whene'er I passed her; but who passed without
Much the same smile? This grew; I gave commands;
Then all smiles stopped together. There she stands
As if alive. Will 't please you rise? We'll meet
The company below, then. I repeat,
The Count your master's known munificence
Is ample warrant that no just pretence
Of mine for dowry will be disallowed;
Though his fair daughter's self, as I avowed
At starting, is my object. Nay, we'll go
Together down, sir. Notice Neptune, though,
Taming a sea-horse, thought a rarity,
Which Claus of Innsbruck cast in bronze for me!

PROSPICE

Fear death? to feel the fog in my throat,
    The mist in my face,
When the snows begin, and the blasts denote
    I am nearing the place,
The power of the night, the press of the storm,
    The post of the foe;
Where he stands, the Arch Fear in a visible form,
    Yet the strong man must go:
For the journey is done and the summit attained,
    And the barriers fall,

Though a battle's to fight ere the guerdon be gained,
   The reward of it all.
I was ever a fighter, so—one fight more,
   The best and the last!
I would hate that death bandaged my eyes, and forbore,
   And bade me creep past.
No! let me taste the whole of it, fare like my peers
   The heroes of old,
Bear the brunt, in a minute pay glad life's arrears
   Of pain, darkness and cold.
For sudden the worst turns the best to the brave,
   The black minute's at end,
And the elements' rage, the fiend-voices that rave,
   Shall dwindle, shall blend,
Shall change, shall become first a peace out of pain,
   Then a light, then thy breast,
O thou soul of my soul! I shall clasp thee again,
   And with God be the rest!

YOUTH AND ART

It once might have been, once only:
   We lodged in a street together,
You, a sparrow on the housetop lonely,
   I, a lone she-bird of his feather.

Your trade was with sticks and clay,
   You thumbed, thrust, patted and polished,
Then laughed 'They will see some day
   Smith made, and Gibson demolished.'

My business was song, song, song;
   I chirped, cheeped, trilled and twittered,
'Kate Brown's on the boards ere long,
   And Grisi's existence embittered!'

I earned no more by a warble
   Than you by a sketch in plaster;
You wanted a piece of marble,
   I needed a music-master.

We studied hard in our styles,
   Chipped each at a crust like Hindoos,
For air, looked out on the tiles,
   For fun, watched each other's windows.

You lounged, like a boy of the South,
    Cap and blouse—nay, a bit of beard too;
Or you got it, rubbing your mouth
    With fingers the clay adhered to.

And I—soon managed to find
    Weak points in the flower-fence facing,
Was forced to put up a blind
    And be safe in my corset-lacing.

No harm! It was not my fault
    If you never turned your eye's tail up
As I shook upon E *in alt*,
    Or ran the chromatic scale up:

For spring bade the sparrows pair,
    And the boys and girls gave guesses,
And stalls in our street looked rare
    With bulrush and watercresses.

Why did not you pinch a flower
    In a pellet of clay and fling it?
hy did not I put a power
    Of thanks in a look, or sing it?

I did look, sharp as a lynx
    (And yet the memory rankles)
When models arrived, some minx
    Tripped up-stairs, she and her ankles.

But I think I gave you as good!
    'That foreign fellow,—who can know
How she pays, in a playful mood,
    For his tuning her that piano?'

Could you say so, and never say
    'Suppose we join hands and fortunes,
And I fetch her from over the way,
    Her, piano, and long tunes and short tunes'?

No, no: you would not be rash,
    Nor I rasher and something over:
You've to settle yet Gibson's hash,
    And Grisi yet lives in clover.

But you meet the Prince at the Board,
    I'm queen myself at *bals-paré*,

I've married a rich old lord,
    And you're dubbed knight and an R.A.

Each life unfulfilled, you see;
    It hangs still, patchy and scrappy:
We have not sighed deep, laughed free,
    Starved, feasted, despaired,—been happy.

And nobody calls you a dunce,
    And people suppose me clever:
This could but have happened once,
    And we missed it, lost it forever.

ONE WORD MORE

TO E. B. B.

Epilogue to *Men and Women*

There they are, my fifty men and women
Naming me the fifty poems finished!
Take them, Love, the book and me together:
Where the heart lies, let the brain lie also.

Rafael made a century of sonnets,
Made and wrote them in a certain volume
Dinted with the silver-pointed pencil
Else he only used to draw Madonnas:
These, the world might view—but one, the volume.
Who that one, you ask? Your heart instructs you.
Did she live and love it all her lifetime?
Did she drop, his lady of the sonnets,
Die, and let it drop beside her pillow
Where it lay in place of Rafael's glory,
Rafael's cheek so duteous and so loving—
Cheek, the world was wont to hail a painter's,
Rafael's cheek, her love had turned a poet's?

You and I would rather read that volume,
(Taken to his beating bosom by it)
Lean and list the bosom-beats of Rafael,
Would we not? then wonder at Madonnas—
Her, San Sisto names, and Her, Foligno,
Her, that visits Florence in a vision,
Her, that's left with lilies in the Louvre—
Seen by us and all the world in circle.

You and I will never read that volume.
Guido Reni, like his own eye's apple
Guarded long the treasure-book and loved it.
Guido Reni dying, all Bologna
Cried, and the world cried too, 'Ours, the treasure!'
Suddenly, as rare things will, it vanished.

Dante once prepared to paint an angel:
Whom to please? You whisper 'Beatrice.'
While he mused and traced it and retraced it,
(Peradventure with a pen corroded
Still by drops of that hot ink he dipped for,
When, his left-hand i' the hair o' the wicked,
Back he held the brow and pricked its stigma,
Bit into the live man's flesh for parchment,
Loosed him, laughed to see the writing rankle,
Let the wretch go festering through Florence)—
Dante, who loved well because he hated,
Hated wickedness that hinders loving,
Dante standing, studying his angel,—
In there broke the folk of his Inferno.
Says he—'Certain people of importance'
(Such he gave his daily dreadful line to)
'Entered and would seize, forsooth, the poet.'
Says the poet—'Then I stopped my painting.'

You and I would rather see that angel,
Painted by the tenderness of Dante,
Would we not?—than read a fresh Inferno.

You and I will never see that picture.
While he mused on love and Beatrice,
While he softened o'er his outlined angel, .
In they broke, those 'people of importance:'
We and Bice bear the loss for ever.

What of Rafael's sonnets, Dante's picture?
This: no artist lives and loves, that longs not
Once, and only once, and for one only,
(Ah, the prize!) to find his love a language
Fit and fair and simple and sufficient—
Using nature that's an art to others,
Not, this one time, art that's turned his nature.
Ay, of all the artists living, loving,
None but would forego his proper dowry,—
Does he paint? he fain would write a poem,—

Does he write? he fain would paint a picture,
Put to proof art alien to the artist's,
Once, and only once, and for one only,
So to be the man and leave the artist,
Gain the man's joy, miss the artist's sorrow.

Wherefore? Heaven's gift takes earth's abatement!
He who smites the rock and spreads the water,
Bidding drink and live a crowd beneath him,
Even he, the minute makes immortal,
Proves, perchance, but mortal in the minute,
Desecrates, belike, the deed in doing.
While he smites, how can he but remember,
So he smote before, in such a peril,
When they stood and mocked—'Shall smiting help us?'
When they drank and sneered—'A stroke is easy!'
When they wiped their mouths and went their journey,
Throwing him for thanks—'But drought was pleasant.'
Thus old memories mar the actual triumph;
Thus the doing savours of disrelish;
Thus achievement lacks a gracious somewhat;
O'er-importuned brows becloud the mandate,
Carelessness or consciousness—the gesture.
For he bears an ancient wrong about him,
Sees and knows again those phalanxed faces,
Hears, yet one time more, the 'customed prelude—
'How shouldst thou, of all men, smite, and save us?'
Guesses what is like to prove the sequel—
'Egypt's flesh-pots—nay, the drought was better.'

Oh, the crowd must have emphatic warrant!
Theirs, the Sinai-forehead's cloven brilliance,
Right-arm's rod-sweep, tongue's imperial fiat.
Never dares the man put off the prophet.

Did he love one face from out the thousands,
(Were she Jethro's daughter, white and wifely,
Were she but the Æthiopian bondslave,)
He would envy yon dumb patient camel,
Keeping a reserve of scanty water
Meant to save his own life in the desert;
Ready in the desert to deliver
(Kneeling down to let his breast be opened)
Hoard and life together for his mistress.

I shall never, in the years remaining,
Paint you pictures, no, nor carve you statues,

Make you music that should all-express me;
So it seems: I stand on my attainment.
This of verse alone, one life allows me;
Verse and nothing else have I to give you.
Other heights in other lives, God willing:
All the gifts from all the heights, your own, Love!

Yet a semblance of resource avails us—
Shade so finely touched, love's sense must seize it.
Take these lines, look lovingly and nearly,
Lines I write the first time and the last time.
He who works in fresco, steals a hair-brush,
Curbs the liberal hand, subservient proudly,
Cramps his spirit, crowds its all in little,
Makes a strange art of an art familiar,
Fills his lady's missal-marge with flowerets.
He who blows thro' bronze, may breathe thro' silver,
Fitly serenade a slumbrous princess.
He who writes, may write for once as I do.

Love, you saw me gather men and women,
Live or dead or fashioned by my fancy,
Enter each and all, and use their service,
Speak from every mouth,—the speech, a poem.
Hardly shall I tell my joys and sorrows,
Hopes and fears, belief and disbelieving:
I am mine and yours—the rest be all men's,
Karshish, Cleon, Norbert and the fifty.
Let me speak this once in my true person,
Not as Lippo, Roland or Andrea,
Though the fruit of speech be just this sentence:
Pray you, look on these my men and women,
Take and keep my fifty poems finished;
Where my heart lies, let my brain lie also!
Poor the speech; be how I speak, for all things.

Not but that you know me! Lo, the moon's self!
Here in London, yonder late in Florence,
Still we find her face, the thrice-transfigured.
Curving on a sky imbued with colour,
Drifted over Fiesole by twilight,
Came she, our new crescent of a hair's-breadth.
Full she flared it, lamping Samminiato,
Rounder 'twixt the cypresses and rounder,
Perfect till the nightingales applauded.
Now, a piece of her old self, impoverished,

Hard to greet, she traverses the house-roofs,
Hurries with unhandsome thrift of silver,
Goes dispiritedly, glad to finish.

What, there's nothing in the moon noteworthy?
Nay: for if that moon could love a mortal,
Use, to charm him (so to fit a fancy),
All her magic ('tis the old sweet mythos),
She would turn a new side to her mortal,
Side unseen of herdsman, huntsman, steersman—
Blank to Zoroaster on his terrace,
Blind to Galileo on his turret,
Dumb to Homer, dumb to Keats—him, even!
Think, the wonder of the moonstruck mortal—
When she turns round, comes again in heaven,
Opens out anew for worse or better!
Proves she like some portent of an iceberg
Swimming full upon the ship it founders,
Hungry with huge teeth of splintered crystals?
Proves she as the paved work of a sapphire
Seen by Moses when he climbed the mountains?
Moses, Aaron, Nadab and Abihu
Climbed and saw the very God, the Highest,
Stand upon the paved work of a sapphire.
Like the bodied heaven in his clearness
Shone the stone, the sapphire of that paved work,
When they ate and drank and saw God also!

What were seen? None knows, none ever shall know.
Only this is sure—the sight were other,
Not the moon's same side, born late in Florence,
Dying now impoverished here in London.
God be thanked, the meanest of his creatures
Boasts two soul-sides, one to face the world with,
One to show a woman when he loves her!

This I say of me, but think of you, Love!
This to you—yourself my moon of poets!
Ah, but that's the world's side, there's the wonder,
Thus they see you, praise you, think they know you!
Out of my own self, I dare to phrase it.
But the best is when I glide from out them,
Cross a step or two of dubious twilight,
Come out on the other side, the novel
Silent silver lights and darks undreamed of,
Where I hush and bless myself with silence.

Oh, their Rafael of the dear Madonnas,
Oh, their Dante of the dread Inferno,
Wrote one song—and in my brain I sing it,
Drew one angel—borne, see, on my bosom!

RABBI BEN EZRA

Grow old along with me!
  The best is yet to be,
The last of life, for which the first was made:
    Our times are in His hand
    Who saith 'A whole I planned,
'Youth shows but half; trust God: see all nor be afraid!'

Not that, amassing flowers,
  Youth signed 'Which rose make ours,
'Which lily leave and then as best recall?'
    Not that, admiring stars,
    It yearned 'Nor Jove, nor Mars;
'Mine be some figured flame which blends, transcends them
    all!'

Not for such hopes and fears
  Annulling youth's brief years,
Do I remonstrate: folly wide the mark!
    Rather I prize the doubt
    Low kinds exist without,
Finished and finite clods, untroubled by a spark.

Poor vaunt of life indeed,
  Were man but formed to feed
On joy, to solely seek and find and feast:
    Such feasting ended, then
    As sure an end to men;
Irks care the crop-full bird? Frets doubt the maw-crammed
    beast?

Rejoice we are allied
  To That which doth provide
And not partake, effect and not receive!
    A spark disturbs our clod;
    Nearer we hold of God
Who gives, than of His tribes that take, I must believe.

Then, welcome each rebuff
  That turns earth's smoothness rough,

Each sting that bids nor sit nor stand but go!
    Be our joys three-parts pain!
    Strive, and hold cheap the strain;
I earn, nor account the pang; dare, never grudge the throe!

    For thence,—a paradox
    Which comforts while it mocks,—
Shall life succeed in that it seems to fail:
    What I aspired to be,
    And was not, comforts me:
A brute I might have been, but would not sink i' the scale.

    What is he but a brute
    Whose flesh has soul to suit,
Whose spirit works lest arms and legs want play?
    To man, propose this test—
    Thy body at its best,
How far can that project thy soul on its lone way?

    Yet gifts should prove their use:
    I own the Past profuse
Of power each side, perfection every turn:
    Eyes, ears took in their dole,
    Brain treasured up the whole;
Should not the heart beat once 'How good to live and learn?'

    Not once beat 'Praise be Thine!
    'I see the whole design,
'I, who saw power, see now love perfect too:
    'Perfect I call Thy plan:
    'Thanks that I was a man!
'Maker, remake, complete,—I trust what Thou shalt do!'

    For pleasant is this flesh;
    Our soul, in its rose-mesh
Pulled ever to the earth, still yearns for rest;
    Would we some prize might hold
    To match those manifold
Possessions of the brute,—gain most, as we did best!

    Let us not always say
    'Spite of this flesh to-day
'I strove, made head, gained ground upon the whole!'
    As the bird wings and sings,
    Let us cry 'All good things
Are ours, nor soul helps flesh more, now, than flesh helps
    soul!'

Therefore I summon age
To grant youth's heritage,
Life's struggle having so far reached its term:
Thence shall I pass, approved
A man, for aye removed
From the developed brute; a god though in the germ.

And I shall thereupon
Take rest, ere I be gone
Once more on my adventure brave and new:
Fearless and unperplexed,
When I wage battle next,
What weapons to select, what armour to indue.

Youth ended, I shall try
My gain or loss thereby;
Leave the fire ashes, what survives is gold:
And I shall weigh the same,
Give life its praise or blame:
Young, all lay in dispute; I shall know, being old.

For note, when evening shuts,
A certain moment cuts
The deed off, calls the glory from the grey:
A whisper from the west
Shoots—'Add this to the rest,
'Take it and try its worth: here dies another day.'

So, still within this life,
Though lifted o'er its strife,
Let me discern, compare, pronounce at last,
'This rage was right i' the main,
'That acquiescence vain:
'The Future I may face now I have proved the Past.'

For more is not reserved
To man, with soul just nerved
To act to-morrow what he learns to-day:
Here, work enough to watch
The Master work, and catch
Hints of the proper craft, tricks of the tool's true play.

As it was better, youth
Should strive, through acts uncouth,
Toward making, then repose on aught found made:
So, better, age, exempt

From strife, should know, than tempt
Further. Thou waitedest age: wait death nor be afraid!

Enough now, if the Right
And Good and Infinite
Be named here, as thou callest thy hand thine own,
With knowledge absolute,
Subject to no dispute
From fools that crowded youth, nor let thee feel alone.

Be there, for once and all,
Severed great minds from small,
Announced to each his station in the Past!
Was I, the world arraigned,
Were they, my soul disdained,
Right? Let age speak the truth and give us peace at last!

Now, who shall arbitrate?
Ten men love what I hate,
Shun what I follow, slight what I receive;
Ten, who in ears and eyes
Match me: we all surmise,
They this thing, and I that: whom shall my soul believe?

Not on the vulgar mass
Called 'work,' must sentence pass,
Things done, that took the eye and had the price;
O'er which, from level stand,
The low world laid its hand,
Found straightway to its mind, could value in a trice:

But all, the world's coarse thumb
And finger failed to plumb,
So passed in making up the main account;
All instincts immature,
All purposes unsure,
That weighed not as his work, yet swelled the man's amount:

Thoughts hardly to be packed
Into a narrow act,
Fancies that broke through language and escaped;
All I could never be,
All, men ignored in me,
This, I was worth to God, whose wheel the pitcher shaped.

Ay, note that Potter's wheel,
That metaphor! and feel

Why time spins fast, why passive lies our clay,—
    Thou, to whom fools propound,
    When the wine makes its round,
Since life fleets, all is change; the Past gone, seize to-day!

    Fool! All that is, at all,
    Lasts ever, past recall;
Earth changes, but thy soul and God stand sure:
    What entered into thee,
    That was, is, and shall be:
Time's wheel runs back or stops: Potter and clay endure.

    He fixed thee mid this dance
    Of plastic circumstance,
This Present, thou, forsooth, wouldst fain arrest:
    Machinery just meant
    To give thy soul its bent,
Try thee and turn thee forth, sufficiently impressed.

    What though the earlier grooves
    Which ran the laughing loves
Around thy base, no longer pause and press?
    What though, about thy rim,
    Skull-things in order grim
Grow out, in graver mood, obey the sterner stress?

    Look not thou down but up!
    To uses of a cup,
The festal board, lamp's flash and trumpet's peal,
    The new wine's foaming flow,
    The Master's lips a-glow!
Thou, heaven's consummate cup, what need'st thou with
    earth's wheel?

    But I need, now as then,
    Thee, God, who mouldest men;
And since, not even while the whirl was worst,
    Did I,—to the wheel of life
    With shapes and colours rife,
Bound dizzily,—mistake my end, to slake Thy thirst:

    So, take and use Thy work:
    Amend what flaws may lurk,
What strain o' the stuff, what warpings past the aim!
    My times be in Thy hand!
    Perfect the cup as planned!
Let age approve of youth, and death complete the same!

ANDREA DEL SARTO

Called "The Faultless Painter"

But do not let us quarrel any more,
No, my Lucrezia; bear with me for once:
Sit down and all shall happen as you wish.
You turn your face, but does it bring your heart?
I'll work then for your friend's friend, never fear,
Treat his own subject after his own way,
Fix his own time, accept too his own price,
And shut the money into this small hand
When next it takes mine. Will it? tenderly?
Oh, I'll content him,—but to-morrow, Love!
I often am much wearier than you think,
This evening more than usual, and it seems
As if—forgive now—should you let me sit
Here by the window with your hand in mine
And look a half-hour forth on Fiesole,
Both of one mind, as married people use,
Quietly, quietly, the evening through,
I might get up to-morrow to my work
Cheerful and fresh as ever. Let us try.
To-morrow, how you shall be glad for this!
Your soft hand is a woman of itself,
And mine the man's bared breast she curls inside.
Don't count the time lost, neither; you must serve
For each of the five pictures we require:
It saves a model. So! keep looking so—
My serpenting beauty, rounds on rounds!
—How could you ever prick those perfect ears,
Even to put the pearl there! oh, so sweet—
My face, my moon, my everybody's moon,
Which everybody looks on and calls his,
And, I suppose, is looked on by in turn,
While she looks—no one's: very dear, no less.
You smile? why, there's my picture ready made,
There's what we painters call our harmony!
A common greyness silvers everything,—
All in a twilight, you and I alike
—You, at the point of your first pride in me
(That's gone, you know),—but I, at every point;
My youth, my hope, my art, being all toned down
To yonder sober pleasant Fiesole.
There's the bell chinking from the chapel-top;
That length of convent-wall across the way

Holds the trees safer, huddled more inside;
The last monk leaves the garden; days decrease
And autumn grows, autumn in everything.
Eh? the whole seems to fall into a shape
As if I saw alike my work and self
And all that I was born to be and do,
A twilight-piece. Love, we are in God's hand.
How strange now, looks the life he makes us lead;
So free we seem, so fettered fast we are!
I feel he laid the fetter: let it lie!
This chamber for example—turn your head—
All that's behind us! You don't understand
Nor care to understand about my art,
But you can hear at least when people speak:
And that cartoon, the second from the door
—It is the thing, Love! so such things should be—
Behold Madonna!—I am bold to say.
I can do with my pencil what I know,
What I see, what at bottom of my heart
I wish for, if I ever wish so deep—
Do easily, too—when I say, perfectly,
I do not boast, perhaps: yourself are judge,
Who listened to the Legate's talk last week,
And just as much they used to say in France.
At any rate 'tis easy, all of it!
No sketches first, no studies, that's long past:
I do what many dream of all their lives,
—Dream? strive to do, and agonize to do,
And fail in doing. I could count twenty such
On twice your fingers, and not leave this town,
Who strive—you don't know how the others strive
To paint a little thing like that you smeared
Carelessly passing with your robes afloat,—
Yet do much less, so much less, Someone says,
(I know his name, no matter) so much less!
Well, less is more, Lucrezia: I am judged.
There burns a truer light of God in them,
In their vexed beating stuffed and stopped-up brain,
Heart, or whate'er else, than goes on to prompt
This low-pulsed forthright craftsman's hand of mine.
Their works drop groundward, but themselves, I know,
Reach many a time a heaven that's shut to me,
Enter and take their place there sure enough,
Though they come back and cannot tell the world.
My works are nearer heaven, but I sit here.
The sudden blood of these men! at a word—

Praise them, it boils, or blame them, it boils too.
I, painting from myself and to myself,
Know what I do, am unmoved by men's blame
Or their praise either. Somebody remarks
Morello's outline there is wrongly traced,
His hue mistaken; what of that? or else,
Rightly traced and well ordered; what of that?
Speak as they please, what does the mountain care?
Ah, but a man's reach should exceed his grasp,
Or what's a heaven for? All is silver-grey,
Placid and perfect with my art: the worse!
I know both what I want and what might gain,
And yet how profitless to know, to sigh
'Had I been two, another and myself,
Our head would have o'erlooked the world!' No doubt.
Yonder's a work, now, of that famous youth
The Urbinate who died five years ago.
('Tis copied, George Vasari sent it me.)
Well, I can fancy how he did it all,
Pouring his soul, with kings and popes to see,
Reaching, that heaven might so replenish him,
Above and through his art—for it gives way;
That arm is wrongly put—and there again—
A fault to pardon in the drawing's lines,
Its body, so to speak: its soul is right,
He means right—that, a child may understand.
Still, what an arm! and I could alter it:
But all the play, the insight and the stretch—
Out of me, out of me! And wherefore out?
Had you enjoined them on me, given me soul,
We might have risen to Rafael, I and you!
Nay, Love, you did give all I asked, I think—
More than I merit, yes, by many times.
But had you—oh, with the same perfect brow,
And perfect eyes, and more than perfect mouth,
And the low voice my soul hears, as a bird
The fowler's pipe, and follows to the snare—
Had you, with these the same, but brought a mind!
Some women do so. Had the mouth there urged
'God and the glory! never care for gain.
The present by the future, what is that?
Live for fame, side by side with Agnolo!
Rafael is waiting: up to God all three!'
I might have done it for you. So it seems:
Perhaps not. All is as God overrules.
Beside, incentives come from the soul's self;

The rest avail not. Why do I need you?
What wife had Rafael, or has Agnolo?
In this world, who can do a thing, will not;
And who would do it, cannot, I perceive:
Yet the will's somewhat—somewhat, too, the power—
And thus we half-men struggle. At the end,
God, I conclude, compensates, punishes.
'Tis safer for me, if the award be strict,
That I am something underrated here,
Poor this long while, despised, to speak the truth.
I dared not, do you know, leave home all day,
For fear of chancing on the Paris lords.
The best is when they pass and look aside;
But they speak sometimes; I must bear it all.
Well may they speak! That Francis, that first time,
And that long festal year at Fontainebleau!
I surely then could sometimes leave the ground,
Put on the glory, Rafael's daily wear,
In that humane great monarch's golden look,—
One finger in his beard or twisted curl
Over his mouth's good mark that made the smile,
One arm about my shoulder, round my neck,
The jingle of his gold chain in my ear,
I painting proudly with his breath on me,
All his court round him, seeing with his eyes,
Such frank French eyes, and such a fire of souls
Profuse, my hand kept plying by those hearts,—
And, best of all, this, this, this face beyond,
This in the background, waiting on my work,
To crown the issue with a last reward!
A good time, was it not, my kingly days?
And had you not grown restless . . . but I know—
'Tis done and past; 'twas right, my instinct said;
Too live the life grew, golden and not grey,
And I'm the weak-eyed bat no sun should tempt
Out of the grange whose four walls make his world.
How could it end in any other way?
You called me, and I came home to your heart.
The triumph was—to reach and stay there; since
I reached it ere the triumph, what is lost?
Let my hands frame your face in your hair's gold,
You beautiful Lucrezia that are mine!
'Rafael did this, Andrea painted that;
The Roman's is the better when you pray,
But still the other's Virgin was his wife—'
Men will excuse me. I am glad to judge

Both pictures in your presence; clearer grows
My better fortune, I resolve to think.
For, do you know, Lucrezia, as God lives,
Said one day Agnolo, his very self,
To Rafael . . . I have known it all these years . . .
(When the young man was flaming out his thoughts
Upon a palace-wall for Rome to see,
Too lifted up in heart because of it)
'Friend, there's a certain sorry little scrub
Goes up and down our Florence, none cares how,
Who, were he set to plan and execute
As you are, pricked on by your popes and kings,
Would bring the sweat into that brow of yours!'
To Rafael's!—And indeed the arm is wrong.
I hardly dare . . . yet, only you to see,
Give the chalk here—quick, thus the line should go!
Ay, but the soul! he's Rafael! rub it out!
Still, all I care for, if he spoke the truth,
(What he? why, who but Michel Agnolo?
Do you forget already words like those?)
If really there was such a chance, so lost,—
Is, whether you're—not grateful—but more pleased.
Well, let me think so. And you smile indeed!
This hour has been an hour! Another smile?
If you would sit thus by me every night
I should work better, do you comprehend?
I mean that I should earn more, give you more.
See, it is settled dusk now; there's a star;
Morello's gone, the watch-lights show the wall,
The cue-owls speak the name we call them by.
Come from the window, love,—come in, at last,
Inside the melancholy little house
We built to be so gay with. God is just.
King Francis may forgive me: oft at nights
When I look up from painting, eyes tired out,
The walls become illumined, brick from brick
Distinct, instead of mortar, fierce bright gold,
That gold of his I did cement them with!
Let us but love each other. Must you go?
That Cousin here again? he waits outside?
Must see you—you, and not with me? Those loans?
More gaming debts to pay? you smiled for that?
Well, let smiles buy me! have you more to spend?
While hand and eye and something of a heart
Are left me, work's my ware, and what's it worth?
I'll pay my fancy. Only let me sit

The grey remainder of the evening out,
Idle, you call it, and muse perfectly
How I could paint, were I but back in France,
One picture, just one more—the Virgin's face,
Not yours this time! I want you at my side
To hear them—that is, Michel Agnolo—
Judge all I do and tell you of its worth.
Will you? To-morrow, satisfy your friend.
I take the subjects for his corridor,
Finish the portrait out of hand—there, there,
And throw him in another thing or two
If he demurs; the whole should prove enough
To pay for this same Cousin's freak. Beside,
What's better and what's all I care about,
Get you the thirteen scudi for the ruff!
Love, does that please you? Ah, but what does he,
The Cousin! what does he to please you more?

I am grown peaceful as old age to-night.
I regret little, I would change still less.
Since there my past life lies, why alter it?
The very wrong to Francis!—it is true
I took his coin, was tempted and complied,
And built this house and sinned, and all is said.
My father and my mother died of want.
Well, had I riches of my own? you see
How one gets rich! Let each one bear his lot.
They were born poor, lived poor, and poor they died:
And I have laboured somewhat in my time
And not been paid profusely. Some good son
Paint my two hundred pictures—let him try!
No doubt, there's something strikes a balance. Yes,
You loved me quite enough, it seems to-night.
This must suffice me here. What would one have?
In heaven, perhaps, new chances, one more chance—
Four great walls in the New Jerusalem
Meted on each side by the angel's reed,
For Leonard, Rafael, Agnolo and me
To cover—the three first without a wife,
While I have mine! So—still they overcome
Because there's still Lucrezia,—as I choose.

Again the Cousin's whistle! Go, my Love.

EMILY BRONTE

(1818-1848)

STANZAS *

Often rebuked, yet always back returning
    To those first feelings that were born with me,
And leaving busy chase of wealth and learning
    For idle dreams of things which cannot be:

To-day, I will seek not the shadowy region;
    Its unsustaining vastness waxes drear;
And visions rising, legion after legion,
    Bring the unreal world too strangely near.

I'll walk, but not in old heroic traces,
    And not in paths of high morality,
And not among the half-distinguished faces,
    The clouded forms of long-past history.

I'll walk where my own nature would be leading:
    It vexes me to choose another guide:
Where the grey flocks in ferny glens are feeding;
    Where the wild wind blows on the mountain-side.

What have those lonely mountains worth revealing?
    More glory and more grief than I can tell:
The earth that wakes *one* human heart to feeling
    Can centre both the worlds of Heaven and Hell.

THE VISIONARY

Silent is the house: all are laid asleep:
One alone looks out o'er the snow-wreaths deep,
Watching every cloud, dreading every breeze
That whirls the 'wildering drift, and bends the groaning
    trees.

* The original manuscript of this poem has never been found, and
some scholars believe that the author is Charlotte, not Emily, Brontë.

Cheerful is the hearth, soft the matted floor;
Not one shivering gust creeps through pane or door;
The little lamp burns straight, its rays shoot strong and far:
I trim it well, to be the wanderer's guiding-star.

Frown, my haughty sire! chide, my angry dame!
Set your slaves to spy; threaten me with shame:
But neither sire nor dame, nor prying serf shall know
What angel nightly tracks that waste of frozen snow.

What I love shall come like visitant of air,
Safe in secret power from lurking human snare;
Who loves me, no word of mine shall e'er betray,
Though for faith unstained my life must forfeit pay.

Burn then, little lamp; glimmer straight and clear—
Hush! a rustling wing stirs, methinks, the air:
He for whom I wait thus ever comes to me:
Strange Power! I trust thy might; trust thou my constancy.

THE NIGHT IS DARKENING ROUND ME

The night is darkening round me,
The wild winds coldly blow;
But a tyrant spell has bound me
And I cannot, cannot go.

The giant trees are bending
Their bare boughs weighed with snow,
And the storm is fast descending
And yet I cannot go.

Clouds beyond clouds above me,
Wastes beyond wastes below;
But nothing drear can move me;
I will not, cannot go.

PLEAD FOR ME

O thy bright eyes must answer now,
When Reason, with a scornful brow,
Is mocking at my overthrow;
O thy sweet tongue must plead for me
And tell why I have chosen thee!

Stern Reason is to judgement come
Arrayed in all her forms of gloom:
Wilt thou my advocate be dumb?
No, radiant angel, speak and say
Why I did cast the world away;

Why I have persevered to shun
The common paths that others run;
And on a strange road journeyed on
Heedless alike of Wealth and Power—
Of Glory's wreath and Pleasure's flower.

These once indeed seemed Beings divine,
And they perchance heard vows of mine
And saw my offerings on their shrine—
But, careless gifts are seldom prized,
And mine were worthily despised;

So with a ready heart I swore
To seek their altar-stone no more,
And gave my spirit to adore
Thee, ever present, phantom thing—
My slave, my comrade, and my King!

A slave because I rule thee still,
Incline thee to my changeful will
And make thy influence good or ill—
A comrade, for by day and night
Thou art my intimate delight—

My Darling Pain that wounds and sears
And wrings a blessing out from tears
By deadening me to real cares;
And yet, a king—though prudence well
Have taught thy subject to rebel.

And am I wrong to worship where
Faith cannot doubt nor Hope despair
Since my own soul can grant my prayer?
Speak, God of Visions, plead for me
And tell why I have chosen thee!

FALL, LEAVES, FALL

Fall, leaves, fall; die, flowers, away;
Lengthen night and shorten day;
Every leaf speaks bliss to me,
Fluttering from the autumn tree.

I shall smile when wreaths of snow
Blossom where the rose should grow;
I shall sing when night's decay
Ushers in a drearier day.

REMEMBRANCE

[R. Alcona to J. Brenzaida]

Cold in the earth, and the deep snow piled above thee!
Far, far removed, cold in the dreary grave!
Have I forgot, my Only Love, to love thee,
Severed at last by Time's all-wearing wave?

Now, when alone, do my thoughts no longer hover
Over the mountains on Angora's shore;
Resting their wings where heath and fern-leaves cover
That noble heart for ever, ever more?

Cold in the earth, and fifteen wild Decembers
From those brown hills have melted into spring—
Faithful indeed is the spirit that remembers
After such years of change and suffering!

Sweet Love of youth, forgive if I forget thee
While the World's tide is bearing me along:
Sterner desires and darker hopes beset me,
Hopes which obscure but cannot do thee wrong.

No other Sun has lightened up my heaven;
No other Star has ever shone for me:
All my life's bliss from thy dear life was given—
All my life's bliss is in the grave with thee.

But when the days of golden dreams had perished
And even Despair was powerless to destroy,
Then did I learn how existence could be cherished,
Strengthened and fed without the aid of joy;

Then did I check the tears of useless passion,
Weaned my young soul from yearning after thine;
Sternly denied its burning wish to hasten
Down to that tomb already more than mine!

And even yet, I dare not let it languish,
Dare not indulge in Memory's rapturous pain;
Once drinking deep of that divinest anguish,
How could I seek the empty world again?

THE TWO CHILDREN

I

Heavy hangs the raindrop
From the burdened spray;
Heavy broods the damp mist
On uplands far away;

Heavy looms the dull sky,
Heavy rolls the sea—
And heavy beats the young heart
Beneath that lonely tree.

Never has a blue streak
Cleft the clouds since morn—
Never has his grim Fate
Smiled since he was born.

Frowning on the infant,
Shadowing childhood's joy,
Guardian angel knows not
That melancholy boy.

Day is passing swiftly
Its sad and sombre prime;
Youth is fast invading
Sterner manhood's time.

All the flowers are praying
For sun before they close,
And he prays too, unknowing,
That sunless human rose!

Blossoms, that the west wind
Has never wooed to blow,
Scentless are your petals,
Your dew as cold as snow.

Soul, where kindred kindness

No early promise woke,
Barren is your beauty
As weed upon the rock.

Wither, Brothers, wither,
You were vainly given—
Earth reserves no blessing
For the unblessed of Heaven!

II

Child of Delight! with sunbright hair,
And seablue, seadeep eyes;
Spirit of Bliss, what brings thee here,
Beneath these sullen skies?

Thou shouldst live in eternal spring,
Where endless day is never dim;
Why, seraph, has thy erring wing
Borne thee down to weep with him?

'Ah, not from heaven am I descended,
And I do not come to mingle tears;
But sweet is day, though with shadows blended;
And, though clouded, sweet are youthful years.

'I, the image of light and gladness,
Saw and pitied that mournful boy,
And I swore to take his gloomy sadness,
And give to him my beamy joy.

'Heavy and dark the night is closing;
Heavy and dark may its biding be:
Better for all from grief reposing,
And better for all who watch like me.

'Guardian angel, he lacks no longer;
Evil fortune he need not fear:
Fate is strong, but Love is stronger;
And more unsleeping than angel's care.'

NO COWARD SOUL IS MINE

No coward soul is mine
No trembler in the world's storm-troubled sphere
I see Heaven's glories shine,
And Faith shines equal arming me from Fear.

O God within my breast,
Almighty ever-present Deity!
Life, that in me hast rest
As I Undying Life, have power in Thee!

Vain are the thousand creeds
That move men's hearts, unutterably vain,
Worthless as withered weeds,
Or idlest froth amid the boundless main

To waken doubt in one
Holding so fast by thy infinity,
So surely anchored on
The steadfast rock of Immortality.

With wide-embracing love
Thy spirit animates eternal years,
Pervades and broods above,
Changes, sustains, dissolves, creates and rears.

Though Earth and moon were gone,
And suns and universes ceased to be,
And thou wert left alone,
Every Existence would exist in thee.

There is not room for Death
Nor atom that his might could render void:
Since thou art Being and Breath,
And what thou art may never be destroyed.

THE OLD STOIC

Riches I hold in light esteem,
   And Love I laugh to scorn;
And lust of Fame was but a dream,
   That vanished with the morn—

And if I pray, the only prayer
   That moves my lips for me
Is—'Leave the heart that now I bear
   And give me liberty!'

Yes, as my swift days near their goal,
   'Tis all that I implore—
In life and death a chainless soul,
   With courage to endure!

THE SUN HAS SET

The sun has set, and the long grass now
    Waves dreamily in the evening wind;
And the wild bird has flown from that old grey stone,
    In some warm nook a couch to find.

In all the lonely landscape round
I see no sight and hear no sound,
Except the wind that far away
Comes sighing o'er the heathy sea.

SLEEP BRINGS NO JOY

Sleep brings no joy to me,
    Remembrance never dies;
My soul is given to misery,
    And lives in sighs.

Sleep bring no strength to me,
    No power renewed to brave
I only sail a wilder sea,
    A darker wave.

Sleep brings no rest to me;
    The shadows of the dead,
My wakening eyes may
      never see,
    Surround my bed.

Sleep brings no friend to me
    To soothe and aid to bear;
They all gaze on, oh, how
      scornfully,
    And I despair.

Sleep brings no strength to me,
    In soundest sleep they come,
And with their doleful imagery
    Deepen the gloom.

Sleep brings no wish to knit
    My harassed heart beneath;
My only wish is to forget
    In the sleep of death.

A LITTLE WHILE, A LITTLE WHILE

A little while, a little while,
    The noisy crowd are barred away;
And I can sing and smile
    A little while I've holiday!

Where wilt thou go, my harassed heart?
    Full many a land invites thee now;
And places near and far apart
    Have rest for thee, my weary brow.

There is a spot 'mid barren hills
    Where winter howls and driving rain,

But if the dreary tempest chills
  There is a light that warms again.

The house is old, the trees are bare,
  And moonless bends the misty dome,
But what on earth is half so dear,
  So longed for as the hearth of home?

The mute bird sitting on the stone,
  The dank moss dripping from the wall,
The garden-walk with weeds o'ergrown,
  I love them—how I love them all!

Shall I go there? or shall I seek
  Another clime, another sky,
Where tongues familiar music speak
  In accents dear to memory?

Yes, as I mused, the naked room,
  The flickering firelight died away
And from the midst of cheerless gloom
  I passed to bright, unclouded day—

A little and a lone green lane
  That opened on a common wide;
A distant, dreamy, dim blue chain
  Of mountains circling every side;

A heaven so clear, an earth so calm,
  So sweet, so soft, so hushed an air
And, deepening still the dream-like charm,
  Wild moor-sheep feeding everywhere—

That was the scene; I knew it well,
  I knew the path-ways far and near
That winding o'er each billowy swell,
  Marked out the tracks of wandering deer.

Could I have lingered but an hour,
  It had well paid a week of toil,
But truth has banished fancy's power;
  I hear my dungeon bars recoil—

Even as I stood with raptured eye,
  Absorbed in bliss so deep and dear,
My hour of rest had fleeted by
  And given me back to weary care.

CASTLE WOOD

The day is done, the winter sun
  Is setting in its sullen sky;
And drear the course that has been run,
  And dim the beams that slowly die.

No star will light my coming night;
  No morn of hope for me will shine;
I mourn not heaven would blast my sight,
  And I ne'er longed for joys divine.

Through Life's hard Task I did not ask
  Celestial aid, celestial cheer;
I saw my fate without its mask,
  And met it too without a tear.

The grief that pressed my aching breast
  Was heavier far than earth can be;
And who would dread eternal rest
  When labour's hour was agony?

Dark falls the fear of this despair
  On spirits born of happiness;
But I was bred the mate of care,
  The foster-child of sore distress.

No sighs for me, no sympathy,
  No wish to keep my soul below;
The heart is dead in infancy,
  Unwept for let the body go.

LOVE AND FRIENDSHIP

Love is like the wild rose-briar,
Friendship like the holly tree—
The holly is dark when the rose-briar blooms
But which will bloom most constantly?

The wild rose-briar is sweet in spring,
Its summer blossoms scent the air;
Yet wait till winter comes again
And who will call the wild-briar fair?

Then scorn the silly rose-wreath now
And deck thee with the holly's sheen,
That when December blights thy brow
He still may leave thy garland green.

I AM THE ONLY BEING

I am the only being whose doom
No tongue would ask, no eye would mourn;
I never caused a thought of gloom,
A smile of joy, since I was born.

In secret pleasure, secret tears,
This changeful life has slipped away,
As friendless after eighteen years,
As lone as on my natal day.

There have been times I cannot hide,
There have been times when this was drear,
When my sad soul forgot its pride
And longed for one to love me here.

But those were in the early glow
Of feelings since subdued by care;
And they have died so long ago,
I hardly now believe they were.

First melted off the hope of youth,
Then fancy's rainbow fast withdrew;
And then experience told me truth
In mortal bosoms never grew.

'Twas grief enough to think mankind
All hollow, servile, insincere;
But worse to trust to my own mind
And find the same corruption there.

METHINKS THIS HEART

Methinks this heart should rest awhile,
So stilly round the evening falls;
The veiled sun sheds no parting smile,
Nor mirth, nor music wakes my halls.

I have sat lonely all the day
Watching the drizzly mist descend
And first conceal the hills in grey
And then along the valleys wend.

And I have sat and watched the trees
And the sad flowers—how drear they blow:
Those flowers were formed to feel the breeze
Wave their light leaves in summer's glow.

Yet their lives passed in gloomy woe
And hopeless comes its dark decline,
And I lament, because I know
That cold departure pictures mine.

THE WIND, I HEAR IT SIGHING

The wind, I hear it sighing
With Autumn's saddest sound;
Withered leaves as thick are lying
As spring-flowers on the ground.

This dark night has won me
To wander far away;
Old feelings gather fast upon me
Like vultures round their prey.

Kind were they once, and cherished,
But cold and cheerless now;
I would their lingering shades had perished
When their light left my brow.

'Tis like old age pretending
The softness of a child,
My altered, hardened spirit bending
To meet their fancies wild.

Yet could I with past pleasures
Past woe's oblivion buy,
That by the death of my dearest treasures
My deadliest pains might die,

O then another daybreak
Might haply dawn above,
Another summer gild my cheek,
My soul, another love.

MATTHEW ARNOLD

(1822-1888)

DOVER BEACH

The sea is calm to-night.
The tide is full, the moon lies fair
Upon the straits;—on the French coast the light
Gleams and is gone; the cliffs of England stand
Glimmering and vast, out in the tranquil bay.
Come to the window, sweet is the night-air!
Only, from the long line of spray
Where the sea meets the moon-blanch'd land,
Listen! you hear the grating roar
Of pebbles which the waves draw back, and fling,
At their return, up the high strand,
Begin, and cease, and then again begin,
With tremulous cadence slow, and bring
The eternal note of sadness in.

Sophocles long ago
Heard it on the Ægean, and it brought
Into his mind the turbid ebb and flow
Of human misery; we
Find also in the sound a thought,
Hearing it by this distant northern sea.

The Sea of Faith
Was once, too, at the full, and round earth's shore
Lay like the folds of a bright girdle furl'd.
But now I only hear
Its melancholy, long, withdrawing roar,
Retreating, to the breath
Of the night-wind, down the vast edges drear
And naked shingles of the world.

Ah, love, let us be true
To one another! for the world, which seems
To lie before us like a land of dreams,

So various, so beautiful, so new,
Hath really neither joy, nor love, nor light,
Nor certitude, nor peace, nor help for pain;
And we are here as on a darkling plain
Swept with confused alarms of struggle and flight,
Where ignorant armies clash by night.

REQUIESCAT

Strew on her roses, roses,
    And never a spray of yew!
In quiet she reposes;
    Ah! would that I did too.

Her mirth the world required;
    She bathed it in smiles of glee.
But her heart was tired, tired,
    And now they let her be.

Her life was turning, turning,
    In mazes of heat and sound.
But for peace her soul was yearning,
    And now peace laps her round.

Her cabin'd, ample spirit,
    It flutter'd and fail'd for breath.
To-night it doth inherit
    The vasty hall of Death.

IN UTRUMQUE PARATUS

If, in the silent mind of One all-pure,
    At first imagined lay
The sacred world; and by procession sure
From those still deeps, in form and colour drest,
Seasons alternating, and night and day,
The long-mused thought to north, south, east, and west,
    Took then its all-seen way;

O waking on a world which thus-wise springs!
    Whether it needs thee count
Betwixt thy waking and the birth of things
Ages or hours—O waking on life's stream!
By lonely pureness to the all-pure fount

(Only by this thou canst) the coloured dream
    Of life remount!

Thin, thin the pleasant human noises grow,
    And faint the city gleams;
Rare the lone pastoral huts—marvel not thou!
The solemn peaks but to the stars are known,
But to the stars, and the cold lunar beams;
Alone the sun arises, and alone
    Spring the great streams.

But, if the wild unfathered mass no birth
    In divine seats hath known;
In the blank, echoing solitude if Earth,
Rocking her obscure body to and fro,
Ceases not from all time to heave and groan,
Unfruitful oft, and at her happiest throe
    Forms, what she forms, alone;

O seeming sole to awake, thy sun-bathed head
    Piercing the solemn cloud
Round thy still dreaming brother-world outspread!
O man, whom Earth, thy long-vext mother, bare
Not without joy—so radiant, so endow'd
(Such happy issue crown'd her painful care)—
    Be not too proud!

Oh when most self-exalted, most alone,
    Chief dreamer, own thy dream!
Thy brother-world stirs at thy feet unknown,
Who hath a monarch's hath no brother's part;
Yet doth thine inmost soul with yearning teem.
—Oh, what a spasm shakes the dreamer's heart!
    'I, too, but seem.'

TO MARGUERITE

Yes! in the sea of life enisled,
    With echoing straits between us thrown,
Dotting the shoreless watery wild,
    We mortal millions live *alone*.
The islands feel the enclasping flow,
And then their endless bounds they know.

But when the moon their hollows lights,
And they are swept by balms of spring,
And in their glens, on starry nights,
The nightingales divinely sing;
And lovely notes, from shore to shore,
Across the sounds and channels pour—

Oh! then a longing like despair
Is to their farthest caverns sent;
For surely once, they feel, we were
Parts of a single continent!
Now round us spreads the watery plain—
Oh might our marges meet again!

Who order'd, that their longing's fire
Should be, as soon as kindled, cooled?
Who renders vain their deep desire?—
A God, a God their severance ruled!
And bade betwixt their shores to be
The unplumb'd, salt, estranging sea.

GROWING OLD

What is it to grow old?
Is it to lose the glory of the form,
The lustre of the eye?
Is it for beauty to forego her wreath?
—Yes, but not this alone.

Is it to feel our strength—
Not our bloom only, but our strength—decay?
Is it to feel each limb
Grow stiffer, every function less exact,
Each nerve more loosely strung?

Yes, this, and more; but not,
Ah, 'tis not what in youth we dreamed 'twould be!
'Tis not to have our life
Mellowed and softened as with sunset-glow,
A golden day's decline.

'Tis not to see the world
As from a height, with rapt prophetic eyes,
And heart profoundly stirred;
And weep, and feel the fulness of the past,
The years that are no more.

It is to spend long days
And not once feel that we were ever young;
It is to add, immured
In the hot prison of the present, month
To month with weary pain.

It is to suffer this,
And feel but half, and feebly, what we feel.
Deep in our hidden heart
Festers the dull remembrance of a change,
But no emotion—none.

It is—last stage of all—
When we are frozen up within, and quite
The phantom of ourselves,
To hear the world applaud the hollow ghost
Which blamed the living man.

YOUTH AND CALM

'Tis death! and peace, indeed, is here,
And ease from shame, and rest from fear.
There's nothing can dismarble now
The smoothness of that limpid brow.
But is a calm like this, in truth,
The crowning end of life and youth,
And when this boon rewards the dead,
Are all debts paid, has all been said?
And is the heart of youth so light,
Its step so firm, its eye so bright,
Because on its hot brow there blows
A wind of promise and repose
From the far grave, to which it goes;
Because it has the hope to come,
One day, to harbour in the tomb?
Ah no, the bliss youth dreams is one
For daylight, for the cheerful sun,
For feeling nerves and living breath—
Youth dreams a bliss on this side death.
It dreams a rest, if not more deep,
More grateful than this marble sleep;
It hears a voice within it tell:
Calm's not life's crown, though calm is well.
'Tis all perhaps which man acquires,
But 'tis not what our youth desires.

SELF-DEPENDENCE

Weary of myself, and sick of asking
What I am, and what I ought to be,
At the vessel's prow I stand, which bears me
Forwards, forwards, oe'r the starlit sea.

And a look of passionate desire
O'er the sea and to the stars I send:
'Ye who from my childhood up have calm'd me,
Calm me, ah, compose me to the end!

'Ah, once more,' I cried, 'ye stars, ye waters,
On my heart your mighty charm renew;
Still, still let me, as I gaze upon you,
Feel my soul becoming vast like you.'

From the intense, clear, star-sown vault of heaven,
Over the lit sea's unquiet way,
In the rustling night-air came the answer:
'Wouldst thou *be* as these are? *Live* as they.

'Unaffrighted by the silence round them,
Undistracted by the sights they see,
These demand not that the things without them
Yield them love, amusement, sympathy.

'And with joy the stars perform their shining,
And the sea its long moon-silvered roll;
For self-poised they live, nor pine with noting
All the fever of some differing soul.

'Bounded by themselves, and unregardful
In what state God's other works may be,
In their own tasks all their powers pouring,
These attain the mighty life you see.'

O air-born voice! long since, severely clear,
A cry like thine in mine own heart I hear.
'Resolve to be thyself: and know that he
Who finds himself, loses his misery!'

A SUMMER NIGHT

In the deserted, moon-blanched street,
How lonely rings the echo of my feet!
Those windows, which I gaze at, frown,
Silent amd white, unopening down,

Repellent as the world:—but see!
A break between the housetops shows
The moon! and, lost behind her, fading dim
Into the dewy dark obscurity
Down at the far horizon's rim,
    Doth a whole tract of heaven disclose.

And to my mind the thought
Is on a sudden brought
Of a past night, and a far different scene.
Headlands stood out into the moonlit deep
As clearly as at noon;
The spring-tide's brimming flow
Heaved dazzlingly between;
Houses with long white sweep,
Girdled the glistening bay;
Behind, through the soft air,
The blue haze-cradled mountains spread away,
That night was far more fair—
But the same restless pacings to and fro,
And the same vainly throbbing heart was there,
And the same bright, calm moon.
And the calm moonlight seems to say:
Hast thou then still the old unquiet breast,
Which neither deadens into rest,
Nor ever feels the fiery glow
That whirls the spirit from itself away,
But fluctuates to and fro,
Never by passion quite possessed
And never quite benumbed by the world's sway?—
And I, I know not if to pray
Still to be what I am, or yield and be
Like all the other men I see.

For most men in a brazen prison live,
Where, in the sun's hot eye,
With heads bent o'er their toil, they languidly
Their lives to some unmeaning taskwork give,
Dreaming of naught beyond their prison-wall.
And as, year after year,
Fresh products of their barren labour fall
From their tired hands, and rest
Never yet comes more near,
Gloom settles slowly down over their breast;
And while they try to stem
The waves of mournful thought by which they are prest,

Death in their prison reaches them,
Unfreed, having seen nothing, still unblest.

And the rest, a few,
Escape their prison, and depart
On the wide ocean of life anew.
There the freed prisoner, where'er his heart
Listeth, will sail;
Nor doth he know how there prevail,
Despotic on that sea,
Trade-winds which cross it from eternity.
Awhile he holds some false way, undebarr'd
By thwarting signs, and braves
The freshening wind and blackening waves.
And then the tempest strikes him; and between
The lightning-bursts is seen
Only a driving wreck,
And the pale master on his spar-strewn deck
With anguished face and flying hair
Grasping the rudder hard,
Still bent to make some port he knows not where,
Still standing for some false, impossible shore.
And sterner comes the roar
Of sea and wind, and through the deepening gloom
Fainter and fainter wreck and helmsman loom,
And he too disappears, and comes no more.

Is there no life, but these alone?
Madman or slave, must man be one?

Plainness and clearness without shadow of stain!
Clearness divine!
Ye heavens, whose pure dark regions have no sign
Of languor, though so calm, and, though so great,
Are yet untroubled and unpassionate;
Who, though so noble, share in the world's toil,
And, though so tasked, keep free from dust and soil!
I will not say that your mild deeps retain
A tinge, it may be, of their silent pain
Who have longed deeply once, and longed in vain—
But I will rather say that you remain
A world above man's head, to let him see
How boundless might his souls' horizons be,
How vast, yet of what clear transparency!
How it were good to sink there, and breathe free;
How fair a lot to fill
Is left to each man still!

THE BURIED LIFE

Light flows our war of mocking words, and yet,
Behold, with tears mine eyes are wet!
I feel a nameless sadness o'er me roll.
Yes, yes, we know that we can jest,
We know, we know that we can smile!
But there's a something in this breast,
To which thy light words bring no rest,
And thy gay smiles no anodyne.
Give me thy hand, and hush awhile,
And turn those limpid eyes on mine,
And let me read there, love! thy inmost soul.

Alas! is even love too weak
To unlock the heart, and let it speak?
Are even lovers powerless to reveal
To one another what indeed they feel?
I knew the mass of men concealed
Their thoughts, for fear that if revealed
They would by other men be met
With blank indifference, or with blame reproved:
I knew they lived and moved
Trick'd in disguises, alien to the rest
Of men, and alien to themselves—and yet
The same heart beats in every human breast.

But we, my love—does a like spell benumb
Our hearts, our voices?—must we too be dumb?

Ah! well for us, if even we,
Even for a moment, can get free
Our heart, and have our lips unchained:
For that which seals them hath been deep ordained.

Fate, which foresaw
How frivolous a baby man would be—
By what distractions he would be possessed,
How he would pour himself in every strife,
And well-nigh change his own identity—
That it might keep from his capricious play
His genuine self, and force him to obey
Even in his own despite his being's law,
Bade through the deep recesses of our breast
The unregarded river of our life
Pursue with indiscernible flow its way;

And that we should not see
The buried stream, and seem to be
Eddying at large in blind uncertainty,
Though driving on with it eternally.

But often, in the world's most crowded streets,
But often, in the din of strife,
There rises an unspeakable desire
After the knowledge of our buried life;
A thirst to spend our fire and restless force
In tracking out our true, original course;
A longing to inquire
Into the mystery of this heart which beats
So wild, so deep in us—to know
Whence our thoughts come and where they go.
And many a man in his own breast then delves,
But deep enough, alas! none ever mines.
And we have been on many thousand lines,
And we have shown, on each, spirit and power;
But hardly have we, for one little hour,
Been on our own line, have we been ourselves—
Hardly had skill to utter one of all
The nameless feelings that course through our breast,
But they course on for ever unexpressed.
And long we try in vain to speak and act
Our hidden self, and what we say and do
Is eloquent, is well—but 'tis not true!
And then we will no more be racked
With inward striving, and demand
Of all the thousand nothings of the hour
Their stupefying power;
Ah yes, and they benumb us at our call!
Yet still, from time to time, vague and forlorn,
From the soul's subterranean depth upborne
As from an infinitely distant land,
Come airs, and floating echoes, and convey
A melancholy into all our day.

Only—but this is rare—
When a belovèd hand is laid in ours,
When, jaded with the rush and glare
Of the interminable hours,
Our eyes can in another's eyes read clear,
When our world-deafened ear
Is by the tones of a loved voice caressed—
A bolt is shot back somewhere in our breast,

And a lost pulse of feeling stirs again.
The eye sinks inward, and the heart lies plain,
And what we mean, we say, and what we would, we know.
A man becomes aware of his life's flow,
And hears its winding murmur; and he sees
The meadows where it glides, the sun, the breeze.

And there arrives a lull in the hot race
Wherein he doth for ever chase
That flying and elusive shadow, rest.
An air of coolness plays upon his face,
And an unwonted calm pervades his breast.
And then he thinks he knows
The hills where his life rose,
And the sea where it goes.

A FAREWELL

My horse's feet beside the lake,
Where sweet the unbroken moonbeams lay,
Sent echoes through the night to wake
Each glistening strand, each heath-fringed bay.
The poplar avenue was passed,
And the roofed bridge that spans the stream;
Up the steep street I hurried fast,
Led by thy taper's starlike beam.

I came! I saw thee rise!—the blood
Pour'd flushing to thy languid cheek.
Locked in each other's arms we stood,
In tears, with hearts too full to speak.

Days flew;—ah, soon I could discern
A trouble in thine altered air!
Thy hand lay languidly in mine,
Thy cheek was grave, thy speech grew rare.

I blame thee not!—this heart, I know,
To be long loved was never framed;
For something in its depths doth glow
Too strange, too restless, too untamed.

And women—things that live and move
Mined by the fever of the soul—
They seek to find in those they love
Stern strength, and promise of control.

They ask not kindness, gentle ways—
These they themselves have tried and known;
They ask a soul which never sways
With the blind gusts that shake their own.

I too have felt the load I bore
In a too strong emotion's sway;
I too have wished, no woman more,
This starting, feverish heart away:

I too have longed for trenchant force,
And will like a dividing spear;
Have praised the keen, unscrupulous course,
Which knows no doubt, which feels no fear.

But in the world I learnt, what there
Thou too wilt surely one day prove,
That will, that energy, though rare,
Are yet far, far less rare than love.

Go then! till time and fate impress
This truth on thee, be mine no more!
They will!—for thou, I feel, not less
Than I, wast destined to this lore.

We school our manners, act our parts—
But He, who sees us through and through,
Knows that the bent of both our hearts
Was to be gentle, tranquil, true.

And though we wear out life, alas!
Distracted as a homeless wind,
In beating where we must not pass,
In seeking what we shall not find;

Yet we shall one day gain, life past,
Clear prospect o'er our being's whole;
Shall see ourselves, and learn at last
Our true affinities of soul.

We shall not then deny a course
To every thought the mass ignore;
We shall not then call hardness force,
Nor lightness wisdom any more.

Then, in the eternal Father's smile,
Our soothed, encouraged souls will dare

To seem as free from pride and guile,
As good, as generous, as they are.

Then we shall know our friends!—though much
Will have been lost—the help in strife,
The thousand sweet, still joys of such
As hand in hand face earthly life—

Though these be lost, there will be yet
A sympathy august and pure;
Ennobled by a vast regret,
And by contrition sealed thrice sure.

And we, whose ways were unlike here,
May then more neighbouring courses ply;
May to each other be brought near,
And greet across infinity.

How sweet, unreached by earthly jars,
My sister! to maintain with thee
The hush among the shining stars,
The calm upon the moonlit sea!

How sweet to feel, on the boon air,
All our unquiet pulses cease!
To feel that nothing can impair
The gentleness, the thirst for peace—

The gentleness too rudely hurled
On this wild earth of hate and fear;
The thirst for peace a raving world
Would never let us satiate here.

THE SCHOLAR GIPSY

Go, for they call you, shepherd, from the hill;
   Go, shepherd, and untie the wattled cotes!
     No longer leave thy wistful flock unfed,
   Nor let thy bawling fellows rack their throats,
     Nor the cropped grasses shoot another head.
       But when the fields are still,
And the tired men and dogs all gone to rest,
   And only the white sheep are sometimes seen
    Cross and recross the strips of moon-blanched green,
Come, shepherd, and again renew the quest.

Here, where the reaper was at work of late—
  In this high field's dark corner, where he leaves
    His coat, his basket, and his earthen cruse,
    And in the sun all morning binds the sheaves,
    Then here, at noon, comes back his stores to use—
      Here will I sit and wait,
  While to my ear from uplands far away
    The bleating of the folded flocks is borne,
    With distant cries of reapers in the corn—
All the live murmur of a summer's day.

Screen'd is this nook o'er the high, half-reaped field,
  And here till sun-down, shepherd! will I be.
    Through the thick corn the scarlet poppies peep,
    And round green roots and yellowing stalks I see
    Pale blue convolvulus in tendrils creep:
      And air-swept lindens yield
  Their scent, and rustle down their perfumed showers
    Of bloom on the bent grass where I am laid,
    And bower me from the August sun with shade;
And the eye travels down to Oxford's towers.

And near me on the grass lies Glanvil's book—
  Come, let me read the oft-read tale again!
    The story of that Oxford scholar poor,
    Of pregnant parts and quick inventive brain,
    Who, tired of knocking at preferment's door,
      One summer-morn forsook
  His friends, and went to learn the gipsy lore,
    And roamed the world with that wild brotherhood,
    And came, as most men deemed, to little good,
But came to Oxford and his friends no more.

But once, years after, in the country-lanes,
  Two scholars whom at college erst he knew,
    Met him, and of his way of life enquired.
    Whereat he answered, that the gipsy-crew,
    His mates, had arts to rule as they desired
      The workings of men's brains,
  And they can bind them to what thoughts they will.
    'And I,' he said, 'the secret of their art,
    When fully learned, will to the world impart;
But it needs heaven-sent moments for this skill.'

This said, he left them, and returned no more.—
  But rumours hung about the country-side

That the lost Scholar long was seen to stray,
  Seen by rare glimpses, pensive and tongue-tied,
    In hat of antique shape, and cloak of grey,
      The same the gipsies wore.
Shepherds had met him on the Hurst in spring;
  At some lone alehouse in the Berkshire moors,
    On the warm ingle-bench, the smock-frocked boors
Had found him seated at their entering,

But, 'mid their drink and clatter, he would fly.
  And I myself seem half to know thy looks,
    And put the shepherds, wanderer! on thy trace;
  And boys who in lone wheatfields scare the rooks
    I ask if thou hast passed their quiet place;
      Or in my boat I lie
Moor'd to the cool bank in the summer-heats,
  'Mid wide grass meadows which the sunshine fills,
    And watch the warm, green-muffled Cumner hills,
And wonder if thou haunt'st their shy retreats.

For most, I know, thou lov'st retired ground!
  Thee, at the ferry Oxford riders blithe,
    Returning home on summer-nights, have met
Crossing the stripling Thames at Bab-lock-hithe,
  Trailing in the cool stream thy fingers wet,
    As the punt's rope chops round;
And leaning backwards in a pensive dream,
  And fostering in thy lap a heap of flowers
    Pluck'd in shy fields and distant Wychwood bowers,
And thine eyes resting on the moonlit stream.

And then they land, and thou art seen no more!—
  Maidens, who from the distant hamlets come
    To dance around the Fyfield elm in May,
Oft through the darkening fields have seen thee roam,
  Or cross a stile into the public way.
    Oft thou hast given them store
Of flowers—the frail-leafed, white anemone,
  Dark bluebells drenched with dews of summer eves,
    And purple orchises with spotted leaves—
But none hath words she can report of thee.

And, above Godstow Bridge, when hay-time's here
  In June, and many a scythe in sunshine flames,
    Men who through those wide fields of breezy grass
Where black-winged swallows haunt the glittering Thames,

To bathe in the abandon'd lasher pass,
    Have often passed thee near
Sitting upon the river bank o'ergrown;
    Mark'd thine outlandish garb, thy figure spare,
    Thy dark vague eyes, and soft abstracted air—
But, when they came from bathing, thou wast gone.

At some lone homestead in the Cumner hills,
    Where at her open door the housewife darns,
        Thou hast been seen, or hanging on a gate
To watch the threshers in the mossy barns.
        Children, who early range these slopes and late
            For cresses from the rills,
    Have known thee eying, all an April-day,
        The springing pastures and the feeding kine;
        And mark'd thee, when the stars come out and shine,
Through the long dewy grass move slow away.

In autumn, on the skirts of Bagley wood—
    Where most the gipsies by the turf-edged way
        Pitch their smoked tents, and every bush you see
With scarlet patches tagg'd and shreds of grey,
        Above the forest ground call'd Thessaly—
            The blackbird, picking food,
    Sees thee, nor stops his meal, nor fears at all;
        So often has he known thee past him stray,
        Rapt, twirling in thy hand a withered spray,
And waiting for the spark from heaven to fall.

And once, in winter, on the causeway chill
    Where home through flooded fields foot-travellers go,
        Have I not passed thee on the wooden bridge,
Wrapt in thy cloak and battling with the snow,
        Thy face tow'rd Hinksey and its wintry ridge?
            And thou hast climbed the hill
    And gained the white brow of the Cumner range;
        Turn'd once to watch, while thick the snowflakes fall,
        The line of festal light in Christ-Church hall—
Then sought thy straw in some sequestered grange.

But what—I dream! Two hundred years are flown
    Since first thy story ran through Oxford halls,
        And the grave Glanvil did the tale inscribe
That thou wert wandered from the studious walls
        To learn strange arts, and join a gipsy-tribe;
            And thou from earth art gone

Long since, and in some quiet churchyard laid—
    Some country-nook, where o'er thy unknown grave
    Tall grasses and white flowering nettles wave,
Under a dark, red-fruited yew-tree's shade.

—No, no, thou hast not felt the lapse of hours!
For what wears out the life of mortal men?
    'Tis that from change to change their being rolls;
    'Tis that repeated shocks, again, again,
        Exhaust the energy of strongest souls
            And numb the elastic powers.
    Till having used our nerves with bliss and teen,
        And tired upon a thousand schemes our wit,
        To the just-pausing Genius we remit
Our worn-out life, and are—what we have been.

Thou hast not lived, why shouldst thou perish, so?
    Thou hadst *one* aim, *one* business, *one* desire;
        Else wert thou long since numbered with the dead!
    Else hadst thou spent, like other men, thy fire!
        The generations of thy peers are fled,
            And we ourselves shall go;
    But thou possessest an immortal lot,
        And we imagine thee exempt from age
        And living as thou liv'st on Glanvil's page,
Because thou hadst—what we, alas, have not!

For early didst thou leave the world, with powers
    Fresh, undiverted to the world without,
        Firm to their mark, not spent on other things;
    Free from the sick fatigue, the languid doubt,
        Which much to have tried, in much been baffled, brings.
            O Life unlike to ours!
    Who fluctuate idly without term or scope,
        Of whom each strives, nor knows for what he strives,
        And each half lives a hundred different lives;
Who wait like thee, but not, like thee, in hope.

Thou waitest for the spark from Heaven! and we,
    Light half-believers of our casual creeds,
        Who never deeply felt, nor clearly willed,
    Whose insight never has borne fruit in deeds,
        Whose vague resolves never have been fulfilled;
            For whom each year we see
    Breeds new beginnings, disappointments new;
        Who hesitate and falter life away,

And lose to-morrow the ground won to-day—
Ah, do not we, wanderer! await it too?

Yes, we await it!—but it still delays,
    And then we suffer! and amongst us one,
        Who most has suffered, takes dejectedly
His seat upon the intellectual throne;
        And all his store of sad experience he
            Lays bare of wretched days;
    Tells us his misery's birth and growth and signs,
        And how the dying spark of hope was fed,
        And how the breast was soothed, and how the head,
And all his hourly varied anodynes.

This for our wisest! and we others pine,
    And wish the long unhappy dream would end,
        And waive all claim to bliss, and try to bear;
With close-lipped patience for our only friend,
        Sad patience, too near neighbour to despair—
            But none has hope like thine!
    Thou through the fields and through the woods dost stray,
        Roaming the country-side, a truant boy,
        Nursing thy project in unclouded joy,
And every doubt long blown by time away.

O born in days when wits were fresh and clear,
    And life ran gaily as the sparkling Thames;
        Before this strange disease of modern life,
With its sick hurry, its divided aims,
        Its heads o'ertaxed, its palsied hearts, was rife—
            Fly hence, our contact fear!
    Still fly, plunge deeper in the bowering wood!
        Averse, as Dido did with gesture stern
        From her false friend's approach in Hades turn,
Wave us away, and keep thy solitude.

Still nursing the unconquerable hope,
    Still clutching the inviolable shade,
        With a free, onward impulse brushing through,
By night, the silvered branches of the glade—
        Far on the forest-skirts, where none pursue,
            On some mild pastoral slope
    Emerge, and resting on the moonlit pales
        Freshen thy flowers as in former years
        With dew, or listen with enchanted ears,
From the dark dingles, to the nightingales.

But fly our paths, our feverish contact fly!
  For strong the infection of our mental strife,
    Which, though it gives no bliss, yet spoils for rest;
And we should win thee from thy own fair life,
    Like us distracted, and like us unblest.
      Soon, soon thy cheer would die,
Thy hopes grow timorous, and unfixed thy powers,
    And thy clear aims be cross and shifting made;
    And then thy glad perennial youth would fade,
Fade, and grow old at last, and die like ours.

Then fly our greetings, fly our speech and smiles!
  —As some grave Tyrian trader, from the sea,
    Descried at sunrise an emerging prow
Lifting the cool-haired creepers stealthily,
    The fringes of a southward-facing brow
      Among the Aegean isles;
And saw the merry Grecian coaster come,
    Freighted with amber grapes, and Chian wine,
    Green, bursting figs, and tunnies steeped in brine;
And knew the intruders on his ancient home,

The young light-hearted masters of the waves—
  And snatched his rudder, and shook out more sail;
    And day and night held on indignantly
O'er the blue Midland waters with the gale,
    Betwixt the Syrtes and soft Sicily,
      To where the Atlantic raves
Outside the western straits; and unbent sails
    There, where down cloudy cliffs, through sheets of foam,
    Shy traffickers, the dark Iberians come;
And on the beach undid his corded bales.

CHRISTINA ROSSETTI

(1830-1894)

A BIRTHDAY

My heart is like a singing bird
   Whose nest is in a watered shoot:
My heart is like an apple-tree
   Whose boughs are bent with thickset fruit;
My heart is like a rainbow shell
   That paddles in a halcyon sea;
My heart is gladder than all these
   Because my love is come to me.

Raise me a daïs of silk and down;
   Hang it with vair and purple dyes;
Carve it in doves and pomegranates,
   And peacocks with a hundred eyes;
Work it in gold and silver grapes,
   In leaves and silver fleurs-de-lys;
Because the birthday of my life
   Is come, my love is come to me.

WHEN I AM DEAD, MY DEAREST

When I am dead, my dearest,
   Sing no sad songs for me;
Plant thou no roses at my head,
   Nor shady cypress tree:
Be the green grass above me
   With showers and dewdrops wet:
And if thou wilt, remember,
   And if thou wilt, forget.

I shall not see the shadows,
   I shall not feel the rain;

I shall not hear the nightingale
    Sing on, as if in pain:
And dreaming through the twilight
    That doth not rise nor set,
Haply I may remember,
    And haply may forget.

ECHO

Come to me in the silence of the night;
    Come in the speaking silence of a dream;
Come with soft rounded cheeks and eyes as bright
    As sunlight on a stream;
        Come back in tears,
O memory, hope, love of finished years.

O dream how sweet, too sweet, too bitter sweet,
    Whose wakening should have been in Paradise,
Where souls brimfull of love abide and meet;
    Where thirsting longing eyes
        Watch the slow door
That opening, letting in, lets out no more.

Yet come to me in dreams, that I may live
    My very life again though cold in death:
Come back to me in dreams, that I may give
    Pulse for pulse, breath for breath:
        Speak low, lean low,
As long ago, my love, how long ago.

GOOD FRIDAY

Am I a stone, and not a sheep,
    That I can stand, O Christ, beneath Thy cross,
    To number drop by drop Thy Blood's slow loss,
And yet not weep?

Not so those women loved
    Who with exceeding grief lamented Thee;
    Not so fallen Peter weeping bitterly;
Not so the thief was moved;

Not so the Sun and Moon
    Which hid their faces in a starless sky.

A horror of great darkness at broad noon—
    I, only I.

Yet give not o'er,
    But seek Thy sheep, true Shepherd of the flock;
Greater than Moses, turn and look once more
    And smite a rock.

UP-HILL

Does the road wind up-hill all the way?
    Yes, to the very end.
Will the day's journey take the whole long day?
    From morn to night, my friend.

But is there for the night a resting-place?
    A roof for when the slow dark hours begin.
May not the darkness hide it from my face?
    You cannot miss that inn.

Shall I meet other wayfarers at night?
    Those who have gone before.
Then must I knock, or call when just in sight?
    They will not keep you standing at that door.

Shall I find comfort, travel-sore and weak?
    Of labour you shall find the sum.
Will there be beds for me and all who seek?
    Yea, beds for all who come.

PASSING AWAY

Passing away, saith the World, passing away:
Chances, beauty, and youth, sapped day by day:
Thy life never continueth in one stay.
Is the eye waxen dim, is the dark hair changing to grey
That hath won neither laurel nor bay?
I shall clothe myself in Spring and bud in May:
Thou, root-stricken, shalt not rebuild thy decay
On my bosom for aye.
Then I answered: Yea.

Passing away, saith my Soul, passing away:
With its burden of fear and hope, of labour and play,

Hearken what the past doth witness and say:
Rust in thy gold, a moth is in thine array,
A canker is in thy bud, thy leaf must decay.
At midnight, at cockcrow, at morning, one certain day
Lo, the Bridegroom shall come and shall not delay;
Watch thou and pray.
Then I answered: Yea.

Passing away, saith my God, passing away:
Winter passeth after the long delay:
New grapes on the vine, new figs on the tender spray,
Turtle calleth turtle in Heaven's May.
Though I tarry, wait for Me, trust Me, watch and pray:
Arise, come away, night is past and lo it is day,
My love, My sister, My spouse, thou shalt hear Me say—
Then I answered: Yea.

REMEMBER

Remember me when I am gone away,
  Gone far away into the silent land;
  When you can no more hold me by the hand,
Nor I half turn to go yet turning stay.
Remember me when no more day by day
  You tell me of our future that you plann'd:
  Only remember me; you understand
It will be late to counsel then or pray.
Yet if you should forget me for a while
  And afterwards remember, do not grieve:
  For if the darkness and corruption leave
    A vestige of the thoughts that once I had,
Better by far you should forget and smile
    Than that you should remember and be sad.

REST

O Earth, lie heavily upon her eyes;
  Seal her sweet eyes weary of watching, Earth;
  Lie close around her; leave no room for mirth
With its harsh laughter, nor for sound of sighs.
She hath no questions, she hath no replies,
  Hushed in and curtained with a blessed dearth
  Of all that irked her from the hour of birth;
With stillness that is almost Paradise.

Darkness more clear than noonday holdeth her,
    Silence more musical than any song;
Even her very heart has ceased to stir:
Until the morning of Eternity
Her rest shall not begin nor end, but be;
    And when she wakes she will not think it long.

A LIFE'S PARALLELS

Never on this side of the grave again,
    On this side of the river,
On this side of the garner of the grain,
    Never.

Ever while time flows on and on and on,
    That narrow noiseless river,
Ever while corn bows heavy-headed, wan,
    Ever.

Never despairing, often fainting, rueing,
    But looking back, ah never!
Faint yet pursuing, faint yet still pursuing
    Ever.

SPRING QUIET

Gone were but the Winter,
    Come were but the Spring,
I would go to a covert
    Where the birds sing;

Where in the whitethorn
    Singeth a thrush,
And a robin sings
    In the holly-bush

Full of fresh scents
    Are the budding boughs
Arching high over
    A cool green house;

Full of sweet scents,
    And whispering air
Which sayeth softly:
    'We spread no snare;

'Here dwell in safety,
    Here dwell alone,
With a clear stream
    And a mossy stone.

'Here the sun shinest
    Most shadily;
Here is heard an echo
    Of the far sea,
    Though far off it be.'

EVE

'While I sit at the door,
Sick to gaze within,
Mine eye weepeth sore
For sorrow and sin:
As a tree my sin stands
To darken all lands;
Death is the fruit it bore.

'How have Eden bowers
    grown
Without Adams to bend
    them?
How have Eden flowers
    blown,
Squandering their sweet
    breath,
Without me to tend them?
The Tree of Life was ours,
Tree twelvefold-fruited,
Most lofty tree that flowers,
Most deeply rooted:
I chose the Tree of Death.

'Hadst thou but said me nay,
Adam, my brother,
I might have pined away—
I, but none other:
God might have let thee stay
Safe in our garden
By putting me away
Beyond all pardon.

'I, Eve, sad mother
Of all who must live,
I, not another,
Plucked bitterest fruit to give
My friend, husband, lover.
O wanton eyes, run over!
Who but I should grieve?
Cain hath slain his brother:
Of all who must die mother,
Miserable Eve!'

Thus she sat weeping,
Thus Eve, our mother,
Where one lay sleeping
Slain by his brother.
Greatest and least
Each piteous beast
To hear her voice
Forgot his joys
And set aside his feast.

The mouse paused in his walk
And dropped his wheaten
    stalk;
Grave cattle wagged their
    heads
In rumination;
The eagle gave a cry
From his cloud station:
Larks on thyme beds
Forbore to mount or sing;
Bees drooped upon the wing;
The raven perched on high
Forgot his ration;
The conies in their rock,
A feeble nation,
Quaked sympathetical;
The mocking-bird left off to
    mock;
Huge camels knelt as if
In deprecation;
The kind hart's tears were
    falling;
Chattered the wistful stork;
Dove-voices with a dying fall
Cooed desolation,
Answering grief by grief.

Only the serpent in the dust,
Wriggling and crawling,
Grinned an evil grin, and
    thrust
His tongue out with its fork.

AMOR MUNDI

'Oh where are you going with your lovelocks flowing,
    On the west wind blowing along this valley track?'

'The down-hill path is easy, come with me an' it please ye,
    We shall escape the up-hill by never turning back.'
So they two went together in glowing August weather,
    The honey-breathing heather lay to their left and right;
And dear she was to doat on, her swift feet seemed to float on
    The air like soft twin pigeons too sportive to alight.

'Oh what is that in heaven where grey cloud-flakes are seven,
    Where blackest clouds hang riven just at the rainy skirt?'
'Oh that's a meteor sent us, a message dumb, portentous,
    An undecipher'd solemn signal of help or hurt.'

'Oh what is that glides quickly where velvet flowers grow
        thickly,
    Their scent comes rich and sickly?' 'A scaled and hooded
        worm.'
'Oh what's that in the hollow, so pale I quake to follow?'
    'Oh, that's a thin dead body which waits the eternal term.'

'Turn again, O my sweetest,—turn again, false and fleetest:
    This beaten way thou beatest, I fear, is hell's own track.'
'Nay, too steep for hill mounting; nay, too late for cost
        counting:
    This down-hill path is easy, but there's no turning back.'

THE CONVENT THRESHOLD

There's blood between us, love, my love,
There's father's blood, there's brother's blood;
And blood's a bar I cannot pass.
I choose the stairs that mount above,
Stair after golden sky-ward stair,
To city and to sea of glass.
My lily feet are soiled with mud,
With scarlet mud which tells a tale
Of hope that was, of guilt that was,
Of love that shall not yet avail;
Alas, my heart, if I could bare
My heart, this selfsame stain is there:
I seek the sea of glass and fire
To wash the spot, to burn the snare;
Lo, stairs are meant to lift us higher:
Mount with me, mount the kindled stair.

Your eyes look earthward, mine look up.
I see the far-off city grand,
Beyond the hills a watered land,
Beyond the gulf a gleaming strand

Of mansions where the righteous sup;
Who sleep at ease among their trees,
Or wake to sing a cadenced hymn
With Cherubim and Seraphim.
They bore the Cross, they drained the cup,
Racked, roasted, crushed, wrenched limb from limb,
They the offscouring of the world:
The heaven of starry heavens unfurled,
The sun before their face is dim.

You looking earthward, what see you?
Milk-white, wine-flushed among the vines,
Up and down leaping, to and fro,
Most glad, most full, made strong with wines,
Blooming as peaches pearled with dew,
Their golden windy hair afloat,
Love-music warbling in their throat,
Young men and women come and go.

You linger, yet the time is short:
Flee for your life, gird up your strength
To flee: the shadows stretched at length
Show that day wanes, that night draws nigh;
Flee to the mountain, tarry not.
Is this a time for smile and sigh,
For songs among the secret trees
Where sudden bluebirds nest and sport?
The time is short and yet you stay:
To-day, while it is called to-day,
Kneel, wrestle, knock, do violence, pray;
To-day is short, to-morrow nigh:
Why will you die? why will you die?

You sinned with me a pleasant sin:
Repent with me, for I repent.
Woe's me the lore I must unlearn!
Woe's me that easy way we went,
So rugged when I would return!
How long until my sleep begin,
How long shall stretch these nights and days?
Surely, clean Angels cry, she prays;
She laves her soul with tedious tears:
How long must stretch these years and years?

I turn from you my cheeks and eyes,

My hair which you shall see no more—
Alas for joy that went before,
For joy that dies, for love that dies.
Only my lips still turn to you,
My livid lips that cry, Repent!
O weary life, O weary Lent,
O weary time whose stars are few!

How should I rest in Paradise,
Or sit on steps of heaven alone?
If Saints and Angels spoke of love,
Should I not answer from my throne,
Have pity upon me, ye my friends,
For I have heard the sound thereof.
Should I not turn with yearning eyes,
Turn earthwards with a pitiful pang?
O save me from a pang in heaven!
By all the gifts we took and gave,
Repent, repent, and be forgiven.
This life is long, but yet it ends;
Repent and purge your soul and save:
No gladder song the morning stars
Upon their birthday morning sang
Than Angels sing when one repents.

I tell you what I dreamed last night.
A spirit with transfigured face
Fire-footed clomb an infinite space.
I heard his hundred pinions clang,
Heaven-bells rejoicing rang and rang,
Heaven-air was thrilled with subtle scents,
Worlds spun upon their rushing cars:
He mounted shrieking 'Give me light!'
Still light was poured on him, more light;
Angels, Archangels he outstripped,
Exultant in exceeding might,
And trod the skirts of Cherubim.
Still 'Give me light,' he shrieked; and dipped
His thirsty face, and drank a sea,
Athirst with thirst it could not slake.
I saw him, drunk with knowledge, take
From arching brows the aureole crown—
His locks writhed like a cloven snake—
He left his throne to grovel down
And lick the dust of Seraphs' feet:
For what is knowledge duly weighed?

Knowledge is strong, but love is sweet;
Yea, all the progress he had made
Was but to learn that all is small
Save love, for love is all in all.

I tell you what I dreamed last night.
It was not dark, it was not light,
Cold dews had drenched my plenteous hair
Through clay; you came to seek me there,
And 'Do you dream of me?' you said.
My heart was dust that used to leap
To you; I answered half asleep:
'My pillow is damp, my sheets are red.
There's a leaden tester to my bed:
Find you a warmer playfellow,
A warmer pillow for your head,
A kinder love to love than mine.'
You wrung your hands; while I, like lead,
Crushed downwards through the sodden earth:
You smote your hands but not in mirth,
And reeled but were not drunk with wine.

For all night long I dreamed of you:
I woke and prayed against my will,
Then slept to dream of you again.
At length I rose and knelt and prayed.
I cannot write the words I said,
My words were slow, my tears were few;
But through the dark my silence spoke
Like thunder. When this morning broke,
My face was pinched, my hair was grey,
And frozen blood was on the sill
Where stifling in my struggle I lay.

If now you saw me you would say:
Where is the face I used to love?
And I would answer: Gone before;
It tarries veiled in Paradise.
When once the morning star shall rise,
When earth with shadow flees away
And we stand safe within the door,
Then you shall lift the veil thereof.
Look up, rise up: for far above
Our palms are grown, our place is set;
There we shall meet as once we met,
And love with old familiar love.

THOMAS HARDY

(1840-1928)

THE DARKLING THRUSH

I leant upon a coppice gate
    When Frost was spectre-grey,
And Winter's dregs made desolate
    The weakening eye of day.
The tangled bine-stems scored the sky
    Like strings of broken lyres,
And all mankind that haunted nigh
    Had sought their household fires.

The land's sharp features seemed to be
    The Century's corpse outleant,
His crypt the cloudy canopy,
    The wind his death-lament.
The ancient pulse of germ and birth
    Was shrunken hard and dry,
And every spirit upon earth
    Seemed fervourless as I.

At once a voice arose among
    The bleak twigs overhead
In a full-hearted evensong
    Of joy illimited;
An agèd thrush, frail, gaunt, and small,
    In blast-beruffled plume,
Had chosen thus to fling his soul
    Upon the growing gloom.

So little cause for carolings
    Of such ecstatic sound
Was written on terrestrial things
    Afar or nigh around,

That I could think there trembled through
    His happy good-night air
Some blessed Hope, whereof he knew
    And I was unaware.

THE SUBALTERNS

'Poor wanderer,' said the leaden sky,
    'I fain would lighten thee,
But there are laws in force on high
    Which say it must not be.'

—'I would not freeze thee, shorn one,' cried
    The North, 'knew I but how
To warm my breath, to slack my stride;
    But I am ruled as thou.'

—'To-morrow I attack thee, wight,'
    Said Sickness. 'Yet I swear
I bear thy little ark no spite,
    But am bid enter there.'

—'Come hither, Son,' I heard Death say;
    'I did not will a grave
Should end thy pilgrimage to-day,
    But I, too, am a slave!'

We smiled upon each other then,
    And life to me had less
Of that fell look it wore ere when
    They owned their passiveness.

HAP

If but some vengeful god would call to me
From up the sky, and laugh: 'Thou suffering thing,
Know that thy sorrow is my ecstasy,
That thy love's loss is my hate's profiting!'
Then would I bear it, clench myself, and die,
Steeled by the sense of ire unmerited;
Half-eased in that a Powerfuller than I
Had willed and meted me the tears I shed.

But not so.   How arrives it joy lies slain,
And why unblooms the best hope ever sown?

—Crass Casualty obstructs the sun and rain,
And dicing Time for gladness casts a moan. . . .
These purblind Doomsters had as readily strown
Blisses about my pilgrimage as pain.

THE TO-BE-FORGOTTEN

I heard a small sad sound,
And stood awhile among the tombs around:
'Wherefore, old friends,' said I, 'are you distrest,
    Now, screened from life's unrest?'

—'O not at being here;
But that our future second death is near;
When, with the living, memory of us numbs,
    And blank oblivion comes!

'These, our sped ancestry,
Lie here embraced by deeper death than we;
Nor shape nor thought of theirs can you descry
    With keenest backward eye.

'They count as quite forgot;
They are as men who have existed not;
Theirs is a loss past loss of fitful breath;
    It is the second death.

'We here, as yet, each day
Are blest with dear recall; as yet, can say
We hold in some soul loved continuance
    Of shape and voice and glance.

'But what has been will be—
First memory, then oblivion's swallowing sea;
Like men foregone, shall we merge into those
    Whose story no one knows.

'For which of us could hope
To show in life that world-awakening scope
Granted the few whose memory none lets die,
    But all men magnify?

'We were but Fortune's sport;
Things true, things lovely, things of good report
We neither shunned nor sought . . . We see our bourne,
    And seeing it we mourn.'

NEUTRAL TONES

We stood by a pond that winter day,
And the sun was white, as though chidden of God,
And a few leaves lay on the starving sod;
    —They had fallen from an ash, and were grey.

Your eyes on me were as eyes that rove
Over tedious riddles of years ago;
And some words played between us to and fro
    On which lost the more by our love.

The smile on your mouth was the deadest thing
Alive enough to have strength to die;
And a grin of bitterness swept thereby
    Like an ominous bird a-wing. . . .

Since then, keen lessons that love deceives,
And wrings with wrong, have shaped to me
Your face, and the God-curst sun, and a tree,
    And a pond edged with greyish leaves.

TO LIZBIE BROWNE

Dear Lizbie Browne,
Where are you now?
In sun, in rain?—
Or is your brow
Past joy, past pain,
Dear Lizbie Browne?

Sweet Lizbie Browne
How you could smile,
How you could sing!—
How archly wile
In glance-giving,
Sweet Lizbie Browne!

And, Lizbie Browne,
Who else had hair
Bay-red as yours,
Or flesh so fair
Bred out of doors,
Sweet Lizbie Browne?

When, Lizbie Browne,
You had just begun
To be endeared
By stealth to one,
You disappeared
My Lizbie Browne!

Ay, Lizbie Browne,
So swift your life,
And mine so slow,
You were a wife
Ere I could show
Love, Lizbie Browne.

Still, Lizbie Browne,
You won, they said,
The best of men
When you were wed. . . .
Where went you then,
O Lizbie Browne?

Dear Lizbie Browne,
I should have thought,
'Girls ripen fast,'
And coaxed and caught
You ere you passed,
Dear Lizbie Browne!

But, Lizbie Browne,
I let you slip;
Shaped not a sign;
Touched never your lip

With lip of mine,
Lost Lizbie Browne!

So, Lizbie Browne,
When on a day
Men speak of me
As not, you'll say,
'And who was he?'—
Yes, Lizbie Browne!

WESSEX HEIGHTS

(1896)

There are some heights in Wessex, shaped as if by a kindly
hand
For thinking, dreaming, dying on, and at crises when I
stand,
Say, on Ingpen Beacon eastward, or on Wylls-Neck west-
wardly,
I seem where I was before my birth, and after death may
be.

In the lowlands I have no comrade, not even the lone man's
friend—
Her who suffereth long and is kind; accepts what he is too
weak to mend:
Down there they are dubious and askance; there nobody
thinks as I,
But mind-chains do not clank where one's next neighbour
is the sky.

In the towns I am tracked by phantoms having weird de-
tective ways—
Shadows of beings who fellowed with myself of earlier
days:
They hang about at places, and they say harsh heavy
things—
Men with a wintry sneer, and women with tart disparagings.

Down there I seem to be false to myself, my simple self that
was,
And is not now, and I see him watching, wondering what
crass cause

Can have merged him into such a strange continuator as
    this,
Who yet has something in common with himself, my
    chrysalis.

I cannot go to the great grey Plain; there's a figure against
    the moon,
Nobody sees it but I, and it makes my breast beat out of
    tune;
I cannot go to the tall-spired town, being barred by the
    forms now passed
For everybody but me, in whose long vision they stand there
    fast.

There's a ghost at Yell'ham Bottom chiding loud at the fall
    of the night,
There's a ghost in Froom-side Vale, thin lipped and vague,
    in a shroud of white,
There is one in the railway train whenever I do not want
    it near,
I see its profile against the pane, saying what I would not
    hear.

As for one rare fair woman, I am not but a thought of hers,
I enter her mind and another thought succeeds me that she
    prefers;
Yet my love for her in its fulness she herself even did not
    know;
Well, time cures hearts of tenderness, and now I can let
    her go.

So I am found on Ingpen Beacon, or on Wylls-Neck to the
    west,
Or else on homely Bulbarrow, or little Pilsdon Crest,
Where men have never cared to haunt, nor women have
    walked with me,
And ghosts then keep their distance; and I know some
    liberty.

CHANNEL FIRING

That night your great guns, unawares,
Shook all our coffins as we lay,
And broke the chancel window-squares,
We thought it was the Judgment-day

And sat upright. While drearisome
Arose the howl of wakened hounds:
The mouse let fall the altar-crumb,
The worms drew back into the mounds,

The glebe cow drooled. Till God called, 'No;
It's gunnery practice out at sea
Just as before you went below;
The world is as it used to be:

'All nations striving strong to make
Red war yet redder. Mad as hatters
They do no more for Christés sake
Than you who are helpless in such matters.

'That this is not the judgment-hour
For some of them's a blessed thing,
For if it were they'd have to scour
Hell's floor for so much threatening. . . .

'Ha, ha. It will be warmer when
I blow the trumpet (if indeed
I ever do; for you are men,
And rest eternal sorely need).'

So down we lay again. 'I wonder,
Will the world ever saner be,'
Said one, 'than when He sent us under
In our indifferent century!'

And many a skeleton shook his head.
'Instead of preaching forty year,'
My neighbour Parson Thirdly said,
'I wish I had stuck to pipes and beer.'

Again the guns disturbed the hour,
Roaring their readiness to avenge,
As far inland as Stourton Tower,
And Camelot, and starlit Stonehenge.

THE LAST CHRYSANTHEMUM

Why should this flower delay so long
        To show its tremulous plumes?
Now is the time of plaintive robin-song,
        When flowers are in their tombs.

Through the slow summer, when the sun
          Called to each frond and whorl
That all he could for flowers was being done,
          Why did it not uncurl?

It must have felt that fervid call
          Although it took no heed,
Waking but now, when leaves like corpses fall,
          And saps all retrocede.

Too late its beauty, lonely thing,
          The season's shine is spent,
Nothing remains for it but shivering
          In tempests turbulent.

Had it a reason for delay,
          Dreaming in witlessness
That for a bloom so delicately gay
          Winter would stay its stress?

—I talk as if the thing were born
          With sense to work its mind;
Yet it is but one mask of many worn
          By the Great Face behind.

THE SOULS OF THE SLAIN

The thick lids of Night closed upon me
          Alone at the Bill
          Of the Isle by the Race—
Many-caverned, bald, wrinkled of face—
And with darkness and silence the spirit was on me
          Too brood and be still.

No wind fanned the flats of the ocean,
          Or promontory sides,
          Or the ooze by the strand,
Or the bent-bearded slope of the land,
Whose base took its rest amid everlong motion
          Of criss-crossing tides.

Soon from out of the Southward seemed nearing
          A whirr, as of wings
          Waved by mighty-vanned flies,
Or by night-moths of measureless size,
And in softness and smoothness well-nigh beyond hearing

Of corporal things.

And they bore to the bluff, and alighted—
    A dim-discerned train
    Of sprites without mould,
Frameless souls none might touch or might hold—
On the ledge by the turreted lantern, far-sighted
    By men of the main.

And I heard them say 'Home!' and I knew them
    For souls of the felled
    On the earth's nether bord
Under Capricorn, whither they'd warred,
And I neared in my awe, and gave heedfulness to them
    With breathings inheld.

Then, it seemed, there approached from the Northward
    A senior soul-flame
    Of the like filmy hue:
And he met them and spake: 'Is it you,
O my men?' Said they, 'Aye! We bear homeward and hearth-
    ward
    To feast on our fame!'

'I've flown there before you,' he said then:
    'Your households are well;
    But—your kin linger less
On your glory and war-mightiness
Than on dearer things.' '—Dearer?' cried these from the
    dead then,
    'Of what do they tell?'

'Some mothers muse sadly, and murmur
    Your doings as boys—
    Recall the quaint ways
Of your babyhood's innocent days.
Some pray that, ere dying, your faith had grown firmer,
    And higher your joys.

'A father broods: "Would I had set him
    to some humble trade,
    And so slacked his high fire,
And his passionate martial desire;
And told him no stories to woo him and whet him
    To this dire crusade!" '

'And, General, how hold out our sweethearts,
    Sworn loyal as doves?'
    —'Many mourn; many think
It is not unattractive to prink
Them in sables for heroes. Some fickle and fleet hearts
    Have found them new loves.'

'And our wives?' quoth another resignedly,
    'Dwell they on our deeds?'
    —'Deeds of home; that live yet
Fresh as new—deeds of fondness or fret;
Ancient words that were kindly expressed, or unkindly,
    These, these have their heeds.'

—'Alas! then it seems that our glory
    Weighs less in their thought
    Than our old homely acts,
And the long-ago commonplace facts
Of our lives—held by us as scarce part of our story,
    And rated as nought!'

Then bitterly some: 'Was it wise now
    To raise such a tomb-door
    For such knowledge? Away!'
But the rest: 'Fame we prized till to-day;
Yet that hearts keep us green for old kindness we prize now
    A thousand times more!'

Thus speaking, the trooped apparitions
    Began to disband
    And resolve them in two:
Those whose record was lovely and true
Bore to northward for home: those of bitter traditions
    Again left the land,

And, towering to seaward in legions,
    They paused at a spot
    Overbending the Race—
That engulphing, ghast, sinister place—
Whither headlong they plunged, to the fathomless regions
    Of myriads forgot.

And the spirits of those who were homing
    Passed on, rushingly,
    Like the Pentecost Wind:
And the whirr of their wayfaring thinned
And surceased on the sky, and but left in the gloaming
    Sea-mutterings and me.

TO AN UNBORN PAUPER CHILD

Breathe not, hid Heart: cease silently,
And though thy birth-hour beckons thee,
    Sleep the long sleep:
    The Doomsters heap
Travails and teens around us here,
And Time-wraiths turn our songsingings to fear.

Heark, how the peoples surge and sigh,
And laughters fails, and greetings die:
    Hopes dwindle; yea,
    Faiths waste away,
Affections and enthusiasms numb;
Thou canst not mend these things if thou dost come.

Had I the ear of wombèd souls
Ere their terrestrial chart unrolls,
    And thou wert free
    To cease, or be,
Then would I tell thee all I know,
And put it to thee: Wilt thou take Life so?

Vain vow! No hint of mine may hence
To theeward fly: to thy locked sense
    Explain none can
    Life's pending plan:
Thou wilt thy ignorant entry make
Though skies spout fire and blood and nations quake.

Fain would I, dear, find some shut plot
Of earth's wide wold for thee, where not
    One tear, one qualm,
    Should break the calm.
But I am weak as thou and bare;
No man can change the common lot to rare.

Must come and bide. And such are we—
Unreasoning, sanguine, visionary—
    That I can hope
    Health, love, friends, scope
In full for thee; can dream thou wilt find
Joys seldom yet attained by humankind!

IN TENEBRIS

I

'Percussus sum sicut foenum, et aruit cor meum.'—Ps. ci.

Wintertime nighs;
But my bereavement-pain
It cannot bring again:
    Twice no one dies.

Leaves freeze to dun;
But friends can not turn cold
This season as of old
    For him with none.

Flower-petals flee;
But, since it once hath been,
No more that severing scene
    Can harrow me.

Tempests may scath;
But love can not make smart
Again this year his heart
    Who no heart hath.

Birds faint in dread:
I shall not lose old strength
In the lone frost's black length:
    Strength long since fled!

Black is night's cope;
But death will not appal
One who, past doubtings all,
    Waits in unhope.

II

'Considerabam ad dexteram, et videbam; et non erat qui cognosceret me. . . . Non est qui requirat animam meam.'—Ps. cxli.

When the clouds' swoln bosoms echo back the shouts of the
    many and strong
That things are all as they best may be, save a few to be right
    ere long,
And my eyes have not the vision in them to discern what to
    these is so clear,
The blot seems straightway in me alone; one better he were
    not here.

The stout upstanders say, All's well with us: ruers have
    nought to rue!
And what the potent say so oft, can it fail to be somewhat
    true?
Breezily go they, breezily come; their dust smokes around
    their career,
Till I think I am one born out of due time, who has no
    calling here.

Their dawns bring lusty joys, it seems; their evenings all
    that is sweet;

Our times are blessed times, they cry: Life shapes it as is
    most meet,
And nothing is much the matter; there are many smiles to
    a tear;
Then what is the matter is I, I say. Why should such an one
    be here? . . .

Let him in whose ears the low-voiced Best is killed by the
    clash of the First,
Who holds that if way to the Better there be, it exacts a full
    look at the Worst,
Who feels that delight is a delicate growth cramped by crook-
    edness, custom, and fear,
Get him up and be gone as one shaped awry; he disturbs
    the order here.

III

*'Heu mihi, quia incolatus meus prolongatus est! Habitavi cum
habitantibus Cedar; multum incola fuit anima mea.'—Ps. cxix.*

There have been times when I well might have passed and
    the ending have come—
Points in my path when the dark might have stolen on me,
    artless, unrueing—
Ere I had learnt that the world was a welter of futile doing:
Such had been times when I well might have passed, and the
    ending have come!

Say, on the noon when the half-sunny hours told that April
    was nigh,
And I upgathered and cast forth the snow from
    the crocus-border,
Fashioned and furbished the soil into a summer-seeming
    order,
Glowing in gladsome faith that I quickened the year thereby.

Or on that loneliest of eves when afar and benighted we
    stood,
She who upheld me and I, in the midmost of Egdon to-
    gether,
Confident I in her watching and ward through the blacken-
    ing heather,
Deeming her matchless in might and with measureless scope
    endued.

Or on that winter-wild night when, reclined by the chim-
ney-nook quoin,
Slowly a drowse overgat me, the smallest and feeblest of
folk there,
Weak from my baptism of pain; when at times and anon I
awoke there—
Heard of a world wheeling on, with no listing or longing to
join.

Even then! while unweeting that vision could vex or that
knowledge could numb,
That sweets to the mouth in the belly are bitter, and tart,
and untoward,
Then, on some dim-coloured scene should my briefly raised
curtain have lowered,
Then might the Voice that is law have said 'Cease!' and the
ending have come.

THE RUINED MAID

'O 'melia, my dear, this does everything crown!
Who could have supposed I should meet you in Town?
And whence such fair garments, such prosperi-ty?'—
'O didn't you know I'd been ruined?' said she.

—'You left us in tatters, without shoes or socks,
Tired of digging potatoes, and spudding up docks;
And now you've gay bracelets and bright feathers three!'—
'Yes: that's how we dress when we're ruined,' said she.

—'At home in the barton you said "thee" and "thou,"
And "thik oon," and "theäs oon," and "t'other"; but now
Your talking quite fits 'ee for high compa-ny!'—
'Some polish is gained with one's ruin,' said she.

—'Your hands were like paws then, your face blue and bleak
But now I'm bewitched by your delicate cheek,
And your little gloves fit as on any la-dy!'—
'We never do work when we're ruined,' said she.

—'You used to call home-life a hag-ridden dream.
And you'd sigh, and you'd sock; but at present you seem
To know not of megrims or melancho-ly!'—
'True. One's pretty lively when ruined,' said she.

—'I wish I had feathers, a fine sweeping gown,
And a delicate face, and could strut about Town!'—
'My dear—a raw country girl, such as you be,
Cannot quite expect that. You ain't ruined,' said she.

A REFUSAL

Said the grave Dean of
 Westminster:
Mine is the best minster
Seen in Great Britain,
As many have written:
So therefore I cannot
Rule here if I ban not
Such liberty-taking
As movements for making
Its greyness environ
The memory of Byron,
Which some are demanding
Who think them of
 standing,
But in my own viewing
Require some subduing
For tendering sugges-
 tions
On Abbey-wall questions
That must interfere here
With my proper sphere
 here,
And bring to disaster
This fane and its master,
Whose dict is but Chris-
 tian
Though nicknamed Philis-
 tian.

A lax Christian charity—
No mental clarity
Ruling its movements
For fabric improvements—
Demands admonition
And strict supervision
When bent on enshrining

Rapscallions, and signing
Their names on God's
 stonework,
As if like His own work
Were their lucubrations:
And passed is my pa-
 tience
That such a creed-scorner
(Not mentioning horner)
Should claim Poet's
 Corner.

'Tis urged that some
 sinners
Are here for worms'
 dinners
Already in person;
That he could not worsen
The walls by a name mere
With men of such fame
 here.
Yet nay; they but leaven
The others in heaven
In just true proportion,
While more mean distor-
 tion.

'Twill next be expected
That I get erected
To Shelley a tablet
In some niche or gablet.
Then—what makes my
 skin burn,
Yea, forehead to chin
 burn—
That I ensconce Swin-
 burne!

THE CONVERGENCE OF THE TWAIN

(*Lines on the loss of the 'Titanic'*)

In a solitude of the sea
Deep from human vanity,
And the Pride of Life that planned her, stilly couches she.

Steel chambers, late the pyres
Of her salamandrine fires,
Cold currents thrid, and turn to rhythmic tidal lyres.

Over the mirrors meant
To glass the opulent
The sea-worm crawls—grotesque, slimed, dumb, indifferent.

Jewels in joy designed
To ravish the sensuous mind
Lie lightless, all their sparkles bleared and black and blind.

Dim moon-eyed fishes near
Gaze at the gilded gear
And query: 'What does this vaingloriousness down here?' . . .

Well: while was fashioning
This creature of cleaving wing,
The Immanent Will that stirs and urges everything

Prepared a sinister mate
For her—so gaily great—
A Shape of Ice, for the time far and dissociate.

And as the smart ship grew
In stature, grace, and hue,
In shadowy silent distance grew the Iceberg too.

Alien they seemed to be:
No mortal eye could see
The intimate welding of their later history.

Or sign that they were bent
By paths coincident
On being anon twin halves of one august event,

Till the Spinner of the Years
Said 'Now!' And each one hears,
And consummation comes, and jars two hemispheres.

NO BUYERS:

A STREET SCENE

A load of brushes and baskets and cradles and chairs
   Labours along the street in the rain:
With it a man, a woman, a pony with whiteybrown hairs.—
   The man foots in front of the horse with a shambling sway
    At a slower tread than a funeral train,
   While to a dirge-like tune he chants his wares,
   Swinging a Turk's-head brush (in a drum-major's way
    When the bandsmen march and play).

A yard from the back of the man is the whiteybrown pony's
    nose:
He mirrors his master in every item of pace and pose:
   He stops when the man stops, without being told,
And seems to be eased by a pause; too plainly he's old,
    Indeed, not strength enough shows
   To steer the disjointed waggon straight,
Which wriggles left and right in a rambling line,
   Deflected thus by its own warp and weight,
And pushing the pony with it in each incline.

   The woman walks on the pavement verge,
    Parallel to the man:
She wears an apron white and wide in span,
And carries a like Turk's-head, but more in nursing-wise:
   Now and then she joins in his dirge,
   But as if her thoughts were on distant things.
   The rain clams her apron till it clings.—
So, step by step, they move with their merchandize,
    And nobody buys.

IN TIME OF 'THE BREAKING OF NATIONS'

   Only a man harrowing clods
    In a slow silent walk
   With an old horse that stumbles and nods
    Half asleep as they stalk.

   Only thin smoke without flame
    From the heaps of couch-grass;
   Yet this will go onward the same
    Though Dynasties pass.

Yonder a maid and her wight
  Come whispering by:
War's annals will fade into night
  Ere their story die.

AFTERWARDS

When the Present has latched its postern behind my tremu-
    lous stay,
  And the May month flaps its glad green leaves like wings,
Delicate-filmed as new-spun silk, will the neighbours say,
  'He was a man who used to notice such things?'

If it be in the dusk when, like an eyelid's soundless blink,
  The dewfall-hawk comes crossing the shades to alight
Upon the wind-warped upland thorn, a gazer may think,
  'To him this must have been a familiar sight.'

If I pass during some nocturnal blackness, mothy and warm,
  When the hedgehog travels furtively over the lawn,
One may say, 'He strove that such innocent creatures should
    come to no harm,
    But he could do little for them; and now he is gone.'

If, when hearing that I have been stilled at last, they stand
    at the door,
  Watching the full-starred heavens that winter sees,
Will this thought rise on those who will meet my face no
    more,
  'He was one who had an eye for such mysteries'?

And will any say when my bell of quittance is heard in the
    gloom,
  And a crossing breeze cuts a pause in its outrollings,
Till they rise again, as they were a new bell's boom,
  'He hears it not now, but used to notice such things'?

THE GOING

Why did you give no hint that night
That quickly after the morrow's dawn,
And calmly, as if indifferent quite,
You would close your term here, up and be gone
  Where I could not follow

With wing of swallow
To gain one glimpse of you ever anon!

    Never to bid good-bye,
        Or lip me the softest call,
Or utter a wish for a word, while I
Saw morning harden upon the wall,
        Unmoved, unknowing
        That your great going
Had place that moment, and altered all.

Why do you make me leave the house
And think for a breath it is you I see
At the end of the alley of bending boughs
Where so often at dusk you used to be;
        Till in darkening dankness
        The yawning blankness
Of the perspective sickens me!

    You were she who abode
        By those red-veined rocks far West,
You were the swan-necked one who rode
Along the beetling Beeny Crest,
        And, reining nigh me,
        Would muse and eye me,
While Life unrolled us its very best.

Why, then, latterly did we not speak,
Did we not think of those days long dead,
And ere your vanishing strive to seek
That time's renewal? We might have said,
        'In this bright spring weather
        We'll visit together
Those places that once we visited.'

    Well, well! All's past amend,
        Unchangeable. It must go.
I seem but a dead man held on end
To sink down soon. . . . O you could not know
        That such swift fleeing
        No soul foreseeing—
Not even I—would undo me so!

THE OXEN

Christmas Eve, and twelve of the clock.
   'Now they are all on their knees,'
An elder said as we sat in a flock
   By the embers in heartside ease.

We pictured the meek mild creatures where
   They dwelt in their strawy pen,
Nor did it occur to one of us there
   To doubt they were kneeling then.

So fair a fancy few would weave
   In these years! Yet, I feel,
If someone said on Christmas Eve,
   'Come; see the oxen kneel,

'In the lonely barton by yonder coomb
   Our childhood used to know,'
I should go with him in the gloom,
   Hoping it might be so.

THE MAN HE KILLED

   'Had he and I but met
     By some old ancient inn,
We should have sat us down to wet
     Right many a nipperkin!

   'But ranged as infantry,
     And staring face to face,
I shot at him as he at me,
     And killed him in his place.

   'I shot him dead because—
     Because he was my foe,
Just so: my foe of course he was;
     That's clear enough; although

   'He thought he'd 'list, perhaps,
     Off-hand like—just as I—
Was out of work—had sold his traps—
     No other reason why.

   'Yes; quaint and curious war is!
     You shoot a fellow down
You'd treat if met where any bar is,
     Or help to half-a-crown.'

AFTER A JOURNEY

Hereto I come to view a voiceless ghost;
   Whither, O whither will its whim now draw me?
Up the cliff, down, till I'm lonely, lost,
   And the unseen waters' ejaculations awe me.
Where you will next be there's no knowing,
   Facing round about me everywhere,
      With your nut-coloured hair,
And grey eyes, and rose-flush coming and going.

Yes: I have re-entered your olden haunts at last;
   Through the years, through the dead scenes I have tracked
      you;
What have you now found to say of our past—
   Scanned across the dark space wherein I have lacked you?
Summer gave us sweets, but autumn wrought division?
   Things were not lastly as firstly well
      With us twain, you tell?
But all's closed now, despite Time's derision.

I see what you are doing: you are leading me on
   To the spots we knew when we haunted here together,
The waterfall, above which the mist-bow shone
   At the then fair hour in the then fair weather,
And the cave just under, with a voice still so hollow
   That it seems to call out to me from forty years ago,
      When you were all aglow,
And not the thin ghost that I now frailly follow!

Ignorant of what there is flitting here to see,
   The waked birds preen and the seals flop lazily,
Soon you will have, Dear, to vanish from me,
   For the stars close their shutters and the dawn whitens
      hazily.
Trust me, I mind not, though Life lours,
   The bringing me here; nay, bring me here again!
      I am just the same as when
Our days were a joy, and our paths through flowers.

THE PHANTOM HORSEWOMAN

Queer are the ways of a man
   I know:
He comes and stands
In a careworn craze,
And looks at the sands
And the seaward haze
With moveless hands
And face and gaze,
Then turns to go . . .

And what does he see when
   he gazes so?
They say he sees as an instant
   thing

More clear than to-day,
A sweet soft scene
That once was in play
By that briny green;
Yes, notes alway
Warm, real, and keen,
What his back years bring—
A phantom of his own
   figuring.

Of this vision of his they
   might say more:
Not only there
Does he see this sight,

But everywhere
In his brain—day, night,
As if on the air
It were drawn rose bright—
Yea, far from that shore
Does he carry this vision
   of heretofore:

A ghost-girl-rider. And
   though, toil-tried,
He withers daily,
Time touches her not,
But she still rides gaily
In his rapt thought
On that shagged and shaly
Atlantic spot,
And as when first eyed
Draws rein and sings to the
   swing of the tide.

WHO'S IN THE NEXT ROOM?

'Who's in the next room?—who?
      I seemed to see
Somebody in the dawning passing through,
      Unknown to me.'
'Nay: you saw nought. He passed invisibly.'

'Who's in the next room?—who?
      I seem to hear
Somebody muttering firm in a language new
      That chills the ear.'
'No: you catch not his tongue who has entered there.'

'Who's in the next room?—who?
      I seem to feel
His breath like a clammy draught, as if it drew
      From the Polar Wheel.'
'No: none who breathes at all does the door conceal.'

'Who's in the next room?—who?
      A figure wan
With a message to one in there of something due?
      Shall I know him anon?'
'Yea he; and, he brought such; and you'll know him anon.'

GERARD MANLEY HOPKINS

(1844-1889)

GOD'S GRANDEUR

The world is charged with the grandeur of God.
  It will flame out, like shining from shook foil;
  It gathers to a greatness, like the ooze of oil
Crushed. Why do men then now not reck his rod?
Generations have trod, have trod, have trod;
  And all is seared with trade; bleared, smeared with toil;
  And wears man's smudge and shares man's smell: the soil
Is bare now, nor can foot feel, being shod.

And for all this, nature is never spent;
  There lives the dearest freshness deep down things;
And though the last lights off the black West went
  Oh, morning, at the brown brink eastward, springs—
Because the Holy Ghost over the bent
  World broods with warm breast and with ah! bright wings.

THE STARLIGHT NIGHT

Look at the stars! look, look up at the skies!
  O look at all the fire-folk sitting in the air!
  The bright boroughs, the circle-citadels there!
Down in dim woods the diamond delves! the elves'-eyes!
The grey lawns cold where gold, where quickgold lies!
  Wind-beat whitebeam! airy abeles set on a flare!
  Flake-doves sent floating forth at a farmyard scare!—
Ah well! it is all a purchase, all is a prize.

Buy then! bid then!—What?—Prayer, patience, alms, vows.
Look, look: a May-mess, like on orchard boughs!
  Look! March-bloom, like on mealed-with-yellow sallows!
These are indeed the barn; withindoors house
The shocks. This piece-bright paling shuts the spouse
  Christ home, Christ and his mother and all his hallows.

SPRING

Nothing is so beautiful as spring—
   When weeds, in wheels, shoot long and lovely and lush;
   Thrush's eggs look little low heavens, and thrush
Through the echoing timber does so rinse and wring
The ear, it strikes like lightnings to hear him sing;
   The glassy peartree leaves and blooms, they brush
   The descending blue; that blue is all in a rush
With richness; the racing lambs too have fair their fling.

What is all this juice and all this joy?
   A strain of the earth's sweet being in the beginning
In Eden garden.—Have, get, before it cloy,
   Before it cloud, Christ, lord, and sour with sinning,
Innocent mind and Mayday in girl and boy,
   Most, O maid's child, thy choice and worthy the winning.

THE LANTERN OUT OF DOORS

Sometimes a lantern moves along the night,
   That interests our eyes. And who goes there?
   I think; where from and bound, I wonder, where,
With, all down darkness wide, his wading light?
Men go by me whom either beauty bright
   In mould or mind or what not else makes rare:
   They rain against our much-thick and marsh air
Rich beams, till death or distance buys them quite.

Death or distance soon consumes them: wind
   What most I may eye after, be in at the end
I cannot, and out of sight is out of mind.
Christ minds; Christ's interest, what to avow or amend
   There, éyes them, heart wánts, care haúnts, foot fól-
      lows kínd,
Their ránsom, théir rescue, ánd first, fást, last friénd.

THE SEA AND THE SKYLARK

On ear and ear two noises too old to end
   Trench—right, the tide that ramps against the shore;
   With a flood or a fall, low lull-off or all roar,
Frequenting there while moon shall wear and wend.
Left hand, off land, I hear the lark ascend,
   His rash-fresh re-winded new-skeinèd score

In his crisps of curl off wild winch whirl, and pour
And pelt music, till none's to spill nor spend.

How these two shame this shallow and frail town!
　　How ɼing right out our sordid turbid time,
Being pure! We, life's pride and cared-for crown,
　　Have lost that cheer and charm of earth's past prime:
Our make and making break, are breaking, down
　　To man's last dust, drain fast towards man's first slime.

THE WINDHOVER:

To Christ our Lord

I caught this morning morning's minion, kingdom of day-
　　　　light's dauphin, dapple-dawn-drawn Falcon, in his
　　　　riding
　　Of the rolling level underneath him steady air, and strid-
　　　　ing
High there, how he rung upon the rein of a wimpling wing
In his ecstasy! then off, off forth on swing,
　　As a skate's heel sweeps smooth on a bow-bend: the hurl
　　　　and gliding
Rebuffed the big wind. My heart in hiding
Stirred for a bird,—the achieve of, the mastery of the thing!

Brute beauty and valour and act, oh, air, pride, plume here
　　Buckle! AND the fire that breaks from thee then, a billion
Times told lovelier, more dangerous, O my chevalier!
　　No wonder of it: shéer plód makes plough down sillion
Shine, and blue-bleak embers, ah my dear,
　　Fall, gall themselves, and gash gold-vermilion.

PIED BEAUTY

Glory be to God for dappled things—
　　For skies of couple-colour as a brinded cow;
　　　　For rose-moles all in stripple upon trout that swim;
Fresh-firecoal chestnut-falls; finches' wings;
　　Landscape plotted and pieced—fold, fallow, and plough;
　　　　And áll trádes, their gear and tackle and trim.
All things counter, original, spare, strange;
　　Whatever is fickle, freckled (who knows how?)
　　　　With swift, slow; sweet, sour; adazzle, dim;
He fathers-forth whose beauty is past change:
　　　　　　　　　Praise him.

HURRAHING IN HARVEST

Summer ends now; now, barbarous in beauty, the stooks arise
    Around; up above, what wind-walks! what lovely behaviour
    Of silk-sack clouds! has wilder, wilful-wavier
Meal-drift moulded ever and melted across skies?
I walk, I lift up, I lift up heart, eyes,
    Down all that glory in the heavens to glean our Saviour;
    And, éyes, heárt, what looks, what lips yet gave you a
Rapturous love's greeting of realer, of rounder replies?

And the azurous hung hills are his world-wielding shoulder
    Majestic—as a stallion stalwart, very-violet-sweet!—
These things, these things were here and but the beholder
    Wanting; which two when they once meet,
The heart réars wíngs bold and bolder
    And hurls for him, O half hurls earth for him off under
        his feet.

THE CAGED SKYLARK

As a dare-gale skylark scanted in a dull cage
    Man's mounting spirit in his bone-house, mean house,
        dwells—
    That bird beyond the remembering his free fells;
This in drudgery, day-labouring-out life's age.
Though aloft on turf or perch or poor low stage,
    Both sing sómetimes the sweetest, sweetest spells,
    Yet both droop deadly sómetimes in their cells
Or wring their barriers in bursts of fear or rage.

Not that the sweet-fowl, song-fowl, needs no rest—
Why, hear him, hear him babble and drop down to his nest,
    But his own nest, wild nest, no prison.

Man's spirit will be flesh-bound when found at best,
But uncumbered: meadow-down is not distressed
    For a rainbow footing it nor he for his bónes rísen.

DUNS SCOTUS'S OXFORD

Towery city and branchy between towers;
Cuckoo-echoing, bell-swarmèd, lark-charmèd, rook-racked,
    river-rounded;
The dapple-eared lily below thee; that country and town did

Once encounter in, here coped and poisèd powers;

Thou hast a base and brickish skirt there, sours
That neighbour-nature thy grey beauty is grounded
Best in; graceless growth, thou hast confounded
Rural rural keeping—folk, flocks, and flowers.

Yet ah! this air I gather and I release
He lived on; these weeds and waters, these walls are what
He haunted who of all men most sways my spirits to peace;

Of realty the rarest-veinèd unraveller; a not
Rivalled insight, be rival Italy or Greece;
Who fired France for Mary without spot.

THE HABIT OF PERFECTION

Elected Silence, sing to me
And beat upon my whorlèd ear,
Pipe me to pastures still and be
The music that I care to hear.

Shape nothing, lips; be lovely-dumb:
It is the shut, the curfew sent
From there where all surrenders come
Which only makes you eloquent.

Be shellèd, eyes, with double dark
And find the uncreated light:
This ruck and reel which you remark
Coils, keeps, and teases simple sight.

Palate, the hutch of tasty lust,
Desire not to be rinsed with wine:
The can must be so sweet, the crust
So fresh that come in fasts divine!

Nostrils, your careless breath that spend
Upon the stir and keep of pride,
What relish shall the censers send
Along the sanctuary side!

O feel-of-primrose hands, O feet
That want the yield of plushy sward,
But you shall walk the golden street
And you unhouse and house the Lord.

And, Poverty, be thou the bride
And now the marriage feast begun,
And lily-coloured clothes provide
Your spouse not laboured-at nor spun.

INVERSNAID

This darksome burn, horseback brown,
His rollrock highroad roaring down,
In coop and in comb the fleece of his foam
Flutes and low to the lake falls home.

A windpuff-bonnet of fáwn-fróth
Turns and twindles over the broth
Of a pool so pitchblack, féll-frówning,
It rounds and rounds Despair to drowning.

Degged with dew, dappled with dew
Are the groins of the braes that the brook treads through,
Wiry heathpacks, flitches of fern,
And the beadbonny ash that sits over the burn.

What would the world be, once bereft
Of wet and of wildness? Let them be left,
O let them be left, wildness and wet;
Long live the weeds and the wilderness yet.

IN THE VALLEY OF THE ELWY

I remember a house where all were good
    To me, God knows, deserving no such thing:
    Comforting smell breathed at very entering,
Fetched fresh, as I suppose, off some sweet wood.
That cordial air made those kind people a hood
    All over, as a bevy of eggs the mothering wing
    Will, or mild nights the new morsels of spring:
Why, it seemed of course; seemed of right it should.

Lovely the woods, waters, meadows, combes, vales,
All the air things wear that build this world of Wales;
    Only the inmate does not correspond:
God, lover of souls, swaying considerate scales,
Complete thy creature dear O where it fails,
    Being mighty a master, being a father and fond.

HENRY PURCELL

*The poet wishes well to the divine genius of Purcell and praises
him that, whereas other musicians have given utterance to the
moods of man's mind, he has, beyond that, uttered in notes the
very make and species of man as created both in him and in all
men generally.*

Have fair fallen, O fair, fair have fallen, so dear
To me, so arch-especial a spirit as heaves in Henry Purcell,
An age is now since passed, since parted; with the reversal
Of the outward sentence low lays him, listed to a heresy, here.
Not mood in him nor meaning, proud fire or sacred fear,
Or love or pity or all that sweet notes not his might nursle:
It is the forgèd feature finds me; it is the rehearsal
Of own, of abrúpt sélf there so thrusts on, so throngs the ear.

Let him oh! with his air of angels then lift me, lay me! only
    I'll
Have an eye to the sakes of him, quaint moonmarks, to his
    pelted plumage under
Wings: so some great stormfowl, whenever he has walked
    his while
The thunder-purple seabeach, plumèd purple-of-thunder,
If a wuthering of his palmy snow-pinions scatter a colossal
    smile
Off him, but meaning motion fans fresh our wits with wonder.

SPRING AND FALL

To a Young Child

Márgarét, are you gríeving
Over Goldengrove unleaving?
Leáves, líke the things of man, you
With your fresh thoughts care for, can you?
Áh! ás the heart grows older
It will come to such sights colder
By and by, nor spare a sigh
Though worlds of wanwood leafmeal lie;
And yet you wíll weep and know why.
Now no matter, child, the name:
Sórrow's spríngs áre the same.
Nor mouth had, no nor mind, expressed
What heart heard of, ghost guessed:
It ís the blight man was born for,
It is Margaret you mourn for.

ANDROMEDA

Now Time's Andromeda on this rock rude,
With not her either beauty's equal or
Her injury's, looks off by both horns of shore,
Her flower, her piece of being, doomed dragon's food.
   Time past she has been attempted and pursued
By many blows and banes; but now hears roar
A wilder beast from West than all were, more
Rife in her wrongs, more lawless, and more lewd.

   Her Perseus linger and leave her tó her extremes?—
Pillowy air he treads a time and hangs
His thoughts on her, forsaken that she seems,
   All while her patience, morselled into pangs,
Mounts; then to alight disarming, no one dreams,
With Gorgon's gear and barebill, thongs and fangs.

FELIX RANDAL

Felix Randal the farrier, O he is dead then? my duty all
   ended,
Who have watched his mould of man, big-boned and hardy-
   handsome
Pining, pining, till time when reason rambled in it and some
Fatal four disorders, fleshed there, all contended?
Sickness broke him. Impatient he cursed at first, but mended
Being anointed and all; though a heavenlier heart began some
Months earlier, since I had our sweet reprieve and ransom
Tendered to him. Ah well, God rest him all road ever he
   offended!

This seeing the sick endears them to us, us too it endears.
My tongue had taught thee comfort, touch had quenched thy
   tears,
Thy tears that touched my heart, child, Felix, poor Felix
   Randal;
How far from then forethought of, all thy more boisterous
   years,
When thou at the random grim forge, powerful amidst peers,
Didst fettle for the great grey drayhorse his bright and
   battering sandal!

THE LEADEN ECHO AND THE GOLDEN ECHO

(Maidens' Song from St. Winefred's Well)

THE LEADEN ECHO

How to kéep—is there any any, is there none such, nowhere
    known some, bow or brooch or braid or brace, láce, latch
    or catch or key to keep
Back beaúty, keep it, beauty, beauty, beauty, . . . from
    vanishing away?
Ó is there no frowning of these wrinkles, rankèd wrinkles
    deep,
Dówn? no waving off of these most mournful messengers,
    still messengers, sad and stealing messengers of grey?
No there's none, there's none, O no there's none,
Nor can you long be, what you now are, called fair,
Do what you may do, what, do what you may,
And wisdom is early to despair:
Be beginning; since, no, nothing can be done
To keep at bay
Age and age's evils, hoar hair,
Ruck and wrinkle, drooping, dying, death's worst, winding
    sheets, tombs and worms and tumbling to decay;
So be beginning, be beginning to despair.
O there's none; no no no there's none:
Be beginning to despair, to despair,
Despair, despair, despair, despair.

THE GOLDEN ECHO

      Spare!
There ís one, yes I have one (Hush there!);
Only not within seeing of the sun,
Not within the singeing of the strong sun,
Tall sun's tingeing, or treacherous the tainting of the earth's
    air,
Somewhere elsewhere there is ah well where! one,
Óne. Yes I cán tell such a key, I dó know such a place,
Where whatever's prized and passes of us, everything that's
    fresh and fast flying of us, seems to us sweet of us and
    swiftly away with, done away with, undone,
Undone, done with, soon done with, and yet dearly and dan-
    gerously sweet
Of us, the wimpled-water-dimpled, not-by-morning-matchèd
    face,

The flower of beauty, fleece of beauty, too too apt to, ah! to
   fleet,
Never fleets móre, fastened with the tenderest truth
To its own best being and its loveliness of youth: it is an ever-
   lastingness of, O it is an all youth!
Come then, your ways and airs and looks, locks, maiden gear,
   gallantry and gaiety and grace,
Winning ways, airs innocent, maiden manners, sweet looks,
   loose locks, long locks, lovelocks, gaygear, going gallant,
   girlgrace—
Resign them, sign them, seal them, send them, motion them
   with breath,
And with sighs soaring, soaring síghs deliver
Them; beauty-in-the-ghost, deliver it, early now, long before
   death
Give beauty back, beauty, beauty, beauty, back to God,
   beauty's self and beauty's giver.
See; not a hair is, not an eyelash, not the least lash lost; every
   hair
Is, hair of the head, numbered.
Nay, what we had lighthanded left in surly the mere mould
Will have waked and have waxed and have walked with the
   wind what while we slept,
This side, that side hurling a heavyheaded hundredfold
What while we, while we slumbered.
O then, weary then whý should we tread? O why are we so
   haggard at the heart, so care-coiled, care-killed, so fagged,
   so fashed, so cogged, so cumbered,
When the thing we freely fórfeit is kept with fonder a care,
Fonder a care kept than we could have kept it, kept
Far with fonder a care (and we, we should have lost it) finer,
   fonder
A care kept.—Where kept? Do but tell us where kept,
   where.—
Yonder.—What high as that! We follow, now we follow.—
   Yonder, yes yonder, yonder,
Yonder.

THE BLESSED VIRGIN COMPARED
TO THE AIR WE BREATHE

Wild air, world-mothering air,
Nestling me everywhere,
That each eyelash or hair
Girdles; goes home betwixt
The fleeciest, frailest-flixed
Snowflake; that's fairly
   mixed
With, riddles, and is rife

In every least thing's life;
This needful, never spent,
And nursing element;
My more than meat and
    drink,
My meal at every wink;
This air, which, by life's law,
My lung must draw and draw
Now but to breathe its
    praise,
Minds me in many ways
Of her who not only
Gave God's infinity
Dwindled to infancy
Welcome in womb and
    breast,
Birth, milk, and all the rest
But mothers each new grace
That does now reach our
    race—
Mary Immaculate,
Merely a woman, yet
Whose presence, power is
Great as no goddess's
Was deemèd, dreamèd; who
This one work has to do—
Let all God's glory through,
God's glory which would go
Through her and from her
    flow
Off, and no way but so.

    I say that we are wound
With mercy round and
    round
As if with air: the same
Is Mary, more by name.
She, wild web, wondrous
    robe,
Mantles the guilty globe,
Since God has let dispense
Her prayers his providence:
Nay, more than almoner,
The sweet alms' self is her
And men are meant to share

Her life as life does air.

    If I have understood,
She holds high motherhood
Towards all our ghostly
    good
And plays in grace her part
About man's beating heart,
Laying, like air's fine flood,
The deathdance in his
    blood;
Yet no part but what will
Be Christ our Saviour still.
Of her flesh he took flesh:
He does take fresh and
    fresh,
Though much the mystery
    how,
Not flesh but spirit now
And makes, O marvellous!
New Nazareths in us,
Where she shall yet con-
    ceive
Him, morning, noon, and
    eve;
New Bethlems, and he born
There, evening, noon, and
    morn—
Bethlem or Nazareth,
Men here may draw like
    breath
More Christ and baffle
    death;
Who, born so, comes to be
New self and nobler me
In each one and each one
More makes, when all is
    done,
Both God's and Mary's Son.
    Again, look overhead
How air is azurèd;
O how! nay do but stand
Where you can lift your
    hand
Skywards: rich, rich it laps
Round the four fingergaps.

Yet such a sapphire-shot,
Charged, steepèd sky will not
Stain light. Yea, mark you this:
It does no prejudice.
The glass-blue days are those
When every colour glows,
Each shape and shadow shows.
Blue be it: this blue heaven
The seven or seven times seven
Hued sunbeam will transmit
Perfect, not alter it.
Or if there does some soft,
On things aloof, aloft,
Bloom breathe, that one breath more
Earth is the fairer for.
Whereas did air not make
This bath of blue and slake
His fire, the sun would shake,
A blear and blinding ball
With blackness bound, and all
The thick stars round him roll
Flashing like flecks of coal,
Quartz-fret, or sparks of salt,
In grimy vasty vault.
　So God was god of old:
A mother came to mould
Those limbs like ours which are
What must make our day-star
Much dearer to mankind;
Whose glory bare would blind
Or less would win man's mind.
Through her we may see him
Made sweeter, not made dim,
And her hand leaves his light
Sifted to suit our sight.
　Be thou then, O thou dear
Mother, my atmosphere;
My happier world, wherein
To wend and meet no sin;
Above me, round me lie
Fronting my froward eye
With sweet and scarless sky;
Stir in my ears, speak there
Of God's love, O live air,
Of patience, penance, prayer:
World-mothering air, air wild,
Wound with thee, in thee isled,
Fold home, fast fold thy child.

TO WHAT SERVES MORTAL BEAUTY?

To what serves mortal beauty ˈ — dangerous; does set danc-
ing blood — the O-seal-that-so ˈ feature, flung prouder form
Than Purcell tune lets tread to? ˈ See: it does this: keeps
　　warm
Men's wits to the things that are; ˈ what good means —
　　where a glance

Master more may than gaze, | gaze out of countenance.
Those lovely lads once, wet-fresh | windfalls of war's storm,
How then should Gregory, a father, | have gleanèd else from
    swarm-
ed Rome? But God to a nation | dealt that day's dear chance.
 To man, that needs would worship | block or barren stone,
Our law says: Love what are | love's worthiest, were all
    known;
World's loveliest — men's selves. Self | flashes off frame and
    face.
What do then? how meet beauty? | Merely meet it; own,
Home at heart, heaven's sweet gift; | then leave, let that
    alone.
Yea, wish that though, wish all, | God's better beauty, grace

SPELT FROM SIBYL'S LEAVES

Earnest, earthless, equal, attuneable, | vaulty, voluminous, . .
    stupendous
Evening strains to be tíme's vást, | womb-of-all, home-of-all,
    hearse-of-all night.
Her fond yellow hornlight wound to the west, | her wild
    hollow hoarlight hung to the height
Waste; her earliest stars, earl-stars, | stárs principal, overbend
    us,
Fíre-féaturing heaven. For earth | her being has unbound, her
    dapple is at an end, as-
tray or aswarm, all throughther, in throngs; | self ín self
    steepèd and páshed—qúite
Disremembering, dísmémbering | áll now. Heart, you round
    me right
With: Óur évening is over us; óur night | whélms, whélms,
    ánd will end us.
Only the beak-leaved boughs dragonish | damask the tool-
    smooth bleak light; black,
Ever so black on it. Óur tale, O óur oracle; | Lét life, wáned,
    ah lét life wind
Off hér once skéined stained véined varíety | upon, áll on
    twó spools; párt, pen, páck
Now her áll in twó flocks, twó folds — black, white; | right,
    wrong; reckon but, reck but, mind
But thése two; wáre of a wórld where bút these | twó tell,
    each off the óther; of a rack
Where, selfwrung, selfstrung, sheathe- and shelterless, |
    thóughts agaínst thoughts ín groans grínd.

THE SOLDIER

Yes. Whý do we áll, seeing of a soldier, bless him? bless
Our redcoats, our tars? Both these being, the greater part,
But frail clay, nay but foul clay. Here it is: the heart,
Since, proud, it calls the calling manly, gives a guess
That, hopes that, makesbelieve, the men must be no less;
It fancies, feigns, deems, dears the artist after his art;
And fain will find as sterling all as all is smart,
And scarlet wear the spirit of wár thére express.

Mark Christ our King. He knows war, served this soldiering
    through;
He of all can reeve a rope best. There he bides in bliss
Now, and séeing somewhére some mán do all that man can
    do,
For love he leans forth, needs his neck must fall on, kiss,
And cry 'O Christ-done deed! So God-made-flesh does too:
Were I come o'er again' cries Christ 'it should be this'.

CARRION COMFORT

Not, I'll not, carrion comfort, Despair, not feast on thee;
Not untwist—slack they may be—these last strands of man
In me ór, most weary, cry I can no more. I can;
Can something, hope, wish day come, not choose not to be.
But ah, but O thou terrible, why wouldst thou rude on me
Thy wring-world right foot rock? lay a lionlimb against me?
    scan
With darksome devouring eyes my bruisèd bones? and fan,
O in turns of tempest, me heaped there; me frantic to avoid
    thee and flee?

    Why? That my chaff might fly; my grain lie, sheer and
    clear.
Nay in all that toil, that coil, since (seems) I kissed the rod,
Hand rather, my heart lo! lapped strength, stole joy, would
    laugh, chéer.
Cheer whom though? the hero whose heaven-handling flung
    me, fóot tród
Me? or me that fought him? O which one? is it each one?
    That night, that year
Of now done darkness I wretch lay wrestling with (my God!)
    my God.

NO WORST, THERE IS NONE

No worst, there is none. Pitched past pitch of grief,
More pangs will, schooled at forepangs, wilder wring.
Comforter, where, where is your comforting?
Mary, mother of us, where is your relief?
My cries heave, herds-long; huddle in a main, a chief
Woe, wórld-sorrow; on an áge-old anvil wince and sing—
Then lull, then leave off. Fury had shrieked 'No ling-
ering! Let me be fell: force I must be brief'.

O the mind, mind has mountains; cliffs of fall
Frightful, sheer, no-man-fathomed. Hold them cheap
May who ne'er hung there. Nor does long our small
Durance deal with that steep or deep. Here! creep,
Wretch, under a comfort serves in a whirlwind: all
Life death does end and each day dies with sleep.

TO SEEM THE STRANGER LIES MY LOT, MY LIFE

To seem the stranger lies my lot, my life
Among strangers. Father and mother dear,
Brothers and sisters are in Christ not near
And he my peace my parting, sword and strife.
   England, whose honour O all my heart woos, wife
To my creating thought, would neither hear
Me, were I pleading, plead nor do I: I wear-
y of idle a being but by where wars are rife.

   I am in Ireland now! now I am at a thírd
Remove. Not but in all removes I can
Kind love both give and get. Only what word
Wisest my heart breeds dark heaven's baffling ban
Bars or hell's spell thwarts. This to hoard unheard,
Heard unheeded, leaves me a lonely began.

I WAKE AND FEEL THE FELL OF DARK, NOT DAY

I wake and feel the fell of dark, not day.
What hours, O what black hoürs we have spent
This night! what sights you, heart, saw; ways you went!
And more must, in yet longer light's delay.
   With witness I speak this. But where I say
Hours I mean years, mean life. And my lament

Is cries countless, cries like dead letters sent
To dearest him that lives alas! away.

I am gall, I am heartburn. God's most deep decree
Bitter would have me taste: my taste was me;
Bones built in me, flesh filled, blood brimmed the curse.
    Selfyeast of spirit a dull dough sours. I see
The lost are like this, and their scourge to be
As I am mine, their sweating selves; but worse.

PATIENCE, HARD THING!

Patience, hard thing! the hard thing but to pray,
But bid for, Patience is! Patience who asks
Wants war, wants wounds; weary his times, his tasks;
To do without, take tosses, and obey.
    Rare patience roots in these, and, these away,
Nowhere. Natural heart's ivy, Patience masks
Our ruins of wrecked past purpose. There she basks
Purple eyes and seas of liquid leaves all day.

We hear our hearts grate on themselves: it kills
To bruise them dearer. Yet the rebellious wills
Of us we do bid God bend to him even so.
    And where is he who more and more distils
Delicious kindness?—He is patient. Patience fills
His crisp combs, and that comes those ways we know.

MY OWN HEART LET ME MORE HAVE PITY ON

My own heart let me more have pity on; let
Me live to my sad self hereafter kind,
Charitable; not live this tormented mind
With this tormented mind tormenting yet.
    I cast for comfort I can no more get
By groping round my comfortless, than blind
Eyes in their dark can day or thirst can find
Thirst's all-in-all in all a world of wet.

Soul, self; come, poor Jackself, I do advise
You, jaded, let be; call off thoughts awhile
Elsewhere; leave comfort root-room; let joy size
At God knows when to God knows what; whose smile
's not wrung, see you; unforeseen times rather—as skies
Betweenpie mountains—lights a lovely mile.

HARRY PLOUGHMAN

Hard as hurdle arms, with a broth of goldish flue
Breathed round; the rack of ribs; the scooped flank; lank
Rope-over thigh; knee-nave; and barrelled shank—
        Head and foot, shoulder and shank—
By a grey eye's heed steered well, one crew, fall to;
Stand at stress. Each limb's barrowy brawn, his thew
That onewhere curded, onewhere sucked or sank—
        Soared or sank—,
Though as a beechbole firm, finds his, as at a roll-call, rank
And features, in flesh, what deed he each must do—
        His sinew-service where do.

He leans to it, Harry bends, look. Back, elbow, and liquid
    waist
In him, all quail to the wallowing o' the plough: 's cheek
    crimsons; curls
Wag or crossbridle, in a wind lifted, windlaced—
        See his wind-lilylocks-laced;
Churlsgrace, too, child of Amansstrength, how it hangs or
    hurls
Them—broad in bluff hide his frowning feet lashed! raced
With, along them, cragiron under and cold furls—
        With-a-fountain's shining-shot furls.

THAT NATURE IS A HERACLITEAN FIRE
AND OF THE
COMFORT OF THE RESURRECTION

Cloud-puffball, torn tufts, tossed pillows ǀ flaunt forth, then
    chevy on an air-
built thoroughfare: heaven-roysterers, in gay-gangs ǀ they
    throng; they glitter in marches.
Down roughcast, down dazzling whitewash, ǀ wherever an
    elm arches,
Shivelights and shadowtackle in long ǀ lashes lace, lance,
    and pair.
Delightfully the bright wind boisterous ǀ ropes, wrestles,
    beats earth bare
Of yestertempest's creases; ǀ in pool and rut peel parches
Squandering ooze to squeezed ǀ dough, crust, dust; stanches,
    starches
Squadroned masks and manmarks ǀ treadmire toil there
Footfretted in it. Million-fuelèd, ǀ nature's bonfire burns
    on.

But quench her bonniest, dearest | to her, her clearest-
    selvèd spark
Man, how fast his firedint, | his mark on mind, is gone!
Both are in an unfathomable, all is in an enormous dark
Drowned. O pity and indig | nation! Manshape, that shone
Sheer off, disseveral, a star, | death blots black out; nor
    mark

              Is any of him at all so stark

But vastness blurs and time | beats level. Enough! the
    Resurrection,
A heart's-clarion! Away grief's gasping, | joyless days,
    dejection.

              Across my foundering deck shone

A beacon, an eternal beam. | Flesh fade, and mortal
    trash
Fall to the residuary worm; | world's wildfire, leave but ash:
              In a flash, at a trumpet crash,
I am all at once what Christ is, | since he was what I
    am, and
This Jack, joke, poor potsherd, | patch, matchwood, immortal
    diamond,

              Is immortal diamond.

THE WRECK OF THE DEUTSCHLAND

*To the happy memory of the five Franciscan Nuns, exiles by the
Falk Laws, drowned between midnight and morning of Dec. 7th,
1875*

I

    Thou mastering me
      God! giver of breath and bread;
    World's strand, sway of the sea;
      Lord of living and dead;
Thou has bound bones and veins in me, fastened me
    flesh,
And after it almost unmade, what with dread,
    Thy doing: and dost thou touch me afresh?
Over again I feel thy finger and find thee.

      I did say yes
    O at lightning and lashed rod;
Thou heardst me truer than tongue confess
    Thy terror, O Christ, O God;
Thou knowest the walls, altar and hour and night:
The swoon of a heart that the sweep and the hurl of thee
    trod

Hard down with a horror of height:
And the midriff astrain with leaning of, laced with fire of
      stress.

      The frown of his face
      Before me, the hurtle of hell
Behind, where, where was a, where was a place?
      I whirled out wings that spell
And fled with a fling of the heart to the heart of the Host.
My heart, but you were dovewinged, I can tell,
      Carrier-witted, I am bold to boast,
To flash from the flame to the flame then, tower from the
      grace to the grace.

      I am soft sift
      In an hourglass—at the wall
Fast, but mined with a motion, a drift,
      And it crowds and it combs to the fall;
I steady as a water in a well, to a poise, to a pane,
      But roped with, always, all the way down from the tall
      Fells or flanks of the voel, a vein
Of the gospel proffer, a pressure, a principle, Christ's gift.

      I kiss my hand
      To the stars, lovely-asunder
Starlight, wafting him out of it; and
      Glow, glory in thunder;
Kiss my hand to the dappled-with-damson west:
Since, tho' he is under the world's splendour and wonder,
      His mystery must be instressed, stressed;
For I greet him the days I meet him, and bless when I under-
      stand.

      Not out of his bliss
      Springs the stress felt
Nor first from heaven (and few know this)
      Swings the stroke dealt—
Stroke and a stress that stars and storms deliver,
That guilt is hushed by, hearts are flushed by and melt—
      But it rides time like riding a river
(And here the faithful waver, the faithless fable and miss).

      It dates from day
      Of his going in Galilee;
Warm-laid grave of a womb-life grey;
      Manger, maiden's knee;
The dense and the driven Passion, and frightful sweat;
Thence the discharge of it, there its swelling to be,

Though felt before, though in high flood yet—
What none would have known of it, only the heart, being
    hard at bay,

            Is out with it! Oh,
        We lash with the best or worst
    Word last! How a lush-kept plush-capped sloe
        Will, mouthed to flesh-burst,
    Gush!—flush the man, the being with it, sour or sweet,
    Brim, in a flash, full!—Hither then, last or first,
        To hero of Calvary, Christ's feet—
Never ask if meaning it, wanting it, warned of it—men go.

            Be adored among men,
        God, three-numberèd form;
    Wring thy rebel, dogged in den,
        Man's malice, with wrecking and storm.
    Beyond saying sweet, past telling of tongue,
    Thou art lightning and love, I found it, a winter and warm;
        Father and fondler of heart thou hast wrung:
Hast thy dark descending and most art merciful then.

            With an anvil-ding
        And with fire in him forge thy will
    Or rather, rather then, stealing as Spring
        Through him, melt him but master him still:
    Whether at once, as once at a crash Paul,
    Or as Austin, a lingering-out swéet skíll,
        Make mercy in all of us, out of us all
Mastery, but be adored, but be adored King.

                    11

        'Some find me a sword; some
        The flange and the rail; flame,
    Fang, or flood' goes Death on drum,
        And storms bugle his fame.
    But wé dream we are rooted in earth—Dust!
    Flesh falls within sight of us, we, though our flower the
        same,
        Wave with the meadow, forget that there must
The sour scythe cringe, and the blear share come.

        On Saturday sailed from Bremen,
        American-outward-bound,
    Take settler and seamen, tell men with women,
        Two hundred souls in the round—

O Father, not under thy feathers nor ever as guessing
    The goal was a shoal, of a fourth the doom to be drowned;
    Yet did the dark side of the bay of thy blessing
Not vault them, the millions of rounds of thy mercy not
      reeve even them in?

      Into the snows she sweeps,
        Hurling the heaven behind,
    The Deutschland, on Sunday; and so the sky keeps,
        For the infinite air is unkind,
And the sea flint-flake, black-backed in the regular blow,
Sitting Eastnortheast, in cursed quarter, the wind;
    Wiry and white-fiery and whirlwind-swivellèd snow
Spins to the widow-making unchilding unfathering deeps.

      She drove in the dark to leeward,
        She struck—not a reef or a rock
    But the combs of a smother of sand: night drew her
        Dead to the Kentish Knock;
And she beat the bank down with her bows and the ride
      of her keel:
The breakers rolled on her beam with ruinous shock;
    And canvas and compass, the whorl and the wheel
Idle for ever to waft her or wind her with, these she endured.

      Hope had grown grey hairs,
        Hope had mourning on,
    Trenched with tears, carved with cares,
        Hope was twelve hours gone;
And frightful a nightfall folded rueful a day
Nor rescue, only rocket and lightship, shone,
    And lives at last were washing away:
To the shrouds they took,—they shook in the hurling and
      horrible airs.

      One stirred from the rigging to save
        The wild woman-kind below,
    With a rope's end round the man, handy and brave—
        He was pitched to his death at a blow,
For all his dreadnought breast and braids of thew:
They could tell him for hours, dandled the to and fro
    Through the cobbled foam-fleece, what could he do
With the burl of the fountains of air, buck and the flood of
      the wave?

      They fought with God's cold—
        And they could not and fell to the deck

(Crushed them) of water (and drowned them) or rolled
    With the sea-romp over the wreck.
Night roared, with the heart-break hearing a heart-broke
        rabble,
The woman's wailing, the crying of child without check—
    Till a lioness arose breasting the babble,
A prophetess towered in the tumult, a virginal tongue told.

    Ah, touched in your bower of bone
    Are you! turned for an exquisite smart,
Have you! make words break from me here all alone,
    Do you!—mother of being in me, heart.
O unteachably after evil, but uttering truth,
    Why, tears! is it? tears; such a melting, a madrigal start!
    Never-eldering revel and river of youth,
What can it be, this glee? the good you have there of your
        own?

    Sister, a sister calling
    A master, her master and mine!—
And the inboard seas run swirling and hawling;
    The rash smart sloggering brine
Blinds her; but she that weather sees one thing, one;
Has one fetch in her: she rears herself to divine
    Ears, and the call of the tall nun
To the men in the tops and the tackle rode over the storm's
        brawling.

    She was first of a five and came
    Of a coifèd sisterhood.
    (O Deutschland, double a desperate name!
    O world wide of its good!
But Gertrude, lily, and Luther, are two of a town,
Christ's lily and beast of the waste wood:
    From life's dawn it is drawn down,
Abel is Cain's brother and breasts they have sucked the
        same.)

    Loathed for a love men knew in them,
    Banned by the land of their birth,
Rhine refused them. Thames would ruin them;
    Surf, snow, river and earth
Gnashed: but thou art above, thou Orion of light;
Thy unchancelling poising palms were weighing the worth,
    Thou martyr-master: in thy sight
Storm flakes were scroll-leaved flowers, lily showers—sweet
        heaven was astrew in them.

Five! the finding and sake
And cipher of suffering Christ.
Mark, the mark is of man's make
And the word of it Sacrificed.
But he scores it in scarlet himself on his own bespoken,
Before-time-taken, dearest prizèd and pricèd—
Stigma, signal, cinquefoil token
For lettering of the lamb's fleece, ruddying of the roseflake.

Joy fall to thee, father Francis,
Drawn to the Life that died;
With the gnarls of the nails in thee, niche of the lance,
his
Lovescape crucified
And seal of his seraph-arrival! and these thy daughters
And five-livèd and leavèd favour and pride,
Are sisterly sealed in wild waters,
To bathe in his fall-gold mercies, to breathe in his all-fire
glances.

Away in the loveable west,
On a pastoral forehead of Wales,
I was under a roof here, I was at rest,
And they the prey of the gales;
She to the black-about air, to the breaker, the thickly
Falling flakes, to the throng that catches and quails
Was calling 'O Christ, Christ, come quickly':
The cross to her she calls Christ to her, christens her wild-
worst Best.

The majesty! what did she mean?
Breathe, arch and original Breath.
Is it love in her of the being as her lover had been?
Breathe, body of lovely Death.
They were else-minded then, altogether, the men
Woke thee with a *we are perishing* in the weather of Gen-
nesareth.
Or is it that she cried for the crown then,
The keener to come at the comfort for feeling the combating
keen?

For how to the heart's cheering
The down-dugged ground-hugged grey
Hovers off, the jay-blue heavens appearing
Of pied and peeled May!
Blue-beating and hoary-glow height; or night, still higher,

With belled fire and the moth-soft Milky Way,
    What by your measure is the heaven of desire,
The treasure never eyesight got, nor was ever guessed what
        for the hearing?

    No, but it was not these.
      The jading and jar of the cart,
Time's tasking, it is fathers that asking for ease
      Of the sodden-with-its-sorrowing heart,
Not danger, electrical horror; then further it finds
The appealing of the Passion is tenderer in prayer apart:
    Other, I gather, in measure her mind's
Burden, in wind's burly and beat of endragonèd seas.

    But how shall I . . . make me room there:
      Reach me a . . . Fancy, come faster—
Strike you the sight of it? look at it loom there,
      Thing that she . . . there then! the Master,
Ipse, the only one, Christ, King, Head:
He was to cure the extremity where he had cast her;
    Do, deal, lord it with living and dead;
Let him ride, her pride, in his triumph, despatch and have
        done with his doom there.

    Ah! there was a heart right
      There was single eye!
Read the unshapeable shock night
      And knew the who and the why;
Wording it how but by him that present and past,
Heaven and earth are word of, worded by?—
    The Simon Peter of a soul! to the blast
Tarpeian-fast, but a blown beacon of light.

    Jesu, heart's light,
      Jesu, maid's son,
What was the feast followed the night
      Thou hadst glory of this nun?—
Feast of the one woman without stain.
For so conceivèd, so to conceive thee is done;
    But here was heart-throe, birth of a brain,
Word, that heard and kept thee and uttered thee outright.

    Well, she has thee for the pain, for the
      Patience; but pity of the rest of them!
Heart, go and bleed at a bitterer vein for the
      Comfortless unconfessed of them—
No not uncomforted: lovely-felicitous Providence

Finger of a tender of, O of a feathery delicacy, the breast
    of the
  Maiden could obey so, be a bell to, ring of it, and
Startle the poor sheep back! is the shipwrack then a harvest,
        does tempest carry the grain for thee?

    I admire thee, master of the tides,
      Of the Yore-flood, of the year's fall;
  The recurb and the recovery of the gulf's sides,
      The girth of it and the wharf of it and the wall;
Stanching, quenching ocean of a motionable mind;
Ground of being, and granite of it: past all
    Grasp God, throned behind
Death with a sovereignty that heeds but hides, bodes but
        abides;

    With a mercy that outrides
      The all of water, an ark
  For the listener; for the lingerer with a love glides
      Lower than death and the dark;
A vein for the visiting of the past-prayer, pent in prison,
  The last-breath penitent spirits—the uttermost mark
    Our passion-plungèd giant risen,
The Christ of the Father compassionate, fetched in the storm
        of his strides.

    Now burn, new born to the world,
      Doubled-naturèd name,
  The heaven-flung, heart-fleshed, maiden-furled
      Miracle-in-Mary-of-flame,
Mid-numbered He in three of the thunder-throne!
Not a dooms-day dazzle in his coming nor dark as he came;
    Kind, but royally reclaiming his own;
A released shower, let flash to the shire, not a lightning of fire
        hard-hurled.

    Dame, at our door
      Drowned, and among our shoals,
  Remember us in the roads, the heaven-haven of the
        Reward:
      Our King back, oh, upon English souls!
Let him easter in us, be a dayspring to the dimness of us,
        be a crimson-cresseted east,
More brightening her, rare-dear Britain, as his reign rolls,
    Pride, rose, prince, hero of us, high-priest,
Our hearts' charity's hearth's fire, our thoughts' chivalry's
        throng's Lord.

JOHN DAVIDSON

(1857-1909)

THIRTY BOB A WEEK

I couldn't touch a stop and turn a screw,
   And set the blooming world a-work for me,
Like such as cut their teeth—I hope, like you—
   On the handle of a skeleton gold key;
I cut mine on a leek, which I eat it every week:
   I'm a clerk at thirty bob as you can see.

But I don't allow it's luck and all a toss;
   There's no such thing as being starred and crossed;
It's just the power of some to be a boss,
   And the bally power of others to be bossed:
I face the music, sir; you bet I ain't a cur;
   Strike me lucky if I don't believe I'm lost!

For like a mole I journey in the dark,
   A-travelling along the underground
From my Pillared Halls and broad Suburban Park,
   To come the daily dull official round;
And home again at night with my pipe all alight,
   A-scheming how to count ten bob a pound.

And it's often very cold and very wet,
   And my missis stitches towels for a hunks;
And the Pillared Halls is half of it to let—
   Three rooms about the size of travelling trunks.
And we cough, my wife and I, to dislocate a sigh,
   When the noisy little kids are in their bunks.

But you never hear her do a growl or whine,
   For she's made of flint and roses, very odd;
And I've got to cut my meaning rather fine,
   Or I'd blubber, for I'm made of greens and sod:

So p'r'aps we are in Hell for all that I can tell,
  And lost and damned and served up hot to God.

I ain't blaspheming, Mr. Silver-tongue;
  I'm saying things a bit beyond your art:
Of all the rummy starts you ever sprung,
  Thirty bob a week's the rummiest start!
With your science and your books and your the'ries about
      spooks,
  Did you ever hear of looking in your heart?

I didn't mean your pocket, Mr., no:
  I mean that having children and a wife,
With thirty bob on which to come and go,
    Isn't dancing to the tabor and the fife:
When it doesn't make you drink, by Heaven! it makes you
      think,
  And notice curious items about life.

I step into my heart and there I meet
  A god-almighty devil singing small,
Who would like to shout and whistle in the street,
  And squelch the passers flat against the wall;
If the whole world was a cake he had the power to take,
  He would take it, ask for more, and eat it all.

And I meet a sort of simpleton beside,
  The kind that life is always giving beans;
With thirty bob a week to keep a bride
  He fell in love and married in his teens:
At thirty bob he stuck; but he knows it isn't luck:
  He knows the seas are deeper than tureens.

And the god-almighty devil and the fool
  That meet me in the High Street on the strike,
When I walk about my heart a-gathering wool,
  Are my good and evil angels if you like.
And both of them together in every kind of weather
  Ride me like a double-seated bike.

That's rough a bit and needs its meaning curled.
  But I have a high old hot un in my mind—
A most engrugious notion of the world,
  That leaves your lightning 'rithmetic behind:
I give it at a glance when I say, 'There ain't no chance,
  Nor nothing of the lucky-lottery kind.'

And it's this way I make it out to be:
  No fathers, mothers, countries, climates—none;
Not Adam was responsible for me.
  Nor society, nor systems, nary one:
A little sleeping seed, I woke—I did, indeed—
  A million years before the blooming sun.

I woke because I thought the time had come;
  Beyond my will there was no other cause;
And every where I found myself at home,
  Because I chose to be the thing I was;
And in whatever shape of mollusc or of ape
  I always went according to the laws.

I was the love that chose my mother out;
  I joined two lives and from the union burst;
My weakness and my strength without a doubt
  Are mine alone for ever from the first:
It's just the very same with a difference in the name
  As 'Thy will be done.' You say it if you durst!

They say it daily up and down the land
  As easy as you take a drink, it's true;
But the difficultest go to understand,
  And the difficultest job a man can do,
Is to come it brave and meek with thirty bob a week,
  And feel that that's the proper thing for you.

It's a naked child against a hungry wolf;
  It's playing bowls upon a splitting wreck;
It's walking on a string across a gulf
  With millstones fore-and-aft about your neck;
But the thing is daily done by many and many a one;
  And we fall, face forward, fighting, on the deck.

A RUNNABLE STAG

When the pods went pop on the broom, green broom,
  And apples began to be golden skinned,
We harbour'd a stag in the Priory coomb,
  And we feather'd his trail up-wind, up-wind,
  We feather'd his trail up-wind—
      A stag of warrant, a stag, a stag,
      A runnable stag, a kingly crop,
      Brow, bay and tray and three on top,
      A stag, a runnable stag.

Then the huntsman's horn rang yap, yap, yap,
   And 'Forwards' we heard the harbourer shout;
But 'twas only a brocket that broke a gap
   In the beechen underwood, driven out,
     From the underwood antler'd out
       By warrant and might of the stag, the stag,
       The runnable stag, whose lordly mind
       Was bent on sleep, though beamed and tined
       He stood, a runnable stag.

So we tufted the covert till afternoon
   With Tinkerman's Pup and Bell-of-the-North;
And hunters were sulky and hounds out of tune
   Before we tufted the right stag forth,
     Before we tufted him forth,
       The stag of warrant, the wily stag,
       The runnable stag with his kingly crop,
       Brow, bay and tray and three on top,
       The royal and runnable stag.

It was Bell-of-the-North and Tinkerman's Pup
   That stuck to the scent till the copse was drawn.
'Tally ho! tally ho!' and the hunt was up,
   The tufters whipped and the pack laid on,
     The resolute pack laid on,
       And the stag of warrant away at last,
       The runnable stag, the same, the same,
       His hoofs on fire, his horns like flame,
       A stag, a runnable stag.

'Let your gelding be: if you check or chide
   He stumbles at once and you're out of the hunt;
For three hundred gentlemen, able to ride,
   On hunters accustom'd to bear the brunt,
     Accustomed to bear the brunt,
       Are after the runnable stag, the stag,
       The runnable stag with his kingly crop,
       Brow, bay and tray and three on top,
       The right, the runnable stag.'

By perilous paths in coomb and dell,
   The heather, the rocks, and the river-bed,
The pace grew hot, for the scent lay well,
   And the runnable stag goes right ahead,
     The quarry went right ahead—
       Ahead, ahead, and fast and far;

His angler'd crest, his cloven hoof,
Brow, bay and tray and three aloof,
The stag, the runnable stag.

For a matter of twenty miles and more,
  By the densest hedge and the highest wall,
Through herds of bullocks he baffled the lore
  Of harbourer, huntsman, hounds and all,
  Of harbourer, hounds and all—
    The stag of warrant, the wily stag,
    For twenty miles, and five and five,
    He ran, and he never was caught alive,
    This stag, this runnable stag.

When he turned at bay in the leafy gloom,
  In the emerald gloom where the brook ran deep,
He heard in the distance the rollers boom,
  And he saw in a vision of peaceful sleep,
  In a wonderful vision of sleep,
    A stag of warrant, a stag, a stag,
    A runnable stag in a jewelled bed,
    Under the sheltering ocean dead,
    A stag, a runnable stag.

So a fateful hope lit up his eye,
  And he opened his nostrils wide again,
And he tossed his branching antlers high
  As he headed the hunt down the Charlock glen,
  As he raced down the echoing glen
    For five miles more, the stag, the stag,
    For twenty miles, and five and five,
    Not to be caught now, dead or alive,
    The stag, the runnable stag.

Three hundred gentlemen, able to ride,
  Three hundred horses as gallant and free,
Beheld him escape on the evening tide,
  Far out till he sank in the Severn Sea,
  Till he sank in the depths of the sea—
    The stag, the buoyant stag, the stag
    That slept at last in a jewelled bed
    Under the sheltering ocean spread,
    The stag, the runnable stag.

A BALLAD OF HELL

'A letter from my love today!
   Oh, unexpected, dear appeal!'
She struck a happy tear away,
   And broke the crimson seal.

'My love, there is no help on earth,
   No help in heaven; the dead-man's bell
Must toll our wedding; our first hearth
   Must be the well-paved floor of hell.'

The colour died from out her face,
   Her eyes like ghostly candles shone;
She cast dread looks about the place,
   Then clenched her teeth and read right on.

'I may not pass the prison door;
   Here must I rot from day to day,
Unless I wed whom I abhor,
   My cousin, Blanche of Valencay.

'At midnight with my dagger keen,
   I'll take my life; it must be so.
Meet me in hell to-night, my queen,
   For weal and woe.'

She laughed although her face was wan,
   She girded on her golden belt,
She took her jewelled ivory fan,
   And at her glowing missal knelt.

Then rose, 'And am I mad?' she said:
   She broke her fan, her belt untied;
With leather girt herself instead,
   And stuck a dagger at her side.

She waited, shuddering in her room,
   Till sleep had fallen on all the house.
She never flinched; she faced her doom:
   They two must sin to keep their vows.

Then out into the night she went,
   And stooping crept by hedge and tree;
Her rose-bush flung a snare of scent,
   And caught a happy memory.

She fell, and lay a minute's space;
  She tore the sward in her distress;
The dewy grass refreshed her face;
  She rose and ran with lifted dress.

She started like a morn-caught ghost
  Once when the moon came out and stood
To watch; the naked road she crossed,
  And dived into the murmuring wood.

The branches snatched her streaming cloak;
  A live thing shrieked; she made no stay!
She hurried to the trysting-oak—
  Right well she knew the way.

Without a pause she bared her breast,
  And drove her dagger home and fell,
And lay like one that takes her rest,
  And died and wakened up in hell.

She bathed her spirit in the flame,
  And near the centre took her post;
From all sides to her ears there came
  The dreary anguish of the lost.

The devil started at her side,
  Comely, and tall, and black as jet.
'I am young Malespina's bride;
  Has he come hither yet?'

'My poppet, welcome to your bed.'
  'Is Malespina here?'
'Not he! To-morrow he must wed
  His cousin Blanche, my dear!'

'You lie, he died with me to-night.'
  'Not he! it was a plot' 'You lie.'
'My dear, I never lie outright.'
  'We died at midnight, he and I.'

The devil went. Without a groan
  She, gathered up on one fierce prayer,
Took root in hell's midst all alone,
  And waited for him there.

She dared to make herself at home
  Amidst the wail, the uneasy stir.

The blood-stained flame that filled the dome,
   Scentless and silent, shrouded her.

How long she stayed I cannot tell;
   But when she felt his perfidy,
She marched across the floor of hell;
   And all the damned stood up to see.

The devil stopped her at the brink:
   She shook him off; she cried, 'Away!'
'My dear, you have gone mad, I think.'
   'I was betrayed: I will not stay.'

Across the weltering deep she ran;
   A stranger thing was never seen:
The damned stood silent to a man;
   They saw the great gulf set between.

To her it seemed a meadow fair;
   And flowers sprang up about her feet;
She entered heaven; she climbed the stair;
   And knelt down at the mercy-seat.

Seraphs and saints with one great voice
   Welcomed that soul that knew not fear;
Amazed to find it could rejoice,
   Hell raised a hoarse half-human cheer.

IN ROMNEY MARSH

As I went down to Dymchurch Wall,
   I heard the South sing o'er the land;
I saw the yellow sunlight fall
   On knolls where Norman churches stand.

And ringing shrilly, taut and lithe,
   Within the wind a core of sound,
The wire from Romney town to Hythe
   Alone its airy journey wound.

A veil of purple vapour flowed
   And trailed its fringe along the Straits;
The upper air like sapphire glowed;
   And roses filled Heaven's central gates.

Masts in the offing wagged their tops;
   The swinging waves pealed on the shore;
The saffron beach, all diamond drops
   And beads of surge, prolonged the roar.

As I came up from Dymchurch Wall,
   I saw above the Downs' low crest
The crimson brands of sunset fall,
   Flicker and fade from out the west.

Night sank: like flakes of silver fire
   The stars in one great shower came down;
Shrill blew the wind; and shrill the wire
   Rang out from Hythe to Romney town.

The darkly shining salt sea drops
   Streamed as the waves clashed on the shore;
The beach, with all its organ stops
   Pealing again, prolonged the roar.

LONDON

Athwart the sky a lowly sigh
   From west to east the sweet wind carried
The sun stood still on Primrose Hill;
   His light in all the city tarried:
The clouds on viewless columns bloomed
Like smouldering lilies unconsumed.

'Oh sweetheart, see! how shadowy,
   Of some occult magician's rearing,
Or swung in space of heaven's grace
   Dissolving, dimly reappearing,
Afloat upon ethereal tides
St Paul's above the city rides!'

A rumour broke through the thin smoke
   Enwreathing abbey, tower, and palace,
The parks, the squares, the thoroughfares,
   The million-peopled lanes and alleys,
An ever-muttering prisoned storm,
The heart of London beating warm.

HOLIDAY AT HAMPTON COURT

Scales of pearly cloud inlay
   North and south the turquoise sky,
While the diamond lamp of day
   Quenchless burns, and time on high
A moment halts upon his way
   Bidding noon again good-bye.

Gaffers, gammers, huzzies, louts,
   Couples, gangs, and families
Sprawling, shake, with Babel-shouts
   Bluff King Hal's funereal trees;
And eddying groups of stare-abouts
   Quiz the sandstone Hercules.

When their tongues and tempers tire,
   Harry and his little lot
Condescendingly admire
   Lozenge-bed and crescent-plot,
Aglow with links of azure fire,
   Pansy and forget-me-not.

Where the emerald shadows rest
   In the lofty woodland aisle,
Chaffing lovers quaintly dressed
   Chase and double many a mile,
Indifferent exiles in the west
   Making love in cockney style.

Now the echoing palace fills;
   Men and women, girls and boys
Trample past the swords and frills,
   Kings and Queens and trulls and toys;
Or listening loll on window-sills,
   Happy amateurs of noise!

That for pictured rooms of state!
   Out they hurry, wench and knave,
Where beyond the palace-gate
   Dusty legions swarm and rave,
With laughter, shriek, inane debate,
   Kentish fire and comic stave.

Voices from the river call;
   Organs hammer tune on tune;

Larks triumphant over all
  Herald twilight coming soon,
For as the sun begins to fall
  Near the zenith gleams the moon.

IMAGINATION

There is a dish to hold the sea,
  A brazier to contain the sun,
A compass for the galaxy,
  A voice to wake the dead and done!

That minister of ministers,
  Imagination, gathers up
The undiscovered Universe,
  Like jewels in a jasper cup.

Its flame can mingle north and south;
  Its accent with the thunder strive;
The ruddy sentence of its mouth
  Can make the ancient dead alive.

The mart of power, the fount of will,
  The form and mold of every star,
The source and bound of good and ill,
  The key of all the things that are,

Imagination, new and strange
  In every age, can turn the year;
Can shift the poles and lightly change
  The mood of men, the world's career

THE OUTCAST

Soul, be your own
  Pleasance and mart,
A land unknown,
  A state apart.

Scowl, and be rude
  Should love entice;
Call gratitude
  The costliest vice.

Deride the ill

By fortune sent;
Be scornful still
If foes repent.

When curse and stone
  Are hissed and hurled,
Aloof, alone
  Disdain the world.

Soul, disregard
  The bad, the good;

Be haughty, hard,
    Misunderstood.
Be neutral; spare
    No humblest lie,
And overbear
    Authority.

Laugh wisdom down;
    Abandon fate;
Shame the renown
    Of all the great.

Dethrone the past;

Deed, vision—naught
Avails at last
    Save your own thouhgt.

Though on all hands
    The powers unsheathe
Their lightning-brands
    And from beneath,

And from above
    One curse be hurled
With scorn, with love
    Affront the world.

THE UNKNOWN

To brave and to know the unknown
    Is the high world's motive and mark,
Though the way with snares be strewn.

The Earth itself alone
    Wheels through the light and the dark
Onward to meet the unknown.

Each soul, upright or prone,
    While the owl sings or the lark,
Must pass where the bones are strewn.

Power on the loftiest throne
    Can fashion no certain ark
That shall stem and outride the unknown.

Beauty must doff her zone,
    Strength trudge unarmed and stark,
Though the way with eyes be strewn.

This only can atone,
    The high world's motive and mark,
To brave and to know the unknown
Though the way with fire be strewn.

A BALLAD OF A NUN

From Eastertide to Eastertide
   For ten long years her patient knees
Engraved the stones—the fittest bride
   Of Christ in all the diocese.

She conquered every earthly lust;
   The abbess loved her more and more;
And, as a mark of perfect trust,
   Made her the keeper of the door.

High on a hill the convent hung,
   Across a duchy looking down,
Where everlasting mountains flung
   Their shadows over tower and town.

The jewels of their lofty snows
   In constellations flashed at night;
Above their crests the moon arose;
   The deep earth shuddered with delight.

Long ere she left her cloudy bed,
   Still dreaming in the orient land,
On many a mountain's happy head
   Dawn lightly laid her rosy hand.

The adventurous sun took heaven by storm;
   Clouds scattered largesses of rain;
The sounding cities, rich and warm,
   Smoldered and glittered in the plain.

Sometimes it was a wandering wind,
   Sometimes the fragrance of the pine,
Sometimes the thought how others sinned,
   That turned her sweet blood into wine.

Sometimes she heard a serenade
   Complaining sweetly far away:
She said, 'A young man woos a maid;'
   And dreamt of love till break of day.

Then she would ply her knotted scourge
   Until she swooned; but evermore
She had the same red sin to purge,
   Poor, passionate keeper of the door!

For still night's starry scroll unfurled,
   And still the day came like a flood:
It was the greatness of the world
   That made her long to use her blood.

In winter-time when Lent drew nigh,
   And hill and plain were wrapped in snow,
She watched beneath the frosty sky
   The nearest city nightly glow.

Like peals of airy bells outworn
   Faint laughter died above her head
In gusts of broken music borne:
   'They keep the Carnival,' she said.

Her hungry heart devoured the town:
   'Heaven save me by a miracle!
Unless God sends an angel down,
   Thither I go though it were Hell.'

She dug her nails deep in her breast,
   Sobbed, shrieked, and straight withdrew the bar:
A fledgling flying from the nest,
   A pale moth rushing to a star.

Fillet and veil in strips she tore;
   Her golden tresses floated wide;
The ring and bracelet that she wore
   As Christ's betrothed, she cast aside.

'Life's dearest meaning I shall probe;
   Lo! I shall taste of love at last!
Away!' She doffed her outer robe,
   And sent it sailing down the blast.

Her body seemed to warm the wind;
   With bleeding feet o'er ice she ran:
'I leave the righteous God behind;
   I go to worship sinful man.'

She reached the sounding city's gate;
   No question did the warder ask:
He passed her in: 'Welcome, wild mate!'
   He thought her some fantastic mask.

Half-naked through the town she went;
   Each footstep left a bloody mark;

Crowds followed her with looks intent;
   Her bright eyes made the torches dark.

Alone and watching in the street
   There stood a grave youth nobly dressed;
To him she knelt and kissed his feet;
   Her face her great desire confessed.

Straight to his house the nun he led:
   'Strange lady, what would you with me?'
'Your love, your love, sweet lord,' she said;
   'I bring you my virginity.'

He healed her bosom with a kiss;
   She gave him all her passion's hoard;
And sobbed and murmured ever, 'This
   Is life's great meaning, dear, my lord.

'I care not for my broken vow;
   Though God should come in thunder soon,
I am sister to the mountains now,
   And sister to the sun and moon.'

Through all the towns of Belmarie
   She made a progress like a queen.
'She is,' they said, 'whate'er she be,
   The strangest woman ever seen.

'From fairyland she must have come,
   Or else she is a mermaiden.'
Some said she was a ghoul, and some
   A heathen goddess born again.

But soon her fire to ashes burned;
   Her beauty changed to haggardness;
Her golden hair to silver turned;
   The hour came of her last caress.

At midnight from her lonely bed
   She rose, and said, 'I have had my will.'
The old ragged robe she donned, and fled
   Back to the convent on the hill.

Half-naked as she went before,
   She hurried to the city wall,
Unnoticed in the rush and roar
   And splendour of the Carnival.

No question did the warder ask:
   Her ragged robe, her shrunken limb,
Her dreadful eyes! 'It is no mask;
   It is a she-wolf, gaunt and grim!'

She ran across the icy plain;
   Her worn blood curdled in the blast;
Each footstep left a crimson stain;
   The white-faced moon looked on aghast.

She said between her chattering jaws,
   'Deep peace is mine, I cease to strive;
Oh, comfortable convent laws,
   That bury foolish nuns alive!

'A trowel for my passing-bell,
   A little bed within the wall,
A coverlet of stones; how well
   I there shall keep the Carnival!'

Like tired bells chiming in their sleep,
   The wind faint peals of laughter bore;
She stopped her ears and climbed the steep,
   And thundered at the convent door.

It opened straight: she entered in,
   And at the wardress' feet fell prone:
'I come to purge away my sin;
   Bury me, close me up in stone.'

The wardress raised her tenderly;
   She touched her wet and fast-shut eyes:
'Look, sister; sister, look at me;
   Look; can you see through my disguise?'

She looked and saw her own sad face,
   And trembled, wondering, 'Who art thou?'
'God sent me down to fill your place:
   I am the Virgin Mary now.'

And with the word, God's mother shone:
   The wanderer whispered, 'Mary, hail!'
The vision helped her to put on
   Bracelet and fillet, ring and veil.

'You are sister to the mountains now,
   And sister to the day and night;

Sister to God.' And on the brow
   She kissed her thrice, and left her sight,

While dreaming in her cloudy bed,
   Far in the crimson orient land,
On many a mountain's happy head
   Dawn lightly laid her rosy hand.

WAR-SONG

In anguish we uplift
   A new unhallowed song:
The race is to the swift;
   The battle to the strong.

Of old it was ordained
   That we, in packs like curs,
Some thirty million trained
   And licensed murderers,

In crime should live and act,
   If cunning folk say sooth
Who flay the naked fact
   And carve the heart of truth.

The rulers cry aloud,
   'We cannot cancel war,
The end and bloody shroud
   Of wrongs the worst abhor,

And order's swaddling band:
   Know that relentless strife
Remains by sea and land
   The holiest law of life.

From fear in every guise,
   From sloth, from lust of pelf,
By war's great sacrifice
   The world redeems itself.

War is the source, the theme
   Of art; the goal, the bent
And brilliant academe
   Of noble sentiment;

The augury, the dawn
   Of golden times of grace;

The true catholicon,
   And blood-bath of the race.

We thirty million trained
   And licensed murderers,
Like zanies rigged, and
chained
   By drill and scourge and
   cures

In shackles of despair
   We know not how to
   break—
What do we victims care
   For art, what interest take

In things unseen, unheard?
   Some diplomat no doubt
Will launch a heedless word,
   And lurking war leap out!

We spell-bound armies then,
   Huge brutes in dumb
   distress
Machines compact of men
   Who once had consciences,

Must trample harvest down—
   Vineyard, and corn and oil;
Dismantle town by town,
   Hamlet and homestead
   spoil

On each appointed path,
   Till lust of havoc light
A blood-red blaze of wrath
   In every frenzied sight.

In many a mountain-pass,
    Or meadow green and fresh,
Mass shall encounter mass
    Of shuddering human flesh;

Opposing ordnance roar
    Across the swaths of slain,
And blood in torrents pour
    In vain—always in vain,
    For war breeds war again!

The shameful dream is past,
    The subtle maze untrod:
We recognize at last
    That war is not of God.

Wherefore we now uplift
    Our new unhallowed song:
The race is to the swift,
    The battle to the strong.

BATTLE

The war of words is done;
    The red-lipped cannon speak;
The battle has begun.

The web your speeches spun
    Tears and blood shall streak;
The war of words is done.

Smoke enshrouds the sun;
    Earth staggers at the shriek
Of battle new begun.
Poltroons and braggarts run:

Woe to the poor, the meek!
The war of words is done.

'And hope not now to shun
    The doom that dogs the
    weak,'
Thunders every gun;

'Victory must be won.'
    When the red-lipped
    cannon speak,
The war of words is done,
    The slaughter has begun.

THE TESTAMENT OF A VIVISECTOR

*'The Testament of a Vivisector . . .' will hardly recommend itself
to Vivisector or Anti-Vivisector; and the new statement of Ma-
terialism which it contains is likely to offend both the religious
and the irreligious mind. This poem, therefore, and its successors,
my 'Testaments,' are addressed to those who are willing to place all
ideas in the crucible, and who are not afraid to fathom what is
subconscious in themselves and others.*

                                          —Note by the Author

Appraise me!—you, Christian of any stock:
Suave Catholic, whose haunting art avails,
Though fires are damped and sophistry undone;
Evangelist, with starved and barren brain,
Preying on evil consciences; or you,
Courageous Anglican, the well-beloved,
Enfeoffed with freehold in the City of God,
And happy here upon commuted tithes—
Your vested interests snug and ancient lights;

Or you, Agnostic, fearing yes and no,
Poltroon upon conviction; you, nor you,
Vendor of poem or philosopheme,
Patriot, gossip, warrior, chapman, all
In profits dabbling and affairs of men—
Not one of you with impulse or intent
To think my thought, how can you judge my life?

Who knows the savour of forbidden fruit,
The zest of inquisition when the world
Delivers whole, unchallenged and exempt;
Who never begs that truth should benefit,
Or be at least innoxious, but frequents
The labyrinthine fires of solitude
Wherein the thinker, parched and charred, outlives
Millenniums in a moment; who reveres
Himself, and with superb despite
Maltreats the loving-kindnesses of men,
Divine ideas and abstractions fond—
He, he alone may measure and endure
My headstrong passion and austerity.
'To love and understand?' The prattlement
Of amorists, begetters, family folk
Inevitably mean, and gall-less hacks
Of wealth who ape imagined Providence!
Chief end of man, the ultimate design
Of intellect, is knowledge undefiled
With use or usufruct. Matter, unknown,
Unknowing, crawled and groped through grade on grade
Of faculty, till Thought came forth at last
With power to sift the elements. Chief end
Of Matter—of the Earth aware in us,
As of that Greater Matter orbed and lit
Throughout Eternal Night—is evermore
Self-Knowledge.

Thought achieved, the unconscious will,
Which Matter is, empowered it and enslaved
With endless lust of life triumphantly,
That knowledge might endure; and tarred it on—
This Thought, or lustful thinker, man—to know
Under a penalty without reprieve,
Of character and title manifold,
Discomfort, pain, affliction, agony.

Inclement skies, antagonism in love,
Engrossing hunger, from the willing earth

Won easy knowledge apt for instant use.
Luxury, fashion, tribal vanity,
Desire of power, disease, the fear of death
Extorted many a secret, quaintly masked,
Embarrassed and provocative, or pent
Inscrutably in substance signetless;
But chiefly Death inspired the slavish Thought
With terror-stricken zeal to penetrate
The only mystery, Matter, mutable,
Eternal, infinite in being, power,
And semblance.

    Matter's drudge, the restless Thought
Knit up with flesh of men, that builds and weaves,
Bakes, brews, and fights, and heals; that *would* express
The very seed of gold, and tamely sought
Elixir—(paragon of vanities,
And Matter's masterpiece in high chicane:
That, not content with offspring, men must scheme
To propagate their own peculiar woe!)—
This helpless Thought, solacing unbeknown
The passion for self-knowledge, crown and flower
Of that unconscious will which Matter is—
(Always the stolid will, Matter supreme!)—
I say, this anguished Thought, this mind of man,
Organ of Matter's consciousness, rebelled,
And with a wanton populace of gods,
A drift of elves, and rout of forms obscene,
Slandered Material truth; more traitorous still,
Perverted and obscured the clear Unknown
With the Immaterial, imagined God
Alone, spirit, and a hereafter—pitched
Sublimely in the empyrean Heaven,
In the abyss profoundly hollowed Hell.
'Salvation or Damnation,' Thought aspired,
'So I escape from Matter's galling yoke!'
Thus the tormented common-mind of man,
A mode of Matter warring with itself.

    But at all times a more reliant Thought,
A strength of brain, a remnant less than man
And greater—in the jargon of the herd,
'Hateful to God and to God's enemies'—
Fulfilled the bent of Matter willingly,
And sought out Knowledge for its very sake:
It might be shrewdly as a livelihood,

Or to delight or help mankind, or make
A name, at first; but in the end to know—
Merely to know was the consuming fire
Of these strong minds, delivered and elect.

In the high sphere of knowledge which I haunt,
When I began to hew the living flesh,
I seemed to seek—I seemed; for who can tell
The drift of aims utility distorts?—
The mitigation of disease. Not long
A bias of humanity deflects
Advancement in the true Materialist!
My Thought that share the contumacy men
Display, effeminate in things Material,
Began to turn to Matter lustfully
With masculine intent . . . You start and stare!
How shall I cut and thrust conviction through
And through you? . . . Now, I know. This impress asks
A sheet unsoiled. Oh, for a sudden end
Of palimpsests! Expunge the o'erscored script
That blurs the mind with poetry and prose
Of every age; and yield it gladly up
For me to carve with knowledge, and to seal
With Matter's signet. Listen now, and think.

Daily I passed a common, chapped and seamed
By weeks of headlong heat. A rotten hack,
Compunctious hideful of rheumatic joints
Larded with dung and clay, gaunt spectacle
Of ringbone, spavin, canker, shambled about,
And grazed the faded, sparse, disrelished tufts
That the sun's tongue of flame had left half-licked:
Family physician, coster, cat's-meat-man—
These, the indifferent fates who ruled his life.
The last had turned him loose to dissipate
A day or two of grace. But when he came—
The raw-faced knacker with his knuckly fists—
I ransomed Dobbin, pitying his case,
He seemed so cheerful maugre destiny.

Enfranchised in my meadow, all his hours
Were golden, till the end with autumn came,
Even while my impulse sundered hisk and shell
Of habit and utility. Two days
He lay a-dying, and could not die. Endowed
With strength, affection, blood, nerve, hearing, sight;
Laden with lust of life for the behoof

Of Matter; gelded, bitted, scourged, starved, dying—
Where could the meaning of the riddle lie?

   Submissively, like a somnambulist
Who solves his problem in a dream, I found
The atonement of it, and became its lord—
Lord of the riddle of the Universe,
Aware at full of Matter's stolid will
In me accomplishing its useless aim.
The whip's-man felt no keener ecstasy
When a fair harlot at the cart's-tail shrieked,
And rags of flesh with blood-soaked tawdry lace
Girdled her shuddering loins. No hallowed awe
That ever rapt a pale inquisitor,
Beholding pangs of stubborn heresy
A-sweat upon the rack, surpassed the fierce
Exalted anguish of my thought. I fixed
The creature, impotent and moribund,
With gag and fetter; sheared his filthy mane;
Cut a foot's length, tissue and tendon, 'twixt
His poll and festering withers, and hammered out
Three arches of his spine. In ropy bulk,
Stripped to my forceps, marrow, Matter's pith
Itself! A twitch, a needle's faint appeal
Recalled the gelding's life, supplied each stop
And register of sense with vibrant power,
And made this faithful, dying, loathsome drudge,
One diapason of intensest pain,
Sublime and terrible in martyrdom.

   I study pain, measure it and invent—
I and my compeers; for I hold again
That every passionate Materialist,
Who rends the living subject, soon is purged
Of vulgar tenderness in diligent
Delighted tormentry of bird and beast;
And, conscious or unconscious of his aim,
Fulfils the will of Matter, cutting out
A path to knowledge, undefiled with use
Or usufruct, by Matter's own resource,
Pain, alkahest of all intelligence.
I study pain—pain only: I broach and tap
The agony of Matter, and work its will,
Detecting useless items—I and those
Who tortured fourscore solipeds to carve
A scale of feeling on the spinal cord;
Quilted with nails, and mangled flights of fowl,

Litters and nests of vermin happily
Throughout a year, discerning in the end
That anguished breath and breath of healthy ease
Differ in function by a jot, perhaps;
Or Pisan doctors whom the Florentine
Furnished with criminals from a gentler doom
Withdrawn to undergo anatomy,
And masters who, before the world grew tame,
Enjoyed the handling in their honoured troughs
Of countless men and women alive and well.

    'Have I no pain?'—I live alone: my wife
Forsook me, and my daughters. In the night,
From silted fountains sprung, insurgent tears
Arouse me, a marauder in the past
Against my will—one of the nightly gang
Impressed by sleep to serve Insomnia,
The queen of waking dreams. Caught in her snare,
The man-trap Memory, towards the recreant hour
When life is at the ebb, I rise and think
To end it now; but always stay my hand,
Because we cannot put an end to that
In which we live and move and have our being,
Nor anywhere escape it: air is Matter;
The interstellar spaces, Matter cold
And thin, the darksome vehicle of light.
To the Materialist there is no Unknown;
All, all is Matter. Pain? I am one ache—
But never when I work; there Matter wins!
And I believe that they who delve the soil,
Who reap the grain, who dig and smelt the ore,
The girl who plucks a rose, the sweetest voice
That thrills the air with sound, give Matter pain:
Think you the sun is happy in his flames,
Or that the cooling earth no anguish feels,
Nor quails from her contraction? Rather say,
The systems, constellations, galaxies
That strew the ethereal waste are whirling there
In agony unutterable. Pain?
It may be Matter in itself is pain,
Sweetened in sexual love that so mankind,
The medium of Matter's consciousness,
May never cease to know—the stolid bent
Of Matter, the infinite vanity
Of the Universe, being evermore
Self-knowledge.

ALFRED EDWARD HOUSMAN

(1859-1936)

WHEN I WAS ONE-AND-TWENTY

When I was one-and-twenty
   I heard a wise man say,
'Give crowns and pounds and guineas
   But not your heart away;
Give pearls away and rubies
   But keep your fancy free.'
But I was one-and-twenty,
   No use to talk to me.

When I was one-and-twenty
   I heard him say again,
'The heart out of the bosom
   Was never given in vain;
'Tis paid with sighs a plenty
   And sold for endless rue.'
And I am two-and-twenty,
   And oh, 'tis true, 'tis true.

OH, WHEN I WAS IN LOVE WITH YOU

Oh, when I was in love with you,
   Then I was clean and brave,
And miles around the wonder grew
   How well did I behave.

And now the fancy passes by,
   And nothing will remain,
And miles around they'll say that I
   Am quite myself again.

LOVELIEST OF TREES

Loveliest of trees, the cherry now
Is hung with bloom along the bough,
And stands about the woodland ride
Wearing white for Eastertide.

Now, of my threescore years and ten,
Twenty will not come again,
And take from seventy springs a score,
It only leaves me fifty more.

And since to look at things in bloom
Fifty springs are little room,
About the woodlands I will go
To see the cherry hung with snow.

REVEILLE

Wake: the silver dusk returning
    Up the beach of darkness brims,
And the ship of sunrise burning
    Strands upon the eastern rims.

Wake: the vaulted shadow shatters,
    Trampled to the floor it spanned,
And the tent of night in tatters
    Straws the sky-pavilioned land.

Up, lad, up, 'tis late for lying:
    Hear the drums of morning play;
Hark, the empty highways crying
    'Who'll beyond the hills away?'

Towns and countries woo together,
    Forelands beacon, belfries call;
Never lad that trod on leather
    Lived to feast his heart with all.

Up, lad: thews that lie and cumber
    Sunlit pallets never thrive;
Morns abed and daylight slumber
    Were not meant for man alive.

Clay lies still, but blood's a rover;
    Breath's a ware that will not keep

> Up, lad: when the journey's over
>   There'll be time enough to sleep.

OH SEE HOW THICK THE GOLDCUP FLOWERS

Oh see how thick the goldcup flowers
    Are lying in field and lane,
With dandelions to tell the hours
    That never are told again.
Oh may I squire you round the meads
    And pick you posies gay?
—'Twill do no harm to take my arm.
    'You may, young man, you may.'

Ah, spring was sent for lass and lad,
    'Tis now the blood runs gold,
And man and maid had best be glad
    Before the world is old.
What flowers to-day may flower to-morrow,
    But never as good as new.
—Suppose I wound my arm right round—
    ' 'Tis true, young man, 'tis true.'

Some lads there are, 'tis shame to say,
    That only court to thieve,
And once they bear the bloom away
    'Tis little enough they leave.
Then keep your heart for men like me
    And safe from trustless chaps.
My love is true and all for you.
    'Perhaps, young man, perhaps.'

Oh, look in my eyes then, can you doubt?
    —Why, 'tis a mile from town.
How green the grass is all about!
    We might as well sit down.
—Ah, life, what is it but a flower?
    Why must true lovers sigh?
Be kind, have pity, my own, my pretty,—
    'Good-bye, young man, good-bye.'

TO AN ATHLETE DYING YOUNG

The time you won your town the race
We chaired you through the market-place;
Man and boy stood cheering by,
And home we brought you shoulder-high.

To-day, the road all runners come,
Shoulder-high we bring you home,
And set you at your threshold down,
Townsman of a stiller town.

Smart lad, to slip betimes away
From fields where glory does not stay
And early though the laurel grows
It withers quicker than the rose.

Eyes the shady night has shut
Cannot see the record cut,
And silence sounds no worse than cheers
After earth has stopped the ears:

Now you will not swell the rout
Of lads that wore their honours out,
Runners whom renown outran
And the name died before the man.

So set, before its echoes fade,
The fleet foot on the sill of shade,
And hold to the low lintel up
The still-defended challenge-cup.

And round that early-laurelled head
Will flock to gaze the strengthless dead,
And find unwithered on its curls
The garland briefer than a girl's.

BREDON HILL

In summertime on Bredon
    The bells they sound so clear;
Round both the shires they ring them
    In steeples far and near,
    A happy noise to hear.

Here of a Sunday morning
    My love and I would lie,
And see the coloured counties,
    And hear the larks so high
    About us in the sky.

The bells would ring to call her
    In valleys miles away:

'Come all to church, good people;
  Good people, come and pray.'
But here my love would stay.

And I would turn and answer
  Among the springing thyme,
'Oh, peal upon our wedding,
  And we will hear the chime,
  And come to church in time.'

But when the snows at Christmas
  On Bredon top were strown,
My love rose up so early
  And stole out unbeknown
  And went to church alone.

They tolled the one bell only,
  Groom there was none to see,
The mourners followed after,
  And so to church went she,
  And would not wait for me.

The bells they sound on Bredon,
  And still the steeples hum.
'Come all to church, good people,'—
  Oh, noisy bells, be dumb;
  I hear you, I will come.

THE LADS IN THEIR HUNDREDS

The lads in their hundreds to Ludlow come in for the fair,
  There's men from the barn and the forge and the mill and
    the fold,
The lads for the girls and the lads for the liquor are there,
  And there with the rest are the lads that will never be old.

There's chaps from the town and the field and the till and the
    cart,
  And many to count are the stalwart, and many the brave,
And many the handsome of face and the handsome of heart,
  And few that will carry their looks or their truth to the
    grave.

I wish one could know them, I wish there were tokens to tell
  The fortunate fellows that now you can never discern;

And then one could talk with them friendly and wish them
    farewell
    And watch them depart on the way that they will not
    return.

But now you may stare as you like and there's nothing to
    scan;
    And brushing your elbow unguessed-at and not to be
    told
They carry back bright to the coiner the mintage of man,
    The lads that will die in their glory and never be old.

IS MY TEAM PLOUGHING

'Is my team ploughing,
    That I was used to drive
And hear the harness jingle
    When I was man alive?'

Ay, the horses trample,
    The harness jingles now;
No change though you lie under
    The land you used to plough.

'Is football playing
    Along the river shore,
With lads to chase the leather,
    Now I stand up no more?'

Ay, the ball is flying,
    The lads play heart and soul;
The goal stands up, the keeper
    Stands up to keep the goal.

'Is my girl happy,
    That I thought hard to leave,
And has she tired of weeping
    As she lies down at eve?'

Ay, she lies down lightly,
    She lies not down to weep:
Your girl is well contented.
    Be still, my lad, and sleep.

'Is my friend hearty,
    Now I am thin and pine,
And has he found to sleep in
    A better bed than mine?'

Yes, lad, I lie easy,
    I lie as lads would choose;
I cheer a dead man's sweetheart,
    Never ask me whose.

OTHERS, I AM NOT THE FIRST

Others, I am not the first,
Have willed more mischief than they durst:
If in the breathless night I too
Shiver now, 'tis nothing new.

More than I, if truth were told,
Have stood and sweated hot and cold,
And through their reins in ice and fire
Fear contended with desire.

Agued once like me were they,
But I like them shall win my way
Lastly to the bed of mould
Where there's neither heat nor cold.

But from my grave across my brow
Plays no wind of healing now,
And fire and ice within me fight
Beneath the suffocating night.

ON WENLOCK EDGE THE WOOD'S IN TROUBLE

On Wenlock Edge the wood's in trouble;
    His forest fleece the Wrekin heaves;
The gale, it plies the saplings double,
    And thick on Severn snow the leaves.

'Twould blow like this through holt and hanger
    When Uricon the city stood:
'Tis the old wind in the old anger,
    But then it threshed another wood.

Then, 'twas before my time, the Roman
    At yonder heaving hill would stare:
The blood that warms an English yeoman,
    The thoughts that hurt him, they were there.

There, like the wind through woods in riot,
    Through him the gale of life blew high;
The tree of man was never quiet:
    Then 'twas the Roman, now 'tis I.

The gale, it plies the saplings double,
    It blows so hard, 'twill soon be gone:
To-day the Roman and his trouble
    Are ashes under Uricon.

WHITE IN THE MOON THE LONG ROAD LIES

White in the moon the long road lies,
    The moon stands blank above;
White in the moon the long road lies
    That leads me from my love.

Still hangs the hedge without a gust,
    Still, still the shadows stay:
My feet upon the moonlit dust
    Pursue the ceaseless way.

The world is round, so travellers tell,
    And straight though reach the track,
Trudge on, trudge on, 'twill all be well,
    The way will guide one back.

But ere the circle homeward hies
    Far, far must it remove:
White in the moon the long road lies
    That leads me from my love.

INTO MY HEART AN AIR THAT KILLS

Into my heart an air that kills
    From yon far country blows:
What are those blue remembered hills,
    What spires, what farms are those?

That is the land of lost content,
   I see it shining plain,
The happy highways where I went
   And cannot come again.

THE IMMORTAL PART

When I meet the morning beam
Or lay me down at night to dream,
I hear my bones within me say,
'Another night, another day.

'When shall this slough of sense be cast,
This dust of thoughts be laid at last,
The man of flesh and soul be slain
And the man of bone remain?

'This tongue that talks, these lungs that shout,
These thews that hustle us about,
This brain that fills the skull with schemes,
And its humming hive of dreams,—

'These to-day are proud in power
And lord it in their little hour:
The immortal bones obey control
Of dying flesh and dying soul.

' 'Tis long till eve and morn are gone:
Slow the endless night comes on,
And late to fulness grows the birth
That shall last as long as earth.

'Wanderers eastward, wanderers west,
Know you why you cannot rest?
'Tis that every mother's son
Travails with a skeleton.

'Lie down in the bed of dust;
Bear the fruit that bear you must;
Bring the eternal seed to light,
And morn is all the same as night.

'Rest you so from trouble sore,
Fear the heat o' the sun no more,
Nor the snowing winter wild,
Now you labour not with child.

'Empty vessel, garment cast,
We that wore you long shall last.
—Another night, another day.'
So my bones within me say.

Therefore they shall do my will
To-day while I am master still,
And flesh and soul, now both are strong,
Shall hale the sullen slaves along,

Before this fire of sense decay,
This smoke of thought blow clean away,
And leave with ancient night alone
The stedfast and enduring bone.

WITH RUE MY HEART IS LADEN

With rue my heart is laden
    For golden friends I had,
For many a rose-lipt maiden
    And many a lightfoot lad.

By brooks too broad for leaping
    The lightfoot boys are laid;
The rose-lipt girls are sleeping
    In fields where roses fade.

YOU SMILE UPON YOUR FRIEND TO-DAY

You smile upon your friend to-day,
    To-day his ills are over;
You hearken to the lover's say,
    And happy is the lover.

'Tis late to hearken, late to smile,
    But better late than never:
I shall have lived a little while
    Before I die for ever.

TERENCE, THIS IS STUPID STUFF

'Terence, this is stupid stuff:
You eat your victuals fast enough;
There can't be much amiss, 'tis clear,
To see the rate you drink your beer.

But oh, good Lord, the verse you make,
It gives a chap the belly-ache.
The cow, the old cow, she is dead;
It sleeps well, the horned head:
We poor lads, 'tis our turn now
To hear such tunes as killed the cow.
Pretty friendship 'tis to rhyme
Your friends to death before their time
Moping melancholy mad:
Come, pipe a tune to dance to, lad.'

    Why, if 'tis dancing you would be,
There's brisker pipes than poetry.
Say, for what were hop-yards meant,
Or why was Burton built on Trent?
Oh many a peer of England brews
Livelier liquor than the Muse,
And malt does more than Milton can
To justify God's ways to man.
Ale, man, ale's the stuff to drink
For fellows whom it hurts to think:
Look into the pewter pot
To see the world as the world's not.
And faith, 'tis pleasant till 'tis past:
The mischief is that 'twill not last.
Oh I have been to Ludlow fair
And left my necktie God knows where,
And carried half-way home, or near,
Pints and quarts of Ludlow beer:
Then the world seemed none so bad,
And I myself a sterling lad;
And down in lovely muck I've lain,
Happy till I woke again.
Then I saw the morning sky:
Heigho, the tale was all a lie;
The world, it was the old world yet,
I was I, my things were wet,
And nothing now remained to do
But begin the game anew.

    Therefore, since the world has still
Much good, but much less good than ill,
And while the sun and moon endure
Luck's a chance, but trouble's sure,
I'd face it as a wise man would,
And train for ill and not for good.

'Tis true, the stuff I bring for sale
Is not so brisk a brew as ale:
Out of a stem that scored the hand
I wrung it in a weary land.
But take it: if the smack is sour,
The better for the embittered hour;
It should do good to heart and head
When your soul is in my soul's stead;
And I will friend you, if I may,
In the dark and cloudy day.

There was a king reigned in the East:
There, when kings will sit to feast,
They get their fill before they think
With poisoned meat and poisoned drink.
He gathered all that springs to birth
From the many-venomed earth;
First a little, thence to more,
He sampled all her killing store;
And easy, smiling, seasoned sound,
Sate the king when healths went round.
They put arsenic in his meat
And stared aghast to watch him eat;
They poured strychnine in his cup
And shook to see him drink it up:
They shook, they stared as white's their shirt:
Them it was their poison hurt.
—I tell the tale that I heard told.
Mithridates, he died old.

I HOED AND TRENCHED AND WEEDED

I hoed and trenched and weeded,
    And took the flowers to fair:
I brought them home unheeded;
    The hue was not the wear.

So up and down I sow them
    For lads like me to find,
When I shall lie below them,
    A dead man out of mind.

Some seed the birds devour,
    And some the season mars,
But here and there will flower
    The solitary stars,

And fields will yearly bear them
  As light-leaved spring comes on,
And luckless lads will wear them
  When I am dead and gone.

THE CHESTNUT CASTS HIS FLAMBEAUX

The chestnut casts his flambeaux, and the flowers
  Stream from the hawthorn on the wind away,
The doors clap to, the pane is blind with showers.
  Pass me the can, lad; there's an end of May.

There's one spoilt spring to scant our mortal lot,
  One season ruined of our little store.
May will be fine next year as like as not:
  Oh ay, but then we shall be twenty-four.

We for a certainty are not the first
  Have sat in taverns while the tempest hurled
Their hopeful plans to emptiness, and cursed
  Whatever brute and blackguard made the world.

It is in truth iniquity on high
  To cheat our sentenced souls of aught they crave,
And mar the merriment as you and I
  Fare on our long fool's-errand to the grave.

Iniquity it is; but pass the can.
  My lad, no pair of kings our mothers bore;
Our only portion is the estate of man:
  We want the moon, but we shall get no more.

If here to-day the cloud of thunder lours
  To-morrow it will hie on far behests;
The flesh will grieve on other bones than ours
  Soon, and the soul will mourn in other breasts.

The troubles of our proud and angry dust
  Are from eternity, and shall not fail.
Bear them we can, and if we can we must.
  Shoulder the sky, my lad, and drink your ale.

THE LAWS OF GOD, THE LAWS OF MAN

The laws of God, the laws of man,
He may keep that will and can;
Not I: let God and man decree
Laws for themselves and not for me;
And if my ways are not as theirs
Let them mind their own affairs.
Their deeds I judge and much condemn,
Yet when did I make laws for them?
Please yourselves, say I, and they
Need only look the other way.
But no, they will not; they must still
Wrest their neighbour to their will,
And make me dance as they desire
With jail and gallows and hell-fire.
And how am I to face the odds
Of man's bedevilment and God's?
I, a stranger and afraid
In a world I never made.
They will be master, right or wrong;
Though both are foolish, both are strong.
And since, my soul, we cannot fly
To Saturn nor to Mercury,
Keep we must, if keep we can,
These foreign laws of God and man.

THE NIGHT IS FREEZING FAST

The night is freezing fast,
   To-morrow comes December;
      And winterfalls of old
Are with me from the past;
   And chiefly I remember
      How Dick would hate the cold.

Fall, winter, fall; for he,
   Prompt hand and headpiece clever,
      Has woven a winter robe,
And made of earth and sea
   His overcoat for ever,
      And wears the turning globe.

REVOLUTION

West and away the wheels of darkness roll,
    Day's beamy banner up the east is borne,
Spectres and fears, the nightmare and her foal,
    Drown in the golden deluge of the morn.

But over sea and continent from sight
    Safe to the Indies has the earth conveyed
The vast and moon-eclipsing cone of night,
    Her towering foolscap of eternal shade.

See, in mid heaven the sun is mounted; hark,
    The belfries tingle to the noonday chime.
'Tis silent, and the subterranean dark
    Has crossed the nadir, and begins to climb.

EPITAPH ON AN ARMY OF MERCENARIES

These, in the day when heaven was falling,
    The hour when earth's foundations fled,
Followed their mercenary calling
    And took their wages and are dead.

Their shoulders held the sky suspended;
    They stood, and earth's foundations stay;
What God abandoned, these defended,
    And saved the sum of things for pay.

WHEN ISRAEL OUT OF EGYPT CAME

When Israel out of Egypt came
    Safe in the sea they trod;
By day in cloud, by night in flame,
    Went on before them God.

He brought them with a stretched out hand
    Dry-footed through the foam,
Past sword and famine, rock and sand,
    Lust and rebellion, home.

I never over Horeb heard
    The blast of advent blow;
No fire-faced prophet brought me word
    Which way behoved me go.

Ascended is the cloudy flame,
    The mount of thunder dumb;
The tokens that to Israel came,
    To me they have not come.

I see the country far away
    Where I shall never stand;
The heart goes where no footstep may
    Into the promised land.

The realm I look upon and die
    Another man will own;
He shall attain the heaven that I
    Perish and have not known.

But I will go where they are hid
    That never were begot,
To my inheritance amid
    The nation that is not.

I DID NOT LOSE MY HEART IN SUMMER'S EVEN

I did not lose my heart in summer's even,
    When roses to the moonrise burst apart:
When plumes were under heel and lead was flying,
    In blood and smoke and flame I lost my heart.

I lost it to a soldier and a foeman,
    A chap that did not kill me, but he tried;
That took the sabre straight and took it striking
    And laughed and kissed his hand to me and died.

INFANT INNOCENCE

The Russian bear is huge and wild,
He has devoured the infant child,
The infant child is not aware
It has been eaten by the bear.

WILLIAM BUTLER YEATS

(1865-1939)

WHEN YOU ARE OLD

When you are old and grey and full of sleep,
And nodding by the fire, take down this book,
And slowly read, and dream of the soft look
Your eyes had once, and of their shadows deep;

How many loved your moments of glad grace,
And loved your beauty with love false or true,
But one man loved the pilgrim soul in you,
And loved the sorrows of your changing face;

And bending down beside the glowing bars,
Murmur, a little sadly, how Love fled
And paced upon the mountains overhead
And hid his face amid a crowd of stars.

THE LAKE ISLE OF INNISFREE

I will arise and go now, and go to Innisfree,
And a small cabin build there, of clay and wattles made:
Nine bean-rows will I have there, a hive for the honeybee,
And live alone in the bee-loud glade.

And I shall have some peace there, for peace comes dropping
    slow,
Dropping from the veils of the morning to where the cricket
    sings;
There midnight's all a glimmer, and noon a purple glow,
And evening full of linnet's wings.

I will arise and go now, for always night and day
I hear lake water lapping with low sounds by the shore;

While I stand on the roadway, or on the pavements grey,
I hear it in the deep heart's core.

DOWN BY THE SALLEY GARDENS

Down by the salley gardens my love and I did meet;
She passed the salley gardens with little snow-white feet.
She bid me take love easy, as the leaves grow on the tree;
But I, being young and foolish, with her would not agree.

In a field by the river my love and I did stand,
And on my leaning shoulder she laid her snow-white hand.
She bid me take life easy, as the grass grows on the weirs;
But I was young and foolish, and now am full of tears.

THE SONG OF WANDERING AENGUS

I went out to the hazel wood,
Because a fire was in my head,
And cut and peeled a hazel wand,
And hooked a berry to a thread;
And when white moths were on the wing,
And moth-like stars were flickering out,
I dropped the berry in a stream
And caught a little silver trout.

When I had laid it on the floor
I went to blow the fire a-flame,
But something rustled on the floor,
And someone called me by my name:
It had become a glimmering girl
With apple blossom in her hair
Who called me by my name and ran
And faded through the brightening air.

Though I am old with wandering
Through hollow lands and hilly lands,
I will find out where she has gone,
And kiss her lips and take her hands;
And walk among long dappled grass,
And pluck till time and times are done
The silver apples of the moon,
The golden apples of the sun.

THE SORROW OF LOVE

The quarrel of the sparrows in the eaves,
The full round moon and the star-laden sky,
And the loud song of the ever-singing leaves,
Had hid away earth's old and weary cry.

And then you came with those red mournful lips,
And with you came the whole of the world's tears,
And all the trouble of her labouring ships,
And all the trouble of her myriad years.

And now the sparrows warring in the eaves,
The curd-pale moon, the white stars in the sky,
And the loud chaunting of the unquiet leaves,
Are shaken with earth's old and weary cry.

HE THINKS OF HIS PAST GREATNESS WHEN A PART OF THE CONSTELLATIONS OF HEAVEN

I have drunk ale from the Country of the Young
And weep because I know all things now:
I have been a hazel tree and they hung
The Pilot Star and the Crooked Plough
Among my leaves in times out of mind:
I became a rush that horses tread:
I became a man, a hater of the wind,
Knowing one, out of all things, alone, that his head
Would not lie on the breast or his lips on the hair
Of the woman that he loves, until he dies;
Although the rushes and the fowl of the air
Cry of his love with their pitiful cries.

O'SULLIVAN RUA TO MARY LAVELL

When my arms wrap you round, I press
My heart upon the loveliness
That has long faded in the world;
The jewelled crowns that kings have hurled
In shadowy pools, when armies fled;
The love-tales wove with silken thread
By dreaming ladies upon cloth
That has made fat the murderous moth;
The roses that of old time were
Woven by ladies in their hair,
The dew-cold lilies ladies bore

Through many a sacred corridor
Where a so sleepy incense rose
That only God's eyes did not close:
For that dim brow and lingering hand
Come from a more dream-heavy land,
A more dream-heavy hour than this;
And, when your sigh from kiss to kiss,
I hear pale Beauty sighing too,
For hours when all must fade like dew,
Till there be naught but throne on throne
Of seraphs, brooding, each alone,
His sword upon a iron knees
On her most lonely mysteries.

THE EVERLASTING VOICES

O sweet everlasting voices be still;
Go to the guards of the heavenly fold
And bid them wander obeying your will
Flame under flame, till Time be no more;
Have you not heard that our hearts are old,
That you call in birds, in wind on the hill,
In shaken boughs, in tide on the shore?
O sweet everlasting Voices be still.

THE SECRET ROSE

Far off, most secret, and inviolate Rose,
Enfold me in my hour of hours; where those
Who sought thee in the Holy Sepulchre,
Or in the wine vat, dwell beyond the stir
And tumult of defeated dreams; and deep
Among pale eyelids, heavy with the sleep
Men have named beauty. Thy great leaves enfold
The ancient beards, the helms of ruby and gold
Of the crowned Magi; and the king whose eyes
Saw the Pierced Hands and Rood of elder rise
In druid vapour and make the torches dim;
Till vain frenzy awoke and he died; and him
Who met Fand walking among flaming dew
By a grey shore where the wind never blew,
And lost the world and Emer for a kiss;
And him who drove the gods out of their liss,
And till a hundred morns had flowered red,
Feasted, and wept the barrows of his dead;
And the proud dreaming king who flung the crown

And sorrow away, and calling bard and clown
Dwelt among wine-stained wanderers in deep woods;
And him who sold tillage, and house, and goods,
And sought through lands and islands numberless years,
Until he found with laughter and with tears,
A woman of so shining loveliness,
That men threshed corn at midnight by a tress,
A little stolen tress. I, too, await
The hour of thy great wind of love and hate.
When shall the stars be blown about the sky,
Like the sparks blown out of a smithy, and die?
Surely thine hour has come, thy great wind blows,
Far-off, most secret, and involate Rose?

PROLOGUE TO RESPONSIBILITIES

Pardon, old fathers, if you still remain
Somewhere in ear-shot for the story's end,
Old Dublin merchant 'free of ten and four'
Or trading out of Galway into Spain;
And country scholar, Robert Emmet's friend,
A hundred-year-old memory to the poor;
Traders or soldiers who have left me blood
That has not passed through any huckster's loin,
Pardon, and you that did not weigh the cost,
Old Butlers when you took to horse and stood
Beside the brackish waters of the Boyne
Till your bad master blenched and all was lost;
You merchant skipper that leaped overboard
After a ragged hat in Biscay Bay,
You most of all, silent and fierce old man
Because you were the spectacle that stirred
My fancy, and set my boyish lips to say,
'Only the wasteful virtues earn the sun';
Pardon that for a barren passion's sake,
Although I have come close on forty-nine
I have no child, I have nothing but a book,
Nothing but that to prove your blood and mine.

A STICK OF INCENSE

Whence did all that fury come?
From empty tomb or Virgin womb?
Saint Joseph thought the world would melt
But liked the way his finger smelt.

A BRONZE HEAD

Here at right of the entrance this bronze head,
Human, superhuman, a bird's round eye,
Everything else withered and mummy-dead.
What great tomb-haunter sweeps the distant sky
(Something may linger there though all else die;)
And finds there nothing to make its terror less
Hysterica passio of its own emptiness?

No dark tomb-haunter once; her form all full
As though with magnanimity of light,
Yet a most gentle woman; who can tell
Which of her forms has shown her substance right?
Or maybe substance can be composite,
Profound McTaggart thought so, and in a breath
A mouthful held the extreme of life and death.

But even at the starting-post, all sleek and new,
I saw the wildness in her and I thought
A vision of terror that it must live through
Had shattered her soul. Propinquity had brought
Imagination to that pitch where it casts out
All that is not itself: I had grown wild
And wandered murmuring everywhere, 'My child, my child!'

Or else I thought her supernatural;
As though a sterner eye looked through her eye
On this foul world in its decline and fall;
On gangling stocks grown great, great stocks run dry,
Ancestral pearls all pitched into a sty,
Heroic reverie mocked by clown and knave,
And wondered what was left for massacre to save.

LAPIS LAZULI

I have heard that hysterical women say
They are sick of the palette and fiddle-bow,
Of poets that are always gay,
For everybody knows or else should know
That if nothing drastic is done
Aeroplane and Zeppelin will come out,
Pitch like King Billy bomb-balls in
Until the town lie beaten flat.

All perform their tragic play,

There struts Hamlet, there is Lear,
That's Ophelia, that Cordelia;
Yet they, should the last scene be there,
The great stage curtain about to drop,
If worthy their prominent part in the play,
Do not break up their lines to weep.
They know that Hamlet and Lear are gay;
Gaiety transfiguring all that dread.
All men have aimed at, found and lost;
Black out; Heaven blazing into the head:
Tragedy wrought to its uttermost.
Though Hamlet rambles and Lear rages,
And all the drop-scenes drop at once
Upon a hundred thousand stages,
It cannot grow by an inch or an ounce.

On their own feet they came, or on shipboard,
Camel-back, horse-back, ass-back, mule-back,
Old civilisations put to the sword.
Then they and their wisdom went to rack:
No handiwork of Callimachus,
Who handled marble as if it were bronze,
Made draperies that seemed to rise
When sea-wind swept the corner, stands;
His long lamp-chimney shaped like the stem
Of a slender palm, stood but a day;
All things fall and are built again,
And those that build them again are gay.

Two Chinamen, behind them a third,
Are carved in lapis lazuli,
Over them flies a long-legged bird,
A symbol of longevity;
The third, doubtless a serving-man,
Carries a musical instrument.

Every discoloration of the stone,
Every accidental crack or dent,
Seems a water-course or an avalanche,
Or lofty slope where it still snows
Though doubtless plum or cherry-branch
Sweetens the little half-way house
Those Chinamen climb towards, and I
Delight to imagine them seated there;
There, on the mountain and the sky,
On all the tragic scene they stare.

One asks for mournful melodies;
Accomplished fingers begin to play.
Their eyes mid many wrinkles, their eyes,
Their ancient, glittering eyes, are gay.

NEWS FOR THE DELPHIC ORACLE

There all the golden codgers lay,
There the silver dew,
And the great water sighed for love,
And the wind sighed too.
Man-picker Niamh leant and sighed
By Oisin on the grass;
There sighed amid his choir of love
Tall Pythagoras.
Plotinus came and looked about,
The salt-flakes on his breast,
And having stretched and yawned awhile
Lay sighing like the rest.

Straddling each a dolphin's back
And steadied by a fin,
Those Innocents re-live their death,
Their wounds open again.
The ecstatic waters laugh because
Their cries are sweet and strange,
Through their ancestral patterns dance,
And the brute dolphins plunge
Until, in some cliff-sheltered bay
Where wades the choir of love
Proffering its sacred laurel crowns,
They pitch their burdens off.

Slim adolescence that a nymph has stripped,
Peleus on Thetis stares.
Her limbs are delicate as an eyelid,
Love has blinded him with tears;
But Thetis' belly listens.
Down the mountain walls
From where Pan's cavern is
Intolerable music falls.
Foul goat-head, brutal arm appear,
Belly, shoulder, bum,
Flash fishlike; nymphs and satyrs
Copulate in the foam.

FOR ANNE GREGORY

'Never shall a young man,
Thrown into despair
By those great honey-coloured
Ramparts at your ear,
Love you for yourself alone
And not your yellow hair.'

'But I can get a hair-dye
And set such colour there,
Brown, or black, or carrot
That young men in despair

May love me for myself alone
And not my yellow hair.'

'I heard an old religious man
But yesternight declare
That he had found a text to
    prove
That only God, my dear,
Could love you for yourself
    alone
And not your yellow hair.'

A PRAYER FOR MY DAUGHTER

Once more the storm is howling, and half hid
Under this cradle-hood and coverlid
My child sleeps on. There is no obstacle
But Gregory's wood and one bare hill
Whereby the haystack- and roof-levelling wind,
Bred on the Atlantic, can be stayed;
And for an hour I have walked and prayed
Because of the great gloom that is in my mind.

I have walked and prayed for this young child an hour
And heard the sea-wind scream upon the tower,
And under the arches of the bridge, and scream
In the elms above the flooded stream;
Imagining in excited reverie
That the future years had come,
Dancing to a frenzied drum,
Out of the murderous innocence of the sea.

May she be granted beauty and yet not
Beauty to make a stranger's eye distraught,
Or hers before a looking-glass, for such,
Being made beautiful overmuch,
Consider beauty a sufficient end,
Lose natural kindness and maybe
The heart-revealing intimacy
That chooses right, and never find a friend.

Helen being chosen found life flat and dull
And later had much trouble from a fool,
While that great Queen, that rose out of the spray,

Being fatherless could have her way
Yet chose a bandy-leggèd smith for man.
It's certain that fine women eat
A crazy salad with their meat
Whereby the Horn of Plenty is undone.

In courtesy I'd have her chiefly learned;
Hearts are not had as a gift but hearts are earned
By those that are not entirely beautiful;
Yet many, that have played the fool
For beauty's very self, has charm made wise,
And many a poor man that has roved,
Loved and thought himself beloved,
From a glad kindness cannot take his eyes.

May she become a flourishing hidden tree
That all her thoughts may like the linnet be,
And have no business but dispensing round
Their magnanimities of sound,
Nor but in merriment begin a chase,
Nor but in merriment a quarrel.
O may she live like some green laurel
Rooted in one dear perpetual place.

My mind, because the minds that I have loved,
The sort of beauty that I have approved,
Prosper but little, has dried up of late,
Yet knows that to be choked with hate
May well be of all evil chances chief.
If there's no hatred in a mind
Assault and battery of the wind
Can never tear the linnet from the leaf.

An intellectual hatred is the worst,
So let her think opinions are accursed.
Have I not seen the loveliest woman born
Out of the mouth of Plenty's horn,
Because of her opinionated mind
Barter that horn and every good
By quiet natures understood
For an old bellows full of angry wind?

Considering that, all hatred driven hence,
The soul recovers radical innocence
And learns at last that it is self-delighting,
Self-appeasing, self-affrighting,

And that its own sweet will is Heaven's will;
She can, though every face should scowl
And every windy quarter howl
Or every bellows burst, be happy still.

And may her bridegroom bring her to a house
Where all's accustomed, ceremonious;
For arrogance and hatred are the wares
Peddled in the thoroughfares.
How but in custom and in ceremony
Are innocence and beauty born?
Ceremony's a name for the rich horn,
And custom for the spreading laurel tree.

A DIALOGUE OF SELF AND SOUL

I

MY SOUL. I summon to the winding ancient stair;
    Set all your mind upon the steep ascent,
    Upon the broken, crumbling battlement,
    Upon the breathless starlit air,
    Upon the star that marks the hidden pole;
    Fix every wandering thought upon
    That quarter where all thought is done:
    Who can distinguish darkness from the soul?

MY SELF. The consecrated blade upon my knees
    Is Sato's ancient blade, still as it was,
    Still razor-keen, still like a looking-glass
    Unspotted by the centuries;
    That flowering, silken, old embroidery, torn
    From some court-lady's dress and round
    The wooden scabbard bound and wound,
    Can, tattered, still protect, faded adorn.

MY SOUL. Why should the imagination of a man
    Long past his prime remember things that are
    Emblematical of love and war?
    Think of ancestral night that can,
    If but imagination scorn the earth
    And intellect its wandering
    To this and that and t' other thing,
    Deliver from the crime of death and birth.

MY SELF. Montashigi, third of his family, fashioned it
    Five hundred years ago, about it lie
    Flowers from I know not what embroidery—
    Heart's purple—and all these I set
    For emblems of the day against the tower
    Emblematical of the night,
    And claim as by a soldier's right
    A charter to commit the crime once more.

MY SOUL. Such fullness in that quarter overflows
    And falls into the basin of the mind
    That man is stricken deaf and dumb and blind,
    For intellect no longer knows
    Is from the *Ought*, or *Knower* from the *Known*—
    That is to say, ascends to Heaven;
    Only the dead can be forgiven;
    But when I think of that my tongue's a stone.

II

MY SELF. A living man is blind and drinks his drop.
    What matter if the ditches are impure?
    What matter if I live it all once more?
    Endure that toil of growing up;
    The ignominy of boyhood; the distress
    Of boyhood changing into man;
    The unfinished man and his pain
    Brought face to face with his own clumsiness;

    The finished man among his enemies?—
    How in the name of Heaven can he escape
    That defiling and disfigured shape
    The mirror of malicious eyes
    Casts upon his eyes until at last
    He thinks that shape must be his shape?
    And what's the good of an escape
    If honour find him in the wintry blast?

    I am content to live it all again
    And yet again, if it be life to pitch
    Into the frog-spawn of a blind man's ditch,
    A blind man battering blind men;
    Or into that most fecund ditch of all,
    The folly that man does
    Or must suffer, if he woos
    A proud woman not kindred of his soul.

I am content to follow to its source,
Every event in action or in thought;
Measure the lot; forgive myself the lot!
When such as I cast out remorse
So great a sweetness flows into the breast
We must laugh and we must sing,
We are blest by everything,
Everything we look upon is blest.

SAILING TO BYZANTIUM

That is no country for old men. The young
In one another's arms, birds in the trees,
—Those dying generations—at their song,
The salmon-falls, the mackerel-crowded seas,
Fish, flesh, or fowl, commend all summer long
Whatever is begotten, born, and dies.
Caught in that sensual music all neglect
Monuments of unageing intellect.

An aged man is but a paltry thing,
A tattered coat upon a stick, unless
Soul clap its hands and sing, and louder sing
For every tatter in its mortal dress,
Nor is there singing school but studying
Monuments of its own magnificence;
And therefore I have sailed the seas and come
To the holy city of Byzantium.

O sages standing in God's holy fire
As in the gold mosaic of a wall,
Come from the holy fire, perne in a gyre,
And be the singing-masters of my soul.
Consume my heart away; sick with desire
And fastened to a dying animal
It knows not what it is; and gather me
Into the artifice of eternity.

Once out of nature I shall never take
My bodily form from any natural thing,
But such a form as Grecian goldsmiths make
Of hammered gold and gold enamelling
To keep a drowsy Emperor awake;
Or set upon a golden bough to sing
To lords and ladies of Byzantium
Of what is past, or passing, or to come.

THE SECOND COMING

Turning and turning in the widening gyre
The falcon cannot hear the falconer;
Things fall apart; the centre cannot hold;
Mere anarchy is loosed upon the world,
The blood-dimmed tide is loosed, and everywhere
The ceremony of innocence is drowned;
The best lack all conviction, while the worst
Are full of passionate intensity.

Surely some revelation is at hand;
Surely the Second Coming is at hand.
The Second Coming! Hardly are those words out
When a vast image out of *Spiritus Mundi*
Troubles my sight: somewhere in sands of the desert
A shape with lion body and the head of a man,
A gaze blank and pitiless as the sun,
Is moving its slow thighs, while all about it
Reel shadows of the indignant desert birds.
The darkness drops again; but now I know
That twenty centuries of stony sleep
Were vexed to nightmare by a rocking cradle,
And what rough beast, its hour come round at last,
Slouches towards Bethlehem to be born?

THE TOWER

I

What shall I do with this absurdity—
O heart, O troubled heart—this caricature,
Decrepit age that has been tied to me
As to a dog's tail?
                    Never had I more
Excited, passionate, fantastical
Imagination, nor an ear and eye
That more expected the impossible—
No, not in boyhood when with rod and fly,
Or the humbler worm, I climbed Ben Bulben's back
And had the livelong summer day to spend.
It seems that I must bid the Muse go pack,
Choose Plato and Plotinus for a friend
Until imagination, ear and eye,
Can be content with argument and deal

In abstract things; or be derided by
A sort of battered kettle at the heel.

II

I pace upon the battlements and stare
On the foundations of a house, or where
Tree, like a sooty finger, starts from the earth;
And send imagination forth
Under the day's declining beam, and call
Images and memories
From ruin or from ancient trees,
For I would ask a question of them all.

Beyond that ridge lived Mrs. French, and once
When every silver candlestick or sconce
Lit up the dark mahogany and the wine,
A serving-man, that could divine
That most respected lady's every wish,
Ran and with the garden shears
Clipped an insolent farmer's ears
And brought them in a little covered dish.

Some few remembered still when I was young
A peasant girl commended by a song,
Who'd lived somewhere upon that rocky place,
And praised the colour of her face,
And had the greater joy in praising her,
Remembering that, if walked she there,
Farmers jostled at the fair
So great a glory did the song confer.

And certain men, being maddened by those rhymes,
Or else by toasting her a score of times,
Rose from the table and declared it right
To test their fancy by their sight;
But they mistook the brightness of the moon
For the prosaic light of day—
Music had driven their wits astray—
And one was drowned in the great bog of Cloone.

Strange, but the man who made the song was blind;
Yet, now I have considered it, I find
That nothing strange; the tragedy began
With Homer that was a blind man,
And Helen has all living hearts betrayed.

O may the moon and sunlight seem
One inextricable beam,
For if I triumph I must make men mad.

And I myself created Hanrahan
And drove him drunk or sober through the dawn
From somewhere in the neighbouring cottages.
Caught by an old man's juggleries
He stumbled, tumbled, fumbled to and fro
And had but broken knees for hire
And horrible splendour of desire;
I thought it all out twenty years ago:

Good fellows shuffled cards in an old bawn;
And when that ancient ruffian's turn was on
He so bewitched the cards under his thumb
That all but the one card became
A pack of hounds and not a pack of cards,
And that he changed into a hare.
Hanrahan rose in frenzy there
And followed up those baying creatures towards—

O towards I have forgotten what—enough!
I must recall a man that neither love
Nor music nor an enemy's clipped ear
Could, he was so harried, cheer;
A figure that has grown so fabulous
There's not a neighbour left to say
When he finished his dog's day:
An ancient bankrupt master of this house.

Before that ruin came, for centuries,
Rough men-at-arms, cross-gartered to the knees
Or shod in iron, climbed the narrow stairs,
And certain men-at-arms there were
Whose images, in the Great Memory stored,
Come with loud cry and panting breast
To break upon a sleeper's rest
While their great wooden dice beat on the board.

As I would question all, come all who can;
Come old, necessitous, half-mounted man;
And bring beauty's blind rambling celebrant;
The red man the juggler sent
Through God-forsaken meadows; Mrs. French,
Gifted with so fine an ear;

The man drowned in a bog's mire,
When mocking Muses chose the country wench.

Did all old men and women, rich and poor,
Who trod upon these rocks or passed this door,
Whether in public or in secret rage
As I do now against old age?
But I have found an answer in those eyes
That are impatient to be gone;
Go therefore; but leave Hanrahan,
For I need all his mighty memories.

Old lecher with a love on every wind,
Bring up out of that deep considering mind
All that you have discovered in the grave,
For it is certain that you have
Reckoned up every unforeknown, unseeing
Plunge, lured by a softening eye,
Or by a touch or a sigh,
Into the labyrinth of another's being;

Does the imagination dwell the most
Upon a woman won or woman lost?
If on the lost, admit you turned aside
From a great labyrinth out of pride,
Cowardice, some silly over-subtle thought
Or anything called conscience once;
And that if memory recur, the sun's
Under eclipse and the day blotted out.

III

It is time that I wrote my will;
I choose upstanding men
That climb the streams until
The fountain leap, and at dawn
Drop their cast at the side
Of dripping stone; I declare
They shall inherit my pride,
The pride of people that were
Bound neither to Cause nor to State,
Neither to slaves that were spat on,
Nor to the tyrants that spat,
The people of Burke and Grattan
That gave, though free to refuse—

Pride, like that of the morn,
When the headlong light is loose,
Or that of the fabulous horn,
Or that of the sudden shower
When all streams are dry,
Or that of the hour
When the swan must fix his eye
Upon a fading gleam,
Float out upon a long
Last reach of glittering stream
And there sing his last song.
And I declare my faith:
I mock Plotinus' thought
And cry in Plato's teeth,
Death and life were not
Till man made up the whole,
Made lock, stock and barrel
Out of his bitter soul,
Aye, sun and moon and star, all,
And further add to that
That, being dead, we rise,
Dream and so create
Translunar Paradise.
I have prepared my peace
With learned Italian things
And the proud stones of Greece,
Poet's imaginings
And memories of love,
Memories of the words of women,
All those things whereof
Man makes a superhuman
Mirror-resembling dream.

As at the loophole there
The daws chatter and scream,
And drop twigs layer upon layer.
When they have mounted up,
The mother bird will rest
On their hollow top,
And so warm her wild nest.

I leave both faith and pride
To young upstanding men
Climbing the mountain-side,
That under bursting dawn
They may drop a fly;

Being of that metal made
Till it was broken by
This sedentary trade.

Now shall I make my soul,
Compelling it to study
In a learned school
Till the wreck of body,
Slow decay of blood,
Testy delirium
Or dull decrepitude,
Or what worse evil come—
The death of friends, or death
Of every brilliant eye
That made a catch in the breath—
Seem but the clouds of the sky
When the horizon fades;
Or a bird's sleepy cry
Among the deepening shades.

AMONG SCHOOL CHILDREN

I walk through the long schoolroom questioning;
A kind old nun in a white hood replies;
The children learn to cipher and to sing,
To study reading-books and history,
To cut and sew, be neat in everything
In the best modern way—the children's eyes
In momentary wonder stare upon
A sixty-year-old smiling public man.

I dream of a Ledaean body, bent
Above a sinking fire, a tale that she
Told of a harsh reproof, or trivial event
That changed some childish day to tragedy—
Told, and it seemed that our two natures blent
Into a sphere from youthful sympathy,
Or else, to alter Plato's parable,
Into the yolk and white of the one shell.

And thinking of that fit of grief or rage
I look upon one child or t'other there
And wonder if she stood so at that age—
For even daughters of the swan can share
Something of every paddler's heritage—

And had that colour upon cheek or hair,
And thereupon my heart is driven wild:
She stands before me as a living child.

Her present image floats into the mind—
Did Quattrocento finger fashion it
Hollow of cheek as though it drank the wind
And took a mess of shadows for its meat?
And I though never of Ledaean kind
Had pretty plumage once—enough of that,
Better to smile on all that smile, and show
There is a comfortable kind of old scarecrow.

What youthful mother, a shape upon her lap
Honey of generation had betrayed,
And that must sleep, shriek, struggle to escape
As recollection or the drug decide,
Would think her son, did she but see that shape
With sixty or more winters on its head,
A compensation for the pang of his birth,
Or the uncertainty of his setting forth?

Plato thought nature but a spume that plays
Upon a ghostly paradigm of things;
Solider Aristotle played the taws
Upon the bottom of a king of kings;
World-famous golden-thighed Pythagoras
Fingered upon a fiddle-stick or strings
What a star sang and careless Muses heard:
Old clothes upon old sticks to scare a bird.

Both nuns and mothers worship images,
But those the candles light are not as those
That animate a mother's reveries,
But keep a marble or a bronze repose.
And yet they too break hearts—O Presences
That passion, piety or affection knows,
And that all heavenly glory symbolise—
O self-born mockers of man's enterprise;

Labour is blossoming or dancing where
The body is not bruised to pleasure soul,
Nor beauty born out of its own despair,
Nor blear-eyed wisdom out of midnight oil.
O chestnut tree, great rooted blossomer,
Are you the leaf, the blossom or the bole?
O body swayed to music, O brightening glance,
How can we know the dancer from the dance?

CRAZY JANE TALKS WITH THE BISHOP

I met the Bishop on the road
And much said he and I.
'Those breasts are flat and fallen now,
Those veins must soon be dry;
Live in a heavenly mansion,
Not in some foul sty.'

'Fair and foul are near of kin,
And fair needs foul,' I cried.
'My friends are gone, but that's a truth
Nor grave nor bed denied,
Learned in bodily lowliness
And in the heart's pride.

'A woman can be proud and stiff
When on love intent;
But Love has pitched his mansion in
The place of excrement;
For nothing can be sole or whole
That has not been rent.'

JOHN KINSELLA'S LAMENT FOR MRS. MARY MOORE

A bloody and a sudden end,
        Gunshot or a noose,
For death who takes what man would keep,
        Leaves what man would lose.
He might have had my sister,
        My cousins by the score,
But nothing satisfied the fool
        But my dear Mary Moore,
None other knows what pleasures man
        At table or in bed.
What shall I do for pretty girls
        Now my old bawd is dead?

Though stiff to strike a bargain,
        Like an old Jew man,
Her bargain struck we laughed and talked
        And emptied many a can;
And O! but she had stories,
        Though not for the priest's ear,
To keep the soul of man alive,
        Banish age and care,

And being old she put a skin
    On everything she said.
What shall I do for pretty girls
    Now my old bawd is dead?

The priests have got a book that says
    But for Adam's sin
Eden's Garden would be there
    And I there within.
No expectation fails there,
    No pleasing habit ends,
No man grows old, no girl grows cold,
    But friends walk by friends.
Who quarrels over halfpennies
    That plucks the trees for bread?
What shall I do for pretty girls
    Now my old bawd is dead?

BYZANTIUM

The unpurged images of day recede;
The Emperor's drunken soldiery are abed;
Night resonance recedes, night-walkers' song
After great cathedral gong;
A starlit or a moonlit dome disdains
All that man is,
All mere complexities,
The fury and the mire of human veins.

Before me floats an image, man or shade,
Shade more than man, more image than a shade;
For Hades' bobbin bound in mummy-cloth
May unwind the winding path;
A mouth that has no moisture and no breath
Breathless mouths may summon;
I hail the superhuman;
I call it death-in-life and life-in-death.

Miracle, bird or golden handiwork,
More miracle than bird or handiwork,
Planted on the star-lit golden bough,
Can like the cocks of Hades crow,
Or, by the moon embittered, scorn aloud
In glory of changeless metal
Common bird or petal
And all complexities of mire or blood.

At midnight on the Emperor's pavement flit
Flames that no faggot feeds, nor steel has lit,
Nor storm disturbs, flames begotten of flame,
Where blood-begotten spirits come
And all complexities of fury leave,
Dying into a dance,
An agony of trance,
An agony of flame that cannot singe a sleeve.

Astraddle on the dolphin's mire and blood,
Spirit after spirit! The smithies break the flood,
The golden smithies of the Emperor!
Marbles of the dancing floor
Break bitter furies of complexity,
Those images that yet
Fresh images beget,
That dolphin-torn, that gong-tormented sea.

TWO SONGS FROM A PLAY

I

I saw a staring virgin stand
Where holy Dionysus died,
And tear the heart out of his side,
And lay the heart upon her hand
And bear that beating heart away;
And then did all the Muses sing
Of Magnus Annus at the spring,
As though God's death were but a play.

Another Troy must rise and set,
Another lineage feed the crow,
Another Argo's painted prow
Drive to a flashier bauble yet.
The Roman Empire stood appalled:
It dropped the reins of peace and war
When that fierce virgin and her Star
Out of the fabulous darkness called.

II

In pity for man's darkening thought
He walked that room and issued thence
In Galilean turbulence;
The Babylonian starlight brought

A fabulous, formless darkness in;
Odour of blood when Christ was slain
Made all Platonic tolerance vain
And vain all Doric discipline.

Everything that man esteems
Endures a moment or a day.
Love's pleasure drives his love away,
The painter's brush consumes his dreams;
The herald's cry, the soldier's tread
Exhaust his glory and his might:
Whatever flames upon the night
Man's own resinous heart has fed.

THE MUNICIPAL GALLERY REVISITED

Around me the images of thirty years:
An ambush; pilgrims at the water-side;
Casement upon trial, half hidden by the bars,
Guarded; Griffith staring in hysterical pride;
Kevin O'Higgins' countenance that wears
A gentle questioning look that cannot hide
A soul incapable of remorse or rest;
A revolutionary soldier kneeling to be blessed;

An Abbot or Archbishop with an upraised hand
Blessing the Tricolour. 'This is not,' I say,
'The dead Ireland of my youth, but an Ireland
The poets have imagined, terrible and gay.'
Before a woman's portrait suddenly I stand,
Beautiful and gentle in her Venetian way.
I met her all but fifty years ago
For twenty minutes in some studio.

Heart-smitten with emotion I sink down,
My heart recovering with covered eyes;
Wherever I had looked I had looked upon
My permanent or impermanent images:
Augusta Gregory's son; her sister's son,
Hugh Lane, 'onlie begetter' of all these;
Hazel Lavery living and dying, that tale
As though some ballad-singer had sung it all;

Mancini's portrait of Augusta Gregory,
'Greatest since Rembrandt,' according to John Synge;
A great ebullient portrait certainly;

But where is the brush that could show anything
Of all that pride and that humility?
And I am in despair that time may bring
Approved patterns of women or of men
But not that selfsame excellence again.

My mediaeval knees lack health until they bend,
But in that woman, in that household where
Honour had lived so long, all lacking found.
Childless I thought, 'My children may find here
Deep-rooted things,' but never foresaw its end,
And now that end has come I have not wept;
No fox can foul the lair the badger swept—

(An image out of Spenser and the common tongue.)
John Synge, I and Augusta Gregory, thought
All that we did, all that we said or sang
Must come from contact with the soil, from that
Contact everything Antaeus-like grew strong.
We three alone in modern times had brought
Everything down to that sole test again,
Dream of the noble and the beggar-man.

And here's John Synge himself, that rooted man,
'Forgetting human words,' a grave deep face.
You that would judge me, do not judge alone
This book or that, come to this hallowed place
Where my friends' portraits hang and look thereon;
Ireland's history in their lineaments trace;
Think where man's glory most begins and ends,
And say my glory was I had such friends.

THE CIRCUS ANIMALS' DESERTION

I

I sought a theme and sought for it in vain,
I sought it daily for six weeks or so.
Maybe at last, being but a broken man,
I must be satisfied with my heart, although
Winter and summer till old age began
My circus animals were all on show,
Those stilted boys, that burnished chariot,
Lion and woman and the Lord knows what.

II

What can I but enumerate old themes?
First that sea-rider Oisin led by the nose
Through three enchanted islands, allegorical dreams,
Vain gaiety, vain battle, vain repose,
Themes of the embittered heart, or so it seems,
That might adorn old songs or courtly shows;
But what cared I that set him on to ride,
I, starved for the bosom of his faery bride?

And then a counter-truth filled out its play,
The Countess Cathleen was the name I gave it;
She, pity-crazed, had given her soul away,
But masterful Heaven had intervened to save it.
I thought my dear must her own soul destroy,
So did fanaticism and hate enslave it,
And this brought forth a dream and soon enough
This dream itself had all my thought and love.

And when the Fool and Blind Man stole the bread
Cuchulain fought the ungovernable sea;
Heart-mysteries there, and yet when all is said
It was the dream itself enchanted me:
Character isolated by a deed
To engross the present and dominate memory.
Players and painted stage took all my love,
And not those things that they were emblems of.

III

Those masterful images because complete
Grew in pure mind, but out of what began?
A mound of refuse or the sweepings of a street,
Old kettles, old bottles, and a broken can,
Old iron, old bones, old rags, that raving slut
Who keeps the till. Now that my ladder's gone,
I must lie down where all the ladders start,
In the foul rag-and-bone shop of the heart.

D. H. LAWRENCE

(1885-1930)

SONG OF A MAN WHO HAS COME THROUGH

Not I, not I, but the wind that blows through me!
A fine wind is blowing the new direction of Time.
If only I let it bear me, carry me, if only to carry me!
If only I am sensitive, subtle, oh, delicate, a winged gift!
If only, most lovely of all, I yield myself and am borrowed
By the fine, fine wind that takes its course through the chaos
    of the world
Like a fine, an exquisite chisel, a wedge-blade inserted;
If only I am keen and hard like the sheer tip of a wedge
Driven by invisible blows,
The rock will split, we shall come at the wonder, we
    shall find the Hesperides.

Oh, for the wonder that bubbles into my soul,
I would be a good fountain, a good well-head,
Would blur no whisper, spoil no expression.

What is the knocking?
What is the knocking at the door in the night?
It is somebody wants to do us harm.

No, no, it is the three strange angels.
Admit them, admit them.

BAVARIAN GENTIANS

Not every man has gentians in his house
in Soft September, at slow, Sad Michaelmas.

Bavarian gentians, big and dark, only dark
darkening the day-time torch-like with the smoking blueness
    of Pluto's gloom,

ribbed and torch-like, with their blaze of darkness spread blue
down flattening into points, flattened under the sweep of
    white day
torch-flower of the blue-smoking darkness, Pluto's dark-blue
    daze,
black lamps from the halls of Dio, burning dark blue,
giving off darkness, blue darkness, as Demeter's pale lamps
    give off light,
lead me then, lead me the way.

Reach me a gentian, give me a torch!
let me guide myself with the blue, forked torch of this flower
down the darker and darker stairs, where blue is darkened on
    blueness.
even where Persephone goes, just now, from the frosted
    September
to the sightless realm where darkness is awake upon the dark
and Persephone herself is but a voice
or a darkness invisible enfolded in the deeper dark
of the arms Plutonic, and pierced with the passion of dense
    gloom,
among the splendour of torches of darkness, shedding
    darkness on the lost bride and her groom.

HUMMING-BIRD

I can imagine, in some otherworld
Primeval-dumb, far back
In that most awful stillness, that only gasped and hummed,
Humming-birds raced down the avenues.

Before anything had a soul,
While life was a heave of Matter, half inanimate,
This little bit chipped off in brilliance
And went whizzing through the slow, vast, succulent stems.

I believe there were no flowers then,
In the world where the humming-bird flashed ahead of
    creation.
I believe he pierced the slow vegetable veins with his long
    beak.

Probably he was big
As mosses, and little lizards, they say, were once big.
Probably he was a jabbing, terrifying monster.

We look at him through the wrong end of the long telescope
    of Time,
Luckily for us.

HOW BEASTLY THE BOURGEOIS IS

How beastly the bourgeois is
especially the male of the species—

Presentable, eminently presentable—
shall I make you a present of him?

Isn't he handsome? isn't he healthy? Isn't he a fine specimen?
doesn't he look the fresh clean englishman, outside?
Isn't it god's own image? tramping his thirty miles a day
after partridges, or a little rubber ball?
wouldn't you like to be like that, well off, and quite the thing?

Oh, but wait!
Let him meet a new emotion, let him be faced with another
    man's need,
let him come home to a bit of moral difficulty, let life face
      him with a new demand on his understanding
and then watch him go soggy, like a wet meringue.
Watch him turn into a mess, either a fool or a bully.
Just watch the display of him, confronted with a new
      demand on his intelligence,
a new life-demand.

How beastly the bourgeois is
especially the male of the species—

Nicely groomed, like a mushroom
standing there so sleek and erect and eyeable—
and like a fungus, living on the remains of bygone life
sucking his life out of the dead leaves of greater life
    than his own.

And even so, he's stale, he's been there too long.
Touch him, and you'll find he's all gone inside
just like an old mushroom, all wormy inside, and hollow
under a smooth skin and an upright appearance.

Full of seething, wormy, hollow feelings
rather nasty—

How beastly the bourgeois is!

Standing in their thousands, these appearances, in damp
    England
what a pity they can't all be kicked over
like sickening toadstools, and left to melt back, swiftly
into the soil of England.

DON'TS

Fight your little fight, my boy,
fight and be a man.
Don't be a good little, good little boy
being as good as you can

and agreeing with all the mealy-mouthed, mealy-mouthed
truths that the sly trot out
to protect themselves and their greedy-mouthed, greedy-
    mouthed
cowardice, every old lout.

Don't live up to the dear little girl who costs
you your manhood, and makes you pay.
Nor the dear old mater who so proudly boasts
that you'll make your way.

Don't earn golden opinions, opinions golden,
or at least worth Treasury notes,
from all sorts of men; don't be beholden
to the herd inside the pen.

Don't long to have dear little, dear little boys
whom you'll have to educate
to earn their living; nor yet girls, sweetjoys
who will find it so hard to mate.

Nor a dear little home, with its cost, its cost
that you have to pay,
earning your living while your life is lost
and dull death comes in a day.

Don't be sucked in by the su-superior,
don't swallow the culture bait,
don't drink, don't drink and get beerier and beerier,
do learn to discriminate.

Do hold yourself together, and fight
with a hit-hit here and a hit-hit there,
and a comfortable feeling at night
that you've let in a little air.

A little fresh air in the money sty,
knocked a little hole in the holy prison,
done your own little bit, made your own little try
that the risen Christ should be risen.

WON'T IT BE STRANGE—?

Won't it be strange, when the nurse brings the newborn
    infant
to the proud father, and shows its little, webbed greenish
    feet
made to smite the waters behind it?
or the round, wild vivid eye of a wild-goose staring
out of fathomless skies and seas?
or when it utters that undaunted little bird-cry
of one who will settle on ice-bergs, and honk across the
    Nile?—

And when the father says: This is none of mine!
Woman, where got you this little beast?—
will there be a whistle of wings in the air, and an icy draught?
will the singing of swans, high up, high up, invisible
break the drums of his ears
and leave him forever listening for the answer?

WHEN I WENT TO THE CIRCUS—

When I went to the circus that had pitched on the waste lot
it was full of uneasy people
frightened of the bare earth and the temporary canvas
and the smell of horses and other beasts
instead of merely the smell of man.

Monkeys rode rather grey and wizened
on curly plump piebald ponies
and the children uttered a little cry—
and dogs jumped through hoops and turned somersaults
and then the geese scuttled in in a little flock
and round the ring they went to the sound of the whip

then doubled, and back, with a funny up-flutter of wings—
and the children suddenly shouted out.
Then came the hush again, like a hush of fear.

The tight-rope lady, pink and blonde and nude-looking,
    with a few gold spangles
footed cautiously out on the rope, turned prettily, spun
                round
bowed, and lifted her foot in her hand, smiled, swung her
                parasol
to another balance, tripped round, poised, and slowly sank
her handsome thighs down, down, till she slept her splendid
                body on the rope.
When she rose, tilting her parasol, and smiled at the cautious
                people
they cheered, but nervously.
The trapeze man, slim and beautiful and like a fish in the air
swung great curves through the upper space, and came down
like a star
—And the people applauded, with hollow, frightened
                applause.

The elephants, huge and grey, loomed their curved bulk
    through the dusk
and sat up, taking strange postures, showing the pink soles
    of their feet
and curling their precious live trunks like ammonites
and moving always with soft slow precision
as when a great ship moves to anchor.
The people watched and wondered, and seemed to resent
    the mystery that lies in beasts.

Horse, gay horses, swirling round and plaiting
in a long line, their heads laid over each other's necks;
they were happy, they enjoyed it;
all the creatures seemed to enjoy the game
in the circus, with their circus people.

But the audience, compelled to wonder
compelled to admire the bright rhythms of moving bodies
compelled to see the delicate skill of flickering human bodies
flesh flamey and a little heroic, even in a tumbling clown,
they were not really happy.
There was no gushing response, as there is at the film.

When modern people see the carnal body dauntless and
    flickering gay

playing among the elements neatly, beyond competition
and displaying no personality,
modern people are depressed.

Modern people feel themselves at a disadvantage.
They know they have no bodies that could play among the
    elements.
They have only their personalities, that are best seen flat,
    on the film,
flat personalities in two dimensions, imponderable and
    touchless.

And they grudge the circus people the swooping gay weight
    of limbs
that flower in mere movement,
and they grudge them the immediate, physical understanding
    they have with their circus beasts,
and they grudge them their circus-life altogether.

Yet the strange, almost frightened shout of delight that comes
    now and then from the children
shows that the children vaguely know how cheated they are
    of their birthright
in the bright wild circus flesh.

THE MOSQUITO KNOWS

The mosquito knows full well, small as he is
he's a beast of prey.
But after all
he only takes his bellyful,
he doesn't put my blood in the bank.

THE ELEPHANT IS SLOW TO MATE

The elephant, the huge old beast,
    is slow to mate;
he finds a female, they show no haste,
    they wait

for the sympathy in their vast shy hearts
    slowly, slowly to rouse
as they loiter along the river-beds
    and drink and browse

and dash in panic through the brake
    of forest with the herd,
and sleep in massive silence, and wake
    together, without a word.

So slowly the great hot elephant hearts
    grow full of desire,
and the great beasts mate in secret at last,
    hiding their fire.

Oldest they are and the wisest of beasts
    so they know at last
how to wait for the loneliest of feasts,
    for the full repast.

They do not snatch, they do not tear;
    their massive blood
moves as the moon-tides, near, more near
    till they touch in flood.

BABY TORTOISE

You know what it is to be born alone,
Baby tortoise!

The first day to heave your feet little by little from the shell,
Not yet awake,
And remain lapsed on earth,
Not quite alive.

A tiny, fragile, half-animate bean.

To open your tiny beak-mouth, that looks as if it would
        never open,
Like some iron door;
To lift the upper hawk-beak from the lower base
And reach your skinny little neck
And take your first bite at some dim bit of herbage,
Alone, small insect,
Tiny bright-eye,
Slow one.

To take your first solitary bite
And move on your slow, solitary hunt.
Your bright, dark little eye,

Your eye of a dark disturbed night,
Under its slow lid, tiny baby tortoise,
So indomitable.

No one ever heard you complain.

You draw your head forward, slowly, from your little wimple
And set forward, slow-dragging, on your four-pinned toes,
Rowing slowly forward.
Whither away, small bird?

Rather like a baby working its limbs,
Except that you make slow, ageless progress
And a baby makes none.

The touch of sun excites you,
And the long ages, and the lingering chill
Make you pause to yawn,
Opening your impervious mouth,
Suddenly beak-shaped, and very wide, like some suddenly
        gaping pincers;
Soft red tongue, and hard thin gums,
Then close the wedge of your little mountain front,
Your face, baby tortoise.

Do you wonder at the world, as slowly you turn your head
        in its wimple
And look with laconic, black eyes?
Or is sleep coming over you again,
The non-life?

You are so hard to wake.

Are you able to wonder?
Or is it just your indomitable will and pride of the first life
Looking round
And slowly pitching itself against the inertia
Which had seemed invincible?

The vast inanimate,
And the fine brilliance of your so tiny eye,
Challenger.

Nay, tiny shell-bird,
What a huge vast inanimate it is, that you must row against,
What an incalculable inertia.

Challenger,
Little Ulysses, fore-runner,
No bigger than my thumb-nail
Buon viaggio.

All animate creation on your shoulder,
Set forth, little Titan, under your battle-shield.
The ponderous, preponderate,
Inanimate universe;
And you are slowly moving, pioneer, you alone.

How vivid your travelling seems now, in the troubled
   sunshine,
Stoic, Ulyssean atom;
Suddenly hasty, reckless, on high toes.

Voiceless little bird,
Resting your head half out of your wimple
In the slow dignity of your eternal pause.
Alone, with no sense of being alone,
And hence six times more solitary;
Fulfilled of the slow passion of pitching through immemorial
   ages
Your little round house in the midst of chaos.

Over the garden earth,
Small bird,
Over the edge of all things.

Traveller,
With your tail tucked a little on one side
Like a gentleman in a long-skirted coat.

All life carried on your shoulder,
Invincible fore-runner.

TORTOISE-SHELL

The Cross, the Cross
Goes deeper in than we know,
Deeper into life;
Right into the marrow
And through the bone.

Along the back of the baby tortoise
The scales are locked in an arch like a bridge,

Scale-lapping, like a lobster's sections
Or a bee's.

Then crossways down his sides
Tiger-stripes and wasp-bands.

Five, and five again, and five again,
And round the edges twenty-five little ones,
The sections of the baby tortoise shell.
Four, and a keystone;
Four, and a keystone;
Four, and a keystone;
Then twenty-four, and a tiny little keystone.

It needed Pythagoras to see life placing her counters on the
    living back
Of the baby tortoise;
Life establishing the first eternal mathematical tablet,
Not in stone, like the Judean Lord, or bronze, but in life-
    clouded, life-rosy tortoise-shell.

The first little mathematical gentleman
Stepping, wee mite, in his loose trousers
Under all the eternal dome of mathematical law.

Fives, and tens,
Threes and fours and twelves,
All the volte face of decimals,
The whirligig of dozens and the pinnacle of seven.

Turn him on his back,
The kicking little beetle,
And there again, on his shell-tender, earth-touching belly,
The long cleavage of division, upright of the eternal cross
And on either side count five,
On each side, two above, on each side, two below
The dark bar horizontal.

The Cross!
It goes right through him, the sprottling insect,
Through his cross-wise cloven psyche,
Through his five-fold complex-nature.

So turn him over on his toes again;
Four pin-point toes, and a problematical thumb-piece,
Four rowing limbs, and one wedge-balancing head,
Four and one makes five, which is the clue to all mathematics.

The Lord wrote it all down on the little slate
Of the baby tortoise.
Outward and visible indication of the plan within,
The complex, manifold involvedness of an individual creature
Blotted out
On this small bird, this rudiment,
This little dome, this pediment
Of all creation,
This slow one.

SNAKE

A snake came to my water-trough
On a hot, hot day, and I in pyjamas for the heat,
To drink there.

In the deep, strange-scented shade of the great dark carob
    tree
I came down the steps with my pitcher
And must wait, must stand and wait, for there he was at
    the trough before me.

He reached down from a fissure in the earth-wall in the
    gloom
And trailed his yellow-brown slackness soft-bellied down,
    over the edge of the stone trough
And rested his throat upon the stone bottom,
And where the water had dripped from the tap, in a small
    clearness,
He sipped with his straight mouth,
Softly drank through his straight gums, into his slack long
    body,
Silently.

Someone was before me at my water-trough,
And I, like a second-comer, waiting.

He lifted his head from his drinking, as cattle do,
And looked at me vaguely, as drinking cattle do,
And flickered his two-forked tongue from his lips, and mused
    a moment,

And stooped and drank a little more,
Being earth-brown, earth-golden from the burning bowels of
    the earth
On the day of Sicilian July, with Etna smoking.

The voice of my education said to me
He must be killed,
For in Sicily the black, black snakes are innocent, the gold
    are venomous.

And voices in me said, If you were a man,
You would take a stick and break him now, and finish him
    off.

But must I confess how I liked him,
How glad I was he had come like a guest in quiet, to drink
    at my water-trough
And depart peaceful, pacified, and thankless,
Into the burning bowels of this earth?

Was it cowardice, that I dared not kill him?
Was it perversity, that I longed to talk to him?
Was it humility, to feel so honoured?
I felt so honoured.

And yet those voices:
If you were not afraid, you would kill him!

And truly I was afraid, I was most afraid,
But even so, honoured still more
That he should seek my hospitality
From out the dark door of the secret earth.

He drank enough
And lifted his head, dreamily, as one who has drunken,
And flickered his tongue like a forked night on the air, so
    black,
Seeming to lick his lips,
And looked around like a god, unseeing, into the air,
And slowly turned his head,
And slowly, very slowly, as if thrice adream
Proceeded to draw his
Slow length curving round
And climb again the broken bank of my wall-face.

And as he put his head into that dreadful hole,
And as he slowly drew up, snake-easing his shoulders, and
    entered farther,
A sort of horror, a sort of protest against his withdrawing
    into that horrid black hole,
Deliberately going into the blackness, and slowly drawing
    himself after,
Overcame me now his back was turned.

I looked around, I put down my pitcher,
I picked up a clumsy log
And threw it at the water-trough with a clatter.

I think it did not hit him,
But suddenly that part of him that was left behind con-
      vulsed in undignified haste,
Writhed like lightning, and was gone
Into the black hole, the earth-lipped fissure in the wall-front
At which, in the intense still noon, I stared with fascination.

And immediately I regretted it.
I thought how paltry, how vulgar, what a mean act!
I despised myself and the voices of my accursed human
      education.
And I thought of the albatross,
And I wished he would come back, my snake.

For he seemed to me again like a king,
Like a king in exile, uncrowned in the underworld,
Now due to be crowned again.

And so, I missed my chance with one of the lords
Of life.
And I have something to expiate:
A pettiness.

KANGAROO

In the northern hemisphere
Life seems to leap at the air, or skim under the wind
Like stags on rocky ground, or pawing horses, or springy
      scut-tailed rabbits.

Or else rush horizontal to charge at the sky's horizon,
Like bulls or bisons or wild pigs.

Or slip like water slippery towards its ends,
As foxes, stoats, and wolves, and prairie dogs.

Only mice, and moles, and rats, and badgers, and beavers,
      and perhaps bears
Seem belly-plumbed to the earth's mid-navel.
Or frogs that when they leap come flop, and flop to the
      centre of the earth.

But the yellow antipodal Kangaroo, when she sits up,
Who can unseat her, like a liquid drop that is heavy, and
    just touches earth.

The downward drip.
The down-urge.
So much denser than cold-blooded frogs.

Delicate mother Kangaroo
Sitting up there rabbit-wise, but huge, plumb-weighted,
And lifting her beautiful slender face, oh! so much more
    gently and finely lined than a rabbit's, or than a hare's,
Lifting her face to nibble at a round white peppermint drop,
    which she loves, sensitive mother Kangaroo.

Her sensitive, long, pure-bred face.
Her full antipodal eyes, so dark,
So big and quiet and remote, having watched so many empty
    dawns in silent Australia.

Her little loose hands, and drooping Victorian shoulders.
And then her great weight below the waist, her vast pale belly
With a thin young yellow little paw hanging out, and strag-
    gle of a long thin ear, like ribbon,
Like a funny trimming to the middle of her belly, thin
    little dangle of an immature paw, and one thin ear.

Her belly, her big haunches
And, in addition, the great muscular python-stretch of her
    tail.

There, she shan't have any more peppermint-drops.
So she wistfully, sensitively sniffs the air, and then turns,
    goes off in slow sad leaps
On the long flat skis of her legs,
Steered and propelled by that steel-strong snake of a tail.

Stops again, half turns, inquisitive to look back.
While something stirs quickly in her belly, and a lean little
    face comes out, as from a window,
Peaked and a bit dismayed,
Only to disappear again quickly away from the sight of the
    world, to snuggle down in the warmth,
Leaving the trail of a different paw hanging out.

Still she watches with eternal, cocked wistfulness!

How full her eyes are, like the full, fathomless, shining eyes
  of an Australian black-boy
Who has been lost so many centuries on the margins of
  existence!

She watches with insatiable wistfulness.
Untold centuries of watching for something to come.
For a new signal from life, in that silent lost land of the
  South.
Where nothing bites but insects and snakes and the sun,
  small life.
Where no bull roared, no cow ever lowed, no stag cried,
  no leopard screeched, no lion coughed, no dog barked,
But all was silent save for parrots occasionally, in the
  haunted blue bush.

Wistfully watching, with wonderful liquid eyes.
And all her weight, all her blood, dripping sack-wise down
  towards the earth's center,
And the live little-one taking in its paw at the door of her
  belly.

Leap then, and come down on the line that draws to the
  earth's deep, heavy centre.

RETORT TO WHITMAN

And whoever walks a mile full of false sympathy
walks to the funeral of the whole human race.

WHALES WEEP NOT!

They say the sea is cold, but the sea contains
the hottest blood of all, and the wildest, the most urgent.

All the whales in the wider deeps, hot are they, as they urge
on and on, and dive beneath the icebergs.
The right whales, the sperm-whales, the hammer-heads, the
  killers
there they blow, there they blow, hot wild white breath out of
  the sea!

And they rock, and they rock, through the sensual ageless
  ages

on the depths of the seven seas,
and through the salt they reel with drunk delight
and in the tropics tremble they with love
and roll with massive, strong desire, like gods.
Then the great bull lies up against his bride
in the blue deep of the sea
as mountain pressing on mountain, in the zest of life:
and out of the inward roaring of the inner red ocean of
    whale blood
the long tip reaches strong, intense, like the maelstrom-
    tip and comes to rest
in the clasp and the soft, wild clutch of a she-whale's fathom-
    less body.

And over the bridge of the whale's strong phallus, linking
    the wonder of whales
the burning archangels under the sea keep passing, back and
    forth,
keep passing archangels of bliss
from him to her, from her to him, great Cherubim
that wait on whales in mid-ocean, suspended in the waves of
    the sea
great heaven of whales in the waters, old hierarchies.
And enormous mother whales lie dreaming suckling their
    whale-tender young
and dreaming with strange whale eyes wide open in the
    waters of the beginning and the end.

And bull-whales gather their women and whale-calves in a
    ring
when danger threatens, on the surface of the ceaseless flood
and range themselves like great fierce Seraphim facing the
    threat
encircling their huddled monsters of love.
And all this happiness in the sea, in the salt
where God is also love, but without words:
and Aphrodite is the wife of whales
most happy, happy she!

and Venus among the fishes skips and is a she-dolphin
she is the gay, delighted porpoise sporting with love and
    the sea
she is the female tunny-fish, round and happy among the
    males
and dense with happy blood, dark rainbow bliss in the sea.

THE SHIP OF DEATH

I

Now it is autumn and the falling fruit
and the long journey towards oblivion.

The apples falling like great drops of dew
to bruise themselves an exit from themselves.

And it is time to go, to bid farewell
to one's own self, and find an exit
from the fallen self.

II

Have you built your ship of death, O have you?
O build your ship of death, for you will need it.

The grim frost is at hand, when the apples will fall
thick, almost thundrous, on the hardened earth.

And death is on the air like a smell of ashes!
Ah! can't you smell it?
And in the bruised body, the frightened soul
finds itself shrinking, wincing from the cold
that blows upon it through the orifices.

III

And can a man his own quietus make
with a bare bodkin?

With daggers, bodkins, bullets, man can make
a bruise or break of exit for his life;
but is that a quietus, O tell me, is it quietus?

Surely not so! for how could murder, even self-murder,
ever a quietus make?

IV

O let us talk of quiet that we know,
that we can know, the deep and lovely quiet
of a strong heart at peace!

How can we this, our own quietus, make?

V

Build then the ship of death, for you must take
the longest journey, to oblivion.

And die the death, the long and painful death
that lies between the old self and the new.

Already our bodies are fallen, bruised, badly bruised,
already our souls are oozing through the exit
of the cruel bruise.

Already the dark and endless ocean of the end
is washing in through the breaches of our wounds,
already the flood is upon us.

O build your ship of death, your little ark
and furnish it with food, with little cakes, and wine
for the dark flight down oblivion.

VI

Piecemeal the body dies, and the timid soul
has her footing washed away, as the dark flood rises.

We are dying, we are dying, we are all of us dying
and nothing will stay the death-flood rising within us
and soon it will rise on the world, on the outside world.

We are dying, we are dying, piecemeal our bodies are dying
and our strength leaves us,
and our soul cowers naked in the dark rain over the flood,
cowering in the last branches of the tree of our life.

VII

We are dying, we are dying, so all we can do
is now to be willing to die, and to build the ship
of death to carry the soul on the longest journey.

A little ship, with oars and food
and little dishes, and all accoutrements
fitting and ready for the departing soul.

Now launch the small ship, now as the body dies
and life departs, launch out, the fragile soul
in the fragile ship of courage, the ark of faith
with its store of food and little cooking pans
and change of clothes,
upon the flood's black waste
upon the waters of the end
upon the sea of death, where still we sail
darkly, for we cannot steer, and have no port.

There is no port, there is nowhere to go
only the deepening blackness darkening still
blacker upon the soundless, ungurgling flood
darkness at one with darkness, up and down
and sideways utterly dark, so there is no direction any more
and the little ship is there; yet she is gone.
She is not seen, for there is nothing to see her by.
She is gone! gone! and yet
somewhere she is there.
Nowhere.

VIII

And everything is gone, the body is gone
completely under, gone, entirely gone.
The upper darkness is heavy as the lower,
between them the little ship
is gone

It is the end, it is oblivion

IX

And yet out of eternity a thread
separates itself on the blackness,
a horizontal thread
that fumes a little with pallor upon the dark.

Is it illusion? or does the pallor fume
a little higher?
Ah wait, wait, for there's the dawn,
the cruel dawn of coming back to life
out of oblivion

Wait, wait, the little ship

drifting, beneath the deathly ashly grey
of a flood-dawn.

Wait, wait! even so, a flush of yellow
and strangely, O chilled wan soul, a flush of rose.

A flush of rose, and the whole thing starts again.

                              x

The flood subsides, and the body, like a worn sea-shell
emerges strange and lovely.
And the little ship wings home, faltering and lapsing
on the pink flood,
and the frail soul steps out, into the house again
filling the heart with peace.

Swings the heart renewed with peace
even of oblivion.

Oh build your ship of death. Oh build it!
for you will need it.
For the voyage of oblivion awaits you.

                 THE END, THE BEGINNING

If there were not an utter and absolute dark
of silence and sheer oblivion
at the core of everything,
how terrible the sun would be,
how ghastly it would be to strike a match, and make a light.

But the very sun himself is pivoted
upon the core of pure oblivion,
so is a candle, even as a match.

And if there were not an absolute, utter forgetting
and a ceasing to know, a perfect ceasing to know
and a silent, sheer cessation of all awareness
how terrible life would be!
how terrible it would be to think and know, to have con-
     sciousness!

But dipped, once dipped in dark oblivion
the soul has peace, inward and lovely peace.

EDWIN MUIR

(1887-1958)

IN LOVE FOR LONG

I've been in love for long
With what I cannot tell
And will contrive a song
For the intangible
That has no mould or shape,
From which there's no escape.

It is not even a name,
Yet is all constancy;
Tried or untried, the same,
It cannot part from me;
A breath, yet as still
As the established hill.

It is not any thing,
And yet all being is;
Being, being, being,
Its burden and its bliss.
How can I ever prove
What it is I love?

This happy happy love
Is sieged with crying sorrows,
Crushed beneath and above
Between to-days and morrows
A little paradise
Held in the world's vice.

And there it is content
And careless as a child,
And in imprisonment
Flourishes sweet and wild;
In wrong, beyond wrong,
All the world's day long.

This love a moment known
For what I do not know
And in a moment gone
Is like the happy doe
That keeps its perfect laws
Between the tiger's paws
And vindicates its cause.

FROM VARIATIONS ON A TIME THEME

At the dead centre of the boundless plain
Does our way end? Our horses pace and pace.
Like steeds for ever labouring on a shield,
Keeping their solitary heraldic courses.

Our horses move on such a ground, for them
Perhaps the progress is all ease and pleasure,
But it is heavy work for us, the riders,

460

Whose hearts have flown so far ahead they are lost
    Long past all finding
While we sit staring at the same horizon.

Time has such curious stretches, we are told,
And generation after generation
May travel them, sad stationary journey,
Of what device, what meaning?
                    Yet these coursers
Have seen all and will see all. Suppliantly
The rocks will melt, the sealed horizons fall
Before their onset—and the places
Our hearts have hid in will be viewed by strangers
Sitting where we are, breathing the foreign air
Of the new realm they have inherited.
But we shall fall here on the plain.

                   It may be
These steeds would stumble and the long road end
(So legend says) if they should lack their riders.
              But then a rider
Is always easy to find. Yet we fill a saddle
At least. We sit where others have sat before us
And others will sit after us.

                 It cannot be
These animals know their riders, mark the change
When one makes way for another. It cannot be
They know this wintry wilderness from spring.
For they have come from regions dreadful past
All knowledge. They have borne upon their saddles
Forms fiercer than the tiger, borne them calmly
As they bear us now.

            And so we do not hope
That their great coal-black glossy hides
Should keep a glimmer of the autumn light
We still remember, when our limbs were weightless
As red leaves on a tree, and our silvery breaths
Went on before us like new-risen souls
Leading our empty bodies through the air.
A princely dream. Now all that golden country
Is razed as bare as Troy. We cannot return,
And shall not see the kingdom of our heirs.

These beasts are mortal, and we who fall so lightly,

Fall so heavily, are, it is said, immortal.
Such knowledge should armour us against all change,
And this monotony. Yet these worn saddles
Have powers to charm us to obliviousness.
They were appointed for us, and the scent of the ancient
    leather
Is strong as a spell. So we must mourn or rejoice
For this our station, our inheritance
As if it were all. This plain all. This journey all.

THE ROAD

There is a road that turning always
        Cuts off the country of Again.
Archers stand there on every side
        And as it runs Time's deer is slain,
        And lies where it has lain.

That busy clock shows never an hour.
        All flies and all in flight must tarry.
The hunter shoots the empty air
        Far on before the quarry,
        Which falls though nothing's there to parry.

The lion couching in the centre
        With mountain head and sunset brow
Rolls down the everlasting slope
        Bones picked an age ago,
        And the bones rise up and go.

There the beginning finds the end
        Before beginning ever can be,
And the great runner never leaves
        The starting and the finishing tree,
        The budding and the fading tree.

There the ship sailing safe in harbour
        Long since in many a sea was drowned.
The treasure burning in her hold
        So near will never be found,
        Sunk past all sound.

There a man on a summer evening
        Reclines at ease upon his tomb
And in his mortal effigy.

And there within the womb,
The cell of doom,

The ancestral deed is thought and done,
    And in a million Edens fall
A million Adams drowned in darkness,
        For small is great and great is small,
        And a blind seed all.

THE ENCHANTED KNIGHT

Lulled by La Belle Dame Sans Merci he lies
    In the bare wood below the blackening hill.
The plough drives nearer now, the shadow flies
    Past him across the plain, but he lies still.

Long since the rust its gardens here has planned,
    Flowering his armour like an autumn field.
From his sharp breast-plate to his iron hand
    A spider's web is stretched, a phantom shield.

When footsteps pound the turf beside his ear
    Armies pass through his dream in endless line,
And one by one his ancient friends appear;
    They pass all day, but he can make no sign.

When a bird cries within the silent grove
    The long-lost voice goes by, he makes to rise
And follow, but his cold limbs never move,
    And on the turf unstirred his shadow lies.

But if a withered leaf should drift
    Across his face and rest, the dread drops start
Chill on his forehead. Now he tries to lift
    The insulting weight that stays and breaks his heart.

THE WAYSIDE STATION

Here at the wayside station, as many a morning,
I watch the smoke torn from the fumy engine
Crawling across the field in serpent sorrow.
Flat in the east, held down by stolid clouds,
The struggling day is born and shines already
On its warm hearth far off. Yet something here

Glimmers along the ground to show the seagulls
White on the furrows' black unturning waves.

But now the light has broadened.
I watch the farmstead on the little hill,
That seems to mutter: 'Here is day again'
Unwillingly. Now the sad cattle wake
In every byre and stall,
The ploughboy stirs in the loft, the farmer groans
And feels the day like a familiar ache
Deep in his body, though the house is dark.
The lovers part
Now in the bedroom where the pillows gleam
Great and mysterious as deep hills of snow,
An inaccessible land. The wood stands waiting
While the bright snare slips coil by coil around it,
Dark silver on every branch. The lonely stream
That rode through darkness leaps the gap of light,
Its voice grown loud, and starts its winding journey
Through the day and time and war and history.

THE RIVER

The silent stream flows on and in its glass
Shows the trained terrors, the well-practised partings,
The old woman standing at the cottage gate,
Her hand upon her grandson's shoulder. He,
A bundle of clouts creased as with tribulations,
Bristling with spikes and spits and bolts of steel,
Bound in with belts, the rifle's snub-nosed horn
Peering above his shoulder, looks across
From this new world to hers and tries to find
Some ordinary words that share her sorrow.
The stream flows on
And shows a blackened field, a burning wood,
A bridge that stops half-way, a hill split open
With scraps of houses clinging to its sides,
Stones, planks and tiles and chips of glass and china
Strewn on the slope as by a wrecking wave
Among the grass and wild-flowers. Darkness falls,
The stream flows through the city. In its mirror
Great oes and capitals and flourishes,
Pillars and towers and fans and gathered sheaves
Hold harvest-home and Judgment Day of fire.
The houses stir and pluck their roofs and walls

Apart as if in play and fling their stones
Against the sky to make a common arc
And fall again. The conflagrations raise
Their mountainous precipices. Living eyes
Glaze instantly in crystal change. The stream
Runs on into the day of time and Europe,
Past the familiar walls and friendly roads,
Now thronged with dumb migrations, gods and altars
That travel towards no destination. Then
The disciplined soldiers come to conquer nothing,
March upon emptiness and do not know
Why all is dead and life has hidden itself.
The enormous winding frontier walls fall down,
Leaving anonymous stone and vacant grass.
The stream flows on into what land, what peace,
Far past the other side of the burning world?

THE RECURRENCE

All things return, Nietzsche said,
The ancient wheel revolves again,
Rise, take up your numbered fate;
The cradle and the bridal bed,
Life and the coffin wait.
All has been that ever can be,
And this sole eternity
Cannot cancel, cannot add
One to your delights or tears,
Or a million million years
Tear the nightmare from the mad.

Have no fear then. You will miss
Achievement by the self-same inch,
When the great occasion comes
And they watch you, you will flinch,
Lose the moment, be for bliss
A footlength short. All done before.
Love's agonies, victory's drums
Cannot huddle the Cross away
Planted on its future hill.
The secret on the appointed day
Will be made known, the ship once more
Hit upon the waiting rock
Or come safely to the shore,
Careless under the deadly tree
The victim drowse, the urgent warning

Come too late, the dagger strike,
Strike and strike through eternity,
And worlds hence the prison clock
Will toll on execution morning,
What is ill be always ill,
Wretches die behind a dike,
And the happy be happy still.

But the heart makes reply:
This is only what the eye
From its tower on the turning field
Sees and sees and cannot tell why,
Quarterings on the turning shield,
The great non-stop heraldic show.
And the heart and the mind know,
What has been can never return,
What is not will surely be
In the changed unchanging reign,
Else the Actor on the Tree
Would loll at ease, miming pain,
And counterfeit mortality.

THE PRIZE

Did we come here, drawn by some fatal thing,
Fly from eternity's immaculate bow
Straight to the heart of time's great turning ring,
That we might win the prize that took us so?
Was it some ordinary sight, a flower,
The white wave falling, falling upon the shore,
The blue of the sky, the grasses' waving green?

Or was it one sole thing, a certain door
Set in a wall, a half-conjectured scene
Of men and women moving as in a play,
A turn in the winding road, a distant tower,
A corner of a field, a single place
Apart, a single house, a single tree,
A look upon one half-averted face
That has been once, or is, or is to be?

We hurried here for some such thing and now
Wander the countless roads to seek our prize,
That far within the maze serenely lies,
While all around each trivial shape exclaims:
'Here is your jewel; this is your longed for day,'
And we forget, lost in the countless names.

THE DEBTOR

I am debtor to all, to all am I bounden,
Fellowman and beast, season and solstice, darkness and light,
And life and death. On the backs of the dead,
See, I am borne, on lost errands led,
By spent harvests nourished. Forgotten prayers
To gods forgotten bring blessings upon me.
Rusted arrow and broken bow, look, they preserve me
Here in this place. The never-won stronghold
That sank in the ground as the years into time,
Slowly with all its men stedfast and watching,
Keeps me safe now. The ancient waters
Cleanse me, revive me. Victor and vanquished
Give me their passion, their peace and the field.
The meadows of Lethe shed twilight around me.
The dead in their silences keep me in memory,
Have me in hold. To all I am bounden.

THE BRIDGE OF DREAD

But when you reach the Bridge of Dread
Your flesh will huddle into its nest
For refuge and your naked head
Creep in the casement of your breast,

And your great bulk grow thin and small
And cower within its cage of bone,
While dazed you watch your footsteps crawl
Toadlike across the leagues of stone.

If they come, you will not feel
About your feet the adders slide,
For still your head's demented wheel
Whirls on your neck from side to side

Searching for danger. Nothing there.
And yet your breath will whistle and beat
As on you push the stagnant air
That breaks in rings about your feet

Like dirty suds. If there should come
Some bodily terror to that place,
Great knotted serpents dread and dumb,
You would accept it as a grace.

Until you see a burning wire
Shoot from the ground. As in a dream
You'll wonder at that flower of fire,
That weed caught in a burning beam.

And you are past. Remember then,
Fix deep within your dreaming head
Year, hour or endless moment when
You reached and crossed the Bridge of Dread.

THE CHILD DYING

Unfriendly friendly universe,
I pack your stars into my purse,
And bid you, bid you so farewell.
That I can leave you, quite go out,
Go out, go out beyond all doubt,
My father says, is the miracle.

You are so great, and I so small:
I am nothing, you are all:
Being nothing, I can take this way.
Oh I need neither rise nor fall,
For when I do not move at all
I shall be out of all your day.

It's said some memory will remain
In the other place, grass in the rain,
Light on the land, sun on the sea,
A flitting grace, a phantom face,
But the world is out. There is no place
Where it and its ghost can ever be.

Father, father, I dread this air
Blown from the far side of despair,
The cold cold corner. What house, what hold,
What hand is there? I look and see
Nothing-filled eternity,
And the great round world grows weak and old.

Hold my hand, oh hold it fast—
I am changing!—until at last
My hand in yours no more will change,
Though yours change on. You here, I there,
So hand in hand, twin-leafed despair—
I did not know death was so strange.

THE LABYRINTH

Since I emerged that day from the labyrinth,
Dazed with the tall and echoing passages,
The swift recoils, so many I almost feared
I'd meet myself returning at some smooth corner,
Myself or my ghost, for all there was unreal
After the straw ceased rustling and the bull
Lay dead upon the straw and I remained,
Blood-splashed, if dead or alive I could not tell
In the twilight nothingness (I might have been
A spirit seeking his body through the roads
Of intricate Hades)—ever since I came out
To the world, the still fields swift with flowers, the trees
All bright with blossom, the little green hills, the sea,
The sky and all in movement under it,
Shepherds and flocks and birds and the young and old,
(I stared in wonder at the young and the old,
For in the maze time had not been with me;
I had strayed, it seemed, past sun and season and change,
Past rest and motion, for I could not tell
At last if I moved or stayed; the maze itself
Revolved around me on its hidden axis
And swept me smoothly to its enemy,
The lovely world)—since I came out that day,
There have been times when I have heard my footsteps
Still echoing in the maze, and all the roads
That run through the noisy world, deceiving streets
That meet and part and meet, and rooms that open
Into each other—and never a final room—
Stairways and corridors and antechambers
That vacantly wait for some great audience,
The smooth sea-tracks that open and close again,
Tracks undiscoverable, indecipherable,
Paths on the earth and tunnels underground,
And bird-tracks in the air—all seemed a part
Of the great labyrinth. And then I'd stumble
In sudden blindness, hasten, almost run,
As if the maze itself were after me
And soon must catch me up. But taking thought,
I'd tell myself, 'You need not hurry. This
Is the firm good earth. All roads lie free before you.'
But my bad spirit would sneer, 'No, do not hurry.
No need to hurry. Haste and delay are equal
In this one world, for there's no exit, none,
No place to come to, and you'll end where you are,

Deep in the centre of the endless maze.'

I could not live if this were not illusion.
It is a world, perhaps; but there's another.
For once in a dream or trance I saw the gods
Each sitting on the top of his mountain-isle,
While down below the little ships sailed by,
Toy multitudes swarmed in the harbours, shepherds drove
Their tiny flocks to the pastures, marriage feasts
Went on below, small birthdays and holidays,
Ploughing and harvesting and life and death,
And all permissible, all acceptable,
Clear and secure as in a limpid dream.
But they, the gods, as large and bright as clouds,
Conversed across the sounds in tranquil voices
High in the sky above the untroubled sea;
And their eternal dialogue was peace
Where all these things were woven; and this our life
Was as a chord deep in that dialogue,
As easy utterance of harmonious words,
Spontaneous syllables bodying forth a world.

That was the real world; I have touched it once,
And now shall know it always. But the lie,
The maze, the wild-wood waste of falsehood, roads
That run and run and never reach an end,
Embowered in error—I'd be prisoned there
But that my soul has birdwings to fly free.

Oh these deceits are strong almost as life.
Last night I dreamt I was in the labyrinth,
And woke far on. I did not know the place.

ONE FOOT IN EDEN

One foot in Eden still, I stand
And look across the other land.
The world's great day is growing late,
Yet strange these fields that we have planted
So long with crops of love and hate.
Time's handiworks by time are haunted,
And nothing now can separate
The corn and tares compactly grown.
The armorial weed in stillness bound
About the stalk; these are our own.

Evil and good stand thick around
In the fields of charity and sin
Where we shall lead our harvest in.

Yet still from Eden springs the root
As clean as on the starting day.
Time takes the foliage and the fruit
And burns the archetypal leaf
To shapes of terror and of grief
Scattered along the winter way.
But famished field and blackened tree
Bear flowers in Eden never known.
Blossoms of grief and charity
Bloom in these darkened fields alone.
What had Eden ever to say
Of hope and faith and pity and love
Until was buried all its day
And memory found its treasure trove?
Strange blessings never in Paradise
Fall from these beclouded skies.

THE ABSENT

They are not here. And we, we are the Others
Who walk by ourselves unquestioned in the sun
Which shines for us and only for us.
For They are not here.
And are made known to us in this great absence
That lies upon us and is between us
Since They are not here.
Now, in this kingdom of summer idleness
Where slowly we the sun-tranced multitudes dream and
    wander
In deep oblivion of brightness
And breathe ourselves out, out into the air—
It is absence that receives us;
We do not touch, our souls go out in the absence
That lies between us and is about us.
For we are the Others,
And so we sorrow for These that are not with us,
Not knowing we sorrow or that this is our sorrow,
Since it is long past thought or memory or device of mourn-
    ing,
Sorrow for loss of that which we never possessed,
The unknown, the nameless,

The ever-present that in their absence are with us
(With us the inheritors, the usurpers claiming
The sun and the kingdom of the sun) that sorrow
And loneliness might bring a blessing upon us.

THE VOYAGE

That sea was greater than we knew.
Week after week the empty round
Went with us; the Unchanging grew,
And we were headed for that bound.

How we came there we could not tell.
Seven storms had piled us in that peace,
Put us in check and barred us well
With seven walls of seven seas.

As one may vanish in a day
In some untravelled fold of space
And there pursue his patient way
Yet never come to any place

Though following still by star and sun,
For every chart is rased and furled,
And he out of this world has run
And wanders now another world,

So we by line and compass steered
And conned the book of sun and star,
Yet where it should no sign appeared
To tell us, You are there or there,

Familiar landfall, slender mast:
We on the ocean were alone.
The busy lanes where fleets had passed
Showed us no sail except our own.

Still south we steered day after day
And only water lay around
As if the land had stolen away
Or sprawled upon the ocean ground.

The sun by day, the stars by night
Had only us to look upon,
Bent on us their collected light,
And followed on as we went on.

Sometimes in utter wonder lost
That loneliness like this could be
We stood and stared until almost
We saw no longer sky or sea,

But only the frame of time and space,
An empty floor, a vacant wall,
And on that blank no line to trace
Movement, if we moved at all.

What thoughts came then! Sometimes it seemed
We long had passed the living by
On other seas and only dreamed
This sea, this journey and this sky,

Or traced a ghostly parallel
That limned the land but could not merge,
And haven and home and harbour bell
Were just behind the horizon verge,

Or the world itself had ended so
Without a cry, and we should sail
To and fro, to and fro,
Long past the lightning and the gale.

O then what crowding fantasies
Poured in from empty sea and sky!
At night we heard the whispering quays,
Line after line, slide softly by.

Delusions in the silent noon;
Fields in the hollows of the waves;
Or spread beneath the yellow moon,
A land of harvests and of graves.

The soft sea-sounds beguiled our ear.
We thought we walked by mountain rills
Or listened half a night to hear
The spring wind hunting on the hills.

And faces, faces, faces came
Across the salt sea-desert air,
And rooms in which a candle flame
Made everything renowned and rare.

The words we knew like our right hand,
Mountain and valley, meadow and grove,

Composed a legendary land
Rich with the broken tombs of love.

Delusion or truth? We were content
Thenceforth to sail the harmless seas
Safe past the Fate and the Accident,
And called a blessing on that peace.

And blessing, we ourselves were blest,
Lauded the loss that brought our gain,
Sang the tumultuous world to rest,
And wishless called it back again.

For loss was then our only joy,
Privation of all, fulfilled desire,
The world our treasure and our toy
In destitution clean as fire.

Our days were then—I cannot tell
How we were then fulfilled and crowned
With life as in a parable,
And sweetly as gods together bound.

Delusion and dream! Our captain knew
Compass and clock had never yet
Failed him; the sun and stars were true.
The mark was there that we should hit.

And it rose up, a sullen stain
Flawing the crystal firmament.
A wound! We felt the familiar pain
And knew the place to which we were sent.

The crowds drew near, the toppling towers;
In hope and dread we drove to birth;
The dream and the truth we clutched as ours,
And gladly, blindly stepped on earth.

WILFRED OWEN

(1893-1918)

MINERS

There was a whispering in my hearth,
   A sigh of the coal,
Grown wistful of a former earth
   It might recall.

I listened for a tale of leaves
   And smothered ferns;
Frond forests; and the low sly lives
   Before the fawns.

My fire might show steam-phantoms simmer
   From Time's old cauldron,
Before the birds made nests in summer,
   Or men had children.

But the coals were murmuring of their mine,
   And moans down there,
Of boys that slept wry sleep, and men
   Writhing for air.

I saw white bones in the cinder-shard,
   Bones without number;
For many hearts with coal are charred,
   And few remember.

I thought of all that worked dark pits
   Of war, and died
Digging the rock where Death reputes
   Peace lies indeed.

Comforted years will sit soft-chaired,
   In rooms of amber,
The years will stretch their hands, well cheered
   By our lives' ember;

The centuries will burn rich loads
   With which we groaned,
Whose warmth shall lull their dreamy lids,
   While songs are crooned.
But they will not dream of us poor lads
   Lost in the ground.

FROM MY DIARY, JULY 1914

Leaves
   Murmuring by myriads in the shimmering trees.
Lives
   Wakening with wonder in the Pyrenees.
Birds
   Cheerily chirping in the early day.
Bards
   Singing of summer scything thro' the hay.
Bees
   Shaking the heavy dews from bloom and frond.
Boys
   Bursting the surface of the ebony pond.
Flashes
   Of swimmers carving thro' the sparkling cold.
Fleshes
   Gleaming with wetness to the morning gold.
A mead
   Bordered about with warbling water brooks.
A maid
   Laughing the love-laugh with me; proud of looks.
The heat
   Throbbing between the upland and the peak.
Her heart
   Quivering with passion to my pressed cheek.
Braiding
   Of floating flames across the mountain brow.
Brooding
   Of stillness; and a sighing of the bough.
Stirs
   Of leaflets in the gloom; soft petal-showers;
Stars
   Expanding with the starr'd nocturnal flowers.

GREATER LOVE

Red lips are not so red
   As the stained stones kissed by the English dead.
Kindness of wooed and wooer
Seems shame to their love pure.
O Love, your eyes lose lure
   When I behold eyes blinded in my stead!

Your slender attitude
  Trembles not exquisite like limbs knife-skewed,
Rolling and rolling there
Where God seems not to care;
Till the fierce Love they bear
  Cramps them in death's extreme decrepitude.

Your voice sings not so soft,—
  Though even as wind murmuring through raftered loft,—
Your dear voice is not dear,
Gentle, and evening clear,
As theirs whom none now hear,
  Now earth has stopped their piteous mouths that coughed.

Heart, you were never hot,
  Nor large, nor full like hearts made great with shot;
And though your hand be pale,
Paler are all which trail
Your cross through flame and hail:
  Weep, you may weep, for you may touch them not.

DULCE ET DECORUM EST

Bent double, like old beggars under sacks,
Knock-kneed, coughing like hags, we cursed through sludge,
Till on the haunting flares we turned our backs,
And towards our distant rest began to trudge.
Men marched asleep. Many had lost their boots,
But limped on, blood-shod. All went lame, all blind;
Drunk with fatigue; deaf even to the hoots
Of gas-shells dropping softly behind.

Gas! GAS! Quick, boys!—An ecstasy of fumbling,
Fitting the clumsy helmets just in time,
But someone still was yelling out and stumbling
And flound'ring like a man in fire or lime.—
Dim through the misty panes and thick green light,
As under a green sea, I saw him drowning.

In all my dreams before my helpless sight
He plunges at me, guttering, choking, drowning.

If in some smothering dreams, you too could pace
Behind the wagon that we flung him in,
And watch the white eyes writhing in his face,
His hanging face, like a devil's sick of sin,
If you could hear, at every jolt, the blood
Come gargling from the froth-corrupted lungs,

Bitter as the cud
Of vile, incurable sores on innocent tongues,—
My friend, you would not tell with such high zest
To children ardent for some desperate glory,
The old Lie: *Dulce et decorum est
Pro patria mori.*

APOLOGIA PRO POEMATE MEO

I, too, saw God through mud—
    The mud that cracked on cheeks when wretches smiled.
    War brought more glory to their eyes than blood,
    And gave their laughs more glee than shakes a child.

Merry it was to laugh there—
    Where death becomes absurd and life absurder.
    For power was on us as we slashed bones bare
    Not to feel sickness or remorse of murder.

I, too, have dropped off fear—
    Behind the barrage, dead as my platoon,
    And sailed my spirit surging, light and clear
    Past the entanglement where hopes lay strewn;

And witnessed exultation—
    Faces that used to curse me, scowl for scowl,
    Shine and lift up with passion of oblation,
    Seraphic for an hour; though they were foul.

I have made fellowships—
    Untold of happy lovers in old song.
    For love is not the binding of fair lips
    With the soft silk of eyes that look and long,

By Joy, whose ribbon slips,—
    But wound with war's hard wire whose stakes are strong;
    Bound with the bandage of the arm that drips;
    Knit in the webbing of the rifle-thong.

I have perceived much beauty
    In the hoarse oaths that kept our courage straight;
    Heard music in the silentness of duty;
    Found peace where shell-storms spouted reddest spate.

Nevertheless, except you share
    With them in hell the sorrowful dark of hell,
    Whose world is but the trembling of a flare,
    And heaven but as the highway for a shell,

You shall not hear their mirth:
    You shall not come to think them well content
    By any jest of mine. These men are worth
    Your tears: You are not worth their merriment.

ANTHEM FOR DOOMED YOUTH

    What passing-bells for these who die as cattle?
        Only the monstrous anger of the guns.
        Only the stuttering rifles' rapid rattle
    Can pattern out their hasty orisons.
    No mockeries for them; no prayers nor bells,
    Nor any voice of mourning save the choirs,—
    The shrill, demented choirs of wailing shells;
    And bugles calling for them from sad shires.

    What candles may be held to speed them all?
        Not in the hands of boys, but in their eyes
    Shall shine the holy glimmers of good-byes.
        The pallor of girls' brows shall be their pall;
    Their flowers the tenderness of patient minds,
    And each slow dusk a drawing-down of blinds.

FUTILITY

    Move him into the sun—
    Gently its touch awoke him once,
    At home, whispering of fields unsown.
    Always it woke him, even in France,
    Until this morning and this snow.
    If anything might rouse him now
    The kind old sun will know.

    Think how it wakes the seeds—
    Woke, once, the clays of a cold star.
    Are limbs so dear-achieved, are sides
    Full-nerved,—still warm,—too hard to stir?
    Was it for this the clay grew tall?
    —O what made fatuous sunbeams toil
    To break earth's sleep at all?

STRANGE MEETING

It seemed that out of battle I escaped
Down some profound dull tunnel, long since scooped
Through granites which titanic wars had groined.
Yet also there encumbered sleepers groaned,

Too fast in thought or death to be bestirred.
Then, as I probed them, one sprang up, and stared
With piteous recognition in fixed eyes,
Lifting distressful hands as if to bless.
And by his smile, I knew that sullen hall,
By his dead smile I knew we stood in Hell.
With a thousand pains that visions face was grained;
Yet no blood reached there from the upper ground,
And no guns thumped, or down the flues made moan.
'Strange friend,' I said, 'here is no cause to mourn.'
'None,' said the other, 'save the undone years,
The hopelessness. Whatever hope is yours,
Was my life also; I went hunting wild
After the wildest beauty in the world,
Which lies not calm in eyes, or braided hair,
But mocks the steady running of the hour,
And if it grieves, grieves richlier than here.
For by my glee might many men have laughed,
And of my weeping something had been left,
Which must die now. I mean the truth untold,
The pity of war, the pity war distilled.
Now men will go content with what we spoiled.
Or, discontent, boil bloody, and be spilled.
They will be swift with swiftness of the tigress,
None will break ranks, though nations trek from progress.
Courage was mine, and I had mystery,
Wisdom was mine, and I had mastery;
To miss the march of this retreating world
Into vain citadels that are not walled.
Then, when much blood had clogged their chariot-wheels
I would go up and wash them from sweet wells,
Even with truths that lie too deep for taint.
I would have poured my spirit without stint
But not through wounds; not on the cess of war.
Foreheads of men have bled where no wounds were.
I am the enemy you killed, my friend.
I knew you in this dark; for so you frowned
Yesterday through me as you jabbed and killed.
I parried; but my hands were loath and cold.
Let us sleep now. . . .'

THE SEND-OFF

Down the close, darkening lanes they sang their way
To the siding-shed,
And lined the train with faces grimly gay.
Their breasts were stuck all white with wreath and spray
As men's are, dead.

Dull porters watched them, and a casual tramp
Stood staring hard,
Sorry to miss them from the upland camp.
Then, unmoved, signals nodded, and a lamp
Winked to the guard.

So secretly, like wrongs hushed-up, they went.
They were not ours:
We never heard to which front these were sent.
Nor there if they yet mock what women meant
Who gave them flowers.

Shall they return to beatings of great bells
In wild train-loads?
A few, a few, too few for drums and yells,
May creep back, silent, to village wells
Up half-known roads.

THE SHOW

We have fallen in the dreams the ever-living
Breathe on the tarnished mirror of the world,
And then smooth out with ivory hands and sigh.
                                                    W. B. YEATS.

My soul looked down from a vague height with Death,
As unremembering how I rose or why,
And saw a sad land, weak with sweats of dearth,
Grey, cratered like the moon with hollow woe,
And pitted with great pocks and scabs of plagues.
Across its beard, that horror of harsh wire,
There moved thin caterpillars, slowly uncoiled.
It seemed they pushed themselves to be as plugs
Of ditches, where they writhed and shrivelled, killed.
By them had slimy paths been trailed and scraped
Round myriad warts that might be little hills.
From gloom's last dregs these long-strung creatures crept,
And vanished out of dawn down hidden holes.
(And smell came up from those foul openings
As out of mouths, or deep wounds deepening.)
On dithering feet upgathered, more and more,
Brown strings, towards strings of grey, with bristling spines,
All migrants from green fields, intent on mire.
Those that were grey, of more abundant spawns,
Ramped on the rest and ate them and were eaten.
I saw their bitten backs curve, loop, and straighten,
I watched those agonies curl, lift, and flatten.
Whereat, in terror what that sight might mean,

I reeled and shivered earthward like a feather.
And Death fell with me, like a deepening moan.
And He, picking a manner of worm, which half had hid
Its bruises in the earth, but crawled no further,
Showed me its feet, the feet of many men,
And the fresh-severed head of it, my head.

ARMS AND THE BOY

Let the boy try along this bayonet-blade
How cold steel is, and keen with hunger of blood;
Blue with all malice, like a madman's flash;
And thinly drawn with famishing for flesh.

Lend him to stroke these blind, blunt bullet-heads
Which long to nuzzle in the hearts of lads,
Or give him cartridges of fine zinc teeth,
Sharp with the sharpness of grief and death.

For his teeth seem for laughing round an apple.
There lurk no claws behind his fingers supple;
And God will grow no talons at his heels,
Nor antlers through the thickness of his curls.

INSENSIBILITY

Happy are men who yet before they are killed
Can let their veins run cold.
Whom no compassion fleers
Or makes their feet
Sore on the alleys cobbled with their brothers.
The front line withers,
But they are troops who fade, not flowers
For poets' tearful fooling:
Men, gaps for filling:
Losses who might have fought
Longer; but no one bothers.

And some cease feeling
Even themselves or for themselves.
Dullness best solves
The tease and doubt of shelling,
And Chance's strange arithmetic
Comes simpler than the reckoning of their shilling.
They keep no check on armies' decimation.

Happy are these who lose imagination:
They have enough to carry with ammunition.
Their spirit drags no pack,

Their old wounds save with cold can not more ache.
Having seen all things red,
Their eyes are rid
Of the hurt of the colour of blood for ever.
And terror's first constriction over,
Their hearts remain small-drawn.
Their senses in some scorching cautery of battle
Now long since ironed,
Can laugh among the dying, unconcerned.

Happy the soldier home, with not a notion
How somewhere, every dawn, some men attack,
And many sighs are drained.
Happy the lad whose mind was never trained:
His days are worth forgetting more than not.
He sings along the march
Which we march taciturn, because of dusk,
The long, forlorn, relentless trend
From larger day to huger night.

We wise, who with a thought besmirch
Blood over all our soul,
How should we see our task
But through his blunt and lashless eyes?
Alive, he is not vital overmuch;
Dying, not mortal overmuch;
Nor sad, nor proud,
Nor curious at all.
He cannot tell
Old men's placidity from his.

But cursed are dullards whom no cannon stuns,
That they should be as stones;
Wretched are they, and mean
With paucity that never was simplicity.
By choice they made themselves immune
To pity and whatever moans in man
Before the last sea and the hapless stars;
Whatever mourns when many leave these shores;
Whatever shares
The eternal reciprocity of tears.

ON SEEING A PIECE OF OUR ARTILLERY
BROUGHT INTO ACTION

Being slowly lifted up, thou long black arm,
Great gun towering toward Heaven, about to curse;
Sway steep against them, and for years rehearse

Huge imprecations like a blasting charm!
Reach at that arrogance which needs thy harm,
And beat it down before its sins grow worse;
Spend our resentment, cannon, yea, disburse
Our gold in shapes of flame, our breaths in storm.

Yet, for men's sakes whom thy vast malison
Must wither innocent of enmity,
Be not withdrawn, dark arm, thy spoilure done,
Safe to the bosom of our prosperity.
But when thy spell be cast complete and whole,
May God curse thee, and cut thee from our soul!

SPRING OFFENSIVE

Halted against the shade of a last hill,
They fed, and, lying easy, were at ease
And, finding comfortable chests and knees,
Carelessly slept. But many there stood still
To face the stark, blank sky beyond the ridge,
Knowing their feet had come to the end of the world.

Marvelling they stood, and watched the long grass swirled
By the May breeze, murmurous with wasp and midge,
For though the summer oozed into their veins
Like an injected drug for their bodies' pains,
Sharp on their souls hung the imminent line of grass,
Fearfully flashed the sky's mysterious glass.

Hour after hour they ponder the warm field—
And the far valley behind, where the buttercup
Had blessed with gold their slow boots coming up,
Where even the little brambles would not yield,
But clutched and clung to them like sorrowing hands;
They breathe like trees unstirred.

Till like a cold gust thrills the little word
At which each body and its soul begird
And tighten them for battle. No alarms
Of bugles, no high flags, no clamorous haste—
Only a lift and flare of eyes that faced
The sun, like a friend with whom their love is done.
O larger shone that smile against the sun,—
Mightier than his whose bounty these have spurned.

So, soon they topped the hill, and raced together
Over an open stretch of herb and heather
Exposed. And instantly the whole sky burned

With fury against them; earth set sudden cups
In thousands for their blood; and the green slope
Chasmed and steepened sheer to infinite space.

. . . . . .

Of them who running on that last high place
Leapt to swift unseen bullets, or went up
On the hot blast and fury of hell's upsurge,
Or plunged and fell away past this world's verge,
Some say God caught them even before they fell.

But what say such as from existence' brink
Ventured but drave too swift to sink,
The few who rushed in the body to enter hell,
And there out-fiending all its fiends and flames
With superhuman inhumanities,
Long-famous glories, immemorial shames—
And crawling slowly back, have by degrees
Regained cool peaceful air in wonder—
Why speak not they of comrades that went under?

EXPOSURE

Our brains ache, in the merciless iced east winds that
        knive us . . .
Wearied we keep awake because the night is silent . . .
Low, drooping flares confuse our memory of the salient . . .
Worried by silence, sentries whisper, curious, nervous,
                But nothing happens.

Watching, we hear the mad gusts tugging on the wire,
Like twitching agonies of men among its brambles,
Northward, incessantly, the flickering gunnery rumbles,
Far off, like a dull rumour of some other war.
                What are we doing here?

The poignant misery of dawn begins to grow . . .
We only know war lasts, rain soaks, and clouds sag stormy.
Dawn massing in the east her melancholy army
Attacks once more in ranks on shivering ranks of gray,
                But nothing happens.

Sudden successive flights of bullets streak the silence.
Less deadly than the air that shudders black with snow,
With sidelong flowing flakes that flock, pause, and renew,
We watch them wandering up and down the wind's
        nonchalance,
                But nothing happens.

Pale flakes with fingering stealth come feeling for our faces—
We cringe in holes, back on forgotten dreams, and stare,
    snow-dazed,
Deep into grassier ditches. So we drowse, sun-dozed,
Littered with blossoms trickling where the blackbird fusses.
        Is it that we are dying?

Slowly our ghosts drag home: glimpsing the sunk fires,
    glozed
With crusted dark-red jewels; crickets jingle there;
For hours the innocent mice rejoice: the house is theirs;
Shutters and doors, all closed: on us the doors are closed,—
        We turn back to our dying.

Since we believe not otherwise can kind fires burn;
Nor ever suns smile true on child, or field, or fruit.
For God's invincible spring our love is made afraid;
Therefore, not loath, we lie out here; therefore were born,
        For love of God seems dying.

To-night, His frost will fasten on this mud and us,
Shrivelling many hands, puckering foreheads crisp.
The burying-party, picks and shovels in their shaking grasp,
Pause over half-known faces. All their eyes are ice,
        But nothing happens.

MENTAL CASES

Who are these? Why sit they here in twilight?
Wherefore rock they, purgatorial shadows,
Drooping tongues from jaws that slob their relish,
Baring teeth that leer like skulls' teeth wicked?
Stroke on stroke of pain,—but what slow panic,
Gouged these chasms round their fretted sockets?
Ever from their hair and through their hands' palms
Misery swelters. Surely we have perished
Sleeping, and walk hell; but who these hellish?

—These are men whose minds the Dead have ravished.
Memory fingers in their hair of murders,
Multitudinous murders they once witnessed.
Wading sloughs of flesh these helpless wander,
Treading blood from lungs that had loved laughter.
Always they must see these things and hear them,
Batter of guns and shatter of flying muscles,
Carnage incomparable, and human squander,
Rucked too thick for these men's extrication.

Therefore still their eyeballs shrink tormented
Back into their brains, because on their sense
Sunlight seems a blood-smear; night comes blood-black;
Dawn breaks open like a wound that bleeds afresh.
—Thus their heads wear this hilarious, hideous,
Awful falseness of set-smiling corpses.
—Thus their hands are plucking at each other;
Picking at the rope-knouts of their scourging;
Snatching after us who smote them, brother,
Pawing us who dealt them war and madness.

DISABLED

He sat in a wheeled chair, waiting for dark,
And shivered in his ghastly suit of grey,
Legless, sewn short at elbow. Through the park
Voices of boys rang saddening like a hymn,
Voices of play and pleasures after day,
Till gathering sleep had mothered them from him.

. . . . . .

About this time Town used to swing so gay
When glow-lamps budded in the light blue trees,
And girls glanced lovelier as the air grew dim,—
In the old times, before he threw away his knees.
Now he will never feel again how slim
Girls' waists are, or how warm their subtle hands;
All of them touch him like some queer disease.

. . . . . .

There was an artist silly for his face,
For it was younger than his youth, last year.
Now, he is old; his back will never brace;
He's lost his colour very far from here,
Poured it down shell-holes till the veins ran dry,
And half his lifetime lapsed in the hot race,
And leap of purple spurted from his thigh.

. . . . . .

One time he liked a blood-smear down his leg,
After the matches, carried shoulder-high.
It was after football, when he'd drunk a peg,
He thought he'd better join.—He wonders why.
Someone had said he'd look a god in kilts,
That's why; and may be, too, to please his Meg;

Aye, that was it, to please the giddy jilts
He asked to join. He didn't have to beg;

. . . . . .

Smiling they wrote his lie; aged nineteen years.
Germans he scarcely thought of; all their guilt,
And Austria's, did not move him. And no fears
Of Fear came yet. He thought of jewelled hilts
For daggers in plaid socks; of smart salutes;
And care of arms; and leave; and pay arrears;
Esprit de corps; and hints for young recruits.
And soon he was drafted out with drums and cheers.

. . . . . .

Some cheered him home, but not as crowds cheer Goal.
Only a solemn man who brought him fruits
Thanked him; and then inquired about his soul.

. . . . . .

Now, he will spend a few sick years in Institutes,
And do what things the rules consider wise,
And take whatever pity they may dole.
To-night he noticed how the women's eyes
Passed from him to the strong men that were whole.
How cold and late it is! Why don't they come
And put him into bed? Why don't they come?

THE NEXT WAR

War's a joke for me and you,
While we know such dreams are true.

SASSOON

Out there, we've talked quite friendly up to Death;
    Sat down and eaten with him, cool and bland,—
    Pardoned his spilling mess-tins in our hand.
We've sniffed the green thick odour of his breath,—
Our eyes wept, but our courage didn't writhe.
    He's spat at us with bullets and he's coughed
    Shrapnel. We chorussed when he sang aloft;
We whistled while he shaved us with his scythe.

Oh, Death was never an enemy of ours!
    We laughed at him, we leagued with him, old chum.
No soldier's paid to kick against his powers.
    We laughed, knowing that better men would come,
And greater wars; when each proud fighter brags
He wars on Death—for Life; not men—for flags.

ROBERT GRAVES

(b. 1895)

ROCKY ACRES

This is a wild land, country of my choice,
With harsh craggy mountain, moor ample and bare.
Seldom in these acres is heard any voice
But voice of cold water that runs here and there
Through rocks and lank heather growing without care.
No mice in the heath run, no song-birds fly
For fear of the buzzard that floats in the sky.

He soars and he hovers, rocking on his wings,
He scans his wide parish with a sharp eye,
He catches the trembling of small hidden things,
He tears them in pieces, dropping them from the sky;
Tenderness and pity the heart will deny,
Where life is but nourished by water and rock—
A hardy adventure, full of fear and shock.

Time has never journeyed to this lost land,
Crakeberry and heather bloom out of date,
The rocks jut, the streams flow singing on either hand,
Careless if the season be early or late,
The skies wander overhead, now blue, now slate;
Winter would be known by his cutting snow
If June did not borrow his armour also.

Yet this is my country, beloved by me best,
The first land that rose from Chaos and the Flood,
Nursing no valleys for comfort or rest,
Trampled by no shod hooves, bought with no blood.
Sempiternal country whose barrows have stood
Stronghold for demigods when on earth they go,
Terror for fat burghers on far plains below.

WARNING TO CHILDREN

Children, if you dare to think
Of the greatness, rareness, muchness,
Fewness of this precious only
Endless world in which you say
You live, you think of things like this:
Blocks of slate enclosing dappled
Red and green, enclosing tawny
Yellow nets, enclosing white
And black acres of dominoes,
Where a neat brown paper parcel
Tempts you to untie the string.
In the parcel a small island,
On the island a large tree,
On the tree a husky fruit.
Strip the husk and pare the rind off:
In the kernel you will see
Blocks of slate enclosed by dappled
Red and green, enclosed by tawny
Yellow nets, enclosed by white
And black acres of dominoes,
Where the same brown paper parcel—
Children, leave the string alone!
For who dares undo the parcel
Finds himself at once inside it,
On the island, in the fruit,
Blocks of slate about his head,
Finds himself enclosed by dappled
Green and red, enclosed by yellow
Tawny nets, enclosed by black
And white acres of dominoes,
With the same brown paper parcel
Still untied upon his knee.
And, if he then should dare to think
Of the fewness, muchness, rareness,
Greatness of this endless only
Precious world in which he says
He lives—he then unties the string.

THE BARDS

The bards falter in shame, their running verse
Stumbles, with marrow-bones the drunken diners
Pelt them for their delay.
It is a something fearful in the song

Plagues them—an unknown grief that like a churl
Goes commonplace in cowskin
And bursts unheralded, crowing and coughing,
An unpilled holly-club twirled in his hand,
Into their many-shielded, samite-curtained,
Jewel-bright hall where twelve kings sit at chess
Over the white-bronze pieces and the gold;
And by a gross enchantment
Flails down the rafters and leads off the queens—
The wild-swan-breasted, the rose-ruddy-cheeked
Raven-haired daughters of their admiration—
To stir his black pots and to bed on straw.

PURE DEATH

We looked, we loved, and therewith instantly
Death became terrible to you and me.
By love we disenthralled our natural terror
From every comfortable philosopher
Or tall, grey doctor of divinity:
Death stood at last in his true rank and order.

It happened soon, so wild of heart were we,
Exchange of gifts grew to a malady:
Their worth rose always higher on each side
Till there seemed nothing but ungivable pride
That yet remained ungiven, and this degree
Called a conclusion not to be denied.

Then we at last bethought ourselves, made shift
And simultaneously this final gift
Gave: each with shaking hands unlocks
The sinister, long, brass-bound coffin-box,
Unwraps pure death, with such bewilderment
As greeted our love's first acknowledgement.

TRAVELLER'S CURSE AFTER MISDIRECTION

(from the Welsh)

May they stumble, stage by stage
On an endless pilgrimage,
Dawn and dusk, mile after mile,
At each and every step, a stile;

At each and every step withal
May they catch their feet and fall;
At each and every fall they take
May a bone within them break;
And may the bone that breaks within
Not be, for variation's sake,
Now rib, now thigh, now arm, now shin,
But always, without fail, THE NECK.

THE READER OVER MY SHOULDER

You, reading over my shoulder, peering beneath
My writing arm—I suddenly feel your breath
  Hot on my hand or on my nape,
So interrupt my theme, scratching these few
Words on the margin for you, namely you,
  Too-human shape fixed in that shape:—

All the saying of things against myself
And for myself I have well done myself.
  What now, old enemy, shall you do
But quote and underline, thrusting yourself
Against me, as ambassador of myself,
  In damned confusion of myself and you?

For you in strutting, you in sycophancy,
Have played too long this other self of me,
  Doubling the part of judge and patron
With that of creaking grind-stone to my wit.
Know me, have done: I am a proud spirit
  And you for ever clay. Have done.

THE LEGS

There was this road,
And it led up-hill,
And it led down-hill,
And round and in and out.

And the traffic was legs,
Legs from the knees down,
Coming and going,
Never pausing.

And the gutters gurgled
With the rain's overflow,
And the sticks on the pavement
Blindly tapped and tapped.

What drew the legs along
Was the never-stopping,
And the senseless, frightening
Fate of being legs.

Legs for the road,
The road for legs,
Resolutely nowhere
In both directions.

My legs at least
Were not in that rout:
On grass by the roadside
Entire I stood,

Watching the unstoppable
Legs go by
With never a stumble
Between step and step.

Though my smile was broad
The legs could not see,
Though my laugh was loud
The legs could not hear.

My head dizzied, then:
I wondered suddenly,
Might I too be a walker
From the knees down?

Gently I touched my shins.
The doubt unchained them:
They had run in twenty puddles
Before I regained them.

SEA SIDE

Into a gentle wildness and confusion,
Of here and there, of one and everyone,
Of windy sandhills by an unkempt sea,
Came two and two in search of symmetry,
Found symmetry of two in sea and sand,
In left foot, right foot, left hand and right hand.

The beast with two backs is a single beast,
Yet by his love of singleness increased
To two and two and two and two again,
Until, instead of sandhills, see, a plain
Patterned in two and two, by two and two—
And the sea parts in horror at a view
Of rows of houses coupling, back to back,
While love smokes from their common chimney-stack
With two-four-eight-sixteenish single same
Re-registration of the duple name.

WELSH INCIDENT

'But that was nothing to what things came out
From the sea-caves of Criccieth yonder.'
'What were they? Mermaids? dragons? ghosts?'
'Nothing at all of any things like that.'
'What were they, then?'
       'All sorts of queer things,
Things never seen or heard or written about,

Very strange, un-Welsh, utterly peculiar
Things. Oh, solid enough they seemed to touch,
Had anyone dared it. Marvellous creation,
All various shapes and sizes, and no sizes,
All new, each perfectly unlike his neighbour,
Though all came moving slowly out together.
'Describe just one of them.'
                            'I am unable.'
'What were their colours?'
                           'Mostly nameless colours,
Colours you'd like to see; but one was puce
Or perhaps more like crimson, but not purplish.
Some had no colour.'
                     'Tell me, had they legs?'
'Not a leg nor foot among them that I saw.'
'But did these things come out in any order?
What o'clock was it? What was the day of the week?
Who else was present? How was the weather?'
'I was coming to that. It was half-past three
On Easter Tuesday last. The sun was shining.
The Harlech Silver Band played *Marchog Jesu*
On thirty-seven shimmering instruments,
Collecting for Caernarvon's (Fever) Hospital Fund.
The populations of Pwllheli, Criccieth,
Portmadoc, Borth, Tremadoc, Penrhyndeudraeth,
Were all assembled. Criccieth's mayor addressed them
First in good Welsh and then in fluent English,
Twisting his fingers in his chain of office,
Welcoming the things. They came out on the sand,
Not keeping time to the band, moving seaward
Silently at a snail's pace. But at last
The most odd, indescribable thing of all,
Which hardly one man there could see for wonder,
Did something recognizably a something.'
'Well, what?'
            'It made a noise.'
                          'A frightening noise?'
'No, no.'
        'A musical noise? A noise of scuffling?'
'No, but a very loud, respectable noise—
Like groaning to oneself on Sunday morning
In Chapel, close before the second psalm.'
'What did the mayor do?'
                          'I was coming to that'.

INTERRUPTION

If ever against this easy blue and silver
Hazed-over countryside of thoughtfulness,
Far behind in the mind and above,
Boots from before and below approach tramping,
Watch how their premonition will display
A forward countryside, low in the distance—
A picture-postcard square of June grass;
Will warm a summer season, trim the hedges,
Cast the river about on either flank,
Start the late cuckoo emptily calling,
Invent a rambling tale of moles and voles,
Furnish a path with stiles.
Watch how the field will broaden, the feet nearing,
Sprout with great dandelions and buttercups,
Widen and heighten. The blue and silver
Fogs at the border of this all-grass.
Interruption looms gigantified,
Lurches against, treads thundering through,
Blots the landscape, scatters all,
Roars and rumbles like a dark tunnel,
Is gone.
            The picture-postcard grass and trees
Swim back to central: it is a large patch,
It is a modest, failing patch of green,
The postage-stamp of its departure,
Clouded with blue and silver, closing in now
To a plain countryside of less and less,
Unpeopled and unfeatured blue and silver,
Before, behind, above.

LOST ACRES

These acres, always again lost
    By every new ordnance-survey
And searched for at exhausting cost
    Of time and thought, are still away.

They have their paper-substitute—
    Intercalation of an inch
At the so-many-thousandth foot:
    And no one parish feels the pinch.

But lost they are, despite all care,
    And perhaps likely to be bound
Together in a piece somewhere,
    A plot of undiscovered ground.

Invisible, they have the spite
    To swerve the tautest measuring-chain
And the exact theodolite
    Perched every side of them in vain.

Yet, be assured, we have no need
    To plot these acres of the mind
With prehistoric fern and reed
    And monsters such as heroes find.

Maybe they have their flowers, their birds,
    Their trees behind the phantom fence,
But of a substance without words:
    To walk there would be loss of sense.

RECALLING WAR

Entrance and exit wounds are silvered clean,
The track aches only when the rain reminds.
The one-legged man forgets his leg of wood,
The one-armed man his jointed wooden arm.
The blinded man sees with his ears and hands
As much or more than once with both his eyes.
Their war was fought these twenty years ago
And now assumes the nature-look of time,
As when the morning traveller turns and views
His wild night-stumbling carved into a hill.

What, then, was war? No mere discord of flags
But an infection of the common sky
That sagged ominously upon the earth
Even when the season was the airiest May.
Down pressed the sky, and we, oppressed, thrust out
Boastful tongue, clenched fist and valiant yard.
Natural infirmities were out of mode,
For Death was young again: patron alone
Of healthy dying, premature fate-spasm.

Fear made fine bed-fellows. Sick with delight
At life's discovered transitoriness,
Our youth became all-flesh and waived the mind.
Never was such antiqueness of romance,
Such tasty honey oozing from the heart.
And old importances came swimming back—
Wine, meat, log-fires, a roof over the head,
A weapon at the thigh, surgeons at call.
Even there was a use again for God—

A word of rage in lack of meat, wine, fire,
In ache of wounds beyond all surgeoning.

War was return of earth to ugly earth,
War was foundering of sublimities,
Extinction of each happy art and faith
By which the world had still kept head in air,
Protesting logic or protesting love,
Until the unendurable moment struck—
The inward scream, the duty to run mad.

And we recall the merry ways of guns—
Nibbling the walls of factory and church
Like a child, piecrust; felling groves of trees
Like a child, dandelions with a switch.
Machine-guns rattle toy-like from a hill,
Down in a row the brave tin-soldiers fall:
A sight to be recalled in elder days
When learnedly the future we devote
To yet more boastful visions of despair.

DOWN, WANTON, DOWN!

Down, wanton, down! Have you no shame
That at the whisper of Love's name,
Or Beauty's, presto! up you raise
Your angry head and stand at gaze?

Poor bombard-captain, sworn to reach
The ravelin and effect a breach—
Indifferent what you storm or why,
So be that in the breach you die!

Love may be blind, but Love at least
Knows what is man and what mere beast;
Or Beauty wayward, but requires
More delicacy from her squires.

Tell me, my witless, whose one boast
Could be your staunchness at the post,
When were you made a man of parts
To think fine and profess the arts?

Will many-gifted Beauty come
Bowing to your bald rule of thumb,
Or Love swear loyalty to your crown?
Be gone, have done! Down, wanton, down!

OGRES AND PYGMIES

Those famous men of old, the Ogres—
They had long beards and stinking arm-pits,
They were wide-mouthed, long-yarded and great-bellied
Yet not of taller stature, Sirs, than you.
They lived on Ogre-Strand, which was no place
But the churl's terror of their vast extent,
Where every foot was three-and-thirty inches
And every penny bought a whole hog.
Now of their company none survive, not one,
The times being, thank God, unfavourable
To all but nightmare shadows of their fame;
Their images stand howling on the hill
(The winds enforced against those wide mouths),
Whose granite haunches country-folk salute
With May Day kisses, and whose knobbed knees.

So many feats they did to admiration:
With their enormous throats they sang louder
Than ten cathedral choirs, with their grand yards
Stormed the most rare and obstinate maidenheads,
With their strong-gutted and capacious bellies
Digested stones and glass like ostriches.
They dug great pits and heaped huge mounds,
Deflected rivers, wrestled with the bear
And hammered judgements for posterity—
For the sweet-cupid-lipped and tassel-yarded
Delicate-stomached dwellers
In Pygmy Alley, where with brooding on them
A foot is shrunk to seven inches
And twelve-pence will not buy a spare rib.
And who would judge between Ogres and Pygmies—
The thundering text, the snivelling commentary—
Reading between such covers he will marvel
How his own members bloat and shrink again.

HISTORY OF THE WORD

The Word that in the beginning was the Word
For two or three, but elsewhere spoke unheard,
Found Words to interpret it, which for a season
Prevailed until ruled out by Law and Reason
Which, by a lax interpretation cursed,
In Laws and Reasons logically dispersed;
These, in their turn, found they could do no better

Than fall to Letters and each claim a letter.
In the beginning then, the Word alone,
But now the various tongue-tied Lexicon
In perfect impotence the day nearing
When every ear shall lose its sense of hearing
And every mind by knowledge be close-shuttered—
But two or three, that hear the Word uttered.

TO JUAN AT THE WINTER SOLSTICE

There is one story and one story only
That will prove worth your telling,
Whether as learned bard or gifted child;
To it all lines or lesser gauds belong
That startle with their shining
Such common stories as they stray into.

Is it of trees you tell, their months and virtues,
Or strange beasts that beset you,
Of birds that croak at you the Triple will?
Or of the Zodiac and how slow it turns
Below the Boreal Crown,
Prison of all true kings that ever reigned?

Water to water, ark again to ark,
From woman back to woman:
So each new victim treads unfalteringly
The never altered circuit of his fate,
Bringing twelve peers as witness
Both to his starry rise and starry fall.

Or is it of the Virgin's silver beauty,
All fish below the thighs?
She in her left hand bears a leafy quince;
When with her right she crooks a finger, smiling,
How may the King hold back?
Royally then he barters life for love.

Or of the undying snake from chaos hatched,
Whose coils contain the ocean,
Into whose chops with naked sword he springs,
Then in black water, tangled by the reeds,
Battles three days and nights,
To be spewed up beside her scalloped shore?

Much snow is falling, winds roar hollowly,
The owl hoots from the elder,
Fear in your heart cries to the loving-cup:

Sorrow to sorrow as the sparks fly upward.
The log groans and confesses:
There is one story and one story only.

Dwell on her graciousness, dwell on her smiling,
Do not forget what flowers
The great boar trampled down in ivy time.
Her brow was creamy as the crested wave,
Her sea-blue eyes were wild
But nothing promised that is not performed.

'¡WELLCOME, TO THE CAVES OF ARTÁ!'

'They are hollowed out in the see coast at the munci-
pal terminal of Capdepera, at nine kilometer from
the town of Artá in the Island of Mallorca, with a
suporizing infinity of graceful colums of 21 meter
and by downward, wich prives the spectator of all
animacion and plunges in dumbness. The way
going is very picturesque, serpentine between style
mountains, til the arrival at the esplanade of the
vallee called "The Spider". There are good enlace-
ments of the railroad with autobuses of excursion,
many days of the week, today actually Wednesday
and Satturday. Since many centuries renown foreing
visitors have explored them and wrote their eulogy
about, included Nort-American geoglogues.' From
a Tourist leaflet.

Such subtile filigranity and nobless of construccion
  Here fraternise in harmony, that respiracion stops.
While all admit their impotence (though autors most formid-
    able)
  To sing in words the excellence of Nature's underprops,
Yet stalactite and stalagmite together with dumb language
  Make hymnes to God wich celebrate the strength of water
    drops.

¿You, also, are you capable to make precise in idiom
  Consideracions magic of ilusions very wide?
Alraedy in the Vestibule of these Grand Caves of Artá
  The spirit of the human verb is darked and stupefyed;
So humildy you trespass trough the forest of the colums
  And listen to the grandess explicated by the guide.

From darkness into darkness, but at measure, now descend-
    ing
  You remark with what esxactitude he designates each
    bent;

'The Saloon of Thousand Banners,' or 'The Tumba of Na-
    poleon,'
'The Grotto of the Rosary,' 'The Club,' 'The Camping Tent.'
And at 'Cavern of the Organ' there are knocking streange
    formacions
    Wich give a nois particular pervoking wonderment.

¡Too far do not adventure, sir! For, further as you wander,
    The every of the stalactites will make you stop and stay.
Grand peril amenaces now, your nostrills aprehending
    An odour least delicious of lamentable decay.
It is some poor touristers, in the depth of obscure cristal,
    Wich deceased of thier emocion on a past excursion day.

THE WHITE GODDESS

All saints revile her, and all sober men
Ruled by the God Apollo's golden mean—
In scorn of which we sailed to find her
In distant regions likeliest to hold her
Whom we desired above all things to know,
Sister of the mirage and echo.

It was a virtue not to stay,
To go our headstrong and heroic way
Seeking her out at the volcano's head,
Among pack ice, or where the track had faded
Beyond the cavern of the seven sleepers:
Whose broad high brow was white as any leper's,
Whose eyes were blue, with rowan-berry lips.
With hair curled honey-coloured to white hips.

Green sap of Spring in the young wood a-stir
Will celebrate the Mountain Mother,
And every song-bird shout awhile for her;
But we are gifted, even in November
Rawest of seasons, with so huge a sense
Of her nakedly worn magnificence
We forget cruelty and past betrayal,
Heedless of where the next bright bolt may fall.

THE NAKED AND THE NUDE

For me, the naked and the nude
(By lexicographers construed
As synonyms that should express
The same deficiency of dress

Or shelter) stand as wide apart
As love from lies, or truth from art.

Lovers without reproach will gaze
On bodies naked and ablaze;
The Hippocratic eye will see
In nakedness, anatomy;
And naked shines the Goddess when
She mounts her lion among men.

The nude are bold, the nude are sly
To hold each treasonable eye.
While draping by a showman's trick
Their dishabille in rhetoric,
They grin a mock-religious grin
Of scorn at those of naked skin.

The naked, therefore, who compete
Against the nude may know defeat;
Yet when they both together tread
The briary pastures of the dead,
By Gorgons with long whips pursued,
How naked go the sometime nude!

LEAVING THE REST UNSAID

Finis, apparent on an earlier page,
With fallen obelisk for colophon,
Must this be here repeated?

Death has been ruefully announced
And to die once is death enough,
Be sure, for any life-time.

Must the book end, as you would end it,
With testamentary appendices
And graveyard indices?

But no, I will not lay me down
To let your tearful music mar
The decent mystery of my progress.

So now, my solemn ones, leaving the rest unsaid,
Rising in air as on a gander's wing
At a careless comma,

GEORGE BARKER

(b. 1913)

ELEGY NO. 1

Those occasions involving the veering of axles
When the wheel's bloody spikes like Arabian armaments
Release Passchendaele on us because it is time, bring
Also with blood to the breast the boon to the bosom:
I saw it happen, had near me the gun and the tear.
Those occasions are all elegiac. The wheel and the wish
Turn in a turtle the chaos of life. It is death,
Death like roulette turning our wish to its will.

I see a scene with a smother of snow over Love.
I know Spring will arise and later the swallow return;
I know, but my torso stands bogged in a load of time,
Like Love lying under the smother of our death and our
Dread. How soon shall the Spring bird arise and the
Summer bells hum with the murmur of our name?
      Soon, soon,
Soon the green room goes blue with the last autumn.

I sip at suicide in bedrooms or dare pessimistic stars,
Keep pigeons with messages or make tame apes
Commemorate in mime the master me who must go;
Or commit crimes of rage or rape to ease the ache:
I promise these cannot propitiate fate. No,
Tomorrow it is not, it is not to-day, it is not
Wednesday or Thursday. It is the greatest day.

That morning not the rose shall rise or dog dance,
Kings with conscience and queens with child sleep long,
For duty is useless; the soldier and sailor glance
Down at their guns with a grin, but they are wrong.
The dodo shall rule for a moment, and the Thames
Remember. Invalids and paralytics shall sing,
      'No more, no more!'
I shall hear the ceremony of heaven and God's roar.

What awaits is the veer of the lever and wheel
When the hands cross at midnight and noon, and the future
Sweeps on with a sigh—but on this occasion Time
Swells like a wave at a wall and bursts to eternity.
I await when the engine of lilies and lakes and love
Reaching its peak of power blows me sky high, and I
      Come down to rest
On the shape I made in the ground where I used to lie.

O widow, do not weep, do not weep! Or wife
Cry in the corner of the window with a child by—
Look how Tottenham and the Cotswolds, with
More mass than a man, lie easy under the sky,
Also awaiting change they cannot understand.
'I have heaven a haven in my hand,' say,
      Like the boy
Cornering butterflies or nothing in cupped hands.

The tragedy is Time foreshadowing its climax.
Thus in the stage of time the minor moth is small
But prophesies the Fokker with marvellous wings
Mottled with my sun's gold and your son's blood.
The crazy anthropoid crawls on time's original
That casts his giant on the contemporary scene:
      That spreadeagled shadow
Covers with horror the green Abyssinian meadow.

Lovers on Sunday in the rear seats of cinemas
Kiss deep and dark, for is it the last kiss?
Children sailing on swings in municipal parks
Swing high, swing high into the reach of the sky,
Leave, leave the sad star that is about to die.
Laugh, my comedians, who may not laugh again—
      Soon, soon,
Soon Jeremiah Job will be walking among men.

MEMORIAL FOR TWO YOUNG SEAMEN

(Lost overboard in a storm in Mid-Pacific, January 1940)

The seagull, spreadeagled, splayed on the wind,
Span backwards shrieking, belly facing upward,
Fled backward with a gimlet in its heart
To see the two youths swimming hand in hand
Through green eternity. O swept overboard

Not could the thirty-foot jaws them part,
Or the flouncing skirts that swept them over
Separate what death pronounced was love.

I saw them, the hand flapping like a flag,
And another like a dolphin with a child
Supporting him. Was I the shape of Jesus
When to me hopeward their eyeballs swivelled,
Saw I was standing in the stance of vague
Horror; paralysed with mere pity's peace?

From thorax of storms the voices of verbs
Shall call to me without sound, like the silence
Round which cyclones rage, to nurse my nerve
And hang my heart midway, where the balance
Meets. I taste sea swilling in my bowels
As I sit shivering in the swing of waves
Like a face in a bubble. As the hull heaves
I and my ghost tread water over hell.

The greedy bitch with sailors in her guts
Green as a dream and formidable as God,
Spitting at stars, gnawing at shores, mad randy,
Riots with us on her abdomen and puts
Eternity in our cabins, pitches our pod
To the mouth of the death for which no one is ready.

At midday they looked up and saw their death
Standing up overhead as loud as thunder
As white as angels and as broad as God:
Then, then the shock, the last gasp of breath,
As grazing the bulwarks they swept over and under,
All the green arms around them that load
Their eyes, their ears, their stomachs with eternals,
Whirled away in a white pool to the stern.
But the most possible of all miracles
Is that the useful tear that did not fall
From the corner of their eyes, was the prize,
The flowers, the gifts, the crystal sepulcher,
The funeral contribution and memorial,
The perfect and non-existent obsequies.

EPISTLE I

Meeting a monster of mourning wherever I go
Who crosses me at morning and evening also,
For whom are you miserable I ask and he murmurs
I am miserable for innumerable man: for him
Who wanders through Woolworth's gazing at tin stars;
I mourn the maternal future tense, Time's mother,
Who has him in her lap, and I mourn also her,
Time whose dial face flashes with scars.

I gave the ghost my money and he smiled and said,
Keep it for the eyeballs of the dead instead.
Why here, I asked, why is it here you come
Breaking into the evening line going to another,
Edging your axe between my pencil fingers,
Twisting my word from a comedy to a crime?
I am the face once seen never forgotten,
Whose human look your dirty page will smother.

I know what it was, he said, that you were beginning;
The rigmarole of private life's belongings.
Birth, boyhood, and the adolescent baloney. So I say
Good go ahead, and see what happens then.
I promise you horror shall stand in your shoes,
And when your register of youth is through
What will it be but about the horror of man?
Try telling about birth and observe the issue.

Epping Forest where the deer and girls
Mope like lost ones looking for Love's gaols—
Among the dilapidated glades my mother wandered
With me as kid, and sadly we saw
The deer in the rain near the trees, the leaf-hidden shit,
The Sunday papers, and the foliage's falling world;
I not knowing nothing was our possession,
Not knowing Poverty my position.

Epping Forest glutted with the green tree
Grew up again like a sweet wood inside me.
I had the deer browsing on my heart,
This was my mother; and I had the dirt.
Inside was well with the green well of love,
Outside privation, poverty, all dearth.
Thus like the pearl I came from hurt,
Like the prize pig I came from love.

Now I know what was wanting in my youth,
It was not water or a loving mouth.
It was what makes the apple-tree grow big,
The mountain fall, and the minnow die.
It was hard cash I needed at my root.
I now know that how I grew was due
To echoing buts and the empty bag—
My song was out of tune for a few notes.

Oh, my ghost cried, the charming chimes of coincidence!
I was born also there where distress collects the rents.
Guttersnipe gutless, I was planted in your guts there,
The tear of time my sperm. I rose from
The woe-womb of the want-raped mind,
Empty hunger cracked with stomach's thunder.
Remember the rags that flattered your frame
Froze hard and formed this flesh my rind.

So close over the chapter of my birth,
Blessed by distress, baptized by dearth.
How I swung myself from the tree's bough
Demonstrating death in my gay play:
How the germ of the sperm of this ghost like a worm
I caught from the cold comfort of never enough.
How by being miserable for myself I began,
And now am miserable for the mass of man.

RESOLUTION OF DEPENDENCE *

We poets in our youth begin in gladness
But thereof come in the end despondency and madness.
                WORDSWORTH: RESOLUTION AND INDEPENDENCE.

I encountered the crowd returning from amusements,
The Bournemouth Pavilion, or the marvellous gardens,
The Palace of Solace, the Empyrean Cinema: and saw
William Wordsworth was once, tawdrily conspicuous,
Obviously emulating the old man of the mountain-moor,
Traipsing along on the outskirts of the noisy crowd.

Remarkable I reflected that after all it is him.
The layers of time falling continually on Grasmere
        Churchyard,
The accumulation of year and year like calendar,

* See p. 54.

The acute superstition that Wordsworth is after all dead,
Should have succeeded in keeping him quiet and cold.
I resent the resurrection when I feel the updraft of fear.

But approaching me with a watch in his hand, he said:
'I fear you are early; I expected a man; I see
That already your private rebellion has been quelled.
Where are the violent gestures of the individualist?
I observe the absence of the erratic, the strange;
Where is the tulip, the rose, or the bird in hand?'

I had the heart to relate the loss of my charms,
The paradise pets I kept in my pocket, the bird,
The tulip trumpet, the penis water pistol;
I had the heart to have mourned them, but no word.
'I have done little reading,' I murmured, 'I have
Most of the time been trying to find an equation.'

He glanced over my shoulder at the evening promenade.
The passing people, like Saint Vitus, averted their eyes:
I saw his eyes like a bent pin searching for eyes
To grip and catch. 'It is a species,' he said,
'I feel I can hardly cope with—it is ghosts,
Trailing, like snails, an excrement of blood.

'I have passed my hand like a postman's into them;
The information I dropped in at once dropped out.'
'No,' I answered, 'they received your bouquet of daffodils,
They speak of your feeling for Nature even now.'
He glanced at his watch. I admired a face.
The town clock chimed like a cat in a well.

'Since the private rebellion, the personal turn,
Leads down to the river with the dead cat and dead dog,
Since the single act of protest like a foggy film
Looks like women bathing, the Irish Lakes, or Saint Vitus,
Susceptible of innumerable interpretations,
I can only advise a suicide or a resolution.'

'I can resolve,' I answered, 'if you can absolve.
Relieve me of my absurd and abysmal past.'
'I cannot relieve or absolve—the only absolution
Is final resolution to fix on the facts.
I mean more and less than Birth and Death; I also mean
The mechanical paraphernalia in between.

'Not you and not him, not me, but all of them.
It is the conspiracy of five hundred million
To keep alive and kick. This is the resolution,
To keep us alive and kicking with strength or joy.
The past's absolution is the present's resolution.
The equation is the interdependence of parts.'

ALLEGORY OF THE ADOLESCENT AND THE ADULT

It was when weather was Arabian I went
Over the downs to Alton where winds were wounded
With flowers and swathed me with aroma, I walked
Like Saint Christopher Columbus through a sea's welter
Of gaudy ways looking for a wonder.

Who was I, who knows, no one when I started,
No more than the youth who takes longish strides,
Gay with a girl and obstreperous with strangers,
Fond of some songs, not unusually stupid,
I ascend hills anticipating the strange.

Looking for a wonder I went on a Monday,
Meandering over the Alton down and moor;
When was it I went, an hour a year or more,
That Monday back, I cannot remember.
I only remember I went in a gay mood.

Hollyhock here and rock and rose there were,
I wound among them knowing they were no wonder;
And the bird with a worm and the fox in a wood
Went flying and flurrying in front, but I was
Wanting a worse wonder, a rarer one.

So I went on expecting miraculous catastrophe.
What is it, I whispered, shall I capture a creature
A woman for a wife, or find myself a king,
Sleep and awake to find Sleep is my kingdom?
How shall I know my marvel when it comes?

Then after long striding and striving I was where
I had so long longed to be, in the world's wind,
At the hill's top, with no more ground to wander
Excepting downward, and I had found no wonder.
Found only the sorrow that I had missed my marvel.

Then I remembered, was it the bird or worm,
The hollyhock, the flower or the strong rock,
Was it the mere dream of the man and woman
Made me a marvel? It was not. It was
When on the hilltop I stood in the world's wind.

The world is my wonder, where the wind
Wanders like wind, and where the rock is
Rock. And man and woman flesh on a dream.
I look from my hill with the woods behind,
And Time, a sea's chaos, below.

DOG, DOG IN MY MANGER

Dog, dog in my manger, drag at my heathen
Heart where the swearing smoke of Love
Goes up as I give everything to the blaze.
Drag at my fires, dog, drag at my altars
Where Aztec I over my tabernacle raise
The Absalom assassination I my murder.

Dog, drag off the gifts too much I load
My life as wishing tree too heavy with:
And, dog, guide you my stray down quiet roads
Where peace is—be my engine of myth
That, dog, so drags me down my time
Sooner I shall rest from my overload.

Dog, is my shake when I come from water,
The cataract of my days, as red as danger?
O my joy has jaws that seize in fangs
The gift and hand of love always I sought for.
They come to me with kingdoms for my paucity—
Dog, why is my tooth red with their charity?

Mourn, dog, mourn over me where I lie
Not dead but spinning on the pinpoint hazard,
The fiftieth angel. Bay, bay in the blizzard
That brings a tear to my snowman's eye
And buries us all in what we most treasured.
Dog, why do we die so often before we die?

Dog, good dog, trick do and make me take
Calmly the consciousness of the crime
Born in the blood simply because we are here.
Your father burns for his father's sake,

So will a son burn in the further time
Under the bush of joy you planted here.

Dog, dog, your bone I am, who tear my life
Tatterdemalion from me. From you I have no peace,
No life at all unless you break my bone,
No bed unless I sleep upon my grief
That without you we are too much alone,
No peace until no peace is a happy home:
O dog my god, how can I cease to praise!

TO MY MOTHER

Most near, most dear, most loved and most far,
Under the window where I often found her
Sitting as huge as Asia, seismic with laughter,
Gin and chicken helpless in her Irish hand,
Irresistible as Rabelais, but most tender for
The lame dogs and hurt birds that surround her,—
She is a procession no one can follow after
But be like a little dog following a brass band.

She will not glance up at the bomber, or condescend
To drop her gin and scuttle to a cellar,
But lean on the mahogany table like a mountain
Whom only faith can move, and so I send
O all my faith, and all my love to tell her
That she will move from mourning into morning.

ELEGY V

I

These errors loved no less than the saint loves arrows
Repeat, Love has left the world. He is not here.
O God, like Love revealing yourself in absence
So that, though farther than stars, like Love that
        sorrows
In separation, the desire in the heart of hearts
To come home to you makes you most manifest.
The booming zero spins as his halo where
Ashes of pride on all the tongues of sense
Crown us with negatives. O deal us in our deserts
The crumb of falling vanity. It is eucharist.

II

Everyone walking everywhere goes in a glow
Of geometrical progression, all meteors, in praise:
Hosannas on the tongues of the dumb shall raise
Roads for the gangs in chains to return to
God. They go hugging the traumas like halleluias
To the bodies that earn this beatitude. The Seven
Seas they crowd like the great sailing clippers,
Those homing migrants that, with their swallow-like
    sails set,
Swayed forward along the loneliness that opposed,
For nothing more than a meeting in heaven.

III

Therefore all things, in all three tenses,
Alone like the statue in an alcove of love,
Moving in obedient machinery, sleeping
Happy in impossible achievements, keeping
Close to each other, because the night is dark;
The great man dreaming on the stones of circum-
    stances,
The small wringing hands because rocks will not move:
The beast in its red kingdom, the star in its arc:
O all things, therefore, in shapes or in senses,
Know that they exist in the kiss of his Love.

IV

Incubus. Anæthetist with glory in a bag,
Foreman with a sweatbox and a whip. Asphyxiator
Of the ecstatic. Sergeant with a grudge
Against the lost lovers in the park of creation,
Fiend behind the fiend behind the fiend behind the
Friend. Mastodon with mastery, monster with an ache
At the tooth of the ego, the dead drunk judge:
Wheresoever Thou art our agony will find Thee
Enthroned on the darkest altar of our heartbreak
Perfect. Beast, brute, bastard. O dog my God!

THE DEATH OF YEATS

That dolphin-torn, that gong-tormented face
With the trumpets of Andromeda rose and spoke,
Blaring the pitiful blast and airing hope

So hope and pity flourished. Now the place
Cold is where he was, and the gold face
Shimmers only through the echoes of a poem.

The swan mourns on the long abandoned lake,
And on the verge gather the great Irish ghosts
Whom only he could from their myth awaken
And make a kingdom. The luckless and the lost
Got glory from the shake of his hand as he passed,
The lunar emperor whom Time could not break.

The boulder where he rested his shoulder is
Luckier than most, who know nothing of
The tremendous gentleness of the poet's kiss,
Thwarted by passion and impelled by love.
But the lost leaf lashed in a March above
Shares sense of action that is also his.

Saints on mountains or animals in the ground
Often found the feather of his wing on their lips
Proving and loving them; stars in their eclipse
Saw his face watching through intervening ground:
And the small fry like fish came up at the sound
Of his voice and listened to his whistling lips.

But now the cloud only shall hear: the ant,
The winter bulb under the ground, and the hidden
Stream be made dumb by his murmur in death,
Lying between the rock and the jealous plant.
No matter how close to the ground I bend, his breath
Is not for me, and all divisions widen.

Remember the lion's head and the blonde angel
Whispering in the chimney; remember the river
Singing sweeter and sweeter as it grows older and older;
Remember the moon sees things from a better angle.
O forget the echoes that go on for ever,
And remember that the great harp-breasted eagle
    Is now a grave.

SECULAR ELEGY V

O Golden Fleece she is where she lies tonight
Trammelled in her sheets like midsummer on a bed,
Kisses like moths flitter over her bright
Mouth, and, as she turns her head,
All space moves over to give her beauty room.

Where her hand, like a bird on the branch of her arm,
Droops its wings over the bedside as she sleeps,
There the air perpetually stays warm
Since, nested, her hand rested there. And she keeps
Under her green thumb life like a growing poem.

My nine-tiered tigress in the cage of sex
I feed with meat that you tear from my side
Crowning your nine months with the paradox:
The love that kisses with a homicide
In robes of red generation resurrects.

The bride who rides the hymenæal waterfall
Spawning all possibles in her pools of surplus,
Whom the train rapes going into a tunnel,
The imperial multiplicator nothing can nonplus:
My mother Nature is the origin of it all.

At Pharaoh's Feast and in the family cupboard,
Gay corpse, bright skeleton, and the fly in amber,
She sits with her laws like antlers from her forehead
Enmeshing everyone, with flowers and thunder
Adorning the head that destiny never worried.

AND NOW THERE IS NOTHING LEFT TO CELEBRATE

And now there is nothing left to celebrate
But the individual death in a ditch or a plane
Like a cock o' the north in a hurricane.
Out of the bogus glory and the synthetic hate,
The welter of nations and the speeches, O step down
You corpse in the gold and blue, out of a cloud,
My dragonfly, step down into your own:
The ditch and the dislocated wings and the cold
Kiss of the not to be monumental stone.

This is the only dignity left, the single
Death without purpose and without understanding
Like birds boys drop with catapults. Not comprehending
Denudes us of the personal aim and angle,
And so we are perfect sacrifice to nothing.

TO ANY MEMBER OF MY GENERATION

What was it you remember—the summer mornings
Down by the river at Richmond with a girl,
And as you kissed, clumsy in bathing costumes,
History guffawed in a rosebush. O what a warning—

If only we had known, if only we had known!
And when you looked in mirrors was this meaning
Plain as the pain in the centre of a pearl?
Horrible tomorrow in Teutonic postures
Making absurd the past we cannot disown?

Whenever we kissed we cocked the future's rifles
And from our wild-oat words, like dragon's teeth,
Death underfoot now arises; when we were gay
Dancing together in what we hoped was life,
Who was it in our arms but the whores of death
Whom we have found in our beds today, today?

NEWS OF THE WORLD 1

Cold shuttered loveless star, skulker in clouds,
   Streetwalker of the sky,
Where can you hide? No one will take you in.
Happy the morning lights up other worlds
As from sleep they turn a family of faces
To the houseproud sun. Outraged, you, outcast,
Leading your one-eyed sister through the night,
From door to door down the locked zodiac,
   Never come home.

'O WHO WILL SPEAK FROM A WOMB OR A CLOUD?'

Not less light shall the gold and the green lie
On the cyclonic curl and diamonded eye, than
Love lay yesterday on the breast like a beast.
Not less light shall God tread my maze of nerve
Than that great dread of tomorrow drove over
My maze of days. Nor less terrible that tread
Stomping upon your grave than I shall tread there.
Who is a god to haunt the tomb but Love?

Therefore I shall be there at morning and midnight,
Not with a straw in my hair and a tear as Ophelia
Floating along my sorrow, but I shall come with
The cabala of things, the cipher of nature, so that
With the mere flounce of a bird's feather crest
I shall speak to you where you sit in all trees,
Where you conspire with all things that are dead.
Who is so far that Love cannot speak to him?

So that no corner can hide you, no autumn of leaves
So deeply close over you that I shall not find you,
To stretch down my hand and sting you with life
Like poison that resurrects. O remember
How once the Lyrae dazzled and how the Novembers
Smoked, so that blood burned, flashed its mica,
And that was life. Now if I dip my hand in your grave
Shall I find it bloody with autumn and bright with stars?
Who is to answer if you will not answer me?

But you are the not yet dead, so cannot answer.
Hung by a hair's breadth to the breath of a lung,
Nothing you know of the hole over which you hang
But that it's dark and deep as tomorrow midnight.
I ask, but you cannot answer except with words
Which show me the mere interior of your fear,
The reverse face of the world. But this,
This is not death, the standing on the head
So that a sky is seen. O who
Who but the not yet born can tell me of my bourne?

Lie you there, lie you there, my never, never,
Never to be delivered daughter, so wise in ways
Where you perch like a bird beyond the horizon,
Seeing but not being seen, above our being?
Then tell me, shall the meeting ever be,
When the corpse dives back through the womb
To clasp his child before it ever was?
Who but the dead can kiss the not yet born?

Sad is space between a start and a finish,
Like the rough roads of stars, fiery and mad.
I go between birth and the urn, a bright ash
Soon blazed to blank, like a fire-ball. But
Nothing I bring from the before, no message,
No clue, no key, no answer. I hear no echo,
Only the sheep's blood dripping from the gun,
The serpent's tear like fire along the branch.
O who will speak from a womb or a cloud?

AT THE WAKE OF DYLAN THOMAS

I cannot take, even for such a purpose
As to honour this death by act of passion,
The word that wore the ring of his married breath.

I will not, where she clasps that curly nothing
Darkly in tears apart and the Dragon mourning,
Vex his cold nurse with a fragmentation of heart.

The vocable flies crying back into September
Away from my hand rather than remember
That speech, like a nagging wife, has been abandoned

By that master of the house so early waking
That the worm and the first bird found him larking
In a Welsh dawn with the paraclete of the word.

The air is full of dead verbs. There are ashes
In every dumbstruck mouth as the dead tide washes
Salt into the ulcer of a torn-out truth.

The merman floats face down on the sea of a poem.
The fish that flew from Wales to the back of doom
Lies cold on the stone of silence. The sea prevails.

Silence is what we hear in the roaring shell.
That first sea whence we rose and to which shall
Go down when all the words and all the heroes

Striking their lyres and attitudes in the middle
Of that burning sea which was a cradle,
Go down under that silence of that sea.

This son of pearl was walking beside water
Taking the pain of sand out of the oyster:
'We will make poems,' he said, 'simply from joy.'

And with the same wonder that the first amoeba
Stepped out of hydrogen and saw God's labour,
He goggled at glory as though it had just begun.

That burning babe! Crying from a bushel
Where he hid all his knowledge in the vessel
Of a divine and a divining image,

He triumphed up the trumpets of a cherub.
What is more for ever and more terrible
Than Abraham's kid and babe singing together?

Where there is a world of wise-eyed infants
Whose innocence has survived all living onslaughts
So that they always look newly arrived:

That cloudy boy harping among the graves
Will lead a doxological choir of loves.
O the dirt sings because all joy is magical.

What is the age of the one who never grieves
But to whom even Grief looks up and gives
An eye as green and new as an Eden leaf?

He is as old as that forsaken garden
Where only he and all the spellbound children
May freely in delight forget a fall.

That corpse of curls! O Dionysian
You will not come back through the door marked Man.
You went the wrong way. And the dawn was black.

But will the bird of fire submit to a lock and key?
The curls dance round the black cap and are free.
And any warty boy can double back.

Blind Harry and Sandy Traill before us
Showed that simply by dying we add to the manic
    chorus
And put the fear of God up all surviving.

And now he's gotten, first of all and foremost,
You, Dylan, too, the one undoubting Thomas,
The whistler in the dark he's taken from us.

Is it you, Cymric, or I who am so cold?
Was it a word and world America killed?
The brainstruck harp lies with its bright wings furled.

And as the winter closes coldly around
This puzzled and bitter necrosis of ground,
The images of death begin to glitter

Like falling icicles of an immanent
End. But I have known, for a moment,
The I undead and the dead who was my friend

Change places. Thus, if this poem speaks
A crown of joy or courage among cold rocks,
It is his spirit that animates my language.

Not in peace rest this whistling jaw now shall

But call and cry from every highblown hill:
'My voice and my grave open. I cannot die.'

But his ghost puts by this poem and goes down
Shaking its locks loudly into the dark,
And every word of the tongue follows him proudly.

TO FATHER GERARD MANLEY HOPKINS, S.J.

Overhead on a wing under heaven, treading
   Bright verbs on silence, writing red on hereafter,
He is for ever his feathers of sunset shedding,
   Bedding all beautiful in the far harder and softer
Breath of his word, bird in a thrash alighting

   All claws for the world that his heart is after,
The wide wonder that, into his talon of writing,
   Rose up, eyes open, to meet her emasculate master.

Father of further sons who wear your plumage
   For the good glory of the word, I speak for
All of us who inherit any merit of your image:
   O long-faced convert, look down and seek for
Worthiness in one of us, and let him speak
   Evangelizing the incomprehensible message.

SESTINA AT 34

I have come down half the overcrowded avenue
O Rhadamanthus, you to whose kingdom I journey
With seven children and several books on my shoulders
All screaming. I have left wounds on some pavements
So that your dogs and furies, hounding the heart to a stone,
Know where I go and where I have left my handmark.

I do not know the purpose of this journey
Between the big breasts and the grounded shoulders
Save that, in some way, by scribbling on pavements,
The man glorifies both himself and the godlike stone.
O morning strike bright along this flashing handmark
I scrawl across Time in its heavenly avenue!

When my love groans with babies and books on its shoulders
This is the proud load of the labouring pavement
Ascending into the sun to burnish a stone.
Christopher, you would know. Saint, set your handmark

On my child-ridden forehead. Water this avenue
With the sweat of an infant-carrier on his journey.

Heavy my heart walks ahead on the pavements
With her high-heel shoe my martyrdom on stone:
Everywhere the red heart lies is a landmark;
I am in the right road, the slaughter's avenue.
Mother of all things, Love, approve my journey
With a fair share of lightning on my shoulders.

I am at midday. Bells rage in the stone
Arch of the chest. The sky wears my handmark
Where I have held it. Summer the avenue
Here where Alighieri started a hotter journey,
Summer more suffering, manhood beating the shoulders,
Than any winter or April. And on the pavements

Fate, photographer, fixing, in shadow, his handwork;
Recording, for ever, in image along the avenue
The lies and the lives we lived. This is a journey
Dollied by the unsleeping eye. No head and shoulders
Shunning the sinning loin, but, naked as pavements,
Every step stopped a monument in stone.

Avenue of myrtles and births! Lovers like statues
Unmoving in evening, all Eden on a pavement!
O journey of hazard and heroes, monster and blizzard,
Who happy unhappy as I when I slip from my shoulders
The heavy bag of the ego, and, dead cat by the pavement,
Lie down under my God's immemorial stone?

THE TRUE CONFESSION OF GEORGE BARKER

BOOK I

Today, recovering from influenza,
      I begin, having nothing worse to do,
This autobiography that ends a
      Half of my life I'm glad I'm through.
O Love, what a bloody hullaballoo
      I look back at, shaken and sober,
When that intemperate life I view
      From this temperate October.

To nineteen hundred and forty-seven
    I pay the deepest of respects,
For during this year I was given
    Some insight into the other sex.
I was a victim, till forty-six,
    Of the rosy bed with bitches in it;
But now, in spite of all pretexes,
    I never sleep a single minute.

O fellow sailor on the tossing sea,
    O fleeting virgin in the night,
O privates, general in lechery,
    Shun, shun the bedroom like a blight:
Evade, O amorous acolyte,
    That pillow where your heart you bury—
For if the thing was stood upright
    It would become a cemetery.

I start with this apostrophe
    To all apostles of true love:
With your devotion visit me,
    Give me the glory of the dove
That dies of dereliction. Give
    True love to me, true love to me,
And in two shakes I will prove
    It's false to you and false to me.

Bright spawner, on your sandbank dwell
    Coldblooded as a plumber's pipe—
The procreatory ocean swell
    Warming, till they're over ripe,
The cockles of your cold heart, will
    Teach us true love can instil
Temperature into any type.

Does not the oyster in its bed
    Open a yearning yoni when
The full moon passes over head
    Feeling for pearls? O nothing, then,
Too low a form of life is, when
    Love, abandoning the cloister,
Can animate the bedded oyster,
    The spawning tiddler, and men.

Thus all of us, the pig and prince,
    The priest and the psychiatrist,

Owe everything to true love, since
    How the devil could we exist
If our parents had never kissed?
    All biographies, therefore,
—No matter what else they evince—
    Open, like prisons, with adore.

Remember, when you love another,
    Who demonstrably is a bitch,
Even Venus had a mother
    Whose love, like a silent aitch,
Incepted your erotic itch.
    Love, Love has the longest history,
For we can tell an ape his father
    Begot him on a mystery.

I, born in Essex thirty-four
    Essentially sexual years ago,
Stepped down, looked around, and saw
    I had been cast a little low
In the social register
    For the friends whom I now know.
Is a constable a mister?
    Bob's your uncle, even so.

Better men than I have wondered
    Why one's father could not see
That at one's birth he had blundered.
    His ill-chosen paternity
Embarrasses the fraternity
    Of one's friends who, living Huysmans,
Understandably have wondered
    At fatherhood permitted policemen.

So I, the son of an administer
    Of the facts of civil laws
Delight in uncivil and even sinister
    Violations. Thus my cause
Is simply, friend, to hell with yours.
    In misdemeanours I was nourished—
Learnt, like altruists in Westminster,
    By what duplicities one flourished.

At five, but feeling rather young,
    With a blue eye beauty over six,
Hand in hand and tongue to tongue
    I took a sin upon my sex.

Sin? It was pleasure. So I told her.
 And ever since, persisting in
Concupiscences no bolder
 My pleasure's been to undress sin.

What's the point of a confession
 If you have nothing to confess?
I follow the perjuring profession
 —O poet, lying to impress!—
But the beautiful lie in a beautiful dress
 Is the least heinous of my transgressions:
When a new one's added, 'O who was it?'
 Sigh the skeletons in my closet.

Ladybird, ladybird, come home, come home:
 Muse and mistress, wherever you are.
The evening is here and in the gloom
 Each bisexual worm burns like a star
And the love of man is crepuscular.
 In the day the world. But, at night, we,
Lonely on egoes dark and far
 Apart as worlds, between sea and sea,

Yearn to each other as the stars hold
 One another in fields together.
O rose of all the world, enfold
 Each weeping worm against the cold
Of the bitter ego's weather:
 To warm our isothermal pride
Cause, sometimes, Love, another
 To keep us by an unselfish side.

The act of human procreation
 —The rutting tongue, the grunt and shudder,
The sweat, the reek of defecation,
 The cradle hanging by the bladder,
The scramble up the hairy ladder,
 And from the thumping bed of Time
Immortality, a white slime,
 Sucking at its mother's udder—

The act of human procreation
 —The sore dug plugging, the lugged out bub,
The small man priming a lactation,
 The grunt, the drooping teat, the rub
Of gum and dug, the slobbing kiss:
 Behold the mater amabilis,

Sow with a saviour, messiah and cow,
　　Virgin and piglet, son and sow:—

The act of human procreation,
　　—O crown and flower, O culmination
Of perfect love throughout creation—
　　What can I compare to it?
O eternal butterflies in the belly,
O trembling of the heavenly jelly,
O miracle of birth! Really
　　We are excreted, like shit.

BOOK II

The Church, mediatrix between heaven
　　And human fallibility
Reminds us that the age of seven
　　Inaugurates the Reason we
Spend our prolonged seniority
　　Transgressing. Of that time I wish
I could recount a better story
　　Than finding a shilling and a fish.

But Memory flirts with seven veils
　　Peekabooing the accidental;
And what the devil it all entails
　　Only Sigmund Freud suspects.
I think my shilling and my fish
　　Symbolised a hidden wish
To sublimate these two affects:
　　Money is nice and so is sex.

The Angel of Reason, descending
　　On my seven year old head
Inscribed this sentence by my bed:
　　The pleasure of money is unending
But sex is satisfied is sex dead.
　　I tested to see if sex died
But, all my effort notwithstanding,
　　Have never found it satisfied.

Abacus of Reason, you have been
　　The instrument of my abuse,
The North Star I have never seen,
　　The trick for which I have no use:
The Reason, gadget of schoolmasters,
　　Pimp of the spirit, the smart alec,

Proud engineer of disasters,
    I see phallic: you, cephalic.

Happy those early days when I
    Attended an elementary school
Where seven hundred infant lives
    Flitted like gadflies on the stool—
(We discovered that contraceptives
    Blown up like balloons, could fly;)
We memorised the Golden Rule:
    Lie, lie, lie, lie.

For God's sake, Barker. This is enough
    Regurgitated obscenities,
Whimsicalities and such stuff.
    Where's the ineffable mystery,
The affiancing to affinities
    Of the young poet? The history
Of an evolving mind's love
    For the miseries and the humanities?

The sulking and son loving Muse
    Grabbed me when I was nine. She saw
It was a question of self abuse
    Or verses. I tossed off reams before
I cared to recognise their purpose.
    While other urchins were blowing up toads
With pipes of straw stuck in the arse,
    So was I, but I also wrote odes.

There was a priest, a priest, a priest,
    A Reverend of the Oratory
Who taught me history. At least
    He taught me the best part of his story.
Fat Father William, have you ceased
    To lead boys up the narrow path
Through the doors of the Turkish bath?
    I hope you're warm in Purgatory.

And in the yard of the tenement
    —The Samuel Lewis Trust—I played
While my father, for the rent,
    (Ten bob a week and seldom paid,)
Trudged London for a job. I went
    Skedaddling up the scanty years,
My learning, like the rent, in arrears,
    But sometimes making the grade.

O boring kids! In spite of Freud
    I find my childhood recollections
Much duller now than when I enjoyed
    It. The whistling affections,
All fitting wrong, toy railway sections
    Running in circles. Cruel as cats
Even the lower beasts avoid
    These inhumanitarian brats.

Since the Age of Reason's seven
    And most of one's friends over eight,
Therefore they're reasonable? Even
    Sensible Stearns or simpleton Stephen
Wouldn't claim that. I contemplate
    A world which, at crucial instants,
Surrenders to adulterant infants
    The adult onus to think straight.

At the bottom of this murky well
    My childhood, like a climbing root,
Nursed in dirt the simple cell
    That pays itself this sour tribute.
Track any poet to a beginning
    And in a dark room you discover
A little boy intent on sinning
    With an etymological lover.

I peopled my youth with the pulchritude
    Of heterae noun-anatomised;
The literature that I prized
    Was anything to do with the nude
Spirit of creative art
    Who whispered to me: 'Don't be queasy.
Simply write about a tart
    And there she is. The rest's easy.'

And thus, incepted in congenial
    Feebleness of moral power
I became a poet. Venial
    As a human misdemeanour,
Still, it gave me, prisoner
    In my lack of character,
Pig to the Circean Muse's honour.
    Her honour? Why, it's lying on her.

Dowered, invested and endowed
    With every frailty is the poet—

Yielding to wickedness because
    How the hell else can he know it?
The tempted poet must be allowed
    All ethical latitude. His small flaws
Bring home to him, in sweet breaches,
    The moral self indulgence teaches.

Where was I? Running, so to speak,
    To the adolescent seed? I
Found my will power rather weak
    And my appetites rather greedy
About the year of the General Strike,
    So I struck, as it were, myself:
Refused to do anything whatsoever, like
    Exercise books on a shelf.

Do Youth and Innocence prevail
    Over that cloudcuckoo clime
Where the seasons never fail
    And the clocks forget the time?
Where the peaks of the sublime
    Crown every thought; where every vale
Has its phantasy and phantasm
    And every midnight its orgasm?

I mooned into my fourteenth year
    Through a world pronouncing harsh
Judgements I could not quite hear
    About my verse, my young moustache
And my bad habits. In Battersea Park
    I almost heard strangers gossip
About my poems, almost remark
    The bush of knowledge on my lip.

Golden Calf, Golden Calf, where are you now
    Who lowed so mournfully in the dense
Arcana of my adolescence?
    No later anguish of bull or cow
Could ever be compared with half
    The misery of the amorous calf
Moonstruck in moonshine. How could I know
    You can't couple Love with any sense?

Poignant as a swallowed knife,
    Abstracted as a mannequin,
Remote as music, touchy as skin,
    Apotheosising life

Into a apocalypse,
    Young Love, taking Grief to wife,
And tasting the bitterness of her lips,
    Forgets it comes from swabbing gin.

The veils descend.   The unknown figure
    Is sheeted in the indecencies
Of shame and boils.   The nose gets bigger.
    The private parts, haired like a trigger,
Cock at a dream.   The infant cries
    Abandoned in its discarded larva,
Out of which steps, with bloodshot eyes,
    The man, the man, crying Ave, Ave!

BOOK III

That Frenchman really had the trick
    Of figure skating in this stanza:
But I, thank God, cannot read Gallic
    And so escape his influenza.
Above my head his rhetoric
    Asks emulation.   I do not answer.
It is as though I had not heard
    Because I cannot speak a word.

But I invoke him, dirty dog,
    As one barker to another:
Lift over me your clever leg,
    Teach me, you snail-swallowing frog,
To make out of a spot of bother
    Verses that shall catalogue
Every exaggerated human claim,
    Every exaggerated human aim.

I entreat you, frank villain,
    Get up out of your bed of dirt
And guide my hand. You are still an
    Irreprehensible expert
At telling Truth she's telling lies.
    Get up, liar; get up, cheat,
Look the bitch square in the eyes
    And you'll see what I entreat.

We share, frog, much the same well.
    I sense your larger spectre down
Here among the social swill
    Moving at ease beside my own

And the muckrakers I have known.
 No, not the magnitude I claim
That makes your shade loom like a tall
 Memorial but the type's the same.

You murdered with a knife, but I
 Like someone out of Oscar Wilde
Commemorate with a child
 The smiling victims as they die
Slewing in kisses and the lie
 Of generation. But we both killed.
I rob the grave you glorify,
 You glorify where I defiled.

O most adult adulterer
 Preside, now, coldly, over
My writing hand, as to it crowd
 The images of those unreal years
That, like a curtain, seem to stir
 Guiltily over what they cover—
Those unreal years, dreamshot and proud,
 When the vision first appears.

The unveiled vision of all things
 Walking towards us as we stand
And giving us, in either hand,
 The knowledge that the world brings
To those her most beloved, those
 Who, when she strikes with her wings,
Stand rooted, turned into a rose
 By terrestial understandings.

Come, sulking woman, bare as water,
 Dazzle me now as you dazzled me
When, blinded by your nudity,
 I saw the sex of the intellect,
The idea of the beautiful.
 The beautiful to which I, later,
Gave only mistrust and neglect,
 The idea no dishonour can annul.

Vanquished aviatrix, descend
 Again, long vanished vision whom
I have not known so long, assume
 Your former bright prerogative,

Illuminate, guide and attend
      Me now. O living vision, give
The grace, the verity; and send
      The spell that makes the poem live.

I sent a letter to my love
      In an envelope of stone,
And in between the letters ran
A crying torrent that began
To grow till it was bigger than
Nyanza or the heart of man.
I sent a letter to my love
      In an envelope of stone.

I sent a present to my love
      In a black bordered box,
A clock that beats a time of tears
As the stricken midnight nears
And my love weeps as she hears
The armageddon of the years.
I sent my love the present
      In a black bordered box.

I sent a liar to my love
      With his hands full of roses
But she shook her yellow and curled
Curled and yellow hair and cried
The rose is dead of all the world
Since my only love has lied.
I sent a liar to my love
      With roses in his hands.

I sent a daughter to my love
      In a painted cradle.
She took her up at her left breast
And rocked her to a mothered rest
Singing a song that what is best
Loves and loves and forgets the rest.
I sent a daughter to my love
      In a painted cradle.

I sent a letter to my love
      On a sheet of stone.
She looked down and as she read
She shook her yellow hair and said
Now he sleeps alone instead

Of many a lie in many a bed.
I sent a letter to my love
    On a sheet of stone.

O long-haired virgin by my tree
    Among whose forks hung enraged
A sexual passion not assuaged
    By you, its victim—knee to knee,
Locked sweating in the muscled dark
    Lovers, as new as we were, spill
The child on grass in Richmond Park.

Crying the calf runs wild among
    Hills of the heart are memories:
Long long the white kiss of the young
    Rides the lip and only dies
When the whole man stalks among
    The crosses where remorse lies—
Then, then the vultures on the tongue
    Rule empires of white memories.

Legendary water, where, within
    Gazing, my own face I perceive,
How can my self-disgust believe
    This was my angel at seventeen?
Stars, stars and the world, seen
    Untouched by crystal. Retrieve
The morning star what culprit can
    Who knows his blood spins in between?

Move backward, loving rover, over
    All those unfeathered instances
I tar with kiss of pitch, the dirty
    Lip-service that a jaded thirty
Renders its early innocences.
    Pointer of recollection, show
The deaths in feather that now cover
    The tarry spot I died below.

What sickening snot-engendered bastard
    Likes making an idiot of himself?
I wish to heaven I had mastered
    The art of living like a dastard
While still admiring oneself.
    About my doings, past and recent,
I hear Disgust—my better half—
    'His only decency's indecent.'

Star-fingered shepherdess of Sleep
  Come, pacify regret, remorse;
And let the suffering black sheep
  Weep on the bed it made. Let pause
The orphic criminal to perceive
  That in the venue of his days
All the crimes look back and grieve
  Over lies no grief allays.

Sleep at my side again, my bride,
  As on our marriage bed you turned
Into a flowering bush that burned
  All the proud flesh away. Beside
Me now, you, shade of my departed
  Broken, abandoned bride, lie still,
And I shall hold you close until
  Even our ghosts are broken hearted.

So trusting, innocent, and unknowing
  What the hazards of the world
Storm and strike a marriage with,
  We did not hear the grinders blowing
But sailed our kisses round the world
  Ignorant of monsters and the vaster
Cemetery of innocence. This wreath
  Dreams over our common disaster.

But bright that nuptials to me now
  As when, the smiling foetus carried
Rose-decked today instead of tomorrow,
  Like country cousins we were married
By the pretty bullying embryo
  And you, my friend: I will not borrow
Again the serge suit that I carried
  Through honey of moon to sup of sorrow.

Loving the hand, gentle the reproving;
  Loving the heart, deeper the understanding;
Deeper the understanding, larger the confiding
  For the hurt heart's hiding.
Forgiving the hand, love without an ending
  Walks back on water; giving and taking
Both sides become by simple comprehending:
  Deeper the love, greater the heart at breaking.

BOOK IV

O Bishop Andrewes, Bishop Berkeley,
    John Peale Bishop and Bishop's Park,
I look through my ego darkly
    But all that I perceive is dark:
Episcopally illuminate
    My parochial testaments
And with your vestal vested vestments
    Tenderly invest my state.

Let Grace, like lace, descend upon me
    And dignify my wingless shoulder:
Let Grace, like space, lie heavy on me
    And make me seem a little older,
A little nobler; let Grace sidle
    Into my shameful bed, and, curling
About me in a psychic bridal,
    Prove that even Grace is a darling.

The moon is graceful in the sky,
    The bird is graceful in the air,
The girl is graceful, too, so why
    The devil should I ever care
Capitulating to despair?
    Since Grace is clearly everywhere
And I am either here or there
    I'm pretty sure I've got my share.

Grace whom no man ever held,
    Whose breast no human hand has pressed,
Grace no lover has undressed
    Because she's naked as a beast—
Grace will either gild or geld,
    Sweet Grace abounding into bed
Jumps to it hot as a springald—
    After a brief prayer is said.

Come to me, Grace, and I will take
    You close into my wicked hands,
And when you come, make no mistake,
    I'll disgrace you at both ends.
We'll grace all long throughout the night
    And as the morning star looks in
And blanches at the state we're in,—
    We'll grace again to be polite.

For Marriage is a state of grace.
    So many mutual sacrifices
Infalliably induce a peace
    Past understanding or high prices.
So many forgivenesses for so many
    Double crossings and double dealings—
I know that the married cannot have any
    But the most unselfish feelings.

But the wise Church, contemplating
    The unnatural demands
That marriage and the art of mating
    Make on egoists, commands
We recognise as sacramental
    A union otherwise destined
To break in every anarchic wind
    Broken by the temperamental.

Off the Tarpeian, for high treason,
    Tied in a bag with a snake and a cock,
The traitor trod the Roman rock.
    But in the bag, for a better reason,
The married lovers, cock and snake,
    Lie on a Mount of Venus. Traitor
Each to each, fake kissing fake,
    So punished by a betrayed creator.

'The willing union of two lives.'
    This is, the Lords of Justice tell us,
The purpose of the connubial knot.
    But I can think of only one
Function that at best contrives
    To join the jealous with the jealous,
And what this function joins is not
    Lives, but the erogenous zone.

I see the young bride move among
    The nine-month trophies of her pride,
And though she is not really young
    And only virtually a bride,
She knows her beauties now belong
    With every other treasure of her
Past and future, to her lover:
    But her babies work out wrong.

I see the bridegroom in his splendour
    Rolling like an unbridalled stallion,

Handsome, powerful and tender,
    And passionate as an Italian—
And nothing I could say would lend a
    Shock of more surprise and pride
Than if I said that this rapscallion
    Was necking with his legal bride.

I knew a beautiful courtesan
    Who, after service, would unbosom
Her prettier memories, like blossom,
    At the feet of the weary man:
'I'm such a sensitive protoplasm,'
    She whispered, when I was not there,
'That I experience an orgasm
    If I *touch* a millionaire.'

Lying with, about, upon,
    Everything and everyone,
Every happy little wife
    Miscegenates once in a life,
And every pardonable groom
    Needs, sometimes, a change of womb,
Because, although damnation may be,
    Society needs every baby.

It takes a sacrament to keep
    Any man and woman together:
Birds of a forgivable feather
    Always flock and buck together:
And in our forgivable sleep
    What birdwatcher will know whether
God Almighty sees we keep
    Religiously to one another?

I have often wondered what method
    Governed the heavenly mind when
It made as audience to God
    The sycophant, the seaman sod,
The solipsist—in short, men.
    Even the circus stepping mare
Lifts her nose into the air
    In the presence of this paragon.

For half a dozen simple years
    We lived happily, so to speak,
On twenty-seven shillings a week;
    And, when worried and in tears,

My mercenary wife complained
    That we could not afford our marriage,
'It's twice as much,' I explained,
    'As MacNeice pays for his garage.'

I entertained the Marxian whore—
    I am concerned with economics,
And naturally felt that more
    Thought should be given to our stomachs.
But when I let my fancy dwell
    On anything below the heart,
I found my thoughts, and hands as well,
    Resting upon some private part.

I sat one morning on the can
    That served us for a lavatory
Composing some laudatory
    Verses on the state of man:
My wife called from the kitchen dresser:
    'There's someone here from Japan.
He wants you out there. As Professor.
    Oh, yes. The War just began.'

So Providence engineered her
    Circumstantial enigmas,
And the crown of the objector
    Was snatched from me. In wars
The conscientious protester
    Preserves, as worlds sink to force,
The dignified particular.
    Particularly one, of course.

'The hackneyed rollcall of chronology'—
    Thus autobiography to de Quincey.
And I can understand it, since he
    Lived like a footnote to philology.
But the archangelic enumeration
    Of unpredictable hejiras,—
These, with a little exaggeration,
    I can adduce for my admirers.

And so, when I saw you, nightmare island,
    Fade into the autumnal night,
I felt the tears rise up for my land,
    But somehow these tears were not quite

As sick as when my belly laughed
    Remembering England had given me
The unconditional liberty
    To do a job for which I starved.

BOOK V

Almighty God, by whose ill will
    I was created with conscience;
By whose merciful malevolence
    I shall be sustained until
My afflictions fulfil
    His victories; by whose dispensation
Whatever I have had of sense
    Has obfuscated my salvation—

Good God, grant that, in reviewing
    My past life, I may remember
Everything I did worth doing
    Seemed rather wicked in persuing:
Grant, Good God, I shall have remitted
    Those earthly pleasures beyond number
I necessarily omitted,
    Exhausted by the ones committed.

Good God, let me recollect
    Your many mercies, tall and short,
The blousy blondes, the often necked,
    And those whom I should not have thought
Given wisely to me; nor let forget
    My grateful memory the odd
Consolers, too frequently brunette,
    Who charged me for your mercies, God.

Good God, let me so recall
    My grave omissions and commissions
That I may repent them all,
    —The places, faces and positions;
Together with the few additions
    A feeble future may instal.
Good God, only mathematicians
    Consider Love an ordinal.

Good God, so wisely you provided
    The loving heart I suffer with,

That I am constantly divided
    By a deep love for all beneath
Me. Every man knows well
    He rides his own whores down to hell,
But, good God, every knackered horse
    Was, originally, yours.

Good God, receive my thanksgiving
    For all the wonders I have seen
(And all the blunders in between)
    In my thirty odd years of living.
I have seen the morning rise
    And I have seen the evening set—
Anything different would surprise
    Me even more profoundly yet.

Good God, receive my gratitude
    For favours undeserved: accept
This truly heartfelt platitude:
    You gave me too much latitude
And so I hanged myself. I kept
    Your mercy, Good God, in a box
But out at midnight Justice crept
    And axed me with a paradox.

O loving kindness of the knife
    That cuts the proud flesh from the rotten
Ego and cuts the rotten life
    Out of the rotten bone! No, not an
Ounce of sparrow is forgotten
    As that butchering surgeon cuts
And rummages among my guts
    To succour what was misbegotten.

I confess, my God, this lonely
    Derelict of a night, when I
And not the conscious I only
    Feel all the responsibility—
(But the simple and final fact
    That we are better than we act,
For this fortunate windfall
    We are not responsible at all)—

I confess, my God, that in
    The hotbed of the monkey sin
I saw you through a guilt of hair

Standing lonely as a mourner
Silent in the bedroom corner
    Knowing you need not be there:
I saw the genetic man had torn
    A face away from your despair.

I confess, my God, my Good,
    I have not wholly understood
The nature of our holiness:
    The striking snake errs even less
Not questioning; the physicist
    Not asking why all things exist
Serves better than those who advance a
    Question to which life's the answer.

But, O my God, the human purpose,
    If at all I can perceive
A purpose in the life I live,
    Is to hide in the glass horse
Of our doubt until the pity
    Of heaven opens up a city
Of absolute belief to us,
    Because our silence is hideous

And our doubt more miserable
    Than certainty of the worst would be.
Like infinitely pitiable
    Ghosts who do not even know
They waver between reality
    And unreality, we go
About our lives and cannot see
    Even why we suffer so.

I know only that the heart
    Doubting every real thing else
Does not doubt the voice that tells
    Us that we suffer. The hard part
At the dead centre of the soul
    Is an age of frozen grief
No vernal equinox of relief
    Can mitigate, and no love console.

Then, O my God, by the hand
    This star-wondering grief takes
The world that does not understand
    Its own miseries and mistakes

And leads it home. Not yet, but later
    To lean an expiated head
On the shoulder of a creator
    Who knows where all troubles lead.

BOOK VI

I looked into my heart to write.
    In that red sepulchre of lies
I saw that all man cherishes
    Goes proud, rots and perishes
Till through that red room pitiless night
    Trails only knife-tongued memories
To whose rags cling, shrieking, bright
    Unborn and aborted glories.

And vinegar the mirages
    That, moaning they were possible
Charge me with the unholy No.
    The unaccomplished issue rages
Round the ringed heart like a bull
    Bellowing for birth. But even so
Remorselessly the clock builds ages
    Over its lifeless embryo.

Ruined empire of dissipated time,
    Perverted aim, abused desire,
The monstrous amoeba cannot aspire
    But sinks down into the cold slime
Of Eden as Ego. It is enough
    To sink back in the primal mud
Of the first person. For what could
    Equal the paradise of Self Love?

The necessary angel is
    The lie. Behind us, all tongue splayed,
The lie triumphant and tremendous
    Shields us from what we are afraid
Of seeing when we turn—the Abyss
    Giving back a face of small
Twisted fear—and this is all,
    To conquer the lie, that we possess.

Come, corybantic self-delusion,
    And whisper such deceptions to
Me now that I will not care who
    Or what you are, save palliation

Of the question marked heart. Let rest
  The harp and horror horned head upon
That green regenerative breast
  By whose great law we still live on.

Now from my window looking down
  I see the lives of those for whom
My love has still a little room
  Go suffering by. I see my own
Stopped, like a stair carpet, at this story
  Not worth the telling. O memory
Let the gilded images of joys known
  Return, and be consolatory!

Bitter and broken as the morning
  Valentine climbs the glaciered sky
With a spike in his foot. The lover's warning
  Blazes a sunrise on our misery:
Look down, look down, and see our grey
  And loveless rendezvous, Valentine:
Fold, then, in grief and cast away
  The love that is not yours or mine.

On this day of the innocent
  And happy lovers, let me praise
The grotesque bestiary of those
  Who love too much. Monsters invent
Monsters, like babies gypsies raise
  In odd bottles for freak shows—
These love too deeply for the skin.
  Whose bottle are you monster in?

The grotesque bestiary where
  Coiled the pythoness of sighs,
To keep a beast within her there
  Crushes him in her clutch of vice
Till, misshapen to her passion, dead,
  The lion of the heart survives
By suffering kisses into knives
  And a spiked pit into a bed.

Stand in your sad and golden haired
  Accusation about me now,
My sweet seven misled into life.
  O had the hot headed seaman spared
Those breast-baring ova on their bough,
  There'd be no aviary of my grief,

No sweet seven standing up in sorrow
    Uttering songs of joy declared

Of joy declared, as birds extol
    The principle of natural pleasure
Not knowing why. Declare to all
    Who disbelieve it, that delight
Naturally inhabits the soul.
    I look down at you to assure
My sense of wrong: but you declare
    Whatever multiplies is right.

I looked into my heart to write.
    But when I saw that cesspit twisted
With the disgusting laws that live
    In royal domination under
The surface of our love, that writhe
    Among our prizes, they attested
The putrefaction of our love
    Spoils the spawner of its grandeur.

BOOK VII

Today the twenty-sixth of February,
    I, halfway to the minute through
The only life I want to know,
    Intend to end this rather dreary
Joke of an autobiography.
    Thirty-five years is quite enough
Of one's own company. I grow
    A bit sick of the terrestrial stuff

And the celestial nonsense. Swill
    Guzzle and copulate and guzzle
And copulate and swill until
    You break up like a jigsaw puzzle
Shattered with smiles. The idiotic
    Beatitude of the sow in summer
Conceals a gibbering neurotic
    Sowing hot oats to get warmer.

Look on your handwork, Adam, now
    As I on mine, and do not weep.
The detritus is us. But how
    Could you and I ever hope to keep
That glittering sibyl bright who first
    Confided to us, perfect, once,

The difference between the best and the worst?
    That vision is our innocence.

But we shall step into our grave
    Not utterly divested of
The innocence our nativity
    Embodies a god in. O bear,
Inheritors, all that you have,
    The sense of good, with much care
Through the dirty street of life
    And the gutter of our indignity.

I sense the trembling in my hand
    Of that which will not ever lower
Its bright and pineal eye and wing
    To any irony, nor surrender
The dominion of my understanding
    To that Apollyonic power
Which, like the midnight whispering
    Sea, surrounds us with dark splendour.

Enisled and visionary, mad,
    Alive in the catacomb of the heart,
O lonely diviner, lovely diviner, impart
    The knowledge of the good and the bad
To us in our need. Emblazon
    Our instincts upon your illumination
So that the rot's revealed, and the reason
    Shown crucified upon our desolation.

You, all whom I coldly took
    And hid my head and horns among,
Shall go caterwauling down with me
    Like a frenzy of chained doves. For, look!
We wailing ride down eternity
    Tongue-tied together. We belong
To those with whom we shook the suck
    And dared an antichrist to be.

Get rags, get rags, all angels, all
    Laws, all principles, all deities,
Get rags, come down and suffocate
    The orphan in its flaming cradle,
Snuff the game and the candle, for our state
    —Insufferable among mysteries—
Makes the worms weep. Abate, abate
    Your justice. Excecute us with mercies!

DYLAN THOMAS

(1914-1953)

ESPECIALLY WHEN THE OCTOBER WIND

Especially when the October wind
With frosty fingers punishes my hair,
Caught by the crabbing sun I walk on fire
And cast a shadow crab upon the land,
By the sea's side, hearing the noise of birds,
Hearing the raven cough in winter sticks,
My busy heart who shudders as she talks
Sheds the syllabic blood and drains her words.

Shut, too, in a tower of words, I mark
On the horizon walking like the trees
The wordy shapes of women, and the rows
Of the star-gestured children in the park.
Some let me make you of the vowelled beeches,
Some of the oaken voices, from the roots
Of many a thorny shire tell you notes,
Some let me make you of the water's speeches.

Behind a pot of ferns the wagging clock
Tells me the hour's word, the neural meaning
Flies on the shafted disk, declaims the morning
And tells the windy weather in the cock.
Some let me make you of the meadow's signs;
The signal grass that tells me all I know
Breaks with the wormy winter through the eye.
Some let me tell you of the raven's sins.

Especially when the October wind
(Some let me make you of autumnal spells,
The spider-tongued, and the loud hill of Wales)
With fists of turnips punishes the land,

Some let me make you of the heartless words.
The heart is drained that, spelling in the scurry
Of chemic blood, warned of the coming fury.
By the sea's side hear the dark-vowelled birds.

A SEQUENCE OF SONNETS

I

ALTARWISE BY OWL-LIGHT IN THE
HALF-WAY HOUSE

Altarwise by owl-light in the half-way house
The gentleman lay graveward with his furies;
Abaddon in the hangnail cracked from Adam,
And, from his fork, a dog among the fairies,
The atlas-eater with a jaw for news,
Bit out the mandrake with to-morrow's scream.
Then, penny-eyed, that gentleman of wounds,
Old cock from nowheres and the heaven's egg,
With bones unbuttoned to the half-way winds,
Hatched from the windy salvage on one leg,
Scraped at my cradle in a walking word
That night of time under the Christward shelter:
I am the long world's gentleman, he said,
And share my bed with Capricorn and Cancer.

II

DEATH IS ALL METAPHORS, SHAPE
IN ONE HISTORY;

Death is all metaphors, shape in one history;
The child that sucketh long is shooting up,
The planet-ducted pelican of circles
Weans on an artery the gender's strip;
Child of the short spark in a shapeless country
Soon sets alight a long stick from the cradle;
The horizontal cross-bones of Abaddon,
You by the cavern over the black stairs,
Rung bone and blade, the verticals of Adam,

And, manned by midnight, Jacob to the stars.
Hairs of your head, then said the hollow agent,
Are but the roots of nettles and of feathers
Over these groundworks thrusting through a pavement
And hemlock-headed in the wood of weathers.

III

FIRST THERE WAS THE LAMB
ON KNOCKING KNEES

First there was the lamb on knocking knees
And three dead seasons on a climbing grave
That Adam's wether in the flock of horns,
Butt of the tree-tailed worm that mounted Eve,
Horned down with skullfoot and the skull of toes
On thunderous pavements in the garden time;
Rip of the vaults, I took my marrow-ladle
Out of the wrinkled undertaker's van,
And Rip Van Winkle from a timeless cradle,
Dipped me breast-deep in the descended bone;
The black ram, shuffling of the year, old winter,
Alone alive among his mutton fold,
We rung our weathering changes on the ladder,
Said the antipodes, and twice spring chimed.

IV

WHAT IS THE METRE OF THE DICTIONARY?

What is the metre of the dictionary?
The size of genesis? the short spark's gender?
Shade without shape? the shape of Pharaoh's echo?
(My shape of age nagging the wounded whisper).
Which sixth of wind blew out the burning gentry?
(Questions are hunchbacks to the poker marrow.)
What of a bamboo man among your acres?
Corset the boneyards for a crooked boy?
Button your bodice on a hump of splinters,
My camel's eyes will needle through the shroud.
Love's reflection of the mushroom features,
Stills snapped by night in the bread-sided field,

Once close-up smiling in the wall of pictures,
Arc-lamped thrown back upon the cutting flood.

V

AND FROM THE WINDY WEST
CAME TWO-GUNNED GABRIEL

And from the windy West came two-gunned Gabriel,
From Jesu's sleeve trumped up the king of spots,
The sheath-decked jacks, queen with a shuffled heart;
Said the fake gentleman in suit of spades,
Black-tongued and tipsy from salvation's bottle.
Rose my Byzantine Adam in the night.
For loss of blood I fell on Ishmael's plain,
Under the milky mushrooms slew my hunger,
A climbing sea from Asia had me down
And Jonah's Moby snatched me by the hair,
Cross-stroked salt Adam to the frozen angel
Pin-legged on pole-hills with a black medusa
By waste seas where the white bear quoted Virgil
And sirens singing from our lady's sea-straw.

VI

CARTOON OF SLASHES ON THE
TIDE-TRACED CRATER

Cartoon of slashes on the tide-traced crater,
He in a book of water tallow-eyed
By lava's light split through the oyster vowels
And burned sea silence on a wick of words.
Pluck, cock, my sea eye, said medusa's scripture,
Lop, love, my fork tongue, said the pin-hilled nettle;
And love plucked out the stinging siren's eye,
Old cock from nowheres lopped the minstrel tongue
Till tallow I blew from the wax's tower
The fats of midnight when the salt was singing;
Adam, time's joker, on a witch of cardboard
Spelt out the seven seas, an evil index,
The bagpipe-breasted ladies in the deadweed
Blew out the blood gauze through the wound of manwax.

VII

NOW STAMP THE LORD'S PRAYER ON A GRAIN OF RICE

Now stamp the Lord's Prayer on a grain of rice,
A Bible-leaved of all the written woods
Strip to this tree: a rocking alphabet,
Genesis is the root, the scarecrow word,
And one light's language in the book of trees.
Doom on deniers at the wind-turned statement.
Time's tune my ladies with the teats of music,
The scaled sea-sawers, fix in a naked sponge
Who sucks the bell-voiced Adam out of magic,
Time, milk, and magic, from the world beginning.
Time is the tune my ladies lend their heartbreak,
From bald pavilions and the house of bread
Time tracks the sound of shape on man and cloud,
On rose and icicle the ringing handprint.

VIII

THIS WAS THE CRUCIFIXION ON THE MOUNTAIN

This was the crucifixion on the mountain,
Time's nerve in vinegar, the gallow grave
As tarred with blood as the bright thorns I wept;
The world's my wound, God's Mary in her grief,
Bent like three trees and bird-papped through her shift,
With pins for teardrops is the long wound's woman.
This was the sky, Jack Christ, each minstrel angle
Drove in the heaven-driven of the nails
Till the three-coloured rainbow from my nipples
From pole to pole leapt round the snail-waked world.
I by the tree of thieves, all glory's sawbones,
Unsex the skeleton this mountain minute,
And by this blowclock witness of the sun
Suffer the heaven's children through my heartbeat.

IX

FROM THE ORACULAR ARCHIVES AND THE PARCHMENT

From the oracular archives and the parchment,
Prophets and fibre kings in oil and letter,
The lamped calligrapher, the queen in splints,
Buckle to lint and cloth their natron footsteps,
Draw on the glove of prints, dead Cairo's henna
Pour like a halo on the caps and serpents.
This was the resurrection in the desert,
Death from a bandage, rants the mask of scholars
Gold on such features, and the linen spirit
Weds my long gentleman to dusts and furies;
With priest and pharaoh bed my gentle wound,
World in the sand, on the triangle landscape,
With stones of odyssey for ash and garland
And rivers of the dead around my neck.

X

LET THE TALE'S SAILOR FROM A CHRISTIAN VOYAGE

Let the tale's sailor from a Christian voyage
Atlaswise hold half-way off the dummy bay
Time's ship-racked gospel on the globe I balance:
So shall winged harbours through the rockbirds' eyes
Spot the blown word, and on the seas I image
December's thorn screwed in a brow of holly.
Let the first Peter from a rainbow's quayrail
Ask the tall fish swept from the bible east,
What rhubarb man peeled in her foam-blue channel
Has sown a flying garden round that sea-ghost?
Green as beginning, let the garden diving
Soar, with its two bark towers, to that Day
When the worm builds with the gold straws of venom
My nest of mercies in the rude, red tree.

AFTER THE FUNERAL

(In memory of Ann Jones)

After the funeral, mule praises, brays,
Windshake of sailshaped ears, muffle-toed tap
Tap happily of one peg in the thick
Grave's foot, blinds down the lids, the teeth in black,
The spittled eyes, the salt ponds in the sleeves,
Morning smack of the spade that wakes up sleep,
Shakes a desolate boy who slits his throat
In the dark of the coffin and sheds dry leaves,
That breaks one bone to light with a judgment clout,
After the feast of tear-stuffed time and thistles
In a room with a stuffed fox and a stale fern,
I stand, for this memorial's sake, alone
In the snivelling hours with dead, humped Ann
Whose hooded, fountain heart once fell in puddles
Round the parched worlds of Wales and drowned each sun
(Though this for her is a monstrous image blindly
Magnified out of praise; her death was a still drop;
She would not have me sinking in the holy
Flood of her heart's fame; she would lie dumb and deep
And need no druid of her broken body).
But I, Ann's bard on a raised hearth, call all
The seas to service that her wood-tongued virtue
Babble like a bellbuoy over the hymning heads,
Bow down the walls of the ferned and foxy woods
That her love sing and swing through a brown chapel,
Bless her bent spirit with four, crossing birds.
Her flesh was meek as milk, but this skyward statue
With the wild breast and blessed and giant skull
Is carved from her in a room with a wet window
In a fiercely mourning house in a crooked year.
I know her scrubbed and sour humble hands
Lie with religion in their cramp, her threadbare
Whisper in a damp word, her wits drilled hollow,
Her fist of a face died clenched on a round pain;
And sculptured Ann is seventy years of stone.
These cloud-sopped, marble hands, this monumental
Argument of the hewn voice, gesture and psalm,
Storm me forever over her grave until
The stuffed lung of the fox twitch and cry Love
And the strutting fern lay seeds on the black sill.

A REFUSAL TO MOURN THE DEATH, BY FIRE, OF A CHILD IN LONDON

Never until the mankind making
Bird beast and flower
Fathering and all humbling darkness
Tells with silence the last light breaking
And the still hour
Is come of the sea tumbling in harness

And I must enter again the round
Zion of the water bead
And the synagogue of the ear of corn
Shall I let pray the shadow of a sound
Or sow my salt seed
In the least valley of sackcloth to mourn

The majesty and burning of the child's death.
I shall not murder
The mankind of her going with a grave truth
Nor blaspheme down the stations of the breath
With any further
Elegy of innocence and youth.

Deep with the first dead lies London's daughter,
Robed in the long friends,
The grains beyond age, the dark veins of her mother,
Secret by the unmourning water
Of the riding Thames.
After the first death, there is no other.

POEM IN OCTOBER

It was my thirtieth year to heaven
Woke to my hearing from harbour and neighbour wood
        And the mussel pooled and the heron
                Priested shore
                The morning beckon
With water praying and call of seagull and rook
And the knock of sailing boats on the net webbed wall
                Myself to set foot
                That second
        In the still sleeping town and set forth.

My birthday began with the water-
Birds and the birds of the winged trees flying my name
  Above the farms and the white horses
    And I rose
    In rainy autumn
And walked abroad in a shower of all my days.
High tide and the heron dived when I took the road
    Over the border
     And the gates
Of the town closed as the town awoke.

  A springful of larks in a rolling
Cloud and the roadside bushes brimming with whistling
  Blackbirds and the sun of October
    Summery
    On the hill's shoulder,
Here were fond climates and sweet singers suddenly
Come in the morning where I wandered and listened
    To the rain wringing
     Wind blow cold
In the wood faraway under me.

  Pale rain over the dwindling harbour
And over the sea wet church the size of a snail
  With its horns through mist and the castle
    Brown as owls
    But all the gardens
Of spring and summer were blooming in the tall tales
Beyond the border and under the lark full cloud.
    There could I marvel
    My birthday
Away but the weather turned around.

  It turned away from the blithe country
And down the other air and the blue altered sky
  Streamed again a wonder of summer
    With apples
    Pears and red currants
And I saw in the turning so clearly a child's
Forgotten mornings when he walked with his mother
    Through the parables
    Of sun light
And the legends of the green chapels

  And the twice told fields of infancy
That his tears burned my cheeks and his heart moved in
   mine.

These were the woods the river and sea
              Where a boy
   In the listening
Summertime of the dead whispered the truth of his joy
To the trees and the stones and the fish in the tide.
              And the mystery
              Sang alive
Still in the water and singingbirds.

And there could I marvel my birthday
Away but the weather turned around.   And the true
   Joy of the long dead child sang burning
              In the sun.
   It was my thirtieth
Year to heaven stood there then in the summer noon
Though the town below lay leaved with October blood.
              O may my heart's truth
              Still be sung
On this high hill in a year's turning.

DO NOT GO GENTLE INTO THAT GOOD NIGHT

Do not go gentle into that good night,
Old age should burn and rave at close of day;
Rage, rage against the dying of the light.

Though wise men at their end know dark is right,
Because their words has forked no lightning they
Do not go gentle into that good night.

Good men, the last wave by, crying how bright
Their frail deeds might have danced in a green bay,
Rage, rage against the dying of the light.

Wild men who caught and sang the sun in flight,
And learn, too late, they grieved it on its way,
Do not go gentle into that good night.

Grave men, near death, who see with blinding sight
Blind eyes could blaze like meteors and be gay,
Rage, rage against the dying of the light.

And you, my father, there on the sad height,
Curse, bless, me now with your fierce tears, I pray.
Do not go gentle into that good night.
Rage, rage against the dying of the light.

FERN HILL

Now as I was young and easy under the apple boughs
About the lilting house and happy as the grass was green,
    The night above the dingle starry,
        Time let me hail and climb
    Golden in the heydays of his eyes,
And honoured among wagons I was prince of the apple
        towns
And once below a time I lordly had the trees and leaves
        Trail with daisies and barley
    Down the rivers of the windfall light.

And as I was green and carefree, famous among the barns
About the happy yard and singing as the farm was home,
    In the sun that is young once only,
        Time let me play and be
    Golden in the mercy of his means,
And green and golden I was huntsman and herdsman, the
        calves
Sang to my horn, the foxes on the hills barked clear and cold,
        And the sabbath rang slowly
    In the pebbles of the holy streams.

All the sun long it was running, it was lovely, the hay
Fields high as the house, the tunes from the chimneys, it
        was air
    And playing, lovely and watery
        And fire green as grass.
And nightly under the simple stars
As I rode to sleep the owls were bearing the farm away,
All the moon long I heard, blessed among stables, the night-
        jars
    Flying with the ricks, and the horses
        Flashing into the dark.

And then to awake, and the farm, like a wanderer white
With the dew, come back, the cock on his shoulder: it was all
    Shining, it was Adam and maiden,
        The sky gathered again
    And the sun grew round that very day.
So it must have been after the birth of the simple light
In the first, spinning place, the spellbound horses walking
        warm
    Out of the whinnying green stable
        On to the fields of praise.

And honoured among foxes and pheasants by the gay house
Under the new made clouds and happy as the heart was long,
    In the sun born over and over,
        I ran my heedless ways,
      My wishes raced through the house high hay
And nothing I cared, at my sky blue trades, that time allows
In all his tuneful turning so few and such morning songs
    Before the children green and golden
        Follow him out of grace,

Nothing I cared, in the lamb white days, that time would
        take me
Up to the swallow thronged loft by the shadow of my hand,
    In the moon that is always rising,
        Nor that riding to sleep
    I should hear him fly with the high fields
And wake to the farm forever fled from the childless land.
Oh as I was young and easy in the mercy of his means,
        Time held me green and dying
    Though I sang in my chains like the sea.

LAMENT

When I was a windy boy and a bit
And the black spit of the chapel fold,
(Sighed the old ram rod, dying of women),
I tiptoed shy in the gooseberry wood,
The rude owl cried like a telltale tit,
I skipped in a blush as the big girls rolled
Ninepin down on the donkeys' common,
And on seesaw sunday nights I wooed
Whoever I would with my wicked eyes,
The whole of the moon I could love and leave
All the green leaved little weddings' wives
In the coal black bush and let them grieve.

When I was a gusty man and a half
And the black beast of the beetles' pews,
(Sighed the old ram rod, dying of bitches),
Not a boy and a bit in the wick-
Dipping moon and drunk as a new dropped calf,
I whistled all night in the twisted flues,
Midwives grew in the midnight ditches,
And the sizzling beds of the town cried, Quick!—

Whenever I dove in a breast high shoal,
Wherever I ramped in the clover quilts,
Whatsoever I did in the coal-
Black night, I left my quivering prints.

When I was a man you could call a man
And the black cross of the holy house,
(Sighed the old ram rod, dying of welcome),
Brandy and ripe in my bright, bass prime,
No springtailed tom in the red hot town
With every simmering woman his mouse
But a hillocky bull in the swelter
Of summer come in his great good time
To the sultry, biding herds, I said,
Oh, time enough when the blood creeps cold,
And I lie down but to sleep in bed,
For my sulking, skulking, coal black soul!

When I was a half of the man I was
And serve me right as the preachers warn,
(Sighed the old ram rod, dying of downfall),
No flailing calf or cat in a flame
Or hickory bull in milky grass
But a black sheep with a crumpled horn,
At last the soul from its foul mousehole
Slunk pouting out when the limp time came;
And I gave my soul a blind, slashed eye,
Gristle and rind, and a roarers' life,
And I shoved it into the coal black sky
To find a woman's soul for a wife.

Now I am a man no more no more
And a black reward for a roaring life,
(Sighed the old ram rod, dying of strangers),
Tidy and cursed in my dove cooed room
I lie down thin and hear the good bells jaw—
For, oh, my soul found a sunday wife
In the coal black sky and she bore angels!
Harpies around me out of her womb!
Chastity prays for me, piety sings,
Innocence sweetens my last black breath,
Modesty hides my thighs in her wings,
And all the deadly virtues plague my death!

A WINTER'S TALE

It is a winter's tale
That the snow blind twilight ferries over the lakes
And floating fields from the farm in the cup of the vales,
Gliding windless through the hand folded flakes,
The pale breath of cattle at the stealthy sail,

And the stars falling cold,
And the smell of hay in the snow, and the far owl
Warning among the folds, and the frozen hold
Flocked with the sheep white smoke of the farm house cowl
In the river wended vales where the tale was told.

Once when the world turned old
On a star of faith pure as the drifting bread,
As the food and flames of the snow, a man unrolled
The scrolls of fire that burned in his heart and head,
Torn and alone in a farm house in a fold

Of fields.   And burning then
In his firelit island ringed by the winged snow
And the dung hills white as wool and the hen
Roosts sleeping chill till the flame of the cock crow
Combs through the mantled yards and the morning men

Stumble out with their spades,
The cattle stirring, the mousing cat stepping shy,
The puffed birds hopping and hunting, the milkmaids
Gentle in their clogs over the fallen sky,
And all the woken farm at its white trades,

He knelt, he wept, he prayed,
By the spit and the black pot in the log bright light
And the cup and the cut bread in the dancing shade,
In the muffled house, in the quick of night,
At the point of love, forsaken and afraid.

He knelt on the cold stones,
He wept from the crest of grief, he prayed to the veiled sky
May his hunger go howling on bare white bones
Past the statues of the stables and the sky roofed sties
And the duck pond glass and the blinding byres alone

Into the home of prayers
And fires where he should prowl down the cloud
Of his snow blind love and rush in the white lairs.

His naked need struck him howling and bowed
Though no sound flowed down the hand folded air

But only the wind strung
Hunger of birds in the fields of the bread of water, tossed
In high corn and the harvest melting on their tongues.
And his nameless need bound him burning and lost
When cold as snow he should run the wended vales among

The rivers mouthed in night,
And drown in the drifts of his need, and lie curled caught
In the always desiring centre of the white
Inhuman cradle and the bride bed forever sought
By the believer lost and the hurled outcast of light.

Deliver him, he cried,
By losing him all in love, and cast his need
Alone and naked in the engulfing bride,
Never to flourish in the fields of the white seed
Or flower under the time dying flesh astride.

Listen. The minstrels sing
In the departed villages. The nightingale,
Dust in the buried wood, flies on the grains of her wings
And spells on the winds of the dead his winter's tale.
The voice of the dust of water from the withered spring

Is telling. The wizened
Stream with bells and baying water bounds. The dew rings
On the gristed leaves and the long gone glistening
Parish of snow. The carved mouths in the rock are wind
    swept strings.
Time sings through the intricately dead snow drop. Listen.

It was a hand or sound
In the long ago land that glided the dark door wide
And there outside on the bread of the ground
A she bird rose and rayed like a burning bride.
A she bird dawned, and her breast with snow and scarlet
    downed.

Look. And the dancers move
On the departed, snow bushed green, wanton in moon light
As a dust of pigeons. Exulting, the grave hooved
Horses, centaur dead, turn and tread the drenched white
Paddocks in the farms of birds. The dead oak walks for love.

The carved limbs in the rock
Leap, as to trumpets. Calligraphy of the old
Leaves is dancing. Lines of age on the stones weave in a
    flock.
And the harp shaped voice of the water's dust plucks in a fold
Of fields. For love, the long ago she bird rises. Look.

And the wild wings were raised
Above her folded head, and the soft feathered voice
Was flying through the house as though the she bird praised
And all the elements of the slow fall rejoiced
That a man knelt alone in the cup of the vales,

In the mantle and calm,
By the spit and the black pot in the log bright light.
And the sky of birds in the plumed voice charmed
Him up and he ran like a wind after the kindling flight
Past the blind barns and byres of the windless farm.

In the poles of the year
When black birds died like priests in the cloaked hedge row
And over the cloth of counties the far hills rode near,
Under the one leaved trees ran a scarecrow of snow
And fast through the drifts of the thickets antlered like deer,

Rags and prayers down the knee-
Deep hillocks and loud on the numbed lakes,
All night lost and long wading in the wake of the she-
Bird through the times and lands and tribes of the slow flakes.
Listen and look where she sails the goose plucked sea,

The sky, the bird, the bride,
The cloud, the need, the planted stars, the joy beyond
The fields of seed and the time dying flesh astride,
The heavens, the heaven, the grave, the burning font.
In the far ago land the door of his death glided wide,

And the bird descended.
On a bread white hill over the cupped farm
And the lakes and floating fields and the river wended
Vales where he prayed to come to the last harm
And the home of prayers and fires, the tale ended.

The dancing perishes
On the white, no longer growing green, and, minstrel dead,

The singing breaks in the snow shoed villages of wishes
That once cut the figures of birds on the deep bread
And over the glazed lakes skated the shapes of fishes

Flying.   The rite is shorn
Of nightingale and centaur dead horse. The springs wither
Back.   Lines of age sleep on the stones till trumpeting dawn.
Exultation lies down.   Time buries the spring weather
That belled and bounded with the fossil and the dew reborn.

For the bird lay bedded
In a choir of wings, as though she slept or died,
And the wings glided wide and he was hymned and wedded,
And through the thighs of the engulfing bride,
The woman breasted and the heaven headed

Bird, he was brought low,
Burning in the bride bed of love, in the whirl-
Pool at the wanting centre, in the folds
Of paradise, in the spun bud of the world.
And she rose with him flowering in her melting snow.

IN MY CRAFT OR SULLEN ART

In my craft or sullen art
Exercised in the still night
When only the moon rages
And the lovers lie abed
With all their griefs in their arms,
I labour by singing light
Not for ambition or bread
Or the strut and trade of charms
On the ivory stages
But for the common wages
Of their most secret heart.

Not for the proud man apart
From the raging moon I write
On these spindrift pages
Nor for the towering dead
With their nightingales and psalms
But for the lovers, their arms
Round the griefs of the ages,
Who pay no praise or wages
Nor heed my craft or art.

ON THE MARRIAGE OF A VIRGIN

Waking alone in a multitude of loves when morning's light
Surprised in the opening of her nightlong eyes
His golden yesterday asleep upon the iris
And this day's sun leapt up the sky out of her thighs
Was miraculous virginity old as loaves and fishes,
Though the moment of a miracle is unending lightning
And the shipyards of Galilee's footprints hide a navy of doves.

No longer will the vibrations of the sun desire on
Her deepsea pillow where once she married alone,
Her heart all ears and eyes, lips catching the avalanche
Of the golden ghost who ringed with his streams her mer-
     cury bone,
Who under the lids of her windows hoisted his golden lug-
     gage,
For a man sleeps where fire leapt down and she learns
     through his arm
That other sun, the jealous coursing of the unrivalled blood.

AUTHOR'S PROLOGUE *

          This day winding down now
          At God speeded summer's end
          In the torrent salmon sun,
          In my seashaken house
          On a breakneck of rocks
          Tangled with chirrup and fruit,
          Froth, flute, fin and quill
          At a wood's dancing hoof,
          By scummed, starfish sands
          With their fishwife cross
          Gulls, pipers, cockles, and sails,
          Out there, crow black, men
          Tackled with clouds, who kneel
          To the sunset nets,
          Geese nearly in heaven, boys
          Stabbing, and herons, and shells
          That speak seven seas,
          Eternal waters away
          From the cities of nine

* To the Collected Edition of his poems, 1952.

Days' night whose towers will catch
In the religious wind
Like stalks of tall, dry straw,
At poor peace I sing
To you strangers (though song
Is a burning and crested act,
The fire of birds in
The world's turning wood,
For my sawn, splay sounds),
Out of these seathumbed leaves
That will fly and fall
Like leaves of trees and as soon
Crumble and undie
Into the dogdayed night.
Seaward the salmon, sucked sun slips,
And the dumb swans drub blue
My dabbed bay's dusk, as I hack
This rumpus of shapes
For you to know
How I, a spinning man,
Glory also this star, bird
Roared, sea born, man torn, blood blest.
Hark: I trumpet the place,
From fish to jumping hill!   Look:
I build my bellowing ark
To the best of my love
As the flood begins,
Out of the fountainhead
Of fear, rage red, manalive,
Molten and mountainous to stream
Over the wound asleep
Sheep white hollow farms

To Wales in my arms.
Hoo, there, in castle keep,
You king singsong owls, who moonbeam
The flickering runs and dive
The dingle furred deer dead!
Huloo, on plumbed bryns,
O my ruffled ring dove
In the hooting, nearly dark
With Welsh and reverent rook,
Coo rooing the woods' praise,
Who moons her blue notes from her nest
Down to the curlew herd!
Ho, hullaballoing clan

Agape, with woe
In your beaks, on the gabbing capes!
Heigh, on horseback hill, jack
Whisking hare! who
Hears, there, this fox light, my flood ship's
Clangour as I hew and smite
(A clash of anvils for my
Hubbub and fiddle, this tune
On a tongued puffball)
But animals thick as thieves
On God's rough tumbling grounds
(Hail to His beasthood!).
Beasts who sleep good and thin,
Hist, in hogsback woods! The haystacked
Hollow farms in a throng
Of waters cluck and cling,
And barnroofs cockcrow war!
O kingdom of neighbours, finned
Felled and quilled, flash to my patch
Work ark and the moonshine
Drinking Noah of the bay,
With pelt, and scale, and fleece:
Only the drowned deep bells
Of sheep and churches noise
Poor peace as the sun sets
And dark shoals every holy field.
We will ride out alone, and then,
Under the stars of Wales,
Cry, Multitudes of arks! Across
The water lidded lands,
Manned with their loves they'll move,
Like wooden islands, hill to hill.
Huloo, my prowed dove with a flute!
Ahoy, old, sea-legged fox,
Tom tit and Dai mouse!
My ark sings in the sun
At God speeded summer's end
And the flood flowers now.

THE FORCE THAT THROUGH THE GREEN FUSE
DRIVES THE FLOWER

The force that through the green fuse drives the flower
Drives my green age; that blasts the roots of trees
Is my destroyer.

And I am dumb to tell the crooked rose
My youth is bent by the same wintry fever.

The force that drives the water through the rocks
Drives my red blood; that dries the mouthing streams
Turns mine to wax.
And I am dumb to mouth unto my veins
How at the mountain spring the same mouth sucks.

The hand that whirls the water in the pool
Stirs the quicksand; that ropes the blowing wind
Hauls my shroud sail.
And I am dumb to tell the hanging man
How of my clay is made the hangman's lime.

The lips of time leech to the fountain head;
Love drips and gathers, but the fallen blood
Shall calm her sores.
And I am dumb to tell a weather's wind
How time has ticked a heaven round the stars.

And I am dumb to tell the lover's tomb
How at my sheet goes the same crooked worm.

I, IN MY INTRICATE IMAGE

I

I, in my intricate image, stride on two levels,
Forged in man's minerals, the grassy orator
Laying my ghost in metal,
The scales of this twin world tread on the double,
My half ghost in armour hold hard in death's corridor,
To my man-iron sidle.

Beginning with doom in the bulb, the spring unravels,
Bright as her spinning-wheels, the colic season
Worked on a world of petals;
She threads off the sap and needles, blood and bubble
Casts to the pine roots, raising man like a mountain
Out of the naked entrail.

Beginning with doom in the ghost, and the springing marvels,
Image of images, my metal phantom

Forcing forth through the harebell,
My man of leaves and the bronze root, mortal, unmortal,
I, in my fusion of rose and male motion,
Create this twin miracle.

This is the fortune of manhood: the natural peril,
A steeplejack tower, bonerailed and masterless,
No death more natural;
Thus the shadowless man or ox, and the pictured devil,
In seizure of silence commit the dead nuisance:
The natural parallel.

My images stalk the trees and the slant sap's tunnel,
No tread more perilous, the green steps and spire
Mount on man's footfall,
I with the wooden insect in the tree of nettles,
In the glass bed of grapes with snail and flower,
Hearing the weather fall.

Intricate manhood of ending, the invalid rivals,
Voyaging clockwise off the symboled harbour,
Finding the water final,
On the consumptives' terrace taking their two farewells,
Sail on the level, the departing adventure,
To the sea-blown arrival.

II

They climb the country pinnacle,
Twelve winds encounter by the white host at pasture,
Corner the mounted meadows in the hill corral;
They see the squirrel stumble,
The haring snail go giddily round the flower,
A quarrel of weathers and trees in the windy spiral.

As they dive, the dust settles,
The cadaverous gravels, falls thick and steadily,
The highroad of water where the seabear and mackerel
Turn the long sea arterial
Turning a petrol face blind to the enemy
Turning the riderless dead by the channel wall.

(Death instrumental,
Splitting the long eye open, and the spiral turnkey,
Your corkscrew grave centred in navel and nipple,

The neck of the nostril,
Under the mask and the ether, they making bloody
The tray of knives, the antiseptic funeral;

Bring out the black patrol,
Your monstrous officers and the decaying army,
The sexton sentinel, garrisoned under thistles,
A cock-on-a-dunghill
Crowing to Lazarus the morning is vanity,
Dust be your saviour under the conjured soil.)

As they drown, the chime travels,
Sweetly the diver's bell in the steeple of spindrift
Rings out the Dead Sea scale;
And, clapped in water till the triton dangles,
Strung by the flaxen whale-weed, from the hangman's raft,

(Turn the sea-spindle lateral,
The grooved land rotating, that the stylus of lightning
Dazzle this face of voices on the moon-turned table,
Let the wax disk babble
Shames and the damp dishonours, the relic scraping.
These are your years' recorders. The circular world stands
    still.)

III

They suffer the undead water where the turtle nibbles,
Come unto sea-stuck towers, at the fibre scaling,
The flight of the carnal skull
And the cell-stepped thimble;
Suffer, my topsy-turvies, that a double angel
Sprout from the stony lockers like a tree on Aran.

Be by your one ghost pierced, his pointed ferrule,
Brass and the bodiless image, on a stick of folly
Star-set at Jacob's angle,
Smoke hill and hophead's valley,
And the five-fathomed Hamlet on his father's coral,
Thrusting the tom-thumb vision up the iron mile.

Suffer the slash of vision by the fin-green stubble,
Be by the ships' sea broken at the manstring anchored
The stoved bones' voyage downward
In the shipwreck of muscle;

Give over, lovers, locking, and the seawax struggle,
Love like a mist or fire through the bed of eels.

And in the pincers of the boiling circle,
The sea and instrument, nicked in the locks of time,
My great blood's iron single
In the pouring town,
I, in a wind on fire, from green Adam's cradle,
No man more magical, clawed out the crocodile.

Man was the scales, the death birds on enamel,
Tail, Nile, and snout, a saddler of the rushes,
Time in the hourless houses
Shaking the sea-hatched skull,
And, as for oils and ointments on the flying grail,
All-hollowed man wept for his white apparel.

Man was Cadaver's masker, the harnessing mantle,
Windily master of man was the rotten fathom,
My ghost in his metal neptune
Forged in man's mineral.
This was the god of beginning in the intricate seawhirl,
And my images roared and rose on heaven's hill.

THE HAND THAT SIGNED THE PAPER

The hand that signed the paper felled a city;
Five sovereign fingers taxed the breath,
Doubled the globe of dead and halved a country;
These five kings did a king to death.

The mighty hand leads to a sloping shoulder,
The finger joints are cramped with chalk;
A goose's quill has put an end to murder
That put an end to talk.

The hand that signed the treaty bred a fever,
And famine grew, and locusts came;
Great is the hand that holds dominion over
Man by a scribbled name.

The five kings count the dead but do not soften
The crusted wound nor stroke the brow;
A hand rules pity as a hand rules heaven;
Hands have no tears to flow.

SHOULD LANTERNS SHINE

Should lanterns shine, the holy face,
Caught in an octagon of unaccustomed light,
Would wither up, and any boy of love
Look twice before he fell from grace.
The features in their private dark
Are formed of flesh, but let the false day come
And from her lips the faded pigments fall,
The mummy cloths expose an ancient breast.

I have been told to reason by the heart,
But heart, like head, leads helplessly;
I have been told to reason by the pulse,
And, when it quickens, alter the actions' pace
Till field and roof lie level and the same
So fast I move defying time, the quiet gentleman
Whose beard wags in Egyptian wind.

I have heard many years of telling,
And many years should see some change.

The ball I threw while playing in the park
Has not yet reached the ground.

AND DEATH SHALL HAVE NO DOMINION

And death shall have no dominion.
Dead men naked they shall be one
With the man in the wind and the west moon;
When their bones are picked clean and the clean bones gone,
They shall have stars at elbow and foot;
Though they go mad they shall be sane,
Though they sink through the sea they shall rise again;
Though lovers be lost love shall not;
And death shall have no dominion.

And death shall have no dominion.
Under the windings of the sea
They lying long shall not die windily;
Twisting on racks when sinews give way,
Strapped to a wheel, yet they shall not break;
Faith in their hands shall snap in two,

And the unicorn evils run them through;
Split all ends up they shan't crack;
And death shall have no dominion.

And death shall have no dominion.
No more may gulls cry at their ears
Or waves break loud on the seashores;
Where blew a flower may a flower no more
Lift its head to the blows of the rain;
Though they be mad and dead as nails,
Heads of the characters hammer through daisies;
Break in the sun till the sun breaks down,
And death shall have no dominion.

TO OTHERS THAN YOU

Friend by enemy I call you out.

You with a bad coin in your socket,
You my friend there with a winning air
Who palmed the lie on me when you looked
Brassily at my shyest secret,
Enticed with twinkling bits of the eye
Till the sweet tooth of my love bit dry,
Rasped at last, and I stumbled and sucked,
Whom now I conjure to stand as thief
In the memory worked by mirrors,
With unforgettably smiling act,
Quickness of hand in the velvet glove
And my whole heart under your hammer,
Were once such a creature, so gay and frank
A desireless familiar
I never thought to utter or think
While you displaced a truth in the air,

That though I loved them for their faults
As much as for their good,
My friends were enemies on stilts
With their heads in a cunning cloud.

THIS SIDE OF THE TRUTH

(for Llewelyn)

This side of the truth,
You may not see, my son,
King of your blue eyes
In the blinding country of youth,
That all is undone,
Under the unminding skies,
Of innocence and guilt
Before you move to make
One gesture of the heart or head,
Is gathered and spilt
Into the winding dark
Like the dust of the dead.

Good and bad, two ways
Of moving about your death
By the grinding sea,
King of your heart in the blind days,
Blow away like breath,
Go crying through you and me
And the souls of all men
Into the innocent
Dark, and the guilty dark, and good
Death, and bad death, and then
In the last element
Fly like the stars' blood,

Like the sun's tears,
Like the moon's seed, rubbish
And fire, the flying rant
Of the sky, king of your six years.
And the wicked wish,
Down the beginning of plants
And animals and birds,
Water and light, the earth and sky,
Is cast before you move,
And all your deeds and words,
Each truth, each lie,
Die in unjudging love.

BALLAD OF THE LONG-LEGGED BAIT

The bows glided down, and the coast
Blackened with birds took a last look
At his thrashing hair and whale-blue eye;
The trodden town rang its cobbles for luck.

Then good-bye to the fishermanned
Boat with its anchor free and fast
As a bird hooking over the sea,
High and dry by the top of the mast,

Whispered the affectionate sand
And the bulwarks of the dazzled quay.
For my sake sail, and never look back,
Said the looking land.

Sails drank the wind, and white as milk
He sped into the drinking dark;
The sun shipwrecked west on a pearl
And the moon swam out of its hulk.

Funnels and masts went by in a whirl.
Good-bye to the man on the sea-legged deck
To the gold gut that sings on his reel
To the bait that stalked out of the sack,

For we saw him throw to the swift flood
A girl alive with his hooks through her lips;
All the fishes were rayed in blood,
Said the dwindling ships.

Good-bye to chimneys and funnels,
Old wives that spin in the smoke,
He was blind to the eyes of candles
In the praying windows of waves

But heard his bait buck in the wake
And tussle in a shoal of loves.
Now cast down your rod, for the whole
Of the sea is hilly with whales,

She longs among horses and angels,
The rainbow-fish bend in her joys,
Floated the lost cathedral
Chimes of the rocked buoys.

Where the anchor rode like a gull
Miles over the moonstruck boat
A squall of birds bellowed and fell,
A cloud blew the rain from its throat;

He saw the storm smoke out to kill
With fuming bows and ram of ice,
Fire on starlight, rake Jesu's stream;
And nothing shone on the water's face

But the oil and bubble of the moon,
Plunging and piercing in his course
The lured fish under the foam
Witnessed with a kiss.

Whales in the wake like capes and Alps
Quaked the sick sea and snouted deep,
Deep the great bushed bait with raining lips
Slipped the fins of those humpbacked tons

And fled their love in a weaving dip.
Oh, Jericho was falling in their lungs!
She nipped and dived in the nick of love,
Spun on a spout like a long-legged ball

Till every beast blared down in a swerve
Till every turtle crushed from his shell
Till every bone in the rushing grave
Rose and crowed and fell!

Good luck to the hand on the rod,
There is thunder under its thumbs;
Gold gut is a lightning thread,
His fiery reel sings off its flames,

The whirled boat in the burn of his blood
Is crying from nets to knives,
Oh the shearwater birds and their boatsized brood
Oh the bulls of Biscay and their calves

Are making under the green, laid veil
The long-legged beautiful bait their wives.
Break the black news and paint on a sail
Huge weddings in the waves,

Over the wakeward-flashing spray
Over the gardens of the floor
Clash out the mounting dolphin's day,
My mast is a bell-spire,

Strike and smoothe, for my decks are drums,
Sing through the water-spoken prow
The octopus walking into her limbs
The polar eagle with his tread of snow.

From salt-lipped beak to the kick of the stern
Sing how the seal has kissed her dead!
The long, laid minute's bride drifts on
Old in her cruel bed.

Over the graveyard in the water
Mountains and galleries beneath
Nightingale and hyena
Rejoicing for that drifting death

Sing and howl through sand and anemone
Valley and sahara in a shell,
Oh all the wanting flesh his enemy
Thrown to the sea in the shell of a girl

Is old as water and plain as an eel;
Always good-bye to the long-legged bread
Scattered in the paths of his heels
For the salty birds fluttered and fed

And the tall grains foamed in their bills;
Always good-bye to the fires of the face,
For the crab-backed dead on the sea-bed rose
And scuttled over her eyes,

The blind, clawed stare is cold as sleet.
The tempter under the eyelid
Who shows to the selves asleep
Mast-high moon-white women naked

Walking in wishes and lovely for shame
Is dumb and gone with his flame of brides.
Sussanah's drowned in the bearded stream
And no-one stirs at Sheba's side

But the hungry kings of the tides;
Sin who had a woman's shape
Sleeps till Silence blows on a cloud
And all the lifted waters walk and leap.

Lucifer that bird's dropping
Out of the sides of the north
Has melted away and is lost
Is always lost in her vaulted breath,

Venus lies star-struck in her wound
And the sensual ruins make
Seasons over the liquid world,
White springs in the dark.

Always good-bye, cried the voices through the shell,
Good-bye always for the flesh is cast
And the fisherman winds his reel
With no more desire than a ghost.

Always good luck, praised the finned in the feather
Bird after dark and the laughing fish
As the sails drank up the hail of thunder
And the long-tailed lightning lit his catch.

The boat swims into the six-year weather,
A wind throws a shadow and it freezes fast.
See what the gold gut drags from under
Mountains and galleries to the crest!

See what clings to hair and skull
As the boat skims on with drinking wings!
The statues of great rain stand still,
And the flakes fall like hills.

Sing and strike his heavy haul
Toppling up the boatside in a snow of light!
His decks are drenched with miracles.
Oh miracle of fishes! The long dead bite!

Out of the urn the size of a man
Out of the room the weight of his trouble
Out of the house that holds a town
In the continent of a fossil

One by one in dust and shawl,
Dry as echoes and insect-faced,
His fathers cling to the hand of the girl
And the dead hand leads the past,

Leads them as children and as air
On to the blindly tossing tops;
The centuries throw back their hair
And the old men sing from newborn lips:

Time is bearing another son.
Kill Time! She turns in her pain!
The oak is felled in the acorn
And the hawk in the egg kills the wren.

He who blew the great fire in
And died on a hiss of flames
Or walked on the earth in the evening
Counting the denials of the grains

Clings to her drifting hair, and climbs;
And he who taught their lips to sing
Weeps like the risen sun among
The liquid choirs of his tribes.

The rod bends low, divining land,
And through the sundered water crawls
A garden holding to her hand
With birds and animals

With men and women and waterfalls
Trees cool and dry in the whirlpool of ships
And stunned and still on the green, laid veil
Sand with legends in its virgin laps

And prophets loud on the burned dunes;
Insects and valleys hold her thighs hard,
Time and places grip her breast bone,
She is breaking with seasons and clouds;

Round her trailed wrist fresh water weaves,
With moving fish and rounded stones
Up and down the greater waves
A separate river breathes and runs;

Strike and sing his catch of fields
For the surge is sown with barley,
The cattle graze on the covered foam,
The hills have footed the waves away,

With wild sea fillies and soaking bridles
With salty colts and gales in their limbs
All the horses of his haul of miracles
Gallop through the arched, green farms,

Trot and gallop with gulls upon them
And thunderbolts in their manes.
O Rome and Sodom To-morrow and London
The country tide is cobbled with towns,

And steeples pierce the cloud on her shoulder
And the streets that the fisherman combed
When his long-legged flesh was a wind on fire
And his loin was a hunting flame

Coil from the thoroughfares of her hair
And terribly lead him home alive
Lead her prodigal home to his terror,
The furious ox-killing house of love.

Down, down, down, under the ground,
Under the floating villages,
Turns the moon-chained and water-wound
Metropolis of fishes,

There is nothing left of the sea but its sound,
Under the earth the loud sea walks,
In deathbeds of orchards the boat dies down
And the bait is drowned among hayricks,

Land, land, land, nothing remains
Of the pacing, famous sea but its speech,
And into its talkative seven tombs
The anchor dives through the floors of a church.

Good-bye, good luck, struck the sun and the moon,
To the fisherman lost on the land.
He stands alone at the door of his home,
With his long-legged heart in his hand.